DIED 1513—BORN 1929

DIED 1513—BORN 1929

The Autobiography of A. J. Stewart

M

ISBN 0 333 22688 7

First published 1978 by
MACMILLAN LONDON LIMITED
4 Little Essex Street London WC2R 3LF
and Basingstoke
Associated companies in New York Dublin
Melbourne Johannesburg and Delhi

Printed in Hong Kong

ACKNOWLEDGEMENT

I CANNOT ESTIMATE THE DEBT I OWE TO LENORE AND LAWRENCE BENZIES whose labour as editors (acting, unpaid) over the last four years of this work have been equal almost to my own; to Isobel Thom (SRN, supposedly retired) who has guarded my health during that period; and to the late Ogilvie Crombie whose faith in my ability to complete the task has achieved what I many times deemed impossible.

I am deeply grateful to all those who, like my mother, have searched memories and obscure personal archives to confirm or correct dates and details which I, no diarist, had not recorded. The names of some will be found in the ensuing narrative, others are anonymous mainly for the reason that they are so numerous. Specifically, however, I would like to mention the enormous amount of trouble taken by people both civil and military who in the course of their normal bureaucratic duties (and possibly some of their spare time) have helped me in my extensive research by verifying dates of minutiae which supplemented personal memory.

I gratefully acknowledge the generosity of those who have let me quote from their correspondence and I thank others who have lent me letters which I wrote to them.

I express my formal appreciation to the Trustees of the late Dr Agnes Mure Mackenzie for permission to quote from her book *The Kingdom of Scotland*, the first paragraph I ever read which told me something about *myself*. Also I am obliged to the late Dr R. L. Mackie who shared my view of the poet Henryson if not of James the 4—an understandable divergence of opinion—and who introduced me to that curious manuscript 'A Mirror for Magistrates' from which I quote the appropriate stanza. Particularly among historians, I would like to thank one G. Gregory Smith, long dead and out of print, for a (to me) priceless small volume *The Days of James IV* from which I have quoted at the end of this book a vitally relevant footnote.

I could list for ever the personalities who have contributed to the making of this story, for no one who has passed through my life has left it unmarked. However one has to stop somewhere, so I shall end at the beginning with the name of my late father, Ernest A. Kay, who taught me to keep an open mind, without which all learning atrophies.

REFERENCES

The Kingdom of Scotland: Agnes Mure Mackenzie (W. & R. Chambers Ltd., 1940)
King James IV of Scotland: R. L. Mackie (Oliver and Boyd, Edinburgh, 1958)
The Days of James IV: G. Gregory Smith (David Nutt, London, 1900)

Who euer knew Christian King in such a case,
As I wretched creature that cannot haue
In Churche or in Churchyard any maner place,
Emong Christen people to lye in a graue:
The earth mee abhorreth, all men mee depraue,
My frends forsake mee, and haue no pity,
The worlde taketh from mee all that hee mee gaue:
Miserere mei Deus & salua mee.

A Mirror For Magistrates

(Quotation from the 1587 Edition, by courtesy of the Huntington Library, San Marino, California.)

THIS BOOK'S ORIGINAL TITLE WAS *Earthe Mee Abhorreth* BUT IF YOU try to say it over the telephone as I have been doing for the past ten years you will see why I finally agreed to let my publishers change it. I am not happy with the new title, suggesting as it does that I am a 'reincarnationist' – by which I mean one who accepts or enjoys the theory or has studied the doctrine. In fact, reincarnation is my least favourite subject for reasons which you may comprehend by the time you have reached the last chapter. In addition, as a rather private person I do not in the least relish having my innermost thoughts and the details of my life read by you, whom I do not know, but I have been aware since 1967 that the presentation of this narrative was an obligation I could not avoid.

There was never a way to tell this story as it should have been told so that you shared to the end my profound perplexity; however, by omitting footnotes I have done what I can to exclude hindsight and amplification by historical reference. Whether or not some acquaintance with Scottish history would have helped me in my youth I cannot say, as there is no way of knowing if I would have connected it with myself. However, of one thing I am certain: had I grown up in a culture which *allowed the possibility* that man has more lives than one, I should have been spared much suffering.

I have done my best to write a readable case-history. I have not enjoyed writing it, and the performance of the task has been as harrowing as that required of me to produce my other autobiography *Falcon – The Autobiography of His Grace, James the 4, King of Scots.* I shall not regret any of it if, at the end, I have left one reader easier in mind, or another more concerned, about what is happening in, or around, him. You, my unknown friend, may be the one for whom I have written.

A. J. Stewart

Edinburgh, 20 June 1977.

1

I WAS BORN ON THE FIFTH DAY OF MARCH 1929, IN THE COUNTY Palatine of Lancaster (which was never to my mind quite the same thing as being English). The great thaw following the historic frost of that year, discharging through the house the melted contents of thirteen burst waterpipes, precipitated my arrival. It was ever after- wards to be identified by my father as the day when he had to deal with a doctor in the bedroom and a plumber in the bathroom.

It was remarked by the nurse who sustained a damaging blow to the eye whilst giving me my first bath, 'This child has a will of iron' – possibly the only compliment she could have paid me, for even by the primitive standards of the newly-born I was not a bonny baby. I had come into the world with a long mane of black pre-natal hair and pointed ears rolled forward like those of an elemental, which caused my startled mother to observe that she had given birth to 'a changeling'.

Sticking plaster trained the ears and the black locks were displaced by an aureole of red-gold curls which gave me the appearance of a sunny child. Inwardly I remained a dark person – dark in my view of life which would, I knew, be a hard one. It always was.

My earliest memories are rarely visual, except for one view from my parked pram of the village grocery store in Tottington. Of the world inside me I seemed to have been aware from the beginning, and my inability to communicate this awareness was a constant vexation. I can remember my frustration when, seated on my mother's knee at bath-time, I tried to use my favourite picture-book, *Chicky-Cluck*, to illustrate aspects of my own life still foremost in my memory. She thought I was screaming because the picture of Chicky-Cluck ship-wrecked beside the duck-pond frightened me, whereas I was trying to make her understand that the limp chicken left for dead beneath a heap of crossed spars looked as I had felt when I went down beneath the blades and staves upon the battlefield. My mother, uncomprehending, finally threatened to put *Chicky-Cluck* upon the proscribed list if I continued so to upset myself at bedtime.

Whether my earliest thought patterns were verbal or intuitive I am unable, now, to say. There is, however, a likelihood that I was to some degree articulate, for there persisted in my head three gutturals (ch, gh and quh) which were to cause problems when I was learning to speak

English. Words used by my parents reminded me of others which had the same meaning but were differently pronounced, and I remember by mother growing desperate in her efforts to train me to say 'walk' instead of 'waak'. My broad vowels and three gratuitous gutturals were foreign even to the dialect of rural Lancashire and bore no resemblance whatever to the English spoken by my parents. The curious thing about the language I was now learning was that it sounded almost, but not quite, familiar; it was, to my ear, a weaker form of a tongue I had known – like a rag of once-bright fabric with all the colour washed away.

When I had mastered the barest sufficiency of vocabulary my reminiscences were unleashed upon an unsuspecting household. Nobody knew what to make of them. I was too young to read and, though the house abounded in books, I was not allowed to play with them. Where we lived on the moor above the village I had no company save that of my parents: who then could have told me these tales of steel-clad men upon a battlefield, of ships, and foreign envoys arriving at court? When taxed with this question my reply was always the same – an exasperated 'I'm telling you because *I was there!*'

Gradually, I perceived in my parents a lack of response to my reiterated 'I was there'. Neither, so far as I can remember, openly expressed incredulity but I had begun to sense it. I was an automatically truthful person (dangerously so at times) reared in a household where deceit was abhorrent, and to have my veracity under question was extremely painful. So I stopped volunteering my anecdotes about my past life. This appeared to relieve my parents who, though rejecting my explanation, had found none of their own satisfactorily to replace it. They held to the orthodox Christian belief in the survival of the spirit *elsewhere*, and there was no place in our household for a changeling with an antique memory. In time I would myself become of the family persuasion (to the extent that twenty years later my mother could raise the subject of my 'fantastic stories' and the reiterated 'I was there!' without wakening in me the slightest interest except for a poignant memory of my own long-ago dismay).

Already, as the patina of new learning obscured the old, the memories themselves were fading. Just a few would stay with me for a lifetime. In my late teens I would still be joking about the 'ridiculous memory' of being hauled by my father's hand through many stone-floored chambers to one where he stood me on his chair to present me to his lords in council. Another was the recollection of myself as a boy nearing fifteen, clad in scarlet with a heavy gold shoulder-chain, riding out through a gateway at the head of small band of horsemen whilst the guard rang out a salute with their pike-butts on the cobbles. I grew to accept the presence in my head of such remembered fragments – like

12

objects in a drawer, which, their purpose forgotten, surface from time to time to be examined and then returned to their obscurity.

So we locked away my ghost where it could damage no one, deep in the recess of my mind where forgotten things are stored. All that remained to torment us was its crying. Once in a while, for no apparent reason, some warped nerve gave out a vibration which nearly sent my parents scampering. No juvenile larynx would normally produce the sound that I made, a great hoarse, bass sobbing, monotonous, endless, like the dull measured tread of the sea. Whence it came I had no idea, but the eerie crying would spill out of me and as suddenly would cease. I had no control over it. While it lasted I felt its grief, grief so enormous that I seemed to be its appendage merely; all I knew was that it was very *old* weeping, yet it was mine. It was entirely different from the natural child's tears I shed at other times.

In the beginning I was just a person, unaware of gender. I can remember my initial perplexity, then annoyance, when people gave me *dolls*. To be a girl I found faintly humiliating, for I was not accustomed to it. My father repaired my broken toys and one day I presented him with a decapitated torso, beseeching him to 'mend it for me, please'. I did not care about the doll per se but the sight of a headless body tumbling from my toy cupboard had brought on an attack of my ghost-tears. Using the head of another broken doll, he created the Hybrid (it never had a name) – a veritable monster with a head too large for its body. To the Hybrid I became immediately attached, and whenever its head came off – as frequently happened – my hoarse weeping would make the house uneasy until my father returned. Watching him make whole again the severed head and decapitated torso gave me immeasurable consolation. He once remarked, 'I think you keep this doll purely for the pleasure of seeing me repair it!' His perception frightened me, for I wanted nobody to know that the headless trunk was identifiable with myself.

When finally the doll was past repair, I had my mother bury it amongst old ceremonial finery in the bottom of the chest where she stored my summer dresses out of season. Opened but twice a year, the chest's lower layer, sown with mothballs, was rarely disturbed. I had my mother's promise that the relics could stay buried *always* – but to be on the safe side I made sure that I was always present when the chest was opened. How long we kept that head and torso I have no idea, but I was into my late childhood before I stopped demanding pledges to safeguard its peace.

The place of the Hybrid was eventually taken by an old novelty perfume bottle of my mother's, shaped like a furry pink monkey with a phial inside the body and a detachable head which served as its stopper. She found it to amuse me on a rainy afternoon, and ever afterwards voiced her amazement that it should become my favourite possession. The great advantage which Monkey had over the Hybrid was that I could assemble body and head for myself. As I grew older, Monkey was to become the focal point of my creative energy and my provision for it was to last until I reached the age of ten or eleven. I clad it in raiment of silk and velvet, made for it coronation robes lavishly embroidered and trimmed with fur; for it I fashioned wigs of silk thread and real hair, and a suit of fifteenth-century plate armour made out of the foil casing from chocolate coins. Before I was finished it was to have forty courtiers of its own size dressed in medieval costume, a palace built of wooden boxes (containing a magnificent medieval kitchen stocked with baked clay comestibles) and a home farm of lead animals to provision the household. (My palace-building ultimately became such a threat to *Lebensraum* that the entire kingdom was banished upstairs to my bedroom.) My plans for the enstatement of Monkey were beyond my powers of execution at the time of which I am writing, but my inspiration to create for it was immediate. Whenever I was asked why I loved it so much, my answer was always the same: 'Because its head comes off.'

We moved to Thornton Cleveleys in the January of 1932, two months short of my third birthday. My father had been appointed to the newly-opened senior school in Thornton, and my parents bought the first of six new houses built on farmland half-way between the two villages of Thornton and Cleveleys. Cleveleys lay at the crossroads of two cultures and civilisation came by tram. The tram-track along the coastline connected Fleetwood and Blackpool, both towns as remote to my infant rural thinking as the caravan terminus of Samarkand. Thornton had the railway, and between these two points of access to the outside world our twin villages slumbered amidst green fields, fish ponds and plots of woodland. A red Ribble bus plied its way harmlessly between Thornton and Cleveleys, and my father, like most other schoolmasters, rode his bicycle to school.

My parents were dedicated cyclists who rode tandem. When my arrival had threatened to impede their wanderlust, they bought a sidecar for me. I detested that sidecar. Every Saturday of my young life and for days on end during the school vacation, all weathers, I was secured with leather straps to travel interminable bumpy miles. The bouncing motion at times upset my time sense, when I would fall asleep and be jolted awake with the certainty that I was riding a horse. I liked least those journeys made in winter when I was wrapped round with many blankets and the performance of filling hot-water bottles delayed our departure; and it was then we came home with the waning end of day, when the huge, red, winter sun travelled with us westward, bringing to my mind calamity. I grew to hate the Fylde Coast with stacks of peat dotting the flat fields, and all its trees humbled by the prevailing wind like old men hunched for shelter – these years later I can see there was wild beauty in that landscape but never as a child could I separate it in my mind from the red sun of a dying day which saw my whole world ended. The only time I enjoyed riding in the sidecar was when it rained and they put up the hood. Then my small, encapsulated existence became exciting while rain drummed on my roof, and my thoughts could go careering back through the tunnel whence I came . . . for there were places still that I remembered, with cobbled or mud streets so narrow between tall houses that my litter had barely room to pass. (I had hated the litter, too, I remembered, using it rarely when I had been old enough to choose my mode of travel). Images of the world which used to lie outside my other travelling box came back to me quite plainly when I concentrated in the closed darkness.

These cycling expeditions usually had a purpose, for my father's other pursuits were photography and brass-rubbing. I never minded how long we waited in old parish churches while my father took photographs, for the smell of hassocks and old hymn books filled me with nostalgia for something once known, now forgotten, nostalgia so acute that its pain was nigh unbearable. I was instinctively well behaved in ecclesiastical surroundings and my parents let me wander off alone; it was in castle ruins where I had to be watched, for there I had a tendency to make myself too much at home in chambers whose floors had perished.

The castles we visited in England and North Wales, albeit open to the skies and floorless, were always home to me in a way that our own neat, small, modern house could never be. I needed high, vaulted ceilings, huge, open fireplaces and windows set high in the wall. Even when I measured less than three feet with my shoes on, the ceilings of our house seemed low enough to crush me. I could never understand what *I* was doing living in a semi-detached house with neither a spiral stair nor a stable-yard. Whenever I expressed dissatisfaction with the house my mother told me not to be silly; I had, she said, no experience of living in a large house too cold in winter and with a dining-room so far removed from the kitchen that any item forgotten from the table was omitted from the meal. My mother's family had lost their money before they lost their sense of grandeur and whenever they could not afford the maintenance of the house in which they were living they moved to one yet larger, acting on the economic principle that great houses were always cheaper because – I quote – 'nobody can afford the upkeep of a big house these days'. Reacting against this paradoxical tradition, my mother had welcomed with joy the advantages of a

15

small house which she could manage herself without assistance. My hope of escaping from Accrington brick and picture rails was doomed from the beginning.

Within twelve months of our arrival in Thornton Cleveleys my maternal grandparents came to establish their household within walking distance of our own. Having, within my own brief lifetime, moved from a very large house into a small one, they sold the latter after a residence so brief as to be a record even by their nomadic standards. In Cleveleys they had found a modest mansion sufficient to their needs, and here came to terms with economic reality. The reason for our tribal migration was the quest for pure, strong air; my grandmother was a chronic asthmatic who found the ozone of the Fylde Coast beneficial. She had come to Cleveleys with the intention of retiring, but with an active head for business she soon found idleness oppressive and so on most days of the week she travelled to and from Blackburn.

My grandparents' house contained, beside my grandmother and grandfather, three aunts and my two male cousins, who were a decade older than I and, for most of the time, away at boarding school. My Aunt Florrie, mother of the boys, was a war widow. My Aunt Anne, the youngest, was unmarried. Aunt Edith was not a blood relation, being the sister of my Aunt Florrie's dead husband who had joined the family initially to nurse the younger of my cousins through an ailing childhood and had stayed on to cook and sew for them all.

I knew one should not have favourite relatives, but the one I liked best was Grandfather Whiteside. We had much in common; facial resemblance, a temper lethal if not suppressed, and our imperviousness to cold. No matter how inclement the weather, he was never known to wear an overcoat or to fasten his jacket. Warned to expect death at sixty, of angina, he was to live to his ninety-third year, walking ten miles a day, and taking in his stride a Second World War during which, as head of the local Fire Watchers, he modestly disowned a decade of his real age and at fourscore shinned any ladder like a lad of forty.

My grandfather had sired four daughters, of whom the eldest, May, was a farmer's wife living on a remote hill farm above Darwen. Whenever we went to stay with my paternal grandparents a visit to Aunt May's farm was the highlight of my holiday. I had not forgiven my parents for taking me away from the bleak moorland terrain which was my native environment, for, though domestic habitations had changed so drastically, scenery had not, and a windswept hill today looks much as it ever did. That may be why on the long walk up to Aunt May's farm I would slip away so often into reminiscent reverie, and that part of our route which lay through oak- and beech-woods is still today in my mind connected with small, humped tents and camp-

16

fires tended by a multitude of men, whom, I know quite well, I never saw upon the moor above Darwen.

This elasticity of memory lasted well into my fourth year when, presumably, my tenancy of current existence had been consolidated. Meanwhile, curious small confusions between what had been and what was puzzled me exceedingly. There was, for example, the matter of my patronym. They said my name was Kay, whereas I was certain it was Stewart. I had not been conscious of my surname until one day my father, when recounting a cycling story, mentioned the name of a companion, Alec Stewart. At once my ear picked up the name with a lurch of excitement which made me almost dizzy: *my* name was Stewart. Or was it? Why was I now called Kay? It was explained to me that children took their father's surname but that did not properly answer my question: why was *my father's* name not Stewart?

My new life never fitted me; it was always like a glove cut and sewn to fit another hand.

I outgrew the knowledge I was born with, and for a short while at the age of four I believed that all adults were born adult, and children were a subject people. This may have been due to the fact that I was outnumbered by adults eleven to one. True, I had two first cousins, but they, as I say, were either at school or at sea through all the years I knew them and as near-men in my eyes could not be counted as juvenile reinforcement. I did not mind adults, who, on the whole, used me with courtesy and consideration, but their numerical superiority was truly daunting. To worsen matters, the population of Cleveleys consisted mainly of elderly, retired people, so my chance of meeting other children was almost non-existent.

My grandmother hardly features at all in my early memory. My few glimpses were of a vigorous lady dressed always fashionably in black, with furs and an immaculate black neck-ribbon. She wore rimless pince-nez clipped to the bridge of an acquiline nose and how she kept them on was to me a mystery. Those spectacles always made me feel that my own wide-bridged nose was terribly plebeian, and it would have comforted me a great deal at the time had I known that the cost of her almost constant spectacle replacement was enormous. On some of the days when she went through to Blackburn my mother and my aunt accompanied her, and there would be talk of 'seeing Smeddles'. I never knew what smeddles were until my mother explained that he was the family laywer. Occasionally they all went to Blackburn, and then I would be left in the charge of Aunt Edith, who set aside her work for the day to make for me what she termed 'doll rags'. I should have looked forward to those afternoons, but never did, because I liked to cut out and sew for myself whereas Aunt Edith preferred to cast me in

17

the role of spectator while she sat busy treddling. She flatly refused to make clothes for a mangy pink monkey three-and-a-half inches tall with a detachable head, and it was her contempt for Monkey which made me hate her. Our afternoons usually ended with my yelling that I wanted to go home, and Aunt Edith accusing me of scattering her precious pins. The fact that it was Aunt Edith who saved me from drowning on the day I was caught in quicksand did nothing to change my feelings.

During the afternoons of my infancy, walks along the sea-shore with my grandfather were life's main event. My mother came with us and one or two of the aunts. We had a choice of two directions – northward towards Fleetwood, and southward towards Blackpool. Both places were just Town to me, the remote centres of commerce visited by tram once in a while on shopping expeditions for commodities unobtainable locally. We never walked further than Bispham or Rossall – though my grandfather promised I could walk with him to Fleetwood when my legs were long enough. Walks with my grandfather were never dull, for he thrived upon adventure. Barbed wire, bulls and 'Private' notices were all to him irrelevant once he had determined his destination. At that time Rossall School owned a strip of the foreshore which they used for swimming exercises, and walkers going to Rossall Point had to make a wide detour back to the main road, returning to the shore via the lane which passed the school farm. My grandfather considered this interruption of his route an imposition and, taking advantage of gaps in dykes and barbed wire, he led us on the path of trespass frequently. Without a blink of shame or any alteration in his leisurely, rythmic pace, he trod firmly past boys and masters swimming in the surf as though it were they and not he who committed the intrusion. My mother's more active conscience caused her to remonstrate angrily, although knowing from a lifetime's experience that argument was wasted on my grandfather. I trudged stoically in grandfather's wake, resigned to the certainty that one day all three of us would go to prison. As we wormed our way through Rossall School's barbed wire, my mother's indignant 'Father, it is *their land*' would be countered by his roared 'Damme, nobody can own *the sea!*'

Cleveleys was never beautiful, but its sea-front had in those years the character peculiar to small sea-side resorts, an atmosphere of eternal old-fashionedness. In summer we left it to the visitors with their Jugs of Tea for the Sands, their plimsolls, rubber caps and picnic-carriers. In winter we had it to ourselves, and I have seen the high tide dash foam and seaweed down the main street in years before they completed the great barricade of tiered promenades to combat erosion. On the south side the promenade ended abruptly at the head of Victoria Road, and one ploughed through sand to the defence work called by us The Steps.

18

The Steps began at Little Bispham but they had not yet reached us, and their iron-rail reinforcement poked out from the end of the concrete structure in a way my mother said was dangerous. They did look uncommonly like iron spears, which made me think once of a wall of *men* advancing down a hillside . . . somewhere . . . once, long ago . . . but my mother marched me firmly past them, and what I had all but remembered was gone. I was allowed to run along The Steps, and that was my first great game, to muster an army, jumping my black stallion from level to level along The Steps.

Northward, the promenade ended by the second sunken garden at Thornton Gate; thereafter there was just a cracked strip of concrete a few feet wide, and a low sea-wall made of large round pebbles stuck in cement like raisins in plum-duff. On the landward side there were small sand dunes planted with marram grass to stop the sand drifting. There one began the detour round Rossall School, or, alternatively, trespassed. On the far side lay the old prep-school building which had not then been demolished, and its ruin stood on a piece of low ground facing the sea-wall across the strip of sand and marram grass. It was there, just at the edge of the shore-path, that I found the flat, blue-green leaved plant with a head like a thistle which is called sea holly. I can remember dropping to my knees beside this flower of my new finding and feeling wind to my hair as I exclaimed, 'Oh, *see!*' to the tall legs of my grandfather standing over me. Half-tearful, half-ecstatic, I wanted to explain that I knew this particualr plant, as I knew vividly the low contours of sand dune and the curve of the coastline at Rossall Point . . . but I could not say why upon this day I saw them differently. The sand thistle and a glimpse of the prep-school roof between sand hummocks resembling a fisherman's hut had reminded me of something once familiar, now forgotten. Using a sandy hand to dash away my tears, I rose from my knees to find Rossall looking like Rossall and nowhere else, and my awareness of belonging had disappeared down my throat like an accidently swallowed acid-drop. On the way home I was listless, dragging my feet. My mother said I was tired and my grandfather picked me up to carry me on his shoulder. I never liked the walk to Rossall Point; and on days when it was possible to see clear across Morcambe Bay to the far hills, I liked it least of all; it was always for me a sad place where I felt exiled.

Having almost lost me once in quicksand my mother never again let me paddle in pools beside the groynes unless she had personally inspected them. In fact, the chance of such a pool being dangerous was so rare that my likelihood of being caught a second time was beyond the range of probability. This concern of my mother's sorely inhibited my inspection of the several wrecked ships which dotted the coastline. The nearest wreck was the *Abana*, a three-masted barque driven aground at Norbreck during a December gale in 1894. By the time we arrived in Cleveleys little remained of her but her green, limpet-encrusted ribs bedded in sand and the tall stem timber which still resisted the many pounding seas of the spring and autumn equinoxes. It was not until I reached the age of five that my grandfather and I persuaded my mother to let me walk out at low tide to the *Abana*. There was another wreck at Pilling, and there one afternoon, when the maternal eye was bent upon the picnic-basket, I set out to explore alone. I was able to walk right inside the wreck and stand looking up at her wooden sides. It was cool and shaded there, and very quiet. A floor of smooth wet sand filled all the hull, in places hollowed out by currents of visiting sea-water like many basins kept topped up at high tide. My memory is of a greenish place, so no doubt there was weed coating the timbers. I stood a long while, my mind making one of its return journeys . . . it seemed not so very long ago that I had been standing within the hull of another ship, built of new, seasoned wood with chisel-marks on her beams cut fresh as of yesterday. . . . When my father appeared against the wreck's holed side it was a second or two before I could recall myself to recognise him. When he saw that all was well he left me to my solitude, but the time-link had been broken: I could never go back to pick up these memories where I had left them.

I had been about three and a half when I had the dream, but the dream itself was older by far than I was. In it, I was walking with my mother along the promenade by the sunken gardens at Thornton Gate when we saw beached high upon the foreshore a huge, black-timbered vessel which I knew was my great warship with her polished brass cannon-mouths lining the deck. Everything about her was in working order, her deck-gear stowed neatly and her sails furled. Enormous pride filled me at the sight of her, and also a terrible pain. The most frightening, and the saddest, thing about her was her silence. Gone were all the shipwrights who had teemed like ants amongst her new timbers when the keel was laid in its mud berth, the caulkers, carpenters and sailmakers whose labours I had watched during those many anxious but exciting months. Gone were the sailors and master gunners I had put aboard her for her great mission. She lay now silent, completed and forgotten by everyone save me; such desolation filled me at the sight of her war-trim so eager, her position so helpless, that even in the dream I shed the tears of many, many years ago. Then something changed about the ship; no longer lifeless, she quickened with an invisible force so that I knew something terrible was about to happen. My mother pulled me by the hand, shouting, 'Run, Ada – run!' and dragged me along the promenade, but even as we ran the black ship exploded into a fountain of flame, like a volcano spitting black parts, but the parts were the heads and severed limbs of men.

These human particles rained down upon us as we ran along the promenade, falling so thickly that in places we had to wade through bloodied mortal debris. We sought shelter at my grandparents' house, which was nearer than our own, but I knew when I saw the door standing open that something there was very wrong. We searched each room on the ground floor, calling their names, but nobody came. Upstairs we found them, laid out neatly on their beds, each member of the family, dead. Pestilence had struck the house. We fled. Running downstairs, led by my mother, I looked back – and there, cascading down the stairs behind me, were the torn limbs and heads of the exploded people from the ship, but all the fragments were *alive*. I had almost reached the safety of the open front door when I went down under a ferocious attack by arms and stamping feet and faces mad with battle-fury. I screamed . . . and my screams brought my mother to my bedside to waken and comfort me.

It was an hour or more before I quietened – though my mother took me downstairs to be dressed by the fire. I can remember standing on my father's big chair, in my embroidered white flannel winter petticoat with its tiny silk bodice, shaking and sobbing so much that my mother could not fasten the buttons. I had to tell her about the dream to expel its horror from my head, but now I was awake I did not know the name of the brass-muzzled things in the ship's side and likened them to the brass-eyelet holes in clogs which were then a familiar sight in rural and urban Lancashire. My mother fussed with buttons and a handkerchief for me to blow my nose when all I wanted was to make known to her what I had been through. I can hear her now – 'Hush, Ada, it's all right, darling. It was just a dream. A *dream*. That's all. It's gone now.'

Gone? I have remembered that dream for over forty years, and the sheer hopelessness of trying to describe it to my mother.

Within twelve months of her arrival in Cleveleys my grandmother had had a minor seizure which ended her visits to Blackburn. Now she rarely left the house and I saw her daily when we called, seated always in her chair and surrounded by the aroma of Lavender Cologne and asthma powder which hung about her like incense. I always knew when her asthma was bad because the pungent smell of asthma powder burnt on a tin plate hit my nostrils the moment we opened the front door. Our relationship had just begun to make progress when she was taken ill with what in those days was called 'a septic appendix'. On the day she was rushed into a nursing home for immediate operation there was turmoil in both households and my mother's problem was to find someone with whom she could leave me while she was visiting the nursing home. Through the kitchen window her eye fell upon Ted Fenton pottering in his orchard, and she rushed out to ask if his sisters

21

would mind a small grass orphan for the day, and that was how I came to meet the world outside my own immediate family circle.

The Fentons formerly owned the land on which our house was built, and their farmhouse seen across the orchard had intrigued me from the beginning. From the side it looked enormous, being very deep from front to back, but narrow, so that from the front it looked to me like half a great house sawn off down the middle. My mother knew Ted Fenton well enough to pass the time of day, and I had been with her when he made her an offering of gooseberries. He may have seen the longing in the eye I applied to a gap in the fence, for thereafter it became an occasional morning occurrence for me to be lifted over the fence to join Ted in his pre-prandial contemplation of his rhubarb or to watch him swat with an old tennis racquet the white butterflies menacing his cabbages. When he discovered I was good at it, he set me to stalk those of his hens suspected of laying astray. A taciturn gentleman, he never fussed me, and our relationship consisted of companionable silence and shared raspberries.

On the day of my grandmother's illness it was a huge adventure to be bundled over the fence and led by the hand to the heavy, timbered gate which I had so many times eyed with interest. On the way Ted let me gather poppies (everything grew in that orchard) so that my arms were filled with them when I stepped through the gate into the farmyard. Across the cobbles I saw two ladies bending low and holding out their arms to me, and one cried, 'Why, it's little Poppy!' and Poppy was to be my name for years at the Fentons. What caught my eye immediately was the sisters' hair, one red-gold, the other black, worn long and pinned by Margaret in a bun and by Alice in plaited 'ear-phones'. It was the first time I had seen what I described to my mother as *real* hair, for I had been born just after the wholesale shingling of the twenties.

My grandmother died of that illness, and there was everywhere quietness, closed curtains and low-lying sadness which, because everyone tried to keep it from me, sank down to my level like a dado round every room. She lay in one of the sitting-rooms downstairs which I passed on my way down from the lavatory and, seeing the door momentarily ajar, I decided it would be a suitable opportunity to pay my respects. Possibly divining my intention, my mother and aunt intercepted me, and I heard above my head a short discussion upon the wisdom of letting small children view the dead, which at the time struck me as being ridiculous for I had seen more corpses in one day upon a battlefield than there was living population in the whole of Cleveleys. I held my tongue because I knew now not to talk about the battlefield. They let me see my grandmother, pushing open the door of the still room where green light filtered through closed curtains. My aunt lifted a white handkerchief covering my grandmother's face, and the fine patrician features had never looked more stately. Death suited her, I thought. I expressed myself satisfied and we left her.

It was to be several months before the sight of my grandmother's empty chair nagged me into awareness that she was *gone*. Walking home in the darkness of the November evening, picking our way carefully through the wheel-ruts and mud of the unmade road, I asked my mother when would I see Granny Whiteside again? My mother replied, 'Oh, one day.' I knew that, but to hear her say it made the appointment definite in time, like a date fixed by a calendar. I can remember looking up at the sky, brilliant with stars, and thinking what a splendid place it was to have as Heaven. I felt envious of my grandmother, gone exploring a sea of silver stars. How much time, I wondered, would I have to put in, ploughing through the slush and puddles of Chester Avenue, my hand gripped firmly in my mother's? Already, at four, I seemed to have been alive for an unconscionably long time.

My grandmother had died in June and it had been for me a busy summer. Picnics in the hayfield with Alice and Margaret Fenton and Laddie the dog had been its highlights. Tumbling in the hay with Laddie while the sisters threw up their arms in laughter; drinking milk still warm from the cow; finding dried-out funerary wreaths of tiny flowers cut down with the hay during reaping; everywhere the smell of heat and dried grass: these were all part and parcel of my childhood summer that I knew would last for ever. It came as a terrible blow to me when Laddie died, far worse than the death of my grandmother.

One day I went into the farmhouse kitchen and Laddie's chair was empty. He did not come romping from the orchard at his dog-dining hour, so I knew the time had come to ask, 'Where's Laddie?' I had dreaded asking the question because I knew the answer: the previous day when I saw Laddie curled on his cushion something odd had happened to my vision; I saw his silhouette carved out of his background, hanging motionless in a single moment stretched to last for ever. Like a camera my mind had taken its last picture of Laddie. Foreknowledge of death was something I took for granted (I thought everyone had it) and it disturbed me less as a child than it was to do in later years when for a while I tried to pretend I did not have it.

My favourite room in the farmhouse was the dining-room, usually called the sewing-room because its great table served for the sisters' dressmaking. Facing west, its wide, sash window gave immediately on to what was known as 'the back orchard', containing only fruit trees, which was small, secret and secluded. I could sit upon the sun-warmed windowsill of sandstone, swinging my legs as I looked out upon apples made rosen by the evening light. Behind me the sisters would move softly, setting the table with old silver and dishes that were never used

23

in the farmhouse kitchen. When we dined there they set me at the head of the table between them, a stately personage in my own right.

It was this magical quality of deference which made the Fenton sisters unique as play-companions. They could enter my inner world without disturbing it by any reminder that I was now a child. My favourite game was centered round the scroll-backed, horse-hair sofa in the sewing-room, which I adopted as my state bed. What I enacted was the procedure of rising and retiring as I remembered it, a performance involving many people whose fortunes depended on their ability to impress me with their thoughtfulness, common sense and perspicacity whilst dressing and undressing me. This memory lingered more clearly than any, I think because it had marked the beginning and end of my every living day. The game involved a great deal more than dressing-up, for I still talked the while about my kingdom, which was the basic purpose behind those royal bedchamber musterings. Margaret and Alice never queried why I was always a king, never a queen or a princess.

On special days in spring we went into the small, walled flower-garden at the front of the farmhouse. The front door was rarely used, except by postmen, being a long way from the main living area of the house, and that particular garden was the reserve of ladies, tended by them and not by Brother who ruled the orchards, farmyard, kitchen patch and what was known as The Field. In the flower-garden grew lily of the valley and a lilac tree. There was a weather-worn old wooden garden seat, and a tiny rockery of white stones gathered from the beach and mollusc-encrusted sea-shells. Those white, smooth pebbles on the grass at dusk reminded me of silver pieces. It was the femininity of this garden, in which I alone was allowed to play, which gently brought to my attention the fact that I was this time a little girl.

My mother had been advised not to have another baby, so the younger brother I had been expecting never materialised. My parents were determined to ensure that, being an only child, I was not spoiled, so each Christmas I had to take my best box of chocolates round our few new neighbours, and if they did happen to pick the hard centres I preferred I was not to show I minded. My toys, too, could be shared, for although I met no children, it was not difficult in the thirties to find young brothers and sisters of my father's pupils whose Christmas had been less affluent than mine. I was well trained to be loving and giving, but the real problem was how to teach me to be loathing and grabbing; alone among adults I had nobody with whom to compete.

One day on our way home from the beach my mother and I passed the garden of a house in Beach Road where several children were playing. Fascinated by the sight of human young at play, I stopped to

24

watch. My mother told me that it was a school. I asked immediately, 'Please may I go to school?' My mother told me that I was not old enough and that I would have to wait until I was five. I said, 'But I've never met children.'

My plight moved my mother to speak to a lady who had just appeared at the door, and it transpired that she was the headmistress of the private school. A few minutes later I had been accepted, despite my lack of years, as a pupil. I asked Mrs Handley, 'Please may I come tomorrow?' My mother explained that there were formalities in regard to starting one's education, one being the purchase of school uniform. Mrs Handley, seeing my face fall, interpolated swiftly, 'If she wants to come tomorrow, let her. Send her in ordinary clothes.'

And that was how, accidently, I began my education in mid-week of mid-term, one whole year before I need have done. As my mother was to point out to me later, I had no one but myself to blame.

The next day I arrived to be initiated into the mysteries of the classroom. We strung beads and drew pictures on stiff, sombre-hued sheets of paper with bright pastel crayons. What I liked best were the cards punched with holes which we embroidered with things like coloured bootlaces, and I stitched a lovely tapestry on mine. It was admired, and then I was told to unpick it. I was appalled by this waste of time and labour. It was explained to me that the empty cards would be required for use again next day. Modern education, I decided, was not for me, and having thanked them for my morning at school I told my mother when she came for me that I had had enough of it. To my indescribable horror I discovered that having joined the club I was expected to remain a member.

What really set me against school, however, was the presence of a terrible, green, papier mâché turnip head exhibited on top of the tall cupboard in the kindergarten. I saw it as soon as I sat down in my small chair, and my whole day darkened with misery. The sight of it made me feel *exposed*. I was amazed that no one had the compassion to take away that poor head and give it decent burial. They all sat there, drawing or threading beads, impervious to its suffering. I never dared ask what it was or why it was there because I was fearful of the answer. I was to suffer its presence for a whole term before, mercifully and unexplained, it vanished.

Temporarily mollified by the pleasure of wearing my new uniform, I endured over a fortnight of school before the dawning of my third Monday made me realise what a terrible number of Mondays there were between me and infinity. I shrieked rebellion – only to be told by my exasperated mother, 'I asked were you *sure* you wanted to begin school. And you said yes. Ada, I did ask you were you sure.' To be reminded that it was my own fault was not the slightest consolation. By this time I loathed the small chairs and low tables of the kindergarten. It bore no resemblance to the picture fixed clearly in my head of a tall stool on which I kneeled to study large, rolled documents and manuscript-books spread on a table. In that memory there were several tutors but no other children. In kindergarten all we seemed to do was play, which to my mind had nothing to do with education.

In my desperation I asked my mother how long would I have to remain at school? She, reaching for the minimum age to console me, replied, 'Fourteen!'

'*Fourteen!*' I gulped down my astonishment. 'Do you mean I shall *grow up?*'

2

AT WHAT AGE I FIRST HEARD GAELIC SPOKEN ON THE RADIO I have no idea, but it seemed to me so natural and familiar that I slipped into the speaker's thought-stream as comfortably as I slid into my bath at night. Neither of my parents spoke Gaelic, nor did anyone else I knew; my father had a smattering of Welsh but I never heard him use it.

By twiddling the knobs on the radio – an illicit entertainment – I had found, I suspect, the Gaelic Children's Hour, then broadcast twice weekly on Scottish Regional in a programme lasting between ten and twenty minutes. Also on the dial was another station called Scottish National which fascinated me irresistibly. By listeners on the north-west coast of England nothing could be heard from Scottish National but atmospheric noises, yet I remained glued to the set when I had the opportunity, waiting for a voice to give me back the only other verbal sound of *home* I knew.

My addiction to the Gaelic Children's Hour was not popular, but it was tolerated. What ended it was my own terrible discovery one day that *I could not understand the words.* I can remember the tidal wave of misery rising inside me to pour out in the terrible lamentation I could never control. My mother said, 'Ernest, switch that off!' but my father, needing no bidding, had already clicked the knob, thus terminating what had been until that time my favourite programme.

Shuddering, I was held in my mother's arms while she asked desperately, 'Child, what *is* it?' – to which I gave no reply but the baying notes of age-old grief. How could I explain that once there had been a time when those words held meaning for me, and that today all that stayed to hold my heart-strings was their sound? Nor could I tell them that I was failing in my duty because I ought to know Gaelic for some reason vital, and now forgotten, which once had been so plain. Then my crying switched off as it began, and I went cheerfully to have my tea. But I never listened to the Gaelic Children's Hour again.

For several years afterwards, when perusing the *Radio Times* to discover details of children's programmes, I would discover passages in Gaelic – and over the mysterious spelling I would pore in anguish and longing, aware of deep loss and the constant sense of banishment. It was like holding in my hand the key to a door when the door itself was lost. I would keep turning back to those pages which held printed Gaelic, for, although incomprehensible, the secret they held was *mine*. At the approach of my parents I would put down the *Radio Times* or feign interest in another page, for I could not suffer any other person to know how deeply my link with Gaelic still affected me.

Written Gaelic worried me less than the spoken word for it had the stamp upon it of modern life. It seemed to me more like a 'foreign' language, whereas the spoken word had cut nearer to my bone. I have often wondered whether at some time in early infancy a Gaelic programme designed for children was, in fact, entirely comprehensible to me, or whether the 'once upon a time' when I had understood it dated back to some point in my infant existence too early for the patina of new learning entirely to cover the older memory. The one thing of which I am certain is that I heard no Gaelic spoken in my native Lancashire.

I had brought with me into modern Lancashire the knowledge that I was born in exile; I knew not to fret or feel hard done by, because my banishment was something I had earned. Also, a sense of duty lingered, and with it the awareness that all my present discomfort was necessary to a purpose. Nobody told me this – indeed, it was the last thing I would have mentioned, for I had learned my lesson when the battlefield memories caused me such embarrassment. I never talked about the things I *knew*, which were secret, and could not be imparted for lack of adequate vocabulary. By the time I had fluency in words the memory of what I knew had gone.

Two certainties lingered, however, like a riddle left to haunt me. I did not belong where I was born. My parents, I knew, were English, but I was not. I came from a different country, away to the north: I was a Scot. I had no wish-games of being stolen by gypsies and adopted; I had never a minute's doubt that my parents were in fact my parents. My singularly clear memory accorded in every detail with the present-life information supplied to me. We had no Scots relations, and it would, in fact, have horrified me had anyone claimed one of those ubiquitous highland grandmothers.

My sensitivity on the subject of Scotland was like a parcel of gelignite left in our house for safe keeping: we lived with it, but we never knew when it was likely to go off. I had never been to Scotland (at that time I had been no further north than Grange-over-Sands or Carnforth), but whenever I passed through Lancaster in my sidecar I always hoped that by some miracle we might lose our way and accidentally ride up to the Border. We never did. The bridge over the Lune carrying all the traffic going north to Carlisle remained for me the portal to paradise – even to see that traffic set me tingling with excitement. When my father's reminiscences of earlier cycling days produced the name Shap Fell ('going over Shap') I crept to the side of his chair, holding my breath, hoping that my silence would encourage him to let slip more crumbs of information. I did not ask to be told about Scotland, ever, for I was jealous of his having been there – and if I had asked I would, I knew, be given all the information which to me was erroneous.

People who returned from holidays in Scotland threw me into confusion. I bitterly resented their right to go where I could not – it was, in fact, the only subject which could provoke me to jealousy, for envy was not one of my natural vices. My mother, usually noted for her tact, once committed the unpardonable error of saying to a newly acquired Scottish friend who had just returned from visiting her family, 'Ada loves Scotland,' with a smile at me intended to make me happy. Scarlet with embarrassment, I fled to the lavatory where I wept and cursed my mother. After that experience I made a point of escaping early from any conversation concerning somebody's experience across the Border.

My awareness of Scotland was devoid entirely of tartan. I knew such material existed – I had been shown a black and yellow scarf and told its name – but it was never connected in my mind with the place that I remembered. Souvenir items which turned up in somebody's drawer, or calendars seen in shops bearing views of highland cattle, filled me with revulsion. I sensed patronage in this English habit of collecting Bonny Scotland trivia, and my rage at it was huge. I liked shortbread, but I had to close my eyes to the decoration on the box; I found Edinburgh rock delicious, provided that it came in a plain cellophane packet. These things gave me a sense of betrayal, as though the offering had been a theft, a cutting away of some part of my own identity.

A strange thing happened once at Thornton railway station. It was early morning during Christmas week, when we were going to spend some days with my paternal grandparents in Darwen. At that hour we were the sole travellers, but the L.M.S. provided a roaring fire in the waiting-room even at small stations like Thornton. I was carrying my new fairy doll, yesterday's Christmas present, shielding it with my gloves so that its silver tissue would not tarnish in the smoky railway-station air. My mother had worked late many nights after I was abed, stitching its many minute frills, to surprise me with it. Now, worrying about the tarnish, I wished she had told me what she was making so that I could have advised her to use cloth of gold, not silver. To sew in

28

silver was an extraordinary extravagance. . . .

I left my parents in the waiting-room and went out to see if the train was coming, still anxiously watching my doll's dress glisten in the station gaslight and hoping no passing train would send its fumes in my direction – and then I saw the poster. . . .

STIRLING CASTLE – the words hit me like a small explosion, leaving me sick with excitement. Military pipers in the foreground meant little; but behind the pipers was the gateway of a castle I *knew*. I stood in the cold, my doll's vulnerable silver tissue quite forgotten, my whole person tensed with longing to be inside the poster. Pain, an actual, physical stab of pain, went through my heart. I knew that it was just a piece of paper stuck upon a board, and behind the board was a wall; I knew it was a routine railway poster, no more imaginative, no more true to life than any other – but to me it was *the* gate. And upon the other side of it was . . . was the reality of *me*. My frustration was too great to bear, the discovery that the entrance was a print upon paper through which my too solid body could not pass. I know I stood for an age staring at the words Stirling Castle. Heaven to me just then would have been to sink to the platform and die at the foot of the L.M.S. poster.

When our train arrived I had to be forcibly removed, my voice protesting against the slam of carriage doors, 'But that's *my Scotland*!'

My Scotland usually identified itself in ways more obtuse. There was the black velvet dinner gown slashed with white satin which my mother had purchased in the afternoon and left at the shop to have the hem shortened. What she described at teatime sounded to me like a garment quartered in black and white, at which I became very quiet and stole away to my room where I confided my feelings to paper in a poem. The dress when it came was indeed magnificent, and much as she had described it – the black flowers in the corsage lying across white satin, and the white satin tail of them falling away across the black velvet; whoever designed it had a sense of heraldry. When I saw it I nearly went demented. That night, when she was dressed to go out with my father, she swept into my room where I lay in bed saying, 'See, Ada!' At the sight of her I screamed. I can remember her kneeling by my bed, in quartered black velvet and white satin, trying to cuddle me as I recoiled from her. *She was wearing my colours* – and there lay something worse behind the flash of memory which burst forth as a gush of ghost-tears.

When I was eight years old my parents went to London to attend a National Savings conference. To reduce my sense of deprivation at being left behind, I had been given two maple brazils (for me the ultimate in grown-up luxury) and the promise that, instead of being farmed out to the aunts, I could spend the weekend with Mrs Collins as her guest. The highlight of my visit was to be the making of a doll's bed,

29

my hostess said – a *small* bed, I had insisted, to fit Monkey. Its base was an eight-inch chocolate box with the lid used as a tester to support the hangings. The material for these I chose myself out of her bag of scraps, selecting the nearest thing I could find to cloth of gold which was a deep yellow taffeta. By teatime on Sunday the bed was complete, a beautiful piece of work. Then Mrs Collins produced what she had intended to be the gift which most pleased me – a doll to fit the bed. It had belonged to her mother and had some claim to be an historic object. The doll itself was perfect in detail, with its delicate porcelain face and eyes which closed. At the sight of it I fell absolutely silent, fighting down what threatened to be a veritable tempest of the ghost-weeping. Mrs Collins, who had been warned by the aunts about my bearlike hug of gratitude, also was silent, plainly wondering what had gone wrong.

What I saw was a doll laid flat with dead, closed eyes – a Scottish doll. It wore a tunic of dark green velvet, with a kilted silk tartan skirt above black-painted stockings. *Those* legs never had to do with tartan, that I knew full well. What repelled me more even than its tartan pattern was the age of the silk; so old, it had split in two places at the knife-edge of the pleats. It reminded me of cerements.

I nearly screamed when Mrs Collins tried to put the doll into the bed. Silently she re-covered it with tissue paper. Then I sat weeping beside the fire as she parcelled up the gifts for me to take away. She could not stop my sobbing; I think it scared her. She begged me not to be crying when my parents came. For her sake I would have stopped, but it was the other sort of cryng over which I had no control.

At my request she wrapped the bed and the doll separately. That way, I reckoned, I could show my mother the splendid bed without having to mention the horrible doll. So it worked out, and I managed to smuggle the doll, still wrapped in its tissue paper, into my toy-cupboard where I gave it decent burial in a far, dark corner beneath a barricade of toys. I lived in dread of the day when we would, inevitably, meet Mrs Collins on Chester Avenue.

The encounter occurred a fortnight later. Mrs Collins did mention the doll, and I, head-hanging, crimson-faced, listened to my mother diplomatically edging round the fact that this was the first she had heard of it. When we parted company I wildly called my mother's attention to everything in the street in my efforts to divert her from the subject of that doll. Chattering ceaselessly, my tactics were successful until bedtime when, as she was going into the kitchen to prepare my hot-water bottle, she said, quite casually, 'You never showed me the doll Mrs Collins gave you.'

I went to my toy-cupboard and dug out the moppet from its burial place. Holding it carefully in its shroud of tissue paper so that my mother would not see its long, black legs and lacerated skirt, I hovered in the kitchen doorway until I saw her fully occupied with the perilous business of transferring boiling water from kettle to hot-water bottle. The moment had been well chosen, for a cursory glance at the doll was the most she could afford. Then I escaped back with it to the cupboard, where I reinterred it as quickly as I could. My mother may have guessed we had some crisis on our hands because she made no further reference to the matter.

For many days the doll lay beneath a mountain of piled toys, but its presence never ceased to haunt me. In the end I resolved the situation by an act of vandalism which in any other circumstances would have horrified me. I purloined a razor blade of my father's and slashed that Balmoral doll's dress down the front from neck to hem. I put aside the garment, wrapped carefully, and then I set to work upon those black-clad legs with two coats of cream enamel. Its brown brogues I eliminated with black paint, so that I had at the end a naked, twentieth-century figure wearing high-heeled black court shoes like a woman.

At that point the doll ceased to worry me. I kept it in a blue and gold chocolate casket together with its savaged dress. The bed I had given to my precious Monkey where it slept solo. After a few months I found a use for the Victorian doll. Clad in silk and velvet of my own making, it became Monkey's consort. When Monkey wore a long-haired wig and gold-embroidered silk gown, the Consort was clad in breeks and doublet; when Monkey donned plate armour, Consort wore a female gown. Life was simple as long as nobody asked me questions. . . . And it was then I began my kingdom-building, with the palace and home farm, and the complement of courtiers brought up to forty, paired, and clad in fifteenth — sixteenth-century dress. So much skilled handiwork had to be shown by my mother to her friends, whose interest I tacitly discouraged.

I knew precisely what I was doing — had the adult world left me unquestioned: I was rebuilding *Scotland*, if they would just let me get on with it in peace.

My grandmother had elected to be buried in Bispham churchyard. From my point of view she could not have made a worse choice. Normally I loved cemeteries and graveyards, but not Bispham. At the very mention of 'taking flowers to Bispham' my symptoms started: sickness, headaches, rheumatism (in those days called 'growing pains'), all quite genuine. With luck, I could sometimes be too ill to go.

It was a pleasant walk to Bispham through the fields, which under other circumstances I enjoyed. The church itself, founded in the twelfth century, I would have liked had it been somewhere else. I did not mind entering the churchyard, bearing left past a row of nineteenth-century headstones, all mossed green, overgrown and quiet: that was fine. My ordeal began at the point where we collected and filled the watering-can.

We went down two damp stone steps to an area approximately four feet square flanked on the right side by a high stone wall on which hung a row of watering-cans above a tap with a lead feed-pipe bracketed to the wall. Beneath the tap was the drain, covered by a metal grill, and the stone flags were always wet and slippery. The worst aspect was the closed door facing me as I came down the steps, then at my left shoulder as I turned to fill the watering-can. Sealed with dirt and damp, blown leaves and cobwebs, it seemed to me that door had not been opened for centuries. Sometimes from the other side of the door could be heard voices – voices I could never reach, and when I descended those steps I had distinctly the feeling that I was approaching the door of a tomb from the inside.

I never mastered my terror sufficiently to ask for an explanation of the human activity behind that door – otherwise I would have learned that it was merely the boiler-room door at the back of the Sunday School. I could see for myself the Church Hall, but those Cubs and Brownies and women with prams whom we saw occasionally issuing from the building adjoining the churchyard were never related in my mind to the door coated in dust and cobwebs. The walled area with the watering-cans seemed to occupy another dimension, and I did not mind it provided I could be there alone. Indeed, I loved it then, and would stand wrapped in serenity beside the watering-cans, listening to those voices playing in a different world from mine. I did not expect to join in their life; I was happy just to know that life continued without me. It was when I had to go into that space with other people that I felt violated. Sometimes it was my mother's presence that suffocated me, or we would find someone else there drawing water. Once there came a workman in dungarees who bade my mother good day and patted me on the head, at which I screamed. We had a lot of sepulchral tears that particular day.

Eventually, I so contrived it – when I was big enough to lift the can – that my mother went on ahead to the grave whilst I went down to get the water. And when we had completed the task, she would take the dead flowers to the refuse bins whilst I returned the can to its place on the wall. When in luck, I would hear those unidentifiable sounds of life from beyond that door, and come away uplifted.

My other tribulation was the walk to the grave. The church was built on a hill, and my grandmother was buried beyond and below the rise. I was perfectly all right while plodding uphill with my watering can, but the scene from the top filled me with panic and extraordinary depression. Looking down the slope I had a vista of contorted angels, funerary urns, pedestals and crosses, all out of alignment – to my mind

32

it was like walking downhill into a petrified battlefield. The hetero-geneous collection of funerary fantasies was exactly like men in combat, frozen forever at the point where life had stopped . . . phantasmagoria.

Also, my mother did things that worried me – like her habit of adding a final douche of water to the vase before we left the newly arranged flowers. I used to watch the water overspilling on to the marble chips and think of all that damp seeping down to the coffin. Did my mother not realise that damp corrupted corpses? I never felt the least concern for my grandmother's remains when torrential rain drove hard into the ground: it was the leaking damp I dreaded.

Once, when cycling through Preston, we passed Woodplumpton graveyard and I asked to be shown where my great-grandmother was buried. Nearby was what was known as the 'witch's grave'. Just an unnamed common boulder marked the place, and in the top of it there still remained the trace of an iron staple which (I was told) once held a length of iron chain securing the stone to the ground, so that its captive could not 'walk' to disturb the peace of honest men. On going to see the witch's grave a second time, I asked what had become of the iron chain – and was told that the chain had been gone a long while before my time. This puzzled me, for I was sure that on my first visit I had actually seen the chain – although my subsequent examination of the rusted staple proved that I must have been wrong about that. It was odd, because I could have sworn that my mind held a clear picture of a length of swinging iron chain as I looked down and heard my mother saying that its owner could not 'walk' again.

My grandmother came of a Catholic family which had ignored Henry Tudor's reformation. Then a period of ecumenical cross-mating had produced the Anglican branch of the family to which I belonged. However, Henry VIII's ecclesiastical interference had never quite disrupted tradition, for most of my maternal relations had 'reverted' – and my Protestant mother and I always betrayed our affiliations when we spoke about a new Catholic as having 'reverted to the Faith'.

On the paternal side I came of a line of Nonconformists so determined to escape the whore of Anglicanism that two of my ancestors insisted on being buried in their own farmyard. My father happily joined the Church of England when he married my mother, but he celebrated their betrothal by walking her miles across the moors to see those two tombstones in a farmyard. 'My lot can fight as well as your lot' may well have been his feeling.

When I was small, I too was taken across the moors to see these tombs of my forefathers. The contemporary owner of the farm had set down on one of them a bucket of pig-swill, a sight which delighted me.

33

To lie in the exact centre of one's home-farm demesne, providing a useful working surface, with the sound of hen-clucking and hoof-plodding on the cobblestones to keep one in touch with earthly continuance, seemed to me a posthumous situation entirely to be envied. I searched for, and found, a chink in one of the tomb chambers, and pressed my face to it with a poignant longing to be inside.

These twin tombs of my ancestors could not be classed as 'forgotten' graves. On the contrary, their presence dominated the farmyard. What always worried me was the grave of someone whose existence had been overlooked. On the foreshore at Pilling were two nameless grave-slabs, by Flukehall, relics of the plague which had raged at Pilling. Disowned by both land and sea, they lay at the edge of the tidefall in a quarantine imposed by nature. Those I did not too much mind, for they lay two together. It was the solitary grave which I could not stand.

On a desolate part of the coastline called Sunderland Point there was a stone slab in the grass of a field, hidden in the shadow of a dry-stone wall. It was the grave of 'Sambo', a negro slave, said to be the last slave imported to these islands. Where he lay the coastline had a wild beauty so much to my taste that I might have envied him his interment there. Yet I hated Sunderland Point. No heat of summer's sun could take from my spine the ice-cold chill which blew from Sambo's grave behind the wall: the grave of a man buried alone in unconsecrated ground, in exile.

Churchyards were for me the happiest of places. Tombstones in churchyards were like a family to me, letting me share their comradeship when I walked among them. I envied those people buried all together, and in consecrated ground. I felt that they belonged to a kind of club which I was forever disqualified from joining. I was happy for them, but I felt my own exclusion keenly. I knew that I had no grave.

My early drawings make plain my tendencies. The houses and gardens which my mother steered my hand to draw became, when I could wield my own pencil, moated dwellings with castellated walls. Any ship I drew became a galleon. My churches, of which I drew many, were all the same – surrounded by a wall enclosing tombstones. I always rushed to finish the tombstones, for I could not bear to see the first one appear alone in my drawing. Sometimes in my haste the closed ranks of headstones would break formation, and then I would panic until I had redrawn them. Those rounded headstones for me represented people.

It was no wonder, really, that I hated the serried ranks of tombstones in Bispham churchyard as we went down the hill.

My SCHOOLING HAD BEEN FROM THE BEGINNING A SUBJECT OF DISSENSION between my parents. My mother herself had been educated privately; Tory in politics, an offshoot of the old faith, she had married my father whose line was Liberal, Congregational and firm in the belief that all children are equal in the eyes of a good elementary school headmaster. They had married for love on the understanding that love allowed them to hold differing opinions. They never quarrelled except upon two subjects – my father's distaste for gardening and my mother's low opinion of Lloyd George. On election day they went amicably together to the polling station to cancel out each other's vote, and on Sunday they knelt side by side at the altar rail in the Church of England. The point on which they could neither agree to differ nor compromise was that of my education.

My father, a schoolmaster by vocation, employed by the Lancashire Education Committee, felt that he betrayed his principles by letting his own child attend a private school. My mother comprehended his dilemma absolutely, but she did not want her daughter to pick up a rough accent and rude manners. During my early formative years she contrived to keep me at the prep school with the suggestion 'Just one more term. . . .' My prep school met my father's educational requirements in all areas save one – the constant turnover of teachers. Personally, I liked seeing new faces, but my mother shared my father's anxiety that this might have a disruptive effect on my learning.

What was finally to put an end to my private education was a social phenomenon later to be identified historically as 'the Thirties'. Both my parents had active consciences, and it seemed to neither of them proper that I should pass my playtime strolling in rose gardens when some of my father's own pupils missed a day's schooling because their one good jersey was in the wash – a contingency euphemised in parental notes as 'Bill is in bed with a cold.' Seated between my parents at our dining table, neat in my prep-school uniform, my up-pricked ears gleaned information about the Depression which is not always recorded in historical texts. Many of my father's boys were the sons of trawler skippers put out of work by the slump in the fishing industry, and men who held a Master's ticket took, when they could get it, a fortnight's work as a deckhand in preference to being on the dole. These were the kind of people whom we tried to help when my father had spotted their predicament, and always our major problem was how to make sharing sound not too much like patronage. My father's salary did not permit us to be bountiful upon a large scale, but he at least was sure of his job and my mother's skilful household management contrived ways of feeding two families for (almost) the price of one. She always had double quantities in the store cupboard, and seeing her make up weekly food parcels – known as 'the hamper' – is one of my clearest memories of that time. I was under oath never to speak of it to anyone, for people's pride might be hurt by my chattering.

Against this background I continued at my prep school until the age of eight. We were taught a variety of useful subjects, including French, but not, at my age, Latin. I can remember my dismay when I discovered that one did not progress immediately from bead-threading to Latin. I could not see how one could be educated in any other subject unless one first mastered that useful tongue. I asked to have pointed out to me those pupils whose studies included Latin and I would pick them out at morning prayers with awe and envy, for to me they were the only true scholars in the school. There was no apparent reason why I should feel so keenly my lack of Latin, for it was not our household language. My father was a Latinist but not a classical scholar, and my mother had long ago forgotten any prayers she might have learned from her grandmother's missal. My recollection of Latin as a spoken language persisted for a long while.

My memories of prep school are not particularly happy. The early days were made hideous by a girl two years my senior who was designated my 'friend' because she lived near enough to walk with me to the point where Fräulein Brücher met us at West Drive tram shelter. I used to pray all the way that Fräulein Brücher would be there when we arrived, to spare me those minutes of deliberate physical torture which otherwise awaited me in that green-painted hut. My companion's objective was to reduce me to tears, a feat in which she never succeeded. The homeward journey was even worse, for then she had three acolytes to help her. I endured this treatment for two years before I finally broke down and told my mother. The result was a school purge which rid me of my tormentors, and I marvelled at the discovery that life could be so simple.

All my real friends were school boarders, and as a day-pupil I could not share their evening activities. This led to an arrangement between my mother and the headmistress that on one or two days of the week I stayed to share the boarders' tea and their period of prep and ensuing recreation. I adapted well to the communal life, except on one occasion when I had a spot of bother of the kind I would today term 'back-head trouble'.

It was the evening when the boarders elected and crowned a Rose Queen. Being a day-pupil disqualified me from candidature but I was admitted to their franchise, and I was highly delighted when the girl for whom I had voted won the contest. The rest of the company assumed supporting roles in the ceremony, and I was cast as 'the Flower Girl'. When raiment from the school-concert trunk had been divided between the various officials, there was nothing left for me, so a senior pupil produced a blue scarf which was pinned round my middle like a sash. The show had started before I learned what were the duties of the Flower Girl: I was expected to strew roses (actually, chickweed) before the feet of the queen. My spontaneous reaction was to jettison my whole load of chickweed on the path, dump my basket beside it, and with ice-cold fury announce to the startled company that I paid homage to *nobody*. Then I stalked off into the empty pavilion where I stood behind the door so that I would not see the coronation.

I had just managed to reach the pavilion before the tears started – not child's tears, the other sort. I could hear the soft, dreadful noise thrumming through the empty building. When my favourite teacher came across to the pavilion I begged to be left alone. There was nothing she could do; I would just have to wait until the weeping stopped of its own accord. I was remorseful for having interrupted the coronation, but I could not have acted in any other way.

At the end of the pageant photographs were taken, and a senior prefect renowed for her diplomacy came to ask did I not wish to be included? I shook my head. The weeping persisted, but quieter now, the rustling desolate sound which, I knew, gave way to silence if I waited. She asked was I crying because the girl chosen was not myself? I shook my head. To stave off more questions I made the excuse that I was 'not properly dressed' in the blue scarf which had been my meagre portion. I hoped that would get rid of her, but she remained, kindly determined. I could feel another crescendo of those frightful sobs imminent and begged her to go away. I can remember beating my head against the doorpost, averring, '*You don't understand . . .!*'

How on earth could I say to her, 'It would be all right for somebody else to scatter flowers beneath the queen's feet, but not for *me* to do it'? The special thing about myself, momentarily remembered, was a duty never to pay homage to another living person; not because I was proud – which, I freely admit, I was – but because my *oath* forbade it.

In our grey and scarlet uniform we were the target for shouts of 'Private school snobs!' When the fields around my home were lost one day to concrete mixers which destroyed our lane, there grew up beside us a housing estate. To live in one of these new houses came a lad of ten or eleven who used to waylay me on my way home from school, barring my path with outstretched arms and grinning at my efforts to elude him. I made a private sallyport by loosening two boards of our back-garden fence which saved me for a while until he spotted it. He pounced on me there one day, catching the end of my scarf as I tried to dodge him, nearly strangling me. When he saw me choking he took fright and ran off.

This incident changed my whole attitude towards being bullied. At our next encounter I chanced to be armed with an umbrella. I shall never be sure what happened. I can remember the red mist rising before my eyes, and then nothing more until I turned and left him. All I know is that he wore an eye-patch for a long while afterwards, and if we met he bade me good day in a courteous and distant fashion.

One victory was all I had needed; nobody bullied me again. On the occasion by Robin's Wood when I was taken hostage by a band of fourteen-year-old youths, the consequences were spectacular. At the field gate my companions were allowed to pass but I was detained by four rough-looking louts, one armed with a cudgel. I was eight years old and frightened, and when their ringleader asked what I would give them in return for letting me go, I offered, ludicrously, to make him a penknife-case adorned with sealing-wax flowers, my hobby of that time. Rejecting my offer, he demanded a second time, 'What will you give us?' Suddenly fear left me. All I saw were those grinning white teeth, half as tall again as I was, and the red mist gathering. A voice came from me, deep and quiet – almost amused, quite unlike my own: I heard it say, 'I will give you *this*!' – and up streaked my clenched fist propelled by a force which almost lifted me off the ground. What happened after that I am not sure, until I found myself on the far side of the gate surrounded by the dumbstruck faces of my comrades. I had my hand to my cheek where at some point the cudgel had struck it. On my knuckles were some scratches and blood not of my shedding. Nearby, three young men had lost all interest in us while they commiserated with their leader, who was spitting out blood and some bits which had been his front teeth. I could not take my eyes off those spat-out teeth, and had to be turned away from the spectacle as we silently set forth for home.

I did not mention these episodes to my parents. When the Great Educational Debate ended with the resolution that I should go to the council school to be 'toughened up', I saw no need to make known the fact that the toughening-up process was already farther advanced than would have met with parental approval.

After the rose gardens and the mugs of cocoa at break-time, I was horrified by the concrete school yard where I had to spend ten minutes after a disgusting refreshment of milk – smelly milk, sucked through a straw from a bottle. There was no school uniform to even out the differences between rich and poor, and it seemed to my mind sheer cruelty to seat together lasses in fine woollen dresses and the few who, literally, wore rags. How did it feel, I wondered, to be frayed-sleeve dipping into an inkwell beside lace-cuff?

On my arrival I was put into a transitional class where there were four people who, though older than myself, had not yet learned to read or to write their names. Because I was young I stayed in that class for a whole year. French was not in the curriculum; we learned the three 'Rs' and some handicraft. My raffia-weaving gained top marks; I completed it ahead of schedule and then set to work privately upon an embroidery sampler which became a showpiece for visiting H.M.I.s. A great deal of my time was spent sitting with my hands folded waiting for the others to catch up, until I was given permission to read when I had finished my exercises. Within a term I had read all the books in the class library which were supposed to last me through the year.

We had an excellent teacher who, while handling a large class of varying ability, contrived to keep me interested; but there was nothing she could do about the lack of competition. My worst lesson was to be learned in due course at my grammar school when I caught up with my own kind and recoiled from the task of competing. Equal must be matched with equal, I had found at eight, otherwise both parties suffer.

At the council school I soon made many friends. Walking home became a pleasure instead of an ordeal, and my new friends, unlike the boarders at my prep school, could come to tea with me. These advantages counterbalanced my dislike of playing in a school yard overlooked by the public.

It was in the playground that a new girl was presented to us: 'This is Sheila.' She wore a blue and white chequered gingham dress, laced up the front by a white cord drawn through bone rings. (This sartorial detail fascinated me.) At the unlovely age of nine, when the rest of us were either pudgy or scrawny, Sheila was beautiful. She had a matching disposition, of which we were less aware at the time; we all liked her because she was hilariously funny.

In later years, once in a while I would catch her in a private moment when her mouth was unsmiling and her eyes had an opaque look which chilled me because sometimes I met it in my own mirror. About four times in our lives I asked, 'Sheila, what's wrong?' Then she would laugh, and say, 'Oh – nothing—Silly!' I think I knew what troubled her. Like myself she had the Sight. We never spoke of it.

Once she unnerved me. We were in the school playground 'dipping' for the leader of a game and holding out our hands to be eliminated. She suddenly remarked, 'Look at Ada's hands!' – and all eyes turned to them. Instinctively, I hid my hands behind my back, demanding to know what was wrong with them.

'There's nothing wrong with them,' said Sheila, 'but they're *different*. Show them – please show them.'

Reluctantly I extended my hands for inspection. My scalp was tingling in the way it did if ever I encountered an adult conversation I did not want to hear. Sheila took my hand and, puzzled, turned it over. Frowning, she made the others show their hands for comparison.

There were stubby hands, chubby hands, square hands, thin hands, short hands and knobbly hands, but there was not another pair like mine: at the end of my plump, child's arms there was a pair of graceful, adult hands which had come with me into the world as a baby.

Beneath the scrutiny of seven pairs of eyes, Sheila examined my hands and turned them over. Even the palms were different, for where the rest were marked by deep lines mine bore only the faintest tracing, like old writing on a stone. I demanded aggressively, 'What's the matter with them?'

'Nothing,' said Sheila, 'They're just – queer.'

The rest of them had lost interest and somebody proposed, 'Let's play.' I reserved my wrath for Sheila. She apologised; she had not meant to offend me. Momentarily apart from the rest, I asked her what had she meant when she said my hands were 'queer'?

She turned bland eyes on me, opaque as frosted glass, then smiled and said, 'I don't know. Truly, *I don't know.*'

I let it go at that. I often wondered if she had spotted what I myself knew about my hands: that they were the hands of another, far older, person.

For my ninth birthday party I promised my guests that I would write a play.

I had been composing poetry for longer than I could write, but my career as a dramatist began at the age of seven when my father bought a typewriter while we were away on holiday, and I had first use of it due to a fortnight's constant rain and the presence of an obnoxious small boy whose life had been in peril more than once because I simply did not know my own strength. Put into the dining-room with the typewriter, a bar of Milky Way and a glass of Tizer, I had written my first real play by lunchtime. ('The play opens on the batlefield where Margets farther is killed. . . .') In the afternoon I had mastered the use of a key marked CAPS, and colons, enabling me to write my second play in dialogue. Then my father reclaimed his typewriter, which inhibited further progress for about two years.

My motive in offering to write a play for my ninth birthday party had nothing whatever to do with Art. My friend Amy had been given for Christmas a tartan kilt and tam-o'-shanter which I coveted inordinately. I had not been interested until she told me its name was Royal Stewart, and then I had gone all breathless and peculiar, as if a drumroll had been played upon the knobbles of my spine. My attitude towards tartan had changed in an instant. Amy would have let me try on her kilt at any time had I asked her, but that would not have been enough: I had to be *entitled* to wear it. So I devised a way of getting that kilt to wear for a whole evening. The only kilted Royal Scot of whom I knew was the Young Pretender, who had never been upon my wavelength until that moment. Having first made sure that I could have the kilt, I set to work on the play: *Bonny Prince Charlie*.

At least, that was the way it should have happened, but that particular play almost proved impossible to write. I found myself unable to relate what was in my head to the small quantity of factual information which, south of the Border, passes for Scottish history. I had never known a similar experience; my mind became totally confused, and there seemed to be a blockage, like a physical lump in my head, whenever I tried to work on the play. (It was, in fact, the first manifestation of a problem I was to encounter years later in a similar situation.) On the eve of my birthday party I was so distressed that I begged my mother to cancel the entire function. Then, after I had actually gone to bed, I went rushing downstairs, grabbed an old schools' musical festival programme of my father's, and on the back of it jotted two scenes consisting of declarations of war, and the single, stark stage direction BATTLE. That I put Edward II of England in the field opposing Charles Edward – I did, in fact, know better – shows my inability to date or name the battle which had flashed suddenly through my head. The sole thing I could remember was my war with England.

When my mother saw the script she removed the ornaments from the drawing-room, shut the door, and left us to it. The two declarations of war we rehearsed and acted once, then devoted the rest of the evening to the third act, BATTLE. Before it began I mustered my Scots to tell them that the outcome rested with us, not with history, and this time they were to *win*. Twice my mother came to warn us about the noise, and on the third occasion arrived just in time to rescue either Sheila or Amy from being clubbed to death with Amy's lead pistol and the vexed cry, 'I've hit her three times but she won't stay dead!' I am unable to say which of them was being slaughtered, for I was occupied in a different part of the field, fighting for my life and heavily outnumbered. I was not playing. This time I meant to get them before they got me. I do not remember what happened after the red mist crossed my eyes, until I became aware of my mother's voice shouting, 'Ada, will you stop this *at once*! *At once*!' as her fingers bit deeply into my arm. Until this time she had known nothing of my record for ferocity under attack, and at bedtime I was subjected to a serious talking-to which ended with a worried, '. . . Child, you could kill somebody.'

My mother's subsequent embargo on battle-scenes diminished the fun of later birthday parties, but the need to substitute a killing line for a sword thrust no doubt speeded my development as a playwright.

*

I had no real interest in organisations of which I had not been the founder member, but anything which savoured of closed orders held for me an irresistible fascination. When I mentioned Brownies, my parents, knowing me, asked, 'Are you *sure* you want to join?' I was not sure at all, but in my new social circle where Sixers and Twicers (or whatever they were called) frequently dominated the conversation with esoteric talk about 'tracking' I felt I simply had to know more about it. It sounded exciting, and I thought one used it to hunt enemies and stalk game. Sadly were my hopes confounded when I arrived at the church hall, already familiar to me as the place wherein I wasted my good Sunday afternoons. I had arrived on the night of the annual festival called Egg Week and, paired with another Brownie, I went from door to door scrounging eggs for hospitals. Returning with our spoils, we had time for just one indoor game before joining hands to make a ring round a papier mâché toadstool where we sang our parting song. Then everyone saluted with the words 'Good night, Brown Owl.' As I was leaving, Brown Owl asked me had I enjoyed it, to which I replied truthfully, 'Not much. Collecting eggs was all right, but the rest of it . . . well, it's a bit childish, isn't it?' This was said in a clear young voice which the acoustics peculiar to church halls amplified, and on my way home several members of the pack wanted to know what I had meant by my parting words to Brown Owl. So I explained, never thinking that my words would leave uneasy the minds of several little Brownies who had never until that moment questioned the usefulness of the cause they served. It so happened that Brown Owl was a colleague of my father's, and thus word reached our tea-table that I had been a disruptive influence, which came as no surprise to my parents. (I had been in trouble before for telling my contemporaries that there was no such person as Father Christmas.) I could not see myself becoming a devotee of the cult, so I was not unduly disturbed to find myself cashiered from the Brownies for preaching treason and sedition.

I had not always escaped so easily. Intrigued by the sight of children flocking past my aunts' house on a Sunday afternoon, I said 'Yes' when my parents asked me would I like to join them. The trap was sprung by the time I realised that my reply had fitted all too well my parents' wish to have me enrolled as a Sunday School member. We sat in horrible small armchairs, torture to my long limbs, and sang 'All Things Bright and Beautiful' with a terrible scroop on the 'bee-ew-tifle' which offended even my not too sensitive musical ear. In the corner was a jingly piano, besides which stood the papier mâché toadstool belonging to the Brownies, and the room was dominated by a framed print of Jesus Christ being friendly to a group of variously coloured children.

There we listened to well-worn tales of Baby Moses and Baby Jesus, about whom I cared nothing until the point where they became grown up and interesting. Those who could endure this martyrdom every Sunday gained stamps, ill-printed pink, blue and yellow seals of virtue to be stuck into a little book which, if completed, earned a Sunday School prize. My own collection was sparse.

My great saviour was Mr Middleton, whose gardening programme on the wireless just after Sunday luncheon sustained my parents' interest sometimes long enough to make them forget the time until it was too late to get me ready for Sunday School. As I grew older I discovered the existence of, and joined, an interdenominational band of outlaws who played truant during the hours of Sunday School. The only thing that troubled my conscience was how to dispose of my collection money. Then I found a sweet-shop which had a collecting box for the Waifs and Strays, who thereafter benefited every week to the tune of fivepence. I often wondered whether the shopkeeper had his suspicions about the Sabbath visitation of five small girls who came not to buy but to donate.

The single good thing about junior Sunday School was a row of black metal candlesticks containing red candles of which an appropriate number was lighted on the Sunday following any member's birthday. To see those candles alight momentarily lifted my spirits, and the thought of having them lighted for me and being prayed for was the only thing that kept me going during my years of affliction. Also, there was the mystery behind the closed, glazed doors of the big hall, whose classes were still in session at the hour when we trooped past after dismissal. At times I heard a booming voice or the clang of a bell, or singing, and it was there, I knew, that older boys and girls learned all about God. God interested me and I looked forward to the day when I could go through those doors to a more esoteric field of instruction. When the time came, however, I discovered it was just another gathering of small groups where well-meaning but unqualified young humans tried to divine for us the meaning of divinity. Where I had expected theology, all we got was more scripture. The nice, simple young woman who taught us seemed dismayed by my string of questions – usually about the soul's progress after death – and advised me to ask the superintendant. I never did. I had no more high hopes of him, either. I was finally allowed to give up Sunday School when an early morning church service for children was started. This was conducted by our vicar, who seemed to know about God and took my questions in his stride as a natural occupational hazard.

I had never minded going to church, real church, with my parents. I loved the tall columns, vaulted roof and the choir singing the anthem; especially, I liked the bit when the two youngest choirboys took the

offering from the choir stalls up to the collecting plate and then bowed
to the altar. To prevent my tendency to restlessness during the sermon,
my father held me in his left arm while his right hand stealthily slipped
into mine, at intervals, three fruit drops. With me cuddled in my
father's arm we must have made a bonny pre-Raphaelite picture; other
members of the congregation who said what a *good* little girl I was
never knew that my father's loving embrace was actually a judo-hold
that could have won him a black belt had he applied it seriously.

The service I really did want to attend was Holy Communion.
Smuggled in by my mother on a week day, I had sat spellbound in the
quiet. Nobody there talked down to me. I was put on my honour to sit
still while she went up to the communion rail, and I never committed
any offence save once, when she had left her fur and gloves beside me in
the pew and I solemnly put them on as vestments, the nearest I could
get to ritual. My mother had difficulty containing her amusement when
she returned and saw me, calling me 'a young imp', but I could not
see why she thought my gesture funny. I knew about the ban on my
receiving bread and wine; it was a fixture in my head like the battlefield
memory. I assumed my mother knew of it too, and when she said I
could not take communion because I was 'too young' I thought she
meant it as an excuse to make my excommunication less embarrassing
for me. When she did finally convince me that there was nothing to
prevent my becoming, one day, a communicant, I surprised her by
bursting into tears.

I had to wait until I was thirteen to be confirmed, and my impatience
became more vociferous with each year as I heard the vicar announce
the start of confirmation classes. When my turn came it was the one
occasion when nobody needed to ask me if I was sure I knew what I was
doing. Before my first class I had learned by heart the entire catechism
and was most disappointed to discover that it was to be merely the
basis of discussion at the classes, and not, as I had anticipated, a formal
duologue between the bishop and myself. It was explained to me that
our dozen communicants would be merely part of a large assembly
coming from all the local churches in the diocese, and that the bishop
would not have time to hear our catechisms individually. I grieved
deeply at this news, for no one knew how much it meant to me to have
the chance of setting my record straight with our bishop. My need
for reconciliation would have to be satisfied with the episcopal
blessing.

My confirmation took place when there was a European war in
progress and formal garb of white cost precious clothing coupons, and
the importance to me of that day is measured by the degree of care
taken by my family to provide me with fitting vestments. From
Fleetwood Market Aunt Edith obtained a length of reduced-coupon

satin which was made up on the wrong side so that no sheen gave frivolity to the occasion. It was a dress made for wearing but the once, with its high collar and long sleeves, and a garment so categorically unadaptable was the extreme of extravagance in wartime. For my white gloves I went to Sweet & Clark's in Blackpool, which was *the* drapers and haberdashers. Even my stockings were white pure silk, an item totally unobtainable in my young lifetime, but they were the pair worn by my mother on her wedding day. My veil I stitched myself, a plain, hemmed square of white net embroidered with one stark white cross which I would wear fastened over my head like a nurse's cap so that not a wisp of curl was given licence. The gold cross and chain were new, a present from my aunt who was my godmother. Many Fylde families had coupon-scraped to give their daughters suitable attire for the occasion, but looking back on that procession I was the only one who came to meet my bishop like a nun dressed for her wedding to the Church. My piety was real, not assumed, and my clothing had to match it.

There was just one flaw in the arrangements, so far as I was concerned. A fortnight before the day the class was told which church, by rotation, would be the scene of our admittance – *Bispham*! Had I known that earlier, it is likely I would have postponed my confirmation. I reflected that it was just my luck to get Bispham. However, I steeled myself, for my appointment with that bishop was so important I would have gone to meet him in hell if necessary.

On the day, which was windy, the Sunday School of the church was put at the disposal of the communicants and their families. Curiously, once inside this building my dread of Bispham left me. It was a friendly, small room, full of bustling mothers with pins and hairgrips in their mouths, fastening daughters' veils firmly against the wind, and changing shoes.

I veiled myself, my mother holding the comb and mirror, and then I set out on the path towards the church, Sheila walking beside me in the long procession of white-clad girls and boys in their best wartime flannels. We kneeled before the Bishop of Lancaster, and I was so happy that I meant to kiss his ring – then realised in the nick of time that kissing his ring had not been part of our instruction. My father, afterwards, prompted me to have him sign my prayer book, which I did – and pored for days over the only autograph which had ever mattered to me, Benjamin Lancaster, *our bishop*. . . .

When all was over and we were about to leave, my mother asked did I mind if she went to grandmother's grave as we happened to be there? – and, far from minding, I actually volunteered to accompany her. Now that I had been admitted to the solemn rite of communion, the sealed door by the watering cans and the petrified battlefield no longer troubled me. Robed in white, still as a marble angel, I stood beside the grave: just for the record, I had come to acquaint my grandmother and everybody else in Bispham churchyard with the news that I too was now entitled to have decent Christian burial.

CHAPTER TWO

1

BETWEEN THE AGES OF EIGHT AND EIGHTEEN I WAS COMPARATIVELY
free from back-head interference. This may have been due to the war,
or to the channelling of my unconscious energy into my writing — or
it may have been simply that the accumulating years' experience buried
my earlier memories. Through the war years even my dedication to
Scotland became displaced by a passionate loyalty to dear, dreadful
Thronton Cleveleys where, in 1938, I helped my father to distribute
gas-masks round all the new houses which had sprung up where the
fields and ponds and bramble hedges used to be.

A child born in 1929 and having access to radio news bulletins had
been, figuratively speaking, within sound of gunfire all its life. I had
been born only a decade and four months after the Armistice of 1918,
and yet my parents' war was to me, I used to say, 'more remote than the
Wars of the Roses'. It was a subject about which I asked questions by
the fireside on winter evenings. Sometimes, if I pleaded, my mother
would bring down the small tin trunk, which was kept beneath the
writing-table in my father's den, and show me yet again the arm-band
emblazoned with a tea-cup which she had worn on voluntary night-
duty on Preston Station, serving tea to troop trains. Also in the trunk
was a pile of newspapers recording such events as the death of King
Edward VII and the sinking of the *Titantic*, and amongst them were
several sheets she did not care to look at which consisted of nothing but
names in columns; almost every man my mother had known when she
was young was listed in those pages.

My father had been too young to serve in the First World War, so
my information about trench warfare had been gleaned from bound
volumes of *The War Illustrated* which were kept in the drawing-room.
The nearest books to hand, they kept me occupied during musical
evenings. My paternal grandparents had come to live in Bispham, and
the two families combined contributed between them an alarming
quantity of musical talent. I had no feeling whatever for the pianoforte,
violin or cello, but I had desperately wanted to learn the harp. My
mother said, 'Child, where would we put a harp in this house?' and my
reply that I had meant the *little* harp was brushed aside as nonsense.
My mother, being English, did not know the clarsach; nor did I by
name, but it appeared in all my drawings of Scottish castle interiors. I
could never sing in tune, a deficiency which grated on my father when

he wanted to use me to try out songs for school musical festivals, and his resigned 'Ginger, go to help your mother with the washing up' was a depressing comment on my vocal ineptitude. The thing I did well was recite, but my mother felt that over-exposure to adult acclaim spoiled the child and made life tedious for guests, so while my grandfather Kay aimed for his top notes I always sat in the corner looking at the pictures in *The War Illustrated*.

When Mr Chamberlain flew back from Munich with the promise that we would have peace in my lifetime, my mother kneeled by the chair in the dining-room to thank God for the reprieve. Dutifully, I imitated her, although I finally gave up trying to tell God that I was anything other than profoundly disappointed.

The peace we were to have lasted just one year, and all of it for me seems compacted into two weeks of summer holiday in 1939 which mark the end of my childhood. It had been a toss-up that year whether we went to Scotland or to South Wales, and I had pleaded hard for us to go to Scotland. My parents continued talking after I had gone to bed, and when my mother came up to tell me that we were going to Wales my ghost-grief wracked the house like a gale. My father told me of the wonderful castles I would see in Pembrokeshire, but even the promise of seeing a real live monastery on Caldy Island evoked no real response. Finally, my mother gave me her word that we could go to Scotland the following year, but of course by that time we were to be at war with Nazi Germany.

I was now aged ten and the phenomenon of double awareness had not troubled me for a couple of years, but I had a dreadful time with it on that holiday in Wales. Whether I visited too many castles, or the sense of impending war stirred the now-forgotten battlefield memory, I do not know, but the disturbance in my head made me irritable and sad without my being able to explain what was the matter with me.

My father had been right about the splendour of Pembrokeshire's castles, and we saw almost all of them. I was deeply impressed by the fortress in Pembroke itself. The most striking feature of Pembroke Castle, apart from its circular keep, was the huge cavern dungeon below it. A natural cave in the rock beneath the castle, it had a hole in the side like a picture window grilled by iron. The view from this 'window' had an extraordinary effect on me; I felt that I was standing in some other castle where the downward view had been similar. I was older there, much taller – not a little girl at all; and my parents had not been present in the remembered scene, when I came to think about it afterwards.

My favourite of the castles was Carew, a lovely, unspoiled ruin in the midst of pastureland. We had it entirely to ourselves on that afternoon when vivid sunshine was intermittently obscured by newly washed and bundled white clouds, so that Carew's mood precisely matched my own; and my father took a photograph of me seated by the moat – or, more likely, composed a picture of the castle using me as a foreground detail to relieve flatness.

Built originally as a medieval fortress, its sixteenth-century owner had converted one side of it into a manor house with mullioned windows, so that it appeared to have stayed forever upon the brink of a new century. It was the nearest I had seen to a building of what I always thought of as 'my time'. All that remained of Carew was the shell and, as we walked along the high parapet formed by the roofless walls, I had distinctly the feeling that *somewhere else* I used frequently a roof walk with a view of greensward not unlike this one, and there I had carried a better head for heights than I had now. (My father, long accustomed to rescuing me from high ladders and rock ledges, remarked subsequently upon my aptitude for altitude that day at Carew.) Once or twice I turned expecting to see roof-slabs, and the sight of roofless and floorless chambers open to the sky startled me.

It was to be many years before I saw and identified the Scottish palace which Carew, in miniature, so much resembled, but on that day in 1939 I had seen the first domestic structure which I could positively identify as 'home'. Pedalling back behind my father on the tandem, I suggested that we should buy Carew Castle and restore it. When my father realised that I was serious, he pointed out that Carew was not for sale, but that did nothing to daunt my enthusiasm. I was to spend many long nights awake planning the renovation of Carew, and my vision, so real, was of a castle *where this had happened.* I could see the restoration work so clearly in my head – even the masons and men with wheelbarrows – that I knew it had happened; and my usually forward-projecting mind concluded that this must be one of the times when I saw things before they came to pass. Hence my extraordinary determination to convert my parents to the idea of buying an inaccessible, ruined Welsh castle in place of our practical residence in North Drive. When my mother, tired of my persistence, pointed out that my father earned our daily bread by teaching in Thornton Cleveleys, I even went so far as to search the columns of *The Schoolmaster* each week to find him a suitable teaching post in Pembrokeshire.

The eagerly awaited visit to Caldy Island to see a functioning Cistercian monastery was a disaster. I had had dreams the previous night of crossing the strand at low water to the shingle on the foreshore of an island where assembled monks waited to welcome me. Caldy Island bore no resemblance to the place I had remembered. We were rowed across to the island in a boat. I was disturbed and distressed all that day by a fusion in my mind between what I actually saw on Caldy

Island and fleeting impressions of monastic life as I had remembered it. Being female, I was not allowed to enter the monastery chapel, but to my inner ear the reason sounded so absurd: whoever thought of *me* as female? But, dimly, I recalled the ban . . . why it had been imposed I had forgotten, but the plight of being forbidden the sacrament was as real to me that day on Caldy Island as it had ever been. My head ached all that day, shivers ran down my spine like a constant trickle of cold water, and I whimpered for the boat to take me back to the mainland. What the monks saw (if they noticed) was a plaintive, badly behaved child, and I blushed for my parents who had to own me. We all agreed that I was 'not myself' that day.

My confusion of memories upon that holiday was not helped by the fact that the village of Penally where we stayed was built around a hill with a ridge leading from it. This set me asking where was 'the square hill where we camped'? I had asked this conundrum many times before in earlier years, to be told by my mother, 'But you have never been camping, child.' I had shouted, then, 'Yes, I have! With lots of men, but you weren't there.' Several times over the intervening years I had set my father searching through all his photographs for my 'square hill' which nobody could identify, but he had never found it.

Only one thing on that holiday gave me enormous happiness. Below the old school house where we stayed was the churchyard and in it was the loveliest tombstone I had seen. It was a large, rectangular structure of mossed-green stone, burst open by a strong young sycamore sapling growing from its dead man's bones. At the end of any troubled day I could restore myself to calm by going to look at that grave.

Our vacation ended abruptly, two days short of the fortnight. I can remember entering the sitting-room of the small Penally guest-house during a thunderstorm to find the proprietors, my parents, and two or three other people grouped round the wireless set, sitting close to hear the news bulletin through the crackling of atmospheric interference. The peculiar yellow cast of storm light threw their intent figures into black silhouette against the window. My mother said 'Ssh, Ada' – I had not spoken – as I tiptoed across the room. This bulletin directly concerned us: all schoolteachers on holiday were recalled to deal with evacuation.

During the following week we saw little of my father, whose task was the billeting of 'evacuees', that new word of our time. On our dangerous family principle of never asking others to do what we would not tackle ourselves, we had offered a home to one child, sex female.

I waited apprehensively, for this was where my part in the war began. The spare bedroom was my father's study. Not only was he an air-raid warden, a billeting officer, and the district secretary of the National Savings movement, he was also the headmaster of a school where the head had to take a full-time class. It was imperative that he should have free access to his study. Another possibility was to put a single bed into my room at the foot of my double one, but we wanted the evacuee to share my life on equal terms. I had whispered, white-faced and stricken, 'She won't have to share my *bed*, will she?' – to which my mother replied, 'Ada! Surely you don't grudge half your bed to a lassie whose parents might get bombed?' Put that way, I could have no objection, but the thought of sharing my bed with a total stranger made me feel physically sick.

My worst memory of the war is that morning, a Saturday, when I helped my mother to prepare my bed for two people. When the ghost tears started a second time my mother, who was ill and trying to do her best for everyone, was in despair. Then she hit on the brilliant idea of putting the bolster down the middle of the bed as a demarcation line. I hugged her for the inspiration.

My father had impressed on us the importance of taking the first child brought to the door – already that morning he and his colleagues had seen too many people expressing preferences. So my mother put her arms round the first that came, and thus Katie joined our family.

My eyes nearly popped out of my head when at luncheon my new sister, ignoring knife and fork, conveyed the food to her mouth in curious small parcels clipped in bread between her fingers. My mother's beacon glare served to steer my eyes back to my own plate, but I made the excuse that I was not hungry. Afterwards, in the kitchen, I was trembling: somewhere, at some time – ages, *ages* ago – I had seen victuals taken by hand in just that same deft fashion: that was what shocked me.

In the afternoon the two of us sat on the see-saw in the garden, sharing a block of Rowntree's Plain York chocolate which had been part of Katie's iron-rations. As we tipped to and fro she taught me the words of 'South of the Border Down Mexico Way' . . . the first and only pop song to invade my classical repertoire. My own talk was chiefly of the coming war, which seemed to be the only thing we had in common. It bonded us in our awkward mutual plight until bedtime.

Katie was three years older than I – something for which my mother had not bargained. Unlike myself, she had many brothers and sisters and had always shared a bed. In fact, she turned out to be a courteous and considerate bedfellow, but nothing took away my horror of that first night when I lay awake listening to the breathing of another human presence on the far side of that bolster. Physical nausea prevented me from sleeping – also, I had moved so far to the edge of the bed that I had to grip the mattress to save myself from falling out. After three nights I had just begun to grow accustomed to the situation – then Katie menstruated. I knew to expect this biological

51

feature myself one day – although to the very end I never believed that anything so bizarre could happen to *me*. The sight of Katie's bloodstained pyjamas, which she took as natural, filled me with terror. To worsen matters, Katie, I soon realised, never used sanitary towels. I went through hell wondering how to tell my mother of this unexpected development but mercifully she discovered it for herself when she made the bed. The same day Katie mentioned the abscess on her head requiring to be dressed, and when my mother looked she found not only the abscess but a lively population of small beasts disporting in the hair roots. Prompt application of the dust-comb to my own hair yielded one awful adult animal, which set me screaming with disgust that anything so hideous and squelchy could inhabit my hair. At this point my mother decided that my contribution to the war-effort had been made, and my father made no protest when the camp-bed was erected for me in his study.

What ended our fostering of Katie was my mother's operation. Before going into the nursing home she searched half of Cleveleys to find the right person to look after Katie. So my temporary sister departed, with a stock of new clothes, trained in hygiene and the use of cutlery, and with an invitation to visit us whenever she wanted. Afterwards, we were to act as transit camp for evacuees during the London blitz, and an entire family of four (thrice-bombed-out) shared our house for a merry fortnight of barrack-life which all of us enjoyed, but I was never asked to share my bed again – except by my mother if the siren went while my father was on A.R.P. duty.

The breakthrough of back-head memory lasted for about a year. It was finally sublimated in my writing and thereafter for a long while ceased to trouble me. What started me writing novels was a serial broadcast in 'Children's Hour' during (I think) the autumn of 1939. My inspiration was not the story – about a fictitious seventeenth-century English highwaymen – but its title, 'The Rider'. At the end of every episode the hero proclaimed his identity – 'the Rider!' – and with the clatter of hooves faded from the air. It was for that final moment I sat glued to the radio every week, my stomach churning with excitement. I knew that somewhere, at some time, *I* had been represented as 'the Rider'.

It is extremely unlikely, but just possible, that a child born and educated in England might at some time have heard of a fifteenth – sixteenth-century Scots coin called the rider because of the equestrian portrait of the King which it bore, but even had she known, why should she connect it with herself?

My inspiration came often the same way, from a name or a title which sparked off in my head a storyline entirely my own. On the night of the first episode I went to bed with that cry, 'the Rider!' still ringing

52

in my ears, and in no time at all my head was filled with the theme for my first great novel. It would be set in modern times, and the hero – now, for my purpose, a heroine – was the leader of a small band of rebels sworn to recover their country from tyrannical rule. Their lair was a huge cavern dungeon beneath a ruined castle – I was drawing on my memory of Pembroke – and their colours were black and white: all the men wore black, their female leader alone being clad in white cavalry uniform and riding a black stallion.

It was thus far a typical child's adventure story, but what was to me the most exciting element of my tale did not fit that genre. Throughout the book I meant to scatter, like choral interpolations, excerpts from Press headlines and radio news bulletins. It was on these my mind was working as I drifted, finally, to sleep. My last conscious recollection is of an entire nation crying the good news that 'The Rider' had been seen here, there, everywhere. . . . My dreams that night became a tangle in which pictures of places and people from the fifteenth – sixteenth-century imposed themselves over my modern story – but the dreams were strange in that the sixteenth-century scenes intruded as complete, clear episodes, within themselves containing no discrepancy.

In the morning I could recall the dreams, but I could no longer see what the 'historical bits' had to do with my story – although I had known just at the moment when I was drifting off to sleep.

Although for many days and nights I constructed my fantasy, I never recaptured the initial excitement. I made a start on it but the book was never completed. One and a half pages set the scene of the mustering in the cavern and registered the equestrienne's colours of black and white. There I left it – possibly having achieved all that my mind considered necessary. To avoid plagiarism of title, I had been obliged to change mine to 'The Phantom Rider' and the intrusion of the word 'phantom' not only displeased me, it broke the link with the name which had originally inspired me.

That first abandoned novel marked the beginning of my compulsive writing. Although it was to be two years before I wrote the first of several complete novels which were to engage me throughout the war years, it was between the ages of ten and eleven that my writing became to me what the pearl is to the oyster, a means of deliverance from discomfort.

I was in my last year at the junior school when reception areas such as ours saw the reintroduction of that archaic custom: part-time edu-cation. Two schools sharing a building, we were taught in shifts, mornings or afternoons. I was happy with the arrangement at first, for my spare time allowed me to pursue my favourite creative hobbies and teach myself new skills. I had just begun to make pillow-lace – using old film spools as bobbins – when authority stepped in to organise these useful hours in ways I found loathsome. The object was 'to keep us off the streets'. (I wondered with interest if anyone I knew was 'on the streets'.)

While good weather prevailed we all trooped off to Rossall Beach to play rounders. I was no good at ball games, and my lot was to stand as deep-fielder amongst the sand-dunes and tufts of marram grass. Nobody but Sheila knew how much I hated Rossall Beach, evocative of dark memories which had plagued my early childhood. Here was the scene of my infant nightmare, where lay the beached black ship with its shining brass gun-mouths. I used to stand at my isolated post, depressed and shivering, and no matter how brightly shone the sun upon the far away rounders' pitch, it never warmed me. Sheila was good at rounders, but she used to play the fool to keep up my spirits. This was naturally deplored by all true sportsmen, and she was moved as far away from me as possible. Thereafter there was nothing to save me from slipping into those dark pools which I remembered afterwards only as blanks in my memory.

When winter ended our sporting activities, various premises were requisitioned to serve as temporary academic accommodation and our luck of the draw was the Working Men's Club in Slinger Road. The unseen presence of those working men lurked everywhere, like their beer-mats and stale beer-fumes – I never opened a door without expecting one to pop out at me. Without, initially, books or blackboards, heroic teachers battled to hold our interest with pastimes which had to be within the grasp of the youngest and the dimmest. Later, when the classes had been sorted out, the best use for the hall was found to be singing and country dancing. I was no asset to any choir, but I enjoyed the dancing and mastered 'Newcastle' well enough to be a member of the prize set which demonstrated to visiting school managers that we were, war regardless, being educated. It was against this background that Sheila and I won our scholarships to the grammar school.

On the last day of term Sheila, Amy and I forgathered for the last time in the ladies' lavatory of the Working Men's Club to enjoy the secret-drinking sessions which had made life there endurable. Our potation was usually my terrible mock-ginger-beer (made of syrup and ground ginger, brewed like tea and, when cold, bottled). None of us liked it, but smuggling the stuff to our meeting-place was the real joy of the exercise. On this occasion Amy had brought for a change a bottle of Rose's lime cordial, but she had forgotten to bring a cup in which to dilute it so we swigged it from the bottle, neat, in a gesture of farewell to Slinger Road and the Working Men's Club.

*

History's watersheds occurred invariably when I was under age, with the result that I grew up rather quickly in sporadic bursts of about ten minutes. The first happened on the morning of the fall of France, in June 1940, when I was eleven. My mother knelt to pray beside a chair in the dining-room, as she had done in 1938, but this time I stood watching her, aware that she would be praying for me. I needed praying for, because if my government surrendered to Germany – which was a possibility that morning – I would have to go to school under the Nazis. It had happened to the rest of Europe's children and now it could be my turn. My thoughts at once had turned to that, because I knew I had no capacity for dissemblance and my record of intractability guaranteed that my life under the Nazis would be a hard and a short one.

We held a council of war, and I required no telling that in the event of invasion my own survival was of paramount importance. My mother was past childbearing and I was the one upon whom our genetic continuance depended. I said I thought that, if the Germans came, my best course would be to hide out somewhere in the Fells. My mother agreed, for she had made up her mind that German paratroops would never occupy our house while she was alive to stop them. I suggested that we should fill my bicycle saddlebag with iron-rations and I would set out to reconnoitre for a suitable hiding place. The first landings could take place at any moment, and there was no time to lose. My mother packed me some sandwiches and waved me off on my bicycle.

An hour's hard pedalling took me to the Fells, no longer signposted. (My father maintained that it would confuse the Germans a great deal more if the Pennine signposts had been left as they were.) Much of my knowledge of the Fells had been acquired through trial and error, and there is no better way to discover old tracks omitted from the Ordnance Survey map. It was for one such that I made now, a marvellous place to hide away in in the event of invasion. On a low plateau of moorland ringed by hills, I stood contemplating a far, tree-lined gully which disappeared into a hillside. That would suit my purpose. Then I looked about me, carefully noting every detail of the immediate landscape: hollows where might lie a clutch of eggs in spring; ledges of earth, barely visible, where rabbit turds were fresh; places where bilberries abounded. I saw it with a hunter's eye, and judged the terrain could support me. The transition from nature lover to predator happened so quickly that all I felt was reassurance to find that I had the instinct to survive as an outlaw.

While I stood there, counting my potential assets, there appeared very high above me a hawk or falcon. All my life the sight of winged predators had set my veins tingling with exhilaration. I had always seemed to *know* hawks and falcons – though my learned knowledge extended no further than a nodding acquaintance with medieval illustrations. I contemplated the hovering bird, wondering whether – if and when I came to be its neighbour – I could trace it to its nest in spring and train its young to do my hunting for me. Intellectually, I had no idea how to 'man' a falcon, but I knew, standing there, the feel of a bird on the flat, broad area of hand formed by thumb and forefinger, where it had been most comfortable for me and for the falcon.

Feeling satisfied with my afternoon's work, I walked my bicycle back to the nearest road and began my journey home to tell my mother that I had found a likely place of refuge. It was only when I pictured myself telling her that the thought occurred to me that, for all I knew, she might no longer be alive for me to tell. I felt solitary and conspicuous riding my bicycle down Victoria Road, glancing to my right and left for any sign that in my absence paratroops had landed. The few people I saw were going about their normal business, but the street seemed curiously quiet. As I rode slowly and warily into North Drive I saw my mother's shadowy figure in the drawing-room window watching for me. She came out to give me a hug.

In September 1940 I started at the grammar school in Fleetwood where at last I would learn Latin. On my first morning, proud and hideous in my green jelly-bag school hat, I set forth in the charge of a senior pupil. Eileen was the daughter of family friends, and just fourteen months previously I had watched enviously her preparation for the school expedition to Switzerland and my mother had consoled me with the promise that my turn would come. By 1940 I knew that my chance of going with the school to the Continent was likely never to materialise. Two other features of grammar-school life to which I had been looking forward were the school magazine and the dramatic society, outlets for my literary and histrionic talents, but the paper shortage had killed the magazine and the blackout put an end to dramatic productions. The only thing not in immediate short supply was Latin, but even that was to become a problem to us during the vital years just before Highers when we had no qualified classics teachers – most of them being male and owned either by boys' public schools or by the army.

The great event of the school social year, I knew, was the Christmas ball traditionally called 'soirée'. For this the girls arrived in long gowns and taxis, and the boys transformed themselves into young men in evening dress. They had a marvellous cold buffet, and another interval for ices, and they danced away the hours until their carriages came for them. . . . I had been dreaming about soirées since about the age of nine.

My first soirée, like those which were to follow it, was a short-frocked, afternoon dance between the hours of two and five so that we

56

could get home by tram before the blackout. Those of us who did not live in Fleetwood had to take our dresses to school in the morning, packed in a suitcase, and change for the party in the school cloakroom smelling of gymshoes. Our refreshment was a sausage-roll and a cress sandwich. No ices. We danced by daylight in the school gymnasium. Half-way through my one dance with a boy for whom I had a term-long secret passion, the air-raid siren sounded. Marched quickly back to the cloakroom, we pulled our black stockings over the silk ones borrowed from our mothers, while Miss Lumsden in stately black stood whistle in hand to exhort the stragglers. My shoe buckle jammed, and I finally hobbled off across the mud of the playing fields wearing one silver shoe and one black, praying that none of my erstwhile partners could see me. In our segregated bunkers twenty-five minutes of our precious utility festival ticked by as we sat in the dark singing 'One Man Went to Mow. . . .'

My first soirée had coincided with the December air attacks on London.

On the morning after the great incendiary attack upon the City of London, I said in anguish to my mother, 'Think of all the churches which have been destroyed!'

My mother retorted angrily, 'Ada, think about the *people*!'

Then I surprised us both by shouting, 'Oh, people can get born again' – by which I meant they could continue reproducing – 'but we can't rebuild the churches. *We can't rebuild the churches*!' Then came one of my attacks of ghost-weeping, so violent that my mother made me sit down while she went to make me a cup of tea. When she returned the gush of tears was over, and I agreed that it was terrible about the people. But my mind's eye carried still a strange, distorted picture of a lone church tower silhouetted against a sky of crimson flames. What it had to do with me personally I had no idea, but it bore no connection whatever with the London blitz.

At the end of our first grammar-school year we moved to our new desks in the second year form-room. There I had trouble with a book. It was supplied to me in the collection of new text-books which were to be our year's study, and I can see it yet – a horrible small book with the name of its previous owner scrawled in spidery writing on the front of the crinkly, brown-paper dustcover. It brought me out in goose-pimples. I hurried to my desk and frantically buried it beneath every other book that I could lay my hands on. I never looked to see what it was, until an English lesson at the beginning of the new term identified it for me as Scott's *Marmion*.

I had never heard of *Marmion*. Despite the presence of two complete sets of Waverley Novels on our bookshelves at home, I had neglected Scott entirely apart from a brief sampling of *The Talisman*, which left me with the feeling that he was an author not upon my wavelength. My father was no Scott enthusiast and my mother had suffered too much of him at school, so there had been no pressure on me to read him.

In fact, I never did discover what *Marmion* was about because I missed those lessons. I was always ill; in the beginning with migraine, and latterly with a strange cardiac manifestation which began that term. A couple of times I tried to get out the book, and on each occasion the sight of that crinkly, brown, protective wrapping made me go cold and sick and my vision blotted out so that I thought I was about to faint, and I asked to be excused. When I came back the lesson was over, and my copy of *Marmion* I put back into my desk, frantically scraping over it a pile of books to give it decent burial. All-through that year its presence in my desk was a nightmare, for occasionally it would surface when I was searching for other books, and the desperate process of burial would start all over again.

I never did read *Marmion* – as I have good cause to know, because I went into the terminal and yearly examinations knowing that in a certain section of the English paper I would be unable to answer a single question. As English was one of the subjects on which I relied for obtaining high marks, that omission was a serious matter.

This strange habit of knowing instinctively which books to avoid *without opening them*, and the curious ritual of burial which accompanied it, will feature more than once in my story. It was not until late 1966 that I discovered, from a scrap of conversation, that Sir Walter Scott's *Marmion* concerned the mustering on the Burgh Muir of Edinburgh for the campaign which ended on the field called Flodden.

2

MY VOCATION SHOWED ITSELF AS FAR BACK AS SEPTEMBER 1939 when, at the outbreak of hostilities, I raised a private army of small girls whom I intended to drill to regulation standard. Mutiny occurred within a month, for my friends could see no purpose in the exercise, refused to march in public, and objected to my autocratic manner. I assured them that the army was like that – any army; my own martial instinct I had taken all my life for granted, and it baffled me to find it lacking in others.

To be a bicycle messenger for the A. R. P. had been one of my early, thwarted ambitions. (That way I might have laid the ghost of the urgent man on a horseback.) The minimum age for A. R. P. messengers was fifteen, but I was sure that, if my father tried, he could persuade the higher echelons to make an exception in my case. He told me it was impossible, but there remained at the back of my mind an absolute certainty that I was one person who had never been designated a minor.

It was my father who recognised my need to participate in the war as an adult. In my role as air-raid warden's mate I helped him to distribute the green canisters we strapped with adhesive tape to the muzzles of the gas-masks we had delivered in 1938. The issue of rubber ear-plugs I took round the houses myself. By this time I was well known as my father's adjutant, and as I grew taller was frequently mistaken for a fully-fledged warden. The more esoteric questions I referred to my father, but in routine precautions I was well briefed. My main contribution was to assure old ladies living alone and elderly disabled couples that *we would win the war*, they had my word for it; and finally my father alloted to me all the barricaded doors which would not open to a man's voice in the blackout. He was not exaggerating when he said he found me useful.

My one official contribution to the war-effort was to run a street savings group which I took on at the age of twelve and continued until I left the neighbourhood. The National Savings movement figured prominently in our family life. The organisation of those annual festivals which began with War Weapons Week and continued to the end of the war was my father's responsibility. He once observed that he would hate to have the Earl Marshal's job, but in fact he had a flair for devising and timing processions which never faltered, even when his prize exhibits were liable to be snatched away at a moment's notice for active service. I witnessed them all, seated with my mother in the enclosure at the saluting base, and for that one afternoon I waited all the year; it was my one great martial occasion.

From the age of ten onwards I had no ambition except to reach the age of seventeen and a half before the war ended so that I could volunteer for the Services.

Our adolescence, like wartime furniture and the clothes we wore, bore a utility label. Even our 'moods' had to be small ones, and any serious complaint received the prompt answer, 'There's a war on.' Twice a school party was taken to the opera, the sum total of our cultural education; museums and swimming-baths were closed; and the question 'Is Your Journey Really Necessary?' posted at railway stations discouraged school outings. The only real treat I can remember was the discovery of eight pre-war exercise-books which had lain forgotten in the school stationery cupboard. They were given to the eight of us who took 'principal' French in the Upper Sixth, and our tutor distributed them with as much solemnity as if they had been prizes. I could have wept for joy over mine, for I had never written an exercise on white, smooth, good quality paper. School stationery was the colour of wholemeal bread, very thin, and of a faintly absorbent texture so that the ink ran if one's nib scratched: I had not noticed how imperceptibly each year its quality had deteriorated until I saw that thick, beautiful, new note-book.

As years passed and we grew, variations appeared in our school uniform so that we never quite looked smart in it like our predecessors. We always had a half-kitted look, a veritable rag-tag-and-bobtail of a scholastic army. My later school blouses were made by Aunt Edith out of shirt-clippings sold off coupons, and they had Peter Pan collars because of the shape of the material. I loathed my Peter Pan collars, which did not sit properly over a tie, but everyone at school had some such secret burden so there was an unspoken understanding never to poke fun at the sartorial imperfections of others. By this time I had spectacles to diminish my negligible charms, and my hair, now growing long, invariably escaped from its plaits by the end of the day. Tie askew, the shoulder of my gabardine dragged down by a satchel-load of books, I really had nothing to say in answer to my mother's frequent, 'Why do you always come home looking so untidy?' Few of my comrades looked any better. Vigilant mothers, who never missed an opportunity to draw our attention to the fate of foolish maidens who fraternised with foreign soldiers, need not have worried: our motley school uniform and our carbohydrate-fed puppy fat put us in a class with nuns. Free Europe's forces gave us no trouble. To the later wave of dame-hungry G. I.s our lack of sex-appeal was no deterrent, and their persistence was astonishing. They harassed us in packs on our way home from school, and once, catching sight of my companions from the rear, the thought crossed my mind, 'My God, they must be desperate for women!' Trained during a war to view all men in uniform as potential rapists, I am only amazed that any of us grew through puberty with our mating instincts intact.

One thing never in short supply was homework. The grammar school had a high academic tradition, and as there was nothing left to do at school but work, intellectually we prospered. A coeducation school, we suffered through the war from a lack of young male teachers – in fact, I never saw one until my last year. The six of us who took Higher Latin struggled on for a year with no tutorial assistance. As our entrance to a university arts faculty depended on Latin, this was a deprivation we felt keenly.

The only person who truly appreciated the particular plight of my generation was my father, who once startled me at tea-time with his sympathetic vehemence. He said, 'Ginger, I *know* what it's like to be at school in wartime. You get none of the fun and none of the excitement. For teachers you get all the old rake-outs from the retired list. Boys who have just left school come back in uniform as heroes. Nobody wants your services for anything, and they all tell you you should be grateful for what you're missing. I know. It's hell to be at school in wartime.'

So that was why he had let me help him on his A. R. P. rounds. . . . I was strangely moved by this outburst, so unlike my father; moved not so much by his understanding of me, as by my understanding of him. Until that moment I had never thought of my father as a sixteen-year-old boy struggling to master his discontent because he had been born too late to be useful. In all our lives we were never so close as at that moment.

It was for my father the second time he had belonged to the wrong age group. Also, he was in a reserved occupation, and as a headmaster teaching full-time he was a great deal more useful to the Lancashire Education Committee than he would have been to the War Office – as he well knew, but he wore the labels 'Over Age' and 'Reserved Occupation' like millstones round his neck. He volunteered for any additional task which was dreary, hard work or potentially dangerous. Near the end of the war, as the age of recruitment crept higher, he did in fact register for military service – and, somewhat to my surprise, expressed a preference for the Air Force. On that day there was a gleam in his eye which he tried unsuccessfully to mask, and we joked that, if the war went on for two more years, he and I would be enlisting simultaneously.

That my time of war would come I never doubted as I pushed each birthday impatiently behind me. All through the years 1939 to 1945 I had a tensed up feeling, like a coiled spring, inside me, that something lay ahead, some testing point for which I must prepare myself; what it was I had no idea, but all my experience seemed like a tempering process. I was shattered when the war in Europe ended fifteen months before I was old enough to join the Army.

However it may have ended in other places, in Thornton Cleveleys the war just fizzled out to the decorous accompaniment of the local brass band playing to an empty promenade and a few noncommittal seagulls. That, for us, was V. E. Day, and a school-friend of mine observed, 'Anyone would think we'd lost the war, not won it.'

Holidays at home were the rule all through the war, and my father used his school vacations as work-time for all his numerous home-front activities. By 1945 his health had been affected, and it was for that reason we decided to take a modest holiday in Derbyshire – albeit with much heart-searching, for we were still at war with Japan. So we were in Tideswell when the news came of the Japanese surrender; there,

61

peace celebrations were spectacular. After a communal tea-party there was a torchlight procession through the streets which featured the Tideswell Processional Morris Dance in which everyone joined, me included, partnered by 'Uncle' Arnold who taught me the steps. Out through the village we danced, up to the beacon hill where the torches were used to ignite a huge bonfire. I remember standing there watching the fire and wishing that my life had got itself over any time prior to 1914.

History's second watershed within my lifetime had occurred some days previously. It had been a normal morning like any other when I came down to breakfast in the farmhouse dining-room. I was the first to arrive, so I was the one to pick up the morning paper from the breakfast table. It bore a headline 'A-Bomb Dropped on Hiroshima.' Some journalistic wag still imbued with wartime spirit had dubbed it 'the Tommy-bomb'. I read two paragraphs and then put down the paper. Two definitions in my first-year physics notebook had been recorded in my head, visually, still in the unformed junior handwriting in which I had set them down and learned them: 'A molecule is the smallest quantity of matter capable of separate existence. An atom is the smallest quantity of matter.' Atoms were, to me, Creation. And we had found a way to split them. We could undo Creation like a piece of knitting.

Until that moment I had grown up in a world where, potentially, one had grandchildren. I or my parents might be killed in a war, but somebody would survive; succeeding generations were a certainty, regardless of who sired or bore them. Also, I wrote books — not consciously for posterity, but there was always the warming thought that possibly a thousand years hence someone might still laugh or weep at something I had written. My sixteen and a half years had not been easy, but I had lived in the secure knowledge that my species had a future.

Now, as I stood by the table and that newspaper in the empty dining-room, I saw my posterity bound away out of the window like a cat.

I waited for other people to come into the room, watching for their reactions as they picked up their newspapers. There was dismay, some shock at the ruthlessness of the new weapon, but I listened in vain for some comment upon the enormity of the change which had taken place in the world overnight. It may be that one had to be sixteen, on the razor-edge between generations, to see what I saw on that morning.

The end of the war left me in a vacuum. In our household there was no extra place to be set at table for a returning member of the family. My two cousins were home on leave for the first time in several years, but I had never known them very well and the gulf had been widened by our

62

differing wartime experiences. Passing in the tram on my way to school those streets where sheet-banners festooned between the houses proclaimed WELCOME HOME TO OUR JIMMIE (Bob/Ted/Bill), it was impossible not to be thankful the war had ended for prisoners in Germany and the Far East. Basically, I was as glad to see the end of hostilities as anyone else, but I was left to find an answer to my major personal question: what was I to do with my life now I had no war to go to?

Writing had been the outlet for all my wartime frustration. A novel a year came from my pen from the age of thirteen onwards. All were tales of human life in a wartime context, their scene contemporary. Romance played its part, for love cannot be separated from war, but it was obvious to any reader that happy endings did not figure anywhere in my vision. I wrote of war from the point of view of those who lost it, the men who died. My love-scenes were skilfully written, using the nineteenth-century technique of leaving much to imagination; I had no personal experience to guide me at that time, and my ability to explore adult emotional feeling gave me a reputation for precocity which I did not deserve. What caused more astonishment was my aptitude for capturing the fear and smell of battlefields, the laconic chat of soldiers.

My writing was patchy, as could be expected of a learner who, in adolescence, wrote only of people half a decade older than herself. Areas of banality I usually rewrote, but there were other passages of which even today I would not be ashamed. I did not set out to 'be a writer'; I just wrote books which ultimately found their way to publishers because there was nothing else to be done with them.

At that time we had upon our hands a war and a paper shortage so severe that even Shakespeare and Rupert Brooke got short shrift on oatmeal-coloured, fly-wing-thin paper. 'Owing to the paper shortage' was the opening or subsequent sentence of every publisher's letter of rejection in those years; . . . 'concentrating upon the classics' . . . 'unable to print the work of new authors. . . .'

Also, I happened to be young when youth was unfashionable.

Rejection slips came invariably accompanied by a letter containing extracts from readers' reports, and usually a request for me to submit my next manuscript. More than one publisher asked me to turn my 'considerable talent' to writing children's books, a field less hard-hit by paper restrictions; but, an adult before my time, I had no real idea of children's tastes in literature. My own juvenile diet had begun with Prescott's *History of the Conquest of Perú* so I did not feel competent to write for children. Nor had I the inclination.

My private battle during the war was to get into print. I learned to live with hope and apprehension every waking morning. The interim letter telling me that my work was being 'considered' lifted my hope too high until there came the day when I travelled grey-spirited to school to break the news of yet another failure.

The unwanted faculty of prescience tripled the distress. I always knew when rejection had been posted. I moped for two days, off my food and deaf to lessons, knowing that a package of manuscript was on its way back to me. I was never wrong. It was usually my father who took in the morning mail, but on the eve of 'doom days' I warned my parents what to expect next morning, and then it was usually my mother who went downstairs in answer to the postman's knock. By that time I would have been cowering beneath the bedclothes for as much as two hours, anticipating every line of dialogue between my mother and the postman – and, when it came, I would hear it, word for word, as I had predicted. Sometimes I could quote from the publisher's letter before I opened it. My parents used to ask me how I could foretell these things with such uncanny accuracy, to which I replied, 'The book is so much part of me, you see; it's only natural that I should know what is happening to it.'

Every writer dies a death when his work is returned. Being prescient, I died several times over at each rejection – which may be why my quota of carnage left me exhausted. I never tried more than three publishers because my nervous system could not stand the manifold degree of suffering. When I read of authors whose best-seller had been rejected by thirty-one publishers, I was awed by their devotion to punishment. But then, I did not set out to be a writer; writing was for me a release, not a prospective profession.

There was not a wide choice of career open to those of us who became sixth formers in September 1945. Due to staff shortages there were no facilities for specialising in individual subjects, and my bent was art, which I could not take beyond School Certificate standard. The aim of the school was to get us, somehow, into university. We had the choice of but two courses, designed to take us into an arts or a science faculty. My School Certificate result was that of a good all-rounder, balanced to such a nicety that it gave no specific directive. What took me into the arts stream was my flair for languages.

'Flair' was the operative word, as I said at the time; I learned them too quickly and then, if practice lapsed, as quickly forgot them. This was to be illustrated in the sixth form where, for a year, we took a cultural course in German. At once the gutturals and strong vowels came back to me like a language remembered, and I could not be satisfied with our dilettante approach to the tongue. Once in a while some lone scholastic lunatic had been known to embark voluntarily upon a serious course in German in addition to working for Highers. I decided to be that year's lunatic. Coached during games periods and half-holidays by a teacher willing to abet me, I matriculated in German after nine months. The only criticism ever levelled at my German was that its style was 'slightly archaic' – a remark which had once been applied to my French. Then the tutor who had helped me took a post in another town, so my German studies ceased. By the time German reappeared officially in the curriculum, I had left school.

Most of those who took a sixth form modern course ended as teachers – at this time a career which offered the best chance of a place in university. In my case the bias was stronger, for teaching was the family profession and my father's eye had remarked me as 'a born instructor of the young'. I had no doubt he was right – I had been instructing people for as long as I could remember – but I had never any real desire to teach. Possibly my own experience of schooling had made me reluctant to inflict it on others.

It was assumed that I would go to university, but I was not enthusiastic about that either. My vision of academic life, distorted by the war years, was one of endless work and no play. No tales of debating societies, students' rag-days or union balls could change my view of university as being like school, but worse. To emerge at the end of it, and a year's teacher-training, merely to go into yet another series of classrooms for the rest of my life was a prospect which filled me with gloom.

Worse than my lack of vocation was my loss of orientation which had occurred during the war. Until 1939 I had had a single clear ambition, somehow to get home to Scotland. Scotland's part in the war was rarely mentioned in news bulletins which focused their attention mainly on London and the surrounding counties. My sole connection with Scottish events had been through the bombing of Clydeside, for my cousin was in the *Sussex* when she was sunk there; otherwise, Scotland never hit the news except for the bizarre occasion when Rudolf Hess landed there asking to see the Duke of Hamilton. After five years' subjection to films like *Mrs Miniver* and such songs as 'There'll Always be an England', I had been thoroughly brainwashed. When the war ended, other people still remained English, but my own allegiance switched off on V. E. Day-plus-one. No other sense of identity came to replace it, for the mysterious homesickness of my childhood had apparently passed.

Then, in 1946, there came to the Odeon a film made on location in the west of Scotland. I went to see it twice in one week – something I never did – and I would have been in the audience every night had I had an adequate excuse and sufficient pocket-money. In it there was a falcon, and a few snippets of Gaelic conversation, and each time I came home from the cinema I was in a trance and went to my room without wanting supper. I even went out of my way to pass the Odeon just to be near that film. On the Saturday night when it left Cleveleys I was bereft, and my ghost-sobs thrummed beneath the bedclothes half the night. Its name was *I Know Where I'm Going*.

Not all the contributory causes which shape our lives can be identified, but one which subtly altered mine was an impetigo germ. The source of infection was not known, for I alone contracted it. The standard treatment of those days was still gentian violet, a slow cure and unsightly. For a week I endured the sight of my purple-blotched visage before, unable to stand it any longer, I asked my doctor, could he think of nothing else? To add to my misery I had simultaneously been stricken by a bout of the spinal trouble which had afflicted me periodically through the years, so I was flat on my back in bed as well as spotty. The new ointment prescribed in place of gentian violet was a compound of mercury and ammonia, and what nobody could have known until I tried it was that I had a mercury allergy. Within hours my face and neck had become a swollen, suppurating travesty of human features, dripping constantly – even, to my disgust, upon my food when I was propped on pillows to eat.

While the doctor debated how best to deal with this new development, I lay contemplating the ceiling as my condition daily worsened. I came to terms with putrefaction by telling myself how much worse than mine was the plight of the leper, and this single thought enabled me to attain a degree of serenity I had not known before. But the new experience had a curious side-effect: it stimulated the return of memories which would surface just when I was going to sleep. These chiefly concerned the pestilence.

My friends came sick-visiting in loyal cohorts. Strict rules of hygiene were observed, and both the doctor and my mother tried to persuade me that there was no danger to my visitors, but I could not be convinced. Even when I had made them set their chairs hard against the wall, as far from my bed as possible, I was not satisfied. It was *against the law* to admit healthy people into a house which was pest-stricken: I knew, because I myself had introduced the legislation.

When my face became so hideous that my mother closed the curtains and put off the light when people came to see me, I used that as an excuse to ban them entirely from the room. In fact, the sight of my disfigurement had become a little too much for me, so I asked my mother to cover the dressing-table mirror – although there was nothing we could do about the mirror on the wardrobe door. Eventually the risk of accidentally seeing myself ceased, for the swelling of my eyelids finally robbed me of sight by the fifth day. Flat on my back, unable to open my eyes, I filled my time by reflecting upon the predicament of the permanently blind: fully to appreciate the

66

blessing of sight can be an illuminating experience.

At this stage there was no knowing how far my condition was due to allergy and how much it owed to the original infection; my doctor decided my case warranted the trial of the new wonder-cure, penicillin, at that time not in general use outside hospitals. Thanks to Alexander Fleming the progress of my disease was checked, and a cure effected.

Meanwhile, I had been obliged to devise my own way of protecting my face from permanent disfigurement. During the day I could lie on my back, but at night I turned on my side when asleep and the excretion from my face stuck to the pillow and set hard like glue. From the beginning my mother had covered the pillow with what I hollowly termed 'drip-mats' — pieces of soft linen, which were constantly changed and destroyed. Even these were of no help to my basic problem, which was, as I put it, how to wake up without leaving half my face behind. It was not merely the discomfort of being awakened by the tearing-away of scab-tissue; I was seriously concerned that the process might, if too often repeated, leave my face permanently scarred.

I then hit upon a bright idea. Using a piece of linen cut from an old pyjama jacket of my father's, I made a mask, cutting slits for eyes and mouth, and affixing tapes to tie behind my head. The device worked. My face stuck merely once, to the mask, which was small enough to be loosened gently with warm water in the morning. We were so glad to find a solution to the problem that we made jokes about 'putting on the face-mask' when my mother was preparing me for the night — although she had early expressed a preference for leaving the room when I did so. I never teased her about the way she scuttled from the room before I donned the mask, for there is always something faintly sinister about a masked face, as everyone knows.

That was not, however, what affected me on the night I came from the bathroom and saw my figure reflected in the mirror on the wardrobe door. I entered the bedroom conscious of this 'thing' over my face — just an encumbrance I could feel, with slits to look through, it was not identified as anything in my mind. Yet when my eyes fell on the mirror what I glimpsed for a fleeting moment was the figure of a man in medieval plate-armour looking through a visor. Then it was gone — if it had ever been there. All that I can say for certain is that I rushed to the mirror for reassurance; to touch my face-mask to make sure that it was only linen. I stood reminding myself: it is a face-mask cut from a pyjama jacket of my father's; I am Ada F. Kay; I am in my bedroom; the year is the *present*.

I returned to my bed where I lay awake a long time wondering why I had been so certain that *I would see* in the mirror a man wearing a visor.

I puzzled for some while, and then warning bells began to ring in my head, telling me to probe no further.

That illness was to cost me an entire term's school studies, but I think it had a still more serious side effect: it had opened the way for revisitation by the inward ghosts which had troubled me in childhood.

Responding to penicillin injections, my face healed quickly, but the dried, peeling scab-tissue kept me housebound – except for brief forays at nightfall, muffled, to take the air. It was during this period I was seized with the idea of presenting the graveyard scene from *Hamlet* at the (hypothetical) end-of-term school concert.

Hamlet had been the one Shakespeare play I had avoided reading – until I met it as a set book for Highers. Its impact upon me was such that I cried, 'But this is *my play*!' – meaning that, if the author had set out to write a play about me, he could not have defined my character more exactly. I have no doubt that many people had reacted similarly to Hamlet to a greater or lesser degree – to gain the self-identification of the audience with the main character is, after all, the dramatist's objective. What I had discovered went a great deal further, for some indefinable link between myself and the play produced repercussions. Whenever *Hamlet* features in my story – as it will, several times – back-head memory stirs, and the prince in black inches forward into my consciousness not as Hamlet but as *myself*.

I consulted nobody at school about my plan to stage the graveyard scene (my favourite). I did not even know if there would, in fact, be a concert, for they were semi-impromptu events devised for our own amusement and dependent upon the goodwill of the headmaster. Yet with no encouragement save wishful thinking, I set out to learn not only the graveyard scene but the entire play. First, however – the pattern is much the same as that of my ninth birthday production – I secured from my mother the remnants of that old black velvet and white dinner-gown which I had coveted in childhood.

After that there was no stopping me. The top of the gown became my doublet, and from my confirmation dress I made the white shirt to wear beneath it. Long black hosen and a shoulder chain of pearls completed the basis of the costume. My dagger – actually a Norwegian fisherman's knife – was one of my most cherished possessions, obtained for me by Amy at a church jumble sale when we were nine. An odd feature of that costume, recurring throughout its history, is the lack of a sword: I knew it no longer had one.

Making off to my bedroom with the substance of my costume and a new pocket edition of *Hamlet*, I was not to be seen for days – except at mealtimes when I appeared frequently in doublet and hosen on the pretext that it helped me to learn my lines. Every day I committed to memory several pages of the text. Alone in my bedroom, acting the part, I was stirred by curious undertones of feeling: a prince who wore black, born of a Danish mother and a king most foully murdered . . . the character was *myself*. Most of all in the graveyard scene, soliloquising over the skull – and making my dramatic leap into Ophelia's grave, demanding burial.

I was blissfully happy. The original object of the exercise had long ago ceased to matter, for it had served its purpose. I clung to the story of the legendary school concert because it gave me an excuse to spend a large part of my day in the bedroom clad in black, medieval, male costume. It was the only clothing I had ever worn in which I felt like a whole person, and totally *myself*.

To the wristbands of the doublet I added, experimentally, a frill of old lace. It had been tacked on hurriedly, and one cuff detached itself when I was wearing it. Rather than take off the doublet, I attempted to repair it on my wrist. I was standing by the dressing-table in the window of my room, and as I looked down, concentrating on my task and my mind for that moment empty of any other thought, I became aware of my own hand, bordered by lace at the end of a black velvet sleeve, with a glimpse of pearls just above it. I flung back my head to reprimand a young girl dressed in green who had just come into the room, 'And the king but newly dead?'

Then, startled, I found myself looking at the window of our house in North Drive. There was no king dead that morning and the young girl clad in bright green did not exist. Who on earth was I, dressed in my black Hamlet gear, standing in a pool of sunlight beside the dressing-table, plying my needle with a hand which I had known *forever*?

Still in my costume, I went downstairs to my mother like a sleepwalker. She remarked that I looked as though I had seen a ghost, and sat me down in a chair whilst she made me a cup of tea. When I had drunk it, I told her what had happened. I concluded, 'All I can tell you is that the dead king was Charles I, but don't ask me who I was because I haven't the faintest idea.' My mother did not say a great deal, for she had seen the state of shock in which I had come downstairs and that was real to her no matter what its cause.

When I returned to school I mentioned this experience to my friends. It was the first time I had had an identifiable flash of memory. The most curious feature of this particular mental image was that it did not fit in with any of the other scraps of memory which had been rattling round my head for a lifetime. It was like finding in a box of dark, old, dirty jig-saw puzzle pieces one stray piece in brilliant colours which belonged to an entirely different picture.

Reincarnation became our primary topic of conversation at school during the next few days, until we had hammered it to death. At intellectual level I found the subject interesting, and quoted Plato vigorously. In doing so I contrived to separate myself from the various uncomfortable, inexplicable experiences which had plagued me for seventeen years. While airing theories one exists at hypothetical level, which is a very comfortable way of revisiting times past with no responsibility, like taking a holiday with no baggage. What turned me off the topic, quite suddenly, was the realisation that, if I had lived before, there was a possibility that I might have to live again. My experience of life was such that I did *not* want a further dose of it. I decided it was preferable not to have reincarnation, and dropped the subject. The strange memory of my hand set against black velvet and lace, and the arrival of the girl in green, I tossed into the rag-bag which accommodated so many other unidentifiable fragments.

I had more serious worries to occupy me when I returned to school. The lost term's work I could make up; what I could not do was put back the clock to become again the person I had been prior to the interruption. Some change had occurred in myself. I could not define it, but it was the way I had felt at the time of my sixteenth birthday. At sixteen I had attained my majority – whatever the law of the land might be, I knew I came of age at sixteen. That for me had always been the age when I assumed adult responsibility, put away my books and went out into the world to see – as I put it – 'how the people lived'. My restlessness at sixteen had been curbed by the need to pass examinations, lulled by the sense of common purpose shared with my fellows; but the break in school routine caused by my illness had given it a chance to re-establish itself.

My inward disturbance coincided with the most serious crisis to overtake our scholastic lives. We were going up to university in the same year as thousands of demobilised service personnel. To give the best possible chance to ex-servicemen, they were allotted ninety-five per cent of all university places: the remaining five per cent had to be distributed among school leavers. We were told reassuringly by our form tutor and the headmaster not to be too discouraged if our applications were turned down; the school would fight on for us, and those who were true academic material would be squeezed into some university, somewhere, even at the last minute.

We had no real choice of university; it was merely a question of guessing who might have room for us, like selecting a likely winner with closed eyes and a pin. I picked Bristol, with Durham as my second choice. There were no Scottish universities on the list, otherwise my future might have turned out differently. One of my school-fellows, a Scot, mentioned St Andrew's in connection with her own career of dentistry, and the name sent a small shock-wave through my head; it was like overhearing one's own surname mentioned in a bus-deck conversation, then realising that it belonged to someone else.

I completed my university application forms late one evening, taking them immediately to the post. It was a clear, frosty night, I can remember, and as I dropped the heavy envelopes into the pillar-box at the top of North Drive they fell with a 'plop' to the bottom. I knew in my bones as I heard them fall that neither Bristol nor Durham would ever see me – it was all a bad dream from which I would awaken. This feeling always came when I had set my foot upon a road which, for me, led nowhere.

I worked hard to make up for my term's lost studies. I should have regained ground easily, for I had the ability. Instead, I floundered, making heavy weather of it, using up my energy too fast. It was as though a part of me had gone missing so that I never really fitted back into school life. In my effort to do so I became nervous, over-anxious. Our family doctor diagnosed 'over-work' and recommended some months' sabbatical.

That, I knew, would be the end of my going to university that year. However, a fourth year in the sixth would guarantee me honours and privileges of which I had dreamed at eleven. I would become head girl. The dramatic society was being revived, which would mean for me a leading role in its first post-war production. The school magazine would be back in circulation, and I would be a likely choice as pupil editor. Most important of all, I would have a relaxed year in which to prepare myself for going up to university as a scholar of realised potential. The golden opportunities all were mine if I took the stipulated rest, then went back to school for one more year.

It was during the first week of my sabbatical that my future was changed by a poster I saw on display in Preston. My mother and I had been visiting her cousin, and on our way to the station to catch our return train we passed, in Pole Street, a shop-window decorated with posters of uniformed women engaged in various military activities. The one which stopped me in my tracks was a picture of an A.T.S. despatch rider. For a moment I was nearly sick with excitement, the urgent man on horseback inside me recognising his equivalent in 1947. I made to move on, for we had a train to catch and our passing the A.T.S. recruiting centre had been purely fortuitous. What my face showed I cannot say, but it caused my mother to stop with the words, 'I know. You want to make enquiries. Go along. I'll wait.'

The moment I stepped across the threshold of that room used by the Army I knew what I had *always* meant to do. Had I been born a boy there would have been no question about it. It took about ten seconds to discover what I wished to know – I doubt the recruiting officer ever made an easier catch – and I was given a handful of explanatory leaflets to take away. An amendment in one of them was made while I waited; it concerned trades, and the photograph of the despatch rider

71

was crossed out in pencil. A.T.S. despatch riders had become a discontinued line that very month. Just my luck. But by that time it made no difference: the Army was the reality, not my fleeting memory of riding over scrawny grass hummocks on some far, forgotten coastline. All the man on horseback ever had to do was to get me through that shop doorway.

It was the next day before I dared tell my father that I wanted to be a private in the A.T.S.

I should not have blamed my father had he wept. So often in the teeth of parental apathy he had fought for the scholastic future of his own pupils. To see me wanting to throw it all away must have broken his heart. But he never mentioned that. What·concerned him was my welfare, the lack of professional qualification which I would have to bear for the rest of my life. My father was a strict disciplinarian, at home and at school, but he never interfered with human liberty. I was free to make my own choice.

On the night of the great decision we talked until midnight, then my father retired, leaving my mother to act as my sounding board. Over the course of a week we had debated the matter from every viewpoint, and I had no doubt in my mind that everything my father said about the advantages of an academic career was correct. At 2 a. m. what my mother and I were still debating was what I *wanted*. At 3 a. m. I, who am not a gambler in anything but vital matters, said, 'Oh, for God's sake let's toss a coin and pray for the right answer. Heads, I join the Army. Tails, I teach.' So my mother prayed while I flipped the coin – I full knowing that it would be heads. It was. I retired to my bed and slept like a soldier after a battle.

I was to be glad that I had tossed the coin, for it gave me the authority, during the weeks that followed, to say a categorical 'no' to everyone trying to save me from myself. I listened while tutors, grandparents and an uncle told me that I was 'throwing away' my abilities and opportunities. Bemused friends questioned my stamina . . . how would I adapt to barrack life and drinking from *tin mugs*? Everywhere I met the question, 'Why?' For my parents' sake I tried to give an answer, and the one I gave had a partial ring of truth to it. It was to be the answer I took into the Army with me, that it was 'the only way in which I could learn how the people lived'.

What I saw during the single day I was in Preston for my medical and intelligence tests was itself a revelation. I had the test papers completed within a matter of minutes, and sat back – to be horrified by the sight of so many adult faces wrestling painfully with questions which were, to my mind, more suitable for primary school children. Afterwards, I was shattered to learn that out of thirty potential recruits only six of us had passed those tests. My estimate of 'average' intelligence had been formed amongst scholars, and it had never entered my mind that half the world consisted of people who could not match together bits of printed patterns.

When I told my tale at the tea-table, my father said grimly, 'Ginger, you don't have to tell me. I know. But are you sure you would not be more useful trying to teach them?'

Possibly I would; but meanwhile I had a very great deal to learn, and to my mind the best finishing school was the Army.

CHAPTER THREE

1

'ON ARRIVAL AT TRAINING CENTRE THE FIRST THING THE NEW
recruit sees is the good hot meal awaiting her at the end of her
journey' – thus read the opening sentence of the A.T.S. recruiting
leaflet, about which we joked bitterly as we queued in the perishing
cold to receive our first issue of small kit. The 'good hot meal' turned
out to be two slices of cold spam, a dollop of piccalilli and a spoonful of
mashed potato crusted over after standing, like ourselves, for the best
part of two hours.

On Tuesday, 8 April 1947, Queen's Camp, Guildford lay in the grip
of a cold spell later to be recorded as historic. A bleak wooden
settlement and some scrawny fir-trees edged a vast, uninviting barrack-
square; it looked and felt like transit camp, Siberia. A piercing wind
whistled round every corner of the buildings outside which we
clustered with chattering teeth awaiting our turn for kit distribution,
medical inspection, and the field postcard on which we sent home our
new army number, address, and a single sentence announcing safe
arrival. That icy wind accounted for several casualties, of
which – inevitably – I was to be the most serious.

Our huts were of the spider design, with linking corridors, and I was
allotted the bed by the door, facing another door, open to the weather,
which took all the main traffic to the block. We were constantly
changing our clothes to match our duties, and at least four times a day I
stripped off standing in a wind tunnel. I had been in the Army just
sixty-four hours when I was packed off to Sick Bay with my small kit
and a gastric chill which cost me five days of my preliminary training.

Not a trace of this suffering appears in my letters home – which have
survived because I meant them to serve as notes for a book about the
A.T.S. Cheerful, juvenile, pedestrian, they are typically the letters of a
new recruit trying to concentrate in a noisy barrack-room during the
few spare minutes allowed in our intensive training programme. Their
tone is Spartan – discomfort is an accepted part of the soldier's life to
which I shall grow accustomed – and their enthusiasm for the Army is
irrepressible. Everyone mentioned is 'frightfully decent', 'great fun' or
part of 'a grand crowd'. There is no doubt I was in the right profession.

As an only child adapting to barrack life, I found my feet almost
immediately. I missed privacy and the opportunity to write, but there
was no longer a need for the latter. It puzzled me that my muse should

have flown so completely, but it had to contend with more than a crowded barrack-room; it knew, I dare say better than I did, that a happy extrovert enjoying a new life has better things to do than sit scribbling.

The recruit next to me in alphabetical order became my closest comrade – Gwen, aged thirty-one, married, took me under her wing as a young person in need of guidance. I had come fresh from school into the company of girls who, at my age, had three years' working life behind them. I was startled by their lack of intellectual development, and they by my total ignorance of the world outside the classroom. There was rarely friction, but once in a while blunders were made by both sides, and then it was Gwen whose diplomacy restored harmony.

The kindness of my comrades, so often mentioned in my letters, was that of older sisters; they would barrack my bed for me, show me how to scrub a floor and give me a hand with any of the rough tasks I had not previously encountered. In return I acted as their scribe, rough-drafting letters to erstwhile boy-friends and previous employers.

There is frequent reference to food – still, in 1947, a subject occupying much of popular attention. Camp food I describe as 'dreadful' – It was! – but I record warmly a meal in the NAAFI – 'had fried rabbit, bread and butter and coffee for 1s. 0½d.' The concession to the Forces of reduced cigarette prices, general throughout the war, ceased during my first month in the Army. It was a small thing, but typical of my mistiming.

My back-head ghosts showed themselves but twice, and that in the vague way experienced by many. Then appear paragraphs in my letters different in style from that documenting military trivia. One was in the barrack-square during drill when I felt myself to belong to *another* army. The second was on the day we went to the male-occupied main part of Queen's Camp for our X-rays. The freak weather had switched from tundra cold to desert hot overnight, and we sat in the shade of a wall as we awaited our turns. Somewhere someone was practising a wind instrument, and for a second I felt I was in a barracks in *India*. Without thinking, I observed to Gwen, 'I've been in the Army before, you know.' Gwen, who had not been listening, said, 'You've what, Ginge?' Then I realised what I had said, and decided not to repeat it. What on earth had made me say something which I knew was simply not true?

I had not left camp, except in a squad, since my arrival on the 8th, and my turn for fire-picket duty fell on the very weekend I had planned to visit my cousin. Claustrophobia had set in, and the weather made another startling volte-face, sending torrential rain to rattle on the roof of the huge, bleak hut where a handful of us were imprisoned. The pop song of the moment was 'April Showers' which I had heard incessantly since my arrival, and they sang it now with droning irony; my nerves, like the joke, had worn thin. I sat on my bed watching the water stream down the window, and wanting so desperately to hear a Bach fugue that I understood for the first time what my father meant by the phrase 'starved of music': music had been something I took for granted at home. For the first and only time my enthusiasm for the Army wilted. Would it always be like this, I wondered? If so, I had to suffer it, for there was no buying one's way out in 1947. I was so depressed, so bored, I took to following the course of individual raindrops down the glass. At 5.15 p.m. on the Sunday fire-picket signed off – and I was free. Driving rain-squalls regardless, I put on my waterproof ground-sheet and set out for a walk. My cape whipped and cracked in the wind like a sail, reminding me of happy times at home with friends, out sailing. The gardens of Guildford were filled with forsythia and Japanese cherry, and one or two had magnolia trees in bloom. I walked on to a crossroads, and there lay all the world before me at the ends of those shining black ribbons of roadmetal. I was filled with exhilaration and the knowledge that my best years lay yet ahead. I returned to camp in a state of euphoria, and took a running jump on to my bed in pure high spirits. Instead of jumping on to it, I jumped at it – and my next letter to my parents records a further visit to the M.O., this time with a badly bruised and scraped shin-bone.

Forbidden to participate in drill and P.T., I spent the time in the library. In fact, I ought to have been in sick bay with my leg up, but this would have jeopardised my prospect of passing out with Number One Company. Within a few days I was back on the parade ground, limping but determined. Two periods of infirmity had reduced my training by exactly half. I caught up with the others, injuries notwithstanding, but I had terrible dreams at night about a mêlée which ensued when soldiers broke formation.

I was on good terms with the Scots girls in camp – as were most of the northern English. We shared their dislike of the pre-sweetened porridge served at breakfast, and they tended to regard Lancashire as a protectorate. We were glad of Scots support because some of the southern English maidens liked to remind us that we were in their territory, which possibly was natural as many of them had never been out of it. I loved to hear the Scots girls singing – and they had one particular song which sent the blood pounding past my ears. It was the Scottish pub and social song 'We're no' awa' tae bide awa' ' which I had never heard before. The verses are mundane, the account of a meeting with Johnnie Scobie and the ensuing pub-crawl, but the refrain held for me a personal message.

We're no' awa' tae bide awa',
We'r no awa' tae leave ye;
We're no' awa' tae bide awa',
We'll aye come back and see ye.

I could never hear enough of that song, and I badgered one of the girls in Holding Unit to teach me the words before I left Guildford.

The Scots mixed well, and I never saw them as being different from ourselves until the night before our seventy-two-hour leave, when Number One Company assembled in the mess for travel instructions. The Scots contingent was leaving twelve hours earlier on the night train from King's Cross, for some of them had to travel great distances. Kitted and dressed for departure, they sat segregated, waiting for the duty truck. It was the first time we had seen them assembled in force, and Guildford mess felt suddenly their *foreignness*. In their greatcoats they seemed curiously overpowering, an army within an army, their voices rising in a medley of regional Scottish accents, cracking indigenous jokes about destinations of which I had never heard. For me suddenly the outline map of Scotland became filled with towns and villages hundreds of miles apart, a living country. I tried to catch the eye of one I knew, but she had no time for me now. At the arrival of their transport they all trooped out singing their homing tune 'We're no' awa' tae bide awa''. I had an extraordinary impulse to jump up and follow – I belonged with *them* – but I mastered it. When they had gone I was desolate, aware of being left behind, in England, and ice-cold shivering seized me. It was a while before I could rouse myself to feel the slightest interest in my own leave.

I had enlisted with the intention of obtaining my commission, but the A.T.S. of 1947 required its members to serve six months in the ranks. Everyone at home, including myself, expected me to be an officer-cadet within a year. With this in mind I had specified clerical work when I took my selection tests, anticipating administrative duties. Whilst I would have sacrificed promotion gladly to be a despatch rider, with that trade closed to me I had no wish to remain in the ranks as, say, a driver or a telephonist. (Reading my letters I feel that in W343451 Pte. Kay, A.F., the Army had a first-class recruiting officer.)

I was a disciplined soldier who never dreamed of breaking rules or disobeying orders – until there cropped up the matter of a nearby medieval grave, and then I acted out of character. For years my father had wanted a rubbing of the memorial brass of Sir John D'Abernon which he had never managed to obtain, and the proximity of Guildford to Stoke d'Abernon was in his eyes probably the one good thing about my decision to join the Army. As I was leaving home to go to the wars, his last words to me were, 'Ginger, you will try to get that brass rubbing for me?' – and my first food parcel sent by my mother was accompanied by a package from my father containing a roll of tracing paper and a lump of his special mixture of wax crayon and cobbler's heel ball.

Passes to travel beyond Guildford were issued only for Saturdays and Sundays, and having spent my first weekend in Sick Bay, my second on fire picket and my third on leave, I had only one chance left to get that rubbing. Then I discovered that no passes were issued on the last weekend before a company left Training Centre, which put Stoke d'Abernon out of bounds.

I picked Gwen as my fellow bounds-breaker, and the two of us set out on a glorious spring afternoon, I smuggling my roll of tracing paper past the guard with a crimson face which Gwen said would have given away the game from the start. At the station it seemed to me that our two khaki-clad figures invited the interest of every red-cap I imagined to be lurking behind the shunting wagons, and in the train I was as nervous as a plate of jelly standing on a shuggly table – causing Gwen to say, 'Argh, Ginge, shut up. Have a fag and enjoy the scenery.' Gwen had quickly picked up the attitude and mannerisms of 'an old sweat' but I still suffered from a schoolgirl conscience. Were I to be caught and questioned, how on earth would I explain that a warrior's grave was more important to me than the heinous offence of deliberately disobeying orders?

Alighting at Stoke d'Abernon we saw in the distance a cricket match in progress on a pitch radiantly green with new spring grass. The white figures invoked for me a memory of English wartime schooldays: I had grown up with young men who wore cricket flannels, and I had been in love with the entire school First Eleven on days when they came into the dining-room dressed for the wicket. Walking through the village I felt an intense sudden fondness for the scene, as though my wartime southern orientation had for a moment been revitalised.

At the vicarage I asked for permission to rub the brass, a request which met with no immediate warmth. I had the feeling that the vicar distrusted our uniform – and then there came into the conversation a brief reference to his having been in the Navy; quickly I realised that in his eyes we rated as 'brown jobs'. (My cousin had made the comment, 'If Ada has to wreck her future, couldn't she at least have joined the Wrens?') So I mentioned my seaworthy connections and, after a few minutes' happy chat, was told that I could rub the brass. As we walked away Gwen, the best diplomat in the squadron, murmured, 'I say, Ginge, how did you manage that one?' I replied, 'Salt in the blood.'

In the empty church, silent with centuries' yellow sunlight, we rolled back the cocoa-matting on the chancel floor and there was Sir John, the azure enamel on his shield almost intact despite nearly seven hundred years' wear beneath the feet of innumerable congregations. . . . Gwen broke my reverie with a brisk, 'Well, come on, Ginge, let's get started.' It was the first time I had taken a brass rubbing, but my father's instruction had been thorough and I had attended many of his lectures on memorial brasses. Gwen held down the paper while I worked the heel ball over it, then, intrigued she said, 'Here, Ginge, let me have a go at that,' and I handed her the wax. After a while she remarked, 'Phew! It's hard work, isn't it?' Between us we completed the rubbing in record time – and later my father was to remark upon our competence.

With a sense of tremendous achievement, we returned to Guildford undetected. We had missed tea and, ravenously hungry, we went up to the NAAFI for a meal of loin chops, new potatoes and green peas (all for 1s. 9d.) which still in my memory tastes better than mutton chops have a right to do. That night, in the barrack-room, Gwen regaled our fellows with an hilarious account of 'how we rubbed Ginge's bloody brass', and I reflected, as I turned to sleep, that I was not the only born teacher who had gone missing in the ranks. It had been a marvellous day, an *English* occasion.

Within four weeks a shamble of civilians had been fashioned into an efficient military unit. The great test lay ahead, our passing-out parade. During one of our lectures on King's Regulations my attention had been riveted upon one particular instruction: a soldier about to faint on parade must first dismiss himself before flopping to the dust. I thought what a splendid thing it would be in battle if on the point of death one had time to give an apologetic salute to those who would be left to carry on the fight with one man less to help them. . . . Recalling myself sharply to listen to the lecturer, I made the resolution that, whoever fell on the parade ground, *it would not be me*. And so it proved on the day, but I took a particular interest in the behaviour of three people thus overcome and felt a huge pride in the Army when I saw one of them turn, make her salute, and only then topple forward. The incident impressed me more than anything I felt that day, and an account of it is included in my letter to my parents.

My letter describing our passing-out parade could have been written by a cadet at the turn of the century. It has to be remembered that it was only two years since the Indian Army had ceased to offer a future to my male contemporaries. Nearly every family I knew contained at least one member who had served or been born on a station in the Empire. Also, the British Army had recently won a war, and the spirit of the war years still lingered in the Services, as did many of those who had fought in it. It was as a very proud *British* soldier I marched with head high on the barrack-square on that May day in 1947.

And it was the Army, having made me British, which as suddenly was to reverse the process.

After preliminary training personnel were despatched to various army schools to learn their trades, and Gwen and I were expecting to go to Gresford in North Wales for our clerical course. At the last moment, for some reason – I think lack of accommodation – our clerical course was cancelled, and we were posted direct to our units. We had been allowed to express preference for location, if any, which would be considered where feasible. I knew my mother was hoping I might be stationed nearer home, perhaps in Preston. I had no desire to go to Preston, but I wanted to escape from southern England. So I compromised by asking for a posting 'to the North'. My mother's letter of 5 May shows her still to be under the impression that I was going to Gresford; however, on the evening of that day, at a meeting in the mess, our postings were read out to us.

The Army had posted me to Scotland.

I sat stunned, unable to believe my ears. Gwen – posted with me to Edinburgh – said, 'Argh, cheer up Ginge! It'll be all right.'

I found my voice to reply, 'No, it's not that. It's. . . .' But I could not explain to anyone how I felt at that moment: it was the greatest piece of good fortune which had ever come my way.

When I went up to the NAAFI to telephone my parents, I tried very hard to keep the elation out of my voice. I felt a terrible hypocrite when I expressed regret that it had not been Preston.

Before I left Guildford I posted off the brass rubbing of Sir John d'Abernon, and the memorial portrait of the dead medieval soldier travelled north simultaneously with myself. I think my Englishness went with him. I went with the Scots contingent, who left twelve hours earlier than the rest, on the night train out of King's Cross station.

2

I HAD NO OPPORTUNITY FOR INTROSPECTION AS THE NINETEEN of us bound for Edinburgh boarded the train with the boisterous high spirits of newly-kitted recruits leaving Training Centre behind. Seven to a compartment, we inspected our haversack rations and then organised our sleeping arrangements with the soldier's talent for improvisation: one to each corner, one on the floor, and the two lightest heaved into the luggage racks. When we had chattered ourselves to weariness, I, like the rest, eventually went to sleep. At Newcastle I wakened, the name teasing my head, and then slid back into a profound slumber.

I was suddenly jolted wide awake by a thought: *I am back in Scotland.* I looked out of the window and saw below scattered reflections of lights upon dark water. The Tweed. My bones knew it as the Tweed. I looked for the sign-board as we came into the station – there it was, Berwick-upon-Tweed. I turned to proclaim to my companions that we were now in Scotland – then found, to my surprise, that they were all sound asleep. The shock which had wakened me had been unfelt by them. Then I realised, isolated in a moment's loneliness, that I had been roused not by any movement of the train: in my head, the Tweed was my Border.

There is extant a letter in which I tried to describe the atmosphere in that railway carriage during my first hour in Scotland. It was as though my comrades and I existed in different dimensions. I sat at the window straining my eyes to identify any outline in the darkness. Turning to look at my companions, I marvelled at the depth and stillness of their slumber; I felt I could not have wakened them had I tried. It was as though they lay under a spell so that none should witness my homecoming. That was how it had to be, I realised, a secret shared between myself and the featureless, grey landscape beyond the window revealing itself in the first cold light of morning. This was my Scotland, unchanged, formidable.

Hungrily, my face pressed against the glass, I watched each field, tree and glimpse of sea go by; I had been waiting all my eighteen years of life to see again this landscape. I knew it was 'again' but I had no time to waste on examining words. Once or twice I turned from the window to see how my comrades fared. Their deep sleep worried me, they were so vulnerable. In the grey light of dawn, shrouded in their greatcoats, how like they were to men asleep before a battle – or dead men after it. Glimpses of memory, like tricks of light at the end of a long corridor, teased my head, then were gone. I was left pained by the huge pang of warmth towards those sleeping figures; I had never felt such profound, protective love in all my life before.

Suddenly I wanted to record my impressions of that homecoming – on paper, while it was still happening; it was an historic event so important that an eyewitness account of it had to be preserved. So I took out writing-pad and pen to start a letter to my parents, which was headed triumphantly, 'Somewhere in Scotland.'

I broke off my letter at the sight of a great rock bathed in the first rays of sunlight. I knew it immediately – the Bass Rock. I knew because I had seen it before – the first major landmark as one came by the coastline towards Edinburgh. My cry of recognition wakened the compartment. Heavy with sleep, stiff and shivering, they stirred; I told them we were approaching Edinburgh. Mercifully, no one asked me how I knew, for I should have been hard put to it to explain how I knew all the landmarks on a route as new to me as it was to them.

That rock bathed in morning sunlight was the first and last sign we were to have that day of May weather in Scotland. A grey, mizzling drench greeted us at Waverley Station, yet to my mind that first glimpse of Edinburgh in the mist and morning rain was the most glorious sight I had ever beheld. I half leaped, half tumbled on to the platform, kit-bag laden, stiff and chilled to the marrow, but my heart filled with a gigantic gladness to be *home*. I can remember even yet putting down my first foot upon Scots ground and feeling a vibration which I was positive came from the earth to me, as though it, too, had waited long for this moment. My high spirits met no response from my cold, travel-weary comrades, Gwen observing, 'Look at her! You wouldn't think she'd been travelling all night. Calm down a bit, Ginge.'

Usually when travelling I let others lead the way, having myself a tendency to get lost at railway stations, but on this morning it was I who took charge, for we were now in my country. A lorry met us, a three-ton Bedford, and bore us away out of town to a warren of huts at Broomfield Camp beside the Forth.

I can remember sitting to unfreeze my bones beside a coke stove in Hut Two – whilst a woman soldier used flat-irons, on a soldier's box covered with an army blanket, to make her starched collars gleam with regimental stiffness; those collars faded almost to cream were the envy of new recruits like myself. I was told that the warmth that morning was a lucky break for me, because the technical shift – it was a Signals Regiment – plus the orderlies' shift had outnumbered empty places, so it was laundry morning in the hut. It reeked with hot damp like a Turkish bath but I was grateful for it. As she heated and used alternately her two flat-irons, she briefed me in camp-lore. Shortage of coke; fires on three evenings of a week only. Not a bad NAAFI; pleasant staff and its chips and spam-fritters were first rate. Hot-water supply minimal – boiler nearly always out of order or flat out of coke. Ablutions' windows locked with rust at 'permanently open'. The camp had been condemned for German prisoners, so they had drafted in the A.T.S. I was told I should have been there before the route from the lavatories to the huts was roofed over with corrugated iron sheeting, and the rain 'came shitting down when you needed to pee in the night'.

Then Gwen came in, murmuring *sotto voce*, 'I say, Ginge, I don't think much of this place, do you?' Not wishing to offend my instructress over by the flat-irons, whose love for her steamy abode had shone through her every word of criticism, I said loudly that I 'rather liked it'. Gwen gave me a look: there were times when my enthusiasm for privation had a hollow ring. My spirits now were ebbing due to lack of sleep, and the constant drum of rain upon the tin-roofed corridor combined with the smell of wet washing did nothing to uplift them. Having the rest of the day off-duty, we decided to go into town, leaving camp by the winding, single-track lane over rain-soaked fields which provoked from my companion a horrified, 'But it's miles from anywhere!' My zest had returned once past the guardroom, and I enthused, 'I know. Isn't it marvellous?'

We found our way by bus to the West End, where we dived into the nearest restaurant. When we had disposed of plaice and chips, we lighted our cigarettes and Gwen conceded, 'This is more like it.' During all my time in Edinburgh I stayed loyal to the West End Restaurant in Shandwick Place for having given me hospitality on my first day in Scotland's capital.

Within a matter of days Gwen and the others were transferred to Number One Squadron at Fairmilehead, the other side of Edinburgh. I should have gone with them, but the barrack-room bruise on my shin-bone brought up from England had now turned into an ulcer. I trotted up to Sick Bay with my small kit, cursing my luck and wondering how long the wretched thing would take to heal. Sick Bay was a large, ground-floor room of Broomfield House, which I had entirely to myself – together with the undivided attention of a dedicated medical orderly, meals cooked in the Officers' Mess, daily visits from its members, and a magnificent view of the red squirrels on the lawn. I could not have fared better in a private clinic.

The main object was to rest my leg, and as the weather turned warmer I took to reclining upon the bed instead of lying in it. My dressing-gown was one I had made from black-out material – coupon-free – with a satin finish; frogged with white cord, it had a high neck and sleeves gathered to the wrist. Instead of pinning up my hair, I let it hang in two plaits over my shoulders, and in those days I used a gold-and-ivory cigarette-holder. The medical orderly, Private Patterson, decided that my name should be Magnolia. I had acquired several nicknames throughout my years, but this one mystified me: I asked her, 'Why *Magnolia*?' She had no idea, except that as she came through the door and saw me reclining gracefully in my black and white upon the bed, there had come into her head a line, 'Magnolia was a lady . . .', though whether it was a line she had read or invented she could not say. I was amused at the time, and accepted the name Magnolia as a Sick Bay joke. It was to be some while before the legend created by Private Patterson caught up with me.

After a fortnight's careful nursing my leg healed and I was packed off in a tilly (utility truck) with my kit-bag to join my comrades at Fairmilehead. At a certain point upon that journey two strange things happened simultaneously; I had the sense that I had just received a tumultuous welcome, as though surrounded by an unseen, cheering crowd, and I realised that *I knew the way*. It was not the streets I recognised but the natural landmarks. Trees and grass to my left with Arthur's Seat in the distance, and to my right, I knew, there should be open water – and there it was, just a far glimpse down a street all lined with houses. It was, I knew, the Forth, but I was puzzled by my own feeling that I should at that moment have seen a great deal *more* of it. I asked, was the green expanse to my left a park? – receiving the reply that it was 'Bruntsfield Links'. The name to me sounded foreign, as though I had expected something else.

That journey, made subsequently many times by tramcar, had always a profoundly disturbing, albeit pleasurable, effect on me. There were three points along the route where I was seized by an intense awareness of my own immediate reality – as I put it then, 'as if all of me came alive simultaneously'.

At Bruntsfield, by the Links, I turned my head always to look at the trees – invariably to be surprised by their sparseness: the memory I carried in my head of this place was a deep belt of woodland . . . I could have sworn, each time I passed, that *last time* I came this way the trees had extended right across the field. And it was here I came to meet those people. . . . Which people? There were no people: there were just the inhabited houses round the Links, and the heads of a few passengers on the top deck of a tram.

The most poignant reaction came always at the top of Church Hill, where I would throw back my head to look at something fluttering metallic above the level of my eyeline – then, where I looked, was every time the tram ceiling above me, and I would be left wondering what trick of light had created the impression of something swinging above me which glinted in the sun. A curious reflex action accompanying my upward glance was to rise in my seat and begin to lift my hand to wave – to *what*? I had no idea. What streamed into my consciousness were elation, pride and warmth so powerful that my spirit soared as though a great bird had made off with it. Then the tram-ceiling obtruded across my vision, almost surprising me.

Beyond Church Hill is a dip in the contour of the land, and the gilt apothecary's sign above a chemist's shop on my left marked for me the third place upon my route where 'all of me came alive simultaneously'. Again, there was the sense that I was in good company; that it was *home*; and once there came into my head a tune – an army song. I hummed cheerfully several bars of it before my effort to recall the words brought flooding the realisation that it was like no army song in the repertoire of a soldier *circa* 1947. Then the music in my head disappeared, as a small, blue-canvas room had disappeared, with an oval of glass upon its wall.

All these impressions held my mind as briefly as the transient patterns in a kaleidoscope constantly shaken. They had been real until I came to think about them consciously, then only the happiness remained.

From the moment of my arrival at Fairmilehead – indeed, from the moment I had passed Bruntsfield in the tilly – I was happier than I had been in all my life. All mention of taking my commission promptly vanished from my letters. Just to be myself on the green slope below the Pentlands seemed to carry rank; I could progress no higher. Number One Squadron had been an all-male unit until the arrival of our contingent of thirteen A.T.S., and I found the predominently masculine atmosphere invigorating – and, curiously, familiar. The camp-site was a large, sloping field, surrounded by oak and beech trees; and sometimes, when I looked down the hill towards the rounded roofs of nissen huts and the bluish smoke of the cookhouse chimney rising in the morning air, some kind of far, dim memory would stir, causing me to catch my breath and feel the smart behind my eyes of a huge love for *my soldiers*.

Once, I was asked by the R.S.M. – a man of twenty-two years' service who knew K.R.s by heart – if I would work late for two or three nights on a special job in the C.O.'s inner sanctum. A team of four – one officer, the R.S.M., a senior male clerk and I – was to prepare a new type of personnel board showing the trade, rank and location of every member of the Royal Corps of Signals serving in Scottish Command. Each man was to be represented by a disc, coloured according to trade, hung on a wall-board. A good deal of cross-checking was required, and the entire job had to be completed within, at most, three evenings when the C. O. was not using the office. Whether I had been chosen for my neatness of hand or because the R.S.M. had spotted my devotion to the Army, I do not know, but the talent which made me uniquely useful on that exercise was my astonishing ability to memorise the name on every disc, and where precisely on the board each had been placed. A man unaccounted for brought from me, then checking the list, the snapped information, 'Posted OSGAR' – (Orkney and Shetland Garrison) – 'he's the third disc on that hook, we put him there last night.' When the C.O. came to view our progress he was told of my feats of memory, and I joked wrily, 'I wish my memory had worked like this when I was learning history notes at school!' Why on these two nights my memory functioned with unprecedented efficiency was not to me a mystery: those names on the personnel board were of men serving in *Scottish Command*, who wore upon their sleeve, as I did, the Lion Rampant, and therefore it was my personal duty to account for every one of them. (The very name 'Scottish Command' set my blood tingling; when I first heard it applied to myself, my mind filled instantly with banners and a great clangour.) The C.O. stayed a short while chatting, and I remember noting that my schoolgirl's voice had deepened and I spoke with the relaxed self-confidence of one accustomed to command. I seemed to be another, older person, who had talked in a similar way with just such another gathering of men, someone whose delivered opinion mattered. I was profoundly disappointed when we completed our task ahead of schedule and no third night's work was required. I had been sublimely happy handling those discs which showed where all my Scots were posted.

Such moments of intense happiness were all the same, dependent not upon personalities but due entirely to a link between the place, the Army and an elusive thread of memory which I could identify only by its feeling. I never chose to examine the phenomenon because to be happy was enough; to analyse why one is happy is like using a sledge-hammer to examine a butterfly.

My new-found contentment did not exclude personal relationships. Soon after my arrival I became friendly with one of the camp wireless operators who shared my artistic interests. He was a member of the drama group at the army study centre in town, currently rehearsing *Hamlet* for presentation at the end of May. My friend was cast as the Player King. To be even thus remotely connected with a production of *Hamlet* filled me with elation. To be in the Army, in Scotland, looking forward to seeing my first production of *Hamlet* was a combination which sent me dizzy with excitement: it was almost too good to be true.

Meanwhile, upon my bright horizon had appeared one small cloud. My mother's letters had become greatly concerned with plans for Whitsuntide. My father had wanted to go to Cheltenham, but she had heard rumours in far-away England that Whitsuntide leave would be granted to the Army. It had been remiss of me not to check earlier whether English holidays were recognised in Scotland, but I had been in the country for a total of only twenty-one days, of which fourteen had been spent in Sick Bay. As a compromise, to see me and to please my father, she suggested they should spend a few days in Edinburgh. Had they suggested taking a holiday near Guildford when I was there I should have been delighted to see them, but the prospect of my parents coming to Scotland filled me with horror. Within three brief weeks I had shed my lifetime's load of English connections – it was already hard to imagine that I had ever lived anywhere but in Scotland. As I travelled on the tramcar past the gilt pestle-and-mortar signs which were *my* Edinburgh – 'Have they survived until *now*?' I had exclaimed on first beholding them – I felt there had to be some way to keep the threatened 'English invasion' out of Edinburgh. I was almost saved by the Church of Scotland Assembly, which filled every hotel and boarding-house in town, and then my mother phoned the news that a schoolfriend of mine, now married to a Scot, had an uncle and aunt who could accommodate them.

When my parents arrived my discomfort became infectious, and how to fill the heavy days became a problem. I was all right when I was on neutral territory – in the living-room at Stenhouse where 'Uncle' Adam and 'Auntie' Mamie were the resident Scots who made both sides welcome: it was when I met them in town that the trouble started. My parents knew Edinburgh better than I did, which in itself galled me. (I had paid no attention to 'historic' Edinburgh; I was happy with camp life and my tramcar up to Fairmilehead.) They knew its castle, which I had avoided, and when they suggested taking me I could offer no rational objection.

Miserable in my soldier's uniform with its Lion Rampant flashes, I entered through the gate and past its sentries trying to disown and be disowned by a procession of holiday people in summer frocks, open-necked shirts and camera straps. Shrinking with embarrassment I managed to creep in with the herd, determined not to let my parents see how much I hated it although I had been ill and temperamental since that morning when the plan was mooted. Silent and sickly, I trekked in the sun past stone walls and through chambers, and the muzz of voices round me grew to be the ice-thick substance of a shroud.

Then – oh my God! – I was crammed into a tower room which held Scotland's regalia. The Honours of Scotland – a crown unworn for centuries and a pair of sceptres never used. They were trapped in a cage of glass, as I was trapped in a stationary file of people unable to retreat or move forward. We had stopped where I was immediately in line with the showcase, then turned to make a close semi-circle, so that I could not even look away from the objects facing me. I pressed my lips together to stop myself from retching. My mind slid away into a wholly alien dimension; in the distance I heard the drone of a guide's voice, but he spoke a tongue foreign to my ears – like a voice on radio, audible but unintelligible. I remember wondering why I did not understand what he was saying. In the dark blank of my mind, I seemed to see another crown – this same crown, but less ornate and lacking arches, and it lay upon a cushion before my hands. . . . Then this picture faded. My link with that crown was intensely personal and so strong that it and I seemed to be alone together; I could feel it appealing to me, almost in words,'*You* will get me out of here.' For a moment I had the wild notion to hurl myself upon its glass case, to smash through it, to seize that poor exploited crown and hug it to me, shielding it from the eyes of all those staring people. Even as the thought came, I knew it to be impossible.

Unable to bear the spectacle, I looked away from the crown. Then my eyes fell upon the sword. I knew that sword, and my reaction was: what on earth is that doing here? – the place for that sword is not with the crown. Then my mind began to see another sword – of steel; it had

run with red, a trickle down the blade upstanding taller than I was. . . .
Then the red was the red of light through my eyelids, and I hoped
frantically that I would not fall. Then the red cleared from my eyes, and
there was nothing but the feel of myself in A.T.S. uniform.

'Are you all right, Ada?' My mother's enquiry reached me from a
great distance, but the note of concern sounded just at my elbow: I
must have looked as bad as I felt. I managed to move my head,
signalling that I could last out if we moved quickly. My father steered
me down the stairs with a grave, 'You'll be all right, Ginger, when you
get outside.'

Then we were in the square of cobbles, and I was holding in my solar
plexus by sheer strength of muscle, until I could hold it no longer. Then
I stood weeping, publicly, in my uniform, a gusher of tears that came
up like vomit from the soul. It was the worst spasm I had ever known.
My mother asked desperately, 'Ada, what *is* it?' I could only shake my
head helplessly. My father stood a short distance from us, showing
embarrassment and concern simultaneously.

There was a brief, tense, family discussion; ought we to leave or to
stay? My mother had particularly wanted me to see the Shrine of
Remembrance, where they had, she had said, a book listing all the
dead. All the dead? I asked, 'Which dead?'

She replied, 'Both wars.'

Then it dawned on me that she meant 1914–18 and 1939–45. My
tears ceased. I could deal with contemporary memorials.

My parents left Edinburgh next day, in time for me to see the
production of *Hamlet* on its last night, 31 May. It was a remarkable
production, the large cast ingeniously deployed upon a minute stage in
what had been the drawing-room of a house in Grosvenor Crescent.
Seated in the front row I was drawn into the atmosphere of the Danish
court so that I forgot my contemporary surroundings. To see Hamlet
portayed by an actor did not diminish my sense, strong as ever, that the
prince soliloquising upon a skull in a graveyard was *myself*.

The deterioration in my health began immediately afterwards.
Heavy depression was accompanied by a curious restlessness, as if
every place in which I found myself was the wrong one. An inexplicable
sense of urgency drove me to wonder what I should be doing. Some
part of me had gone missing, so that I was no longer the complete
person who had been so happy at Fairmilehead Camp just a few days
previously. These psychological symptoms were accompanied by a
return of the mysterious cardiac disturbance which had temporarily
afflicted me at school.

When I blacked out in the orderly room while waiting to go on
morning sick-parade to Redford Barracks – we had no resident M.O.
at Fairmilehead – I was sent to Camp Reception Station, Strathearn

Road, for observation. Thence, to my horror, I was packed off to Cowglen Military Hospital by Glasgow.

At Cowglen, once more all tests proved negative. It was observed, however, that I had abnormally slow blood-circulation, most noticeable in my hands which have almost no subcutaneous tissue. Further tests were made, involving the freezing of my hands in crushed ice and water. What this disclosed I never knew, but there was a sudden shift of interest when one of the doctors remarked upon my manual bone-structure. Picking my hand out of the ice, he held it frozen and dripping while he demonstrated to his colleagues the low thumb emplacement which gave my hand its enormous span. Asked, was I a musician, I replied that I had briefly studied the pianoforte but with no real enthusiasm. They considered this a great pity; and I watched with amusement as my hand was passed from one to the other as though it had been a skeleton at medical school. The incident had a curious sequel the following day, when a male medical orderly paid a visit to the ward solely to ask me, 'Please may I see your hands?' I showed them to him, and after studying them silently for a few moments he thanked me and departed, apparently satisfied.

My depressions I never mentioned. These had worsened considerably since my arrival at Cowglen, a fact which I attributed to my unwanted stay in hospital; I had no means of knowing when I should get out, and every day was a life sentence. I marvelled at the stamina of long-term patients who could view that ward and the distant NAAFI hearth as home.

The conditions at Cowglen were, as far as I could see, exemplary. The A.T.S. ward was a huge nissen hut, with snow-white interior walls and a black floor polished as jet; it was summer, and the two great, black stoves were enamelled and heaped with flowers like twin altars. It had for me a curious likeness to a monastic dwelling, particularly noticeable when patients were resting and it was quiet.

The food was superb — I had tasted nothing like it since my pre-war childhood — and it came in unlimited quantity. In 1947 everything was still on points, on coupons or unobtainable; it was the year when the Minister of Food, Mr Strachey, was answering parliamentary questions about 'the grave food crisis' and the civilian daily ration was 2700 calories. For seven years my one egg per fortnight had been a dietary luxury, and I marvelled when at Cowglen a second and a third egg appeared on my plate during the course of a single meal. When this was followed by a surfeit of *tinned peaches* I was stricken speechless: nobody squandered precious points on tinned peaches except on anniversaries, or when relatives came home on leave.

Ambulant patients were given the task of serving the food and washing dishes, and it so happened that my first spell of sink-duty coincided with this remarkable meal of poached eggs and peaches. When I asked what to do with the surplus food I was told to throw it away. My horrified protest brought the laconic reply from my departing instructress, 'Then eat them yourself.' When she had gone I stood beside those wasted army rations and began to cry. The enormity of my grief filled the empty, small, ward kitchen like a tornado, casting me aside like some object in its path. When it had abated and I regained control of the personality from which it had emerged, I set to work to scour the empty food containers fired with a resolve to take up the matter of wasted provisions. When the orderlies came to take away the containers, I was ready with as many questions as a visitor from the War Office. The explanation was simply that food supplied to the wards was proportioned according to the number of beds, not the number of patients. I was relieved to know that the surplus of that week was exceptional, and I could see that cooks in faraway kitchens preparing meals for thousands of patients could not be informed daily of changes in numbers. The orderly-in-charge remarked with pleasure on my interest, and there the matter should have ended – but I pursued it relentlessly up the scale of administration. Had I stayed longer at Cowglen there was no doubt I would have pressed my enquiry to the full and until the day I left I was still trying to work out an alternative system.

After two and a half weeks I received the glad news that I was to be returned to my unit. I was so anxious to get back to Fairmilehead that I made a thorough mess of packing my kitbag and had to put the surplus into a paper carrier.

It is that paper carrier bag I remember, standing upon a table in the waiting-room of Queen Street Station in Glasgow, while I stared at a poster on the wall facing me. On it was a map of the Kyles of Bute and Lochalsh. A single name hit my eye – Rothesay. Why on earth did the name Rothesay make me think immediately of *myself*? And Bute – why should Bute send through my head a multiplicity of tiny flashes? I had no idea. But it was the second time in my life that a railway poster had conjured up for me the identity of *my* Scotland.

The ominous portent, unseen by myself at the time, lay in my recognition of 'my' Scotland being different from the Scotland in which I currently dwelled.

The joy of my return to Fairmilehead was short-lived. Within a couple of days I was summoned to the C.O.'s office to be told that I was being transferred to Broomfield. At my exclamation of horror it was explained to me, sympathetically, that I was a lady of doubtful health in a camp where robust males predominated, and that if I fell ill again there was no one on the camp-site to look after me; whereas at Broomfield there was a visiting M.O., a comfortable Sick Bay, and a medical orderly of my own sex. I protested, 'But I'm not ill now!' – and would have added, 'But I shall be if you send me to Broomfield,' except that it might have sounded like an attempt at moral blackmail. My pleas disregarded, I was transported by tilly back to Broomfield – the camp on the edge of the sea with a view of Fife across the water, which set me thinking of my infant dream about a great black ship with polished gun-mouths. . . .

For the first fortnight of my new posting I went back to Fairmilehead every evening – a long journey which used up most of my visiting time. I went mainly for the ride by tramcar, to feel just for those few seconds the sense of being fully alive – although this pleasure now reminded me chiefly of exile from the Pentlands. Through the rest of the day I pined for the lost proximity of the Pentlands which had made any job at Fairmilehead seem important. Pushing my pen in Broomfield troop office I was bored to death. I came alive there only in the late afternoon, very briefly, when the despatch riders went zooming out of camp upon their various routes. The best rider in the Don R. Troop was a man called Prince, and once I was electrified by a snatch of routine office conversation:

'Who's Perth courier today?'

'Prince.'

The association of the two names 'Prince' and 'Perth' set my mind spinning with a succession of images, one clear and vivid: assembled banners and tall stone columns stretching before me, and some kind of weight around my head which very slightly wobbled so that I must walk carefully. When I looked down at my desk I was startled to see my hand in a khaki sleeve: why was it not *black*? After that, I always listened for the Perth courier setting out on his mission, the sound of his motor-cycle a momentary link with 'my' Scotland.

I did not stay long a clerk in troop office. Private Patterson, due to be demobbed, had her eye on me as a likely successor in the M.I. Room. When the senior commander asked me what I knew about first aid, I replied that I had as much knowledge as 'the average person'. My notion of average was as usual rather high – which was fortunate for the personnel of Broomfield Camp, whose lives would be in my hands as of 00.01 hours on Sunday morning.

My medical training had been a crash course fragmented over several days. Private Patterson initiated me in the mysteries of her medicaments cupboard, preparing sick reports, compiling the weekly register, sterilising instruments, and igniting the malevolent stove which heated the surgery. The only thing still worrying me on the Sunday was that cupboard – to which now I formally held the key – containing such powerful remedies as strychnine, which I was anxious to use correctly. True to her word, my mentor, imperturbable as ever, arrived at the M.I. Room at the last minute to record for me on paper which medicaments I was to apply to which maladies. Then with a cheerful, 'Good luck, Magnolia – you'll do it!' she departed to catch her train to Civvy Street. I pinned the sheet behind the cupboard door, locked the M.I. Room, and went to my bed praying that nobody would die before morning.

I was up at six to wrestle with that abominable stove – I finally cured its pranks by using extravagant firelighters made of cotton-wool and surgical spirit – and when I had washed the smuts from my hands and face I donned my white overall and prepared the sick report. I greeted the M.O. with a wild cry, 'I don't know how to do this job!' to which he replied calmly, 'Give it a week, Magnolia. You'll learn.'

It was then I inherited the full legacy left by Private Patterson, poet extraordinary and creator of camp legend. I was to spend many weeks trying to convince the personnel of Broomfield that my baptismal name was not Magnolia – nobody could be called *Magnolia Kay*! I found I was stuck with it (I could have cursed Private Patterson). Eventually I gave up trying to disillusion the M.O. Possibly to him the name suggested someone who was still, serene, and shining in the rain – qualities highly desirable in the Medical Orderly i/c Broomfield Camp, and no doubt present in my predecessor: mine was a different style.

Within a week I knew my job well enough not to be afraid of it. I never took risks. The Army with its curious talent for ordering square pegs to volunteer for square holes had, somewhere along the line, spotted in me the secret medico screaming to get out. (I still carried in my head from schooldays all my notes and diagrams made during my year's course in physiology.) Also, I had spent more time in sick bays and hospitals than anyone of my intake, and not a minute had been wasted. I had always carried an innate, obscure sense of responsibility towards the health of people, which now had outlet. I would never like Broomfield Camp, but I would have job-satisfaction.

Mine was an autonomous position like that of the education instructor and the hairdresser whose two establishments flanked mine at the intersection of the main drive and the path which ran parallel with the sea to the cookhouse. Our front doors overlooked the barrack-huts and the main camp area, and our back doors were conveniently connected by a path well-screened by the tangle of trees on the shore. Between us we had the best early-warning system in the Squadron – invaluable during formal inspections.

In addition to independence, I had in the M.I. Room a place of solitude where I could go to write poetry as well as sick reports. That this facility failed to induce my lost muse to return worried me a good deal for I felt guilty when I was not writing; merely to do my job well and enjoy it seemed to me perilously like self-indulgence. My most pleasant duty was going to collect medical supplies from Strathearn Road, by Church Hill – maintaining my link with that area; the least pleasant, syringing ears – a service required almost invariably on Tuesday afternoons when we had egg and chips for tea. I liked the unpredictability of the work, the constant state of emergency in which I lived; the drawback was that I had no relief orderly to whom I could hand over when, ostensibly, off-duty. Theoretically, my hours were those of the clerical staff, except when I had patients in Sick Bay; accidents and illness, however, do not conform to a timetable, so that news of a hand caught in the bread-slicer terminated my NAAFI break in the same way that an appendix grumbling in the night would call me out to go with an ambulance across Edinburgh. My weekends and evenings were, again in theory, my own (provided I did not have patients in Sick Bay) but I never liked to leave camp even for an hour for fear that pestilence might strike during my absence. I knew that Private Patterson had not made such heavy weather of her responsibility (I had an anxious nature) but I had not seen her enjoy much free time, either.

There was no resident M.O. – it was a small camp – and sick parade was taken by a retired doctor from Davidson's Mains, who came to camp for a couple of hours each morning. Anyone taken ill outwith those hours depended on me for survival. If I diagnosed an ailment which would keep till morning, I put the sufferer to bed in the Sick Bay. If I suspected something more serious, the procedure was to telephone C.R.S. Strathearn Road for an ambulance. In the case of the men – of whom we had a few, Don R. Troop and an Infantry unit who did guard duty – there were no facilities for nursing, except in their own hut, so it was usually for male patients I required the ambulance.

The trouble with our camp was that almost nobody could find it except those of us who lived there. Magnificently camouflaged by trees, it lay at the remote end of a farm lane which included a fearsome S-bend over a hill, the hill itself affording excellent cover. Finding the entrance to the lane depended upon how well one knew the avenues of Davidson's Mains. Being able to give navigational instructions to an ambulance was as necessary as knowing when to send for one. In the end I gave up trying to explain on the telephone; whenever I encountered a driver who had not been out to Broomfield before, I went out myself to meet the ambulance on the lane and pilot it safely past a farm entrance and the several cunningly concealed field gates which had misled many newcomers. On clear nights I could safely board the vehicle; on pitch-dark nights or when the haar blew in from the sea, I would walk a few yards ahead using the beam of my torch as a beacon.

Men on guard duty, solicitous for my safety, were sometimes puzzled by my determination to brave the elements, alone, at all hours of the night. The only real menace was a farm dog who, for a short period, terrorised our girls walking back to camp, but he had been a friend of mine since our first meeting when I clouted his muzzle and snarled back at him. I had nothing to fear but pneumonia as I stood shivering on the hilltop, clad in a pair of slacks, battle-top and greatcoat pulled hurriedly over my pyjamas. My shivering was not due entirely to cold; an extraordinary excitement filled me up there alone in the dark, eyes straining for the first glimpse of headlights on the road. The real challenge lay in getting my patient safely to hospital, but my vigil on the hilltop represented for me something else as well; what that was I could never determine, except that it had to do with responsibility for the lives of *people in an army camp* – and when I felt it, all of me came alive simultaneously.

When I had patients in Sick Bay or a heavy influx of customers for my 5 p.m. treatment parade, I took my tea late with the Don R. Troop. The despatch riders were a close-knit group, existing apart from the rest, using the NAAFI snuggery which was predominantly male, and taking their meals at hours which suited their duties. To eat my tea in solitary state with the Don Rs gave me an extraordinarily deep satisfaction. I hardly ever spoke to them. It was sufficient merely to be in the same room with those booted young men, their helmets beside them, taking food before setting out with their despatches across the kingdom. Hearing them discuss their rota of destinations, I became almost dizzy with excitement – Stirling, Glasgow, Perth, a roll-call of names which brought vividly alive *my* Scotland. Some hazy, curious conviction lurked in me that these were my couriers, setting out upon my business – and once there came into my head the clatter of hoof-beats, but I told myself that was imagination. What we had in common, I knew, was our duty after tea; and we all belonged to Scottish Command. To be asked, 'Got many patients, Magnolia?' gave me a huge surge of belonging.

3

THE YEAR I CAME TO SCOTLAND WAS THE YEAR OF ITS AWAKENING. In 1947 one took for granted the greyness of post-war life and the continuing 'austerity' restrictions. I was accustomed to seeing hotels and public buildings requisitioned by various Ministries, in use as offices or billets. They wore a drab, patchy look, due to the number of high windows still covered with black-out paint. I had grown up in a world where public baths were closed to all but the Forces, where museum treasures were stored away and their premises occupied by civil servants, and I did not feel unduly deprived to find Edinburgh's museums and galleries closed – in fact, it did not even occur to me to find out if any of them were open.

I arrived in Scotland's capital in the May, unaware that I was just in time for the renaissance. Local news, which must have featured in headlines earlier in the year, had been relegated to small paragraphs by the time I came back from Cowglen. (I had been incarcerated in various Sick Bays for a total of six weeks out of my three months in Scotland.) The first I heard about the Edinburgh Festival of Music and Drama of 1947 was at the army study centre where the members of the drama group (which I had now joined) were discussing their bookings for various programmes. A late comer to the scene, I must have sounded curiously ill-informed when I asked, 'Do you mean the Exhibition?'

There was some excuse for my confusion because the two events had been timed to run concurrently, and it was 'Enterprise Scotland' which had most publicity at that particular time. Trade fairs were of no real interest to me, but that one had caught my attention on 6 August when runners bearing fiery crosses – the traditional call to the clansmen, my evening paper informed me – had been despatched from Edinburgh Castle to all parts of the world, proclaiming Scotland's revival. The thought of those fiery crosses going out from the castle filled me with a disturbing and powerful elation.

The Festival of Edinburgh when it opened took me entirely by surprise. The word 'festival' meant, to my mind, an event similar to the schools' musical festivals which so much involved my father during the brief years of my pre-war childhood: for me to visualise any kind of large-scale public activity devoted to enjoyment was like expecting a child of four in 1945 to imagine the taste of a banana.

One day I went into the West End on my way to pick up medical supplies, and I found the clock in Shandwick Place had become an island of flowers. I stood gazing in incredulous delight. I can remember my thought: So the war is really over! People spoke to each other on the corner by Binns, all of us moved by the sight of so much colour. At once I became excited about the new Festival. It was then that I discovered why the members of the drama group had booked tickets months in advance. I did manage to see the film *Les Enfants du Paradis*. Otherwise, I had to make do with glimpses of other people's enjoyment, which were picturesque enough. For the first time since my childhood I saw people in the street clad in long evening dress. One night a piper in full garb lifted me down from the back of the T.C.V. (How on earth did women help to fight a war wearing those tight box skirts?) I mixed with the crowd, saw the flowers, smelled ladies' perfume and heard foreign tongues; like a child I was entranced.

I would have nothing whatever to do with the exhibition 'Enterprise Scotland'. Seething with wrath, I stalked past shop windows on Princes Street filled with magnificent clothes such as we had not seen for years, all marked 'For sale to overseas customers only.' That I should be *in Scotland* forbidden to purchase goods manufactured in my own country was something I took as a personal insult. I do not think it would have worried me so much in England. I came to look upon the foreign buyers as invaders and plunderers, who occupied too much space in our trams and on our pavements, and I could not wait to see the back of them.

After a long debate, the Minister of Fuel and Power, Mr Shinwell, relaxed the ban on floodlighting for just four nights of the Festival so that the castle could be illuminated. I saw it from the back of an army lorry bringing home the cast of *Hamlet* from Newbattle Abbey. Newbattle Abbey, Dalkeith, was then used by the Army as Number One Formation College, and the production of *Hamlet* was presented there for one night at the end of the Festival. As an appendage of the Danish court, I was invited to go with them.

The performance was held in a small theatre built in the Abbey grounds, and we were taken straight to it. Our transport had been late when we set out, so the cast rushed away to their dressing-rooms, leaving me alone in the auditorium. A junior officer arrived to keep me company, and we sat on the front row reserved for the college staff and guests.

Normally I was a shy person (except when dedicated to a cause) but on that night there occurred an extraordinary fusion of my entire personality. It was similar to the sensation I experienced when I worked at the personnel board in the C.O.'s office at Fairmilehead, but on this evening it went much deeper. As the rest of the staff arrived I became the centre of a great deal of attention, and the senior A.T.S. officer present accused the others of commandeering my company. At this I laughed heartily, and allowed myself to be placed in the central seat, beside the C.O., where all of them could share me. I knew *here* to expect this competition because it had always happened. I did not know Newbattle, but Newbattle certainly knew me: I could feel its welcome from the ground beneath me.

I did not see the abbey. It was dark when the show ended, and the players and I climbed into the waiting army lorry. The vehicle was stationary for some while because we had lost Hamlet, and Gertrude led the company in a choral rendering of 'Why are we waiting?' Privately, I wished our waiting could go on forever, with the members of the Danish court around me, and a single light upon the path and some bushes our only landmark. Out there, in the dark, quite near, was a medieval Cistercian monastery. . . . In fact, there was no such thing – as I had been told by a member of the staff when I asked if the abbey was 'as it used to be'. This knowledge did not intrude upon my conviction, as I sat in the lorry, that nearby it stood intact. I knew the abbey was there because *I had seen it*. There must be two buildings in the grounds, the Cistercian monastery and the more recent structure. With nobody there to contradict me, it was easy to assume that my informant and I had been talking at cross purposes.

On the homeward route from Dalkeith I saw suddenly Edinburgh Castle, floodlit, in the distance, a shining fortress floating in the sky. The rest of the company were talking, so for some moments I had the miraculous spectacle entirely to myself. Then someone else called attention to it, and it ceased to be 'my' castle.

From July onward I had become increasingly agitated by news of another quite different event, the betrothal of Princess Elizabeth. Like all English people, I though of the monarch as the King of England, and therefore to me his daughter was 'the English Princess'. Indeed, the only time I ever felt hostility towards the royal family was when I heard mention of them in a Scottish context; then a great hot anger filled me, because my Scotland, I felt, was no concern of English monarchs. The existence of that English princess had worried me during all the years we had been simultaneously growing up, though why I should feel that constituted a threat to my personal happiness and security was totally inexplicable. Now, the news that she was to be married filled me with alarm.

It was extremely difficult to escape the reverberations of the royal marriage, for the newspapers carried a blow by blow account of the preparations. My feelings came to a head one autumn evening when all A.T.S. personnel were assembled in the mess. There we were told that the Service, collectively, would donate a wedding present. Our personal contribution was to be one shilling per head, surrendered during pay-parade. It was assumed that we were all willing volunteers, but any objectors would be heard. My immediate reaction was an impulse to leap to my feet, declaring 'We wull have no marriage of English princesses!' The words rang in my head, in my own voice but deeper than I knew it and with a broad Scots accent – rang so clearly that I looked about me in consternation, convinced that I had spoken aloud. However, nobody had turned to look at me, so presumably the voice had spoken only in my own head, yet I could *hear* its echo.

One brave girl rose to her feet, voicing her objection. Asked why, she replied with a slight wriggle of embarrassment, 'Because I don't believed in monarchy and things like that.'

'Anyone else objecting?'

I sat frozen to my seat, thrown out of countenance to discover that objectors must give reasons. How on earth could I say that the marriage of an English princess *constituted a menace to Scotland*? — which was the sole instinctive thought in my head at that moment. While I was still trying to think of a rational reason for my refusal, my silence was taken as assent.

Later, on our way to the NAAFI, a great deal was said which should properly have been aired at the meeting, but soldiers are trained to obey orders and to voice an opinion contrary to the decision of High Command does not come naturally. One shilling out of twenty-six was a sizeable sum of money to those girls who sent home part of their pay. What irked most people was the way in which our enthusiasm had been taken too readily for granted. I made the observation that it would have been a happier arrangement for everyone if those wishing to subscribe had been the ones to stand up and be counted. I was furious with myself for not having thought of this earlier.

The problem posed by that wedding present hung over me all the week. So strongly did I feel about it that I would — in my own words of the time — have died rather than contribute to it. Alone in the M.I. Room. I racked my brains to discover why I felt so passionately. I was not anti-monarchist; it was a constitutional system of the land which I accepted with no strong feelings. I grudged nobody marital happiness. I gave subscriptions readily on any public flag-day, so my objection was not to the disbursement of a shilling. I was baffled. Finally, I decided that at pay-parade, when I refused to subscribe, I would say that I objected to the way in which our acquiescence had been assumed. I knew that this criticism of military procedure would be less welcome than a statement of republican sympathies, but my blood was up. Many people would have paid one shilling for a quiet life and thought no more about it, but I could not do that. The situation required from me some enormous personal statement. Why, I knew not. The nearest I came to identifying what troubled me was the spontaneous, curious thought that 'this time' I would not be coerced into something to do with 'the English Princess'.

At night I slept badly, having confused dreams of a royal marriage which I was desperate to escape. I had worked myself into a frightful state of nerves by the time Thursday came. When I was due to go on pay-parade I was detained by the arrival at the M.I. Room of a casualty. When this happened my pay was kept for me and I collected it from Troop Office when it was convenient. I was still composing my refusal when I set out grimly in the afternoon to get my pay. As it turned out, the wedding present was never mentioned. I escaped back to the M.I. Room where I was attacked by a fit of ghost-weeping which then turned into the most extraordinary euphoria because 'this time' I had escaped from some monumental catastrophe threatening myself

98

and Scotland.

In fact, how far I had escaped remains debatable. The nightmare of that wedding was to hound my days and nights until November. The local papers were saturated with reports and pictures of royal engagements taking place in Scotland. At one point I actually broke down and cried because it seemed so unfair that 'all this' had to coincide with my own arrival in Scotland. I gave up trying to read newspapers. My work in the M.I. Room gave me an excuse to be alone and think of other matters, but the sense of urgency never left me, the curious feeling that I was myself involved in a marriage which I did not want and could not stop. I reminded myself many times that it was not *my* wedding but there persisted a feeling that I was in some terrible way connected with it.

During October I had one more encounter with my ghost-self in black, the man who wrestled with his conscience about his father's death. There was to be a Halloween fancy-dress dance at Fairmilehead. Others planned to hire their costumes, but my mind was not on fancy dress: I had seen a glorious opportunity to wear, in Scotland, my right and proper clothes. I sent home for the fifteenth-century black costume I had made to wear as Hamlet. When it arrived I set to work to give it more an air of royalty. On the black cloak I fixed a collar of ermine made of cotton-wool painted with tails of indian ink, and added a border of white bandage stitched with fleur-de-lis cut out of black stuff, with four sequins composed like a jewel in each centre. Why I thought of fleur-de-lis as *my* royal emblem was something I had never questioned. My excitement as I worked on these alterations was unbounded – something akin to relief that for once I could appear as *myself* at the camp below the Pentland hills.

At the start of the parade I was asked to identify myself. Startled, I said I had no 'character' in mind – did it matter? It was explained to me that I needed some title for the benefit of the judges. This sent my mind reeling: it had not occurred to me that I required to explain who I was. Surely, *everyone knew that*? A name? I groped through a blank part of my mind, trying to remember who I was. By this time I was holding up the parade. I said, 'Well, originally I made this costume to wear as Hamlet. . . .' They said that would do. So I said, unwillingly, 'Announce me as Hamlet, Prince of Denmark,' stressing the last title, which was the only part that seemed to fit me.

Trapped into presenting myself as Shakespeare's character, I held out my right hand to support an imaginary skull – an unnecessary contrivance, but I had to focus quickly back to the character in the play, and my immediate thought was *a head*. As we circled the NAAFI recreational hall, a jolly girl behind me tried to lift my cloak like a train, and I snapped at her, 'Don't do that!' She let it drop. I could not bear the feel of hands lifting the weight of a garment from my shoulders. I remembered that I always wore my robes of a length manageable by myself, and scooped them into the crook of my left arm, spreading them like a fan when I sat down. At the end of the parade I apologised to the girl for snarling, while she apologised for having tried to be my courtier. I said, 'That's all right. But I cannot stand train-bearers. I never could.'

I won second prize for my costume. Afterwards, I learned that it would have been first, but the judges felt that the skull I carried should have been a real one. (My piece of mime must have been successful.) They were right, so it should. But then, I had not gone to the dance dressed as Hamlet. When I set off for the Pentlands in an army lorry dressed in fifteenth-century black, I had gone as *myself*.

4

WINTER CAME LIKE A SCOURGE TO BROOMFIELD WHEN Q-STORES ran out of khaki woollen gloves and I had had three pairs successively uplifted by the cold-fisted, I sent home for the wrist-buttoned kid gloves left over from my schooldays. Nobody stole those. I wore them overtly but I was never charged with breach of regulations – the glove famine being, I suspect, an embarrassment to the Army. My greatcoat issued to me at Training Centre was not, like the rest, in the current princess-line style, but of the old, half-belted variety, designed like an officer's greatcoat but of coarser material; it was much coveted by my comrades who did not have to wear the thing or, worse, attempt to bend in it. I used the brown bakelite cap badge, the alternative to the brass one which I considered flashy. The addition of the kid gloves completed the inadvertant officer-image which in the beginning had embarrassed me; now I had grown used to it, and when saluted on Princes Street by privates from other camps I returned the salute automatically. Ignoring it would have left someone with the impression of a very rude officer, and to go to the length of stopping a perfect stranger to point out that I wore no pips would merely have made the situation a good deal more trying for all.

I went into town more frequently these days, having lost my fear that if I left camp for half an hour somebody would die. I always told the duty telephonist when I was going out, so that no one wasted precious minutes looking for me. My visits to Edinburgh were usually to see Uncle Adam and Auntie Mamie, or, more regularly, to attend rehearsals at the army study centre where I had been given the second female role in *L'Ame en Peine*. The cinema was a popular recreation for Broomfield inmates as it afforded a few hours' respite from the bitter cold of camp. The friend whose taste in films I shared was a telephonist at the castle, and when she was on afternoon shift I usually met her either in the Church of Scotland canteen at the Bridges or on the Castle Esplanade. She had often suggested that I should go into the exchange to collect her, but I was loath to do that, not merely because I would be an unauthorised visitor – I had still unpleasant memories of an encounter with a crown. Finally, I agreed to go into the castle if she would ensure that my presence there had official recognition. So she arranged with the duty officer a formal invitation for me to visit the exchange.

It was lunchtime on a clear day when I first went up there. Summer's hordes of civilian sightseers were gone, and the castle was closed to all but military personnel. (It was H.Q. Scottish Command, and that year all the Highland regiments were home simultaneously.) My steel-tipped heels clipped briskly along Half-Moon Battery as I headed straight for the barracks entrance with only a brief, incurious glance at the historic edifice on my left. My ordeal in the jewel room seemed remote to me now, as though the shrinking girl with English parents, trying to hide away an A.T.S. uniform, was somebody with whom I had long since parted company. As I neared the entrance to the military quarters my step quickened, as though heading for home, and I had the just-vanished sensation that the castle as I knew it was much smaller than the present establishment – more domestic, and, in an odd way, bore more resemblance to the barrack-block I was approaching than to the actual fortress; also, the area of rock seemed smaller now than it used to be, and I missed the periphery of greensward which had been a feature in my day. There was, to my surprise, no smithy – which I had expected, due possibly to the clangour of hammers on metal which just then rang so clearly in my head.

I was received by the duty officer and one of the engineers who was to escort me through the warren of passages. On the way I was told of extensions made recently to the exchange, and I listened with great interest, asking many questions. It had been my rule personally to inspect any alterations at the castle, and I had instinctively retained the habit. At ease within this context, I was startled to meet my friend at the switchboard, for I had temporarily forgotten her. When finally we all emerged into the pale sunlight, and I was thanking the duty officer for his courtesy, I made off confidently in the wrong direction. Everyone laughed, including myself, yet I remained convinced that I had been going the right way – which, in fact, I had, if we had been making for the old west sallyport, no longer extant.

Thereafter I made my own way up to the castle exchange. In camp, when making plans to see a film, my heart still sank at the suggestion, 'Meet me at the castle.' I had a real dread of being stopped by the guard and questioned. What would I say? My fear amused the telephonists: 'Just tell them you're going to the exchange.' This answer never sounded right to me; I was sure there was some other reason, now lost in my head, which might tumble out if ever I were challenged.

This unease would last until I reached the Lawnmarket, where another personality took over. Confident and purposeful, I would go striding across the Esplanade, past the sentries, heading through the darkness towards the barracks, my footsteps ringing on the cobbles. I felt the welcome of the place like a warm tent around me. My right to be there was something I never questioned, once inside. Afterwards, thinking about it, I would be awed by my own temerity; but this was the waning thought of a waning personality: even in camp I had grown to realise that whatever answer I gave if challenged, *it would be the right one*. And so, indeed, it turned out on the one occasion when I *was* challenged, in the dark, crossing Half-Moon Battery, by a courteous, 'Excuse me—?'

I rapped, 'Yes?'

The voice said, 'Oh – I'm sorry, ma'am,' and the speaker stepped back to salute.

Returning the salute, I said pleasantly, 'That's all right' – and went my way.

I cannot have visited the exchange very often, yet on each occasion I entered the castle gate I was aware of having passed that way hundreds of times. My feeling was of going home, or of attending to some official matter. I even knew the view from a certain high window – although no longer sure whether any part of the existing castle still contained that particular chamber. That this view contained a greater proportion of water and green grass than would be seen anywhere round modern Edinburgh did not strike me as the least bit strange. Yet I think there must have been a time when my double awareness of Edinburgh Castle obtruded sufficiently to require some explanation. And there was, of course, one which came to me automatically: I was merely seeing my own future. It was something which had happened to me before on several occasions, so there was nothing unusual about it.

There was just one flaw in this line of reasoning: A.T.S. personnel were never billeted at the castle. Then I discovered that the Army Educational Corps operated from there, some of its male personnel lived in the barracks, and the female A.E.C. instructors billeted at the Langdon Hotel could use the castle's sergeants' mess. I was relieved: the explanation of my *future* presence at the castle had now been slotted, albeit creakingly, into place.

My transfer to the Army Educational Corps was not a new idea. It had, however, come recently to prominence due to the impending demobilisation of my neighbour at Broomfield, the A.E.C. instructor, who had suggested my becoming her successor. I had no desire to stay at Broomfield but, now that I 'saw' myself as one of the instructors housed in the Langdon and commanded from the castle, a period of service as education sergeant at Broomfield was merely a step in the right direction. It was ironic that I should now turn to teaching, the profession I had rejected, but to be a teacher in the Army was an ideal combination of talent and vocation. I made my application, the education instructor put in her word, and the administrative machinery set to work to transfer me to the Army Educational Corps.

Whilst awaiting my formal transfer and the two months' training course at Buchanan Castle, I continued as trainee lecturer in the education hut, taking the classes on alternate weeks. As I was still the camp medical orderly the preparation of my lectures was an additional load of work, but I enjoyed it all. My sole complaint was lack of time.

Lack of time had served usefully to explain why my knowledge of Edinburgh remained extraordinarily limited, being confined entirely to those areas which I traversed during the course of my working or social life. My movements about Edinburgh all had to be justified on grounds of utility – that way I belonged to my surroundings: to step outwith these confines put me in danger of feeling like an English visitor, or, worse, feeling too familiar to be comfortable. Going only where obligation took me, I was safe.

My boundary on the north side of Edinburgh was Princes Street. I seemed unable to recognise the existence of the New Town, a curious sort of blindness for an avowed admirer of Georgian domestic architecture. Glancing to my left up the many intersections, I was aware of George Street upon what I termed 'the ridge' but I never troubled to venture the few yards to discover what lay beyond it. My mind already knew what lay beyond it – marshland where the bittern boomed and distant small lochen reflected back like discs of lead the winter sky. It had been a superb place to hunt wildfowl. One day I would go there on a tram which turned off Princes Street and chugged its way up to 'the ridge', bearing the name Granton. I knew the landscape had not changed because I had seen it from the castle.

What, in fact, I saw from the castle on the many occasions when I stood beside Haig's horse, patting its fetlock, was a built-up area. I knew that. But the view from the castle which I carried away in my head was rural. I made no attempt to reconcile these contradictory impressions: I just stayed clear of the north side of Edinburgh.

The exceptions to this rule were when I went to the army study centre – which I approached from the Haymarket; or when I accompanied a friend to mass at St Mary's Cathedral in Broughton Street. I was quite happy going there, because to my mind Broughton was a place that *existed*. Once I was asked by a visitor, where was Queen

Street? I was nonplussed; then I heard myself say, 'There isn't one.' Seeing a puzzled face, I quickly recollected myself and recommended the querist to the service of another passer-by. I fled, feeling faintly queasy after the experience.

My links with Church Hill had been restored – thanks to my job as medical orderly. Going to Strathearn Road for medical supplies I had the use of a duty vehicle to take me there, but I prefered to go by tram if I did not have too much to carry. The journey still afforded me an echo of the same exquisite happiness I had known when going up to Fairmilehead. I took my army collars to be starched at Church Hill Laundry, and I reflected when leaving or collecting them what a good thing it was to have a link which would continue when my connection with Strathearn Road had ended.

One part of Edinburgh from which I disassociated myself entirely was the environs of Holyrood House – in fact, I doubt whether I could have brought myself to pass that way even in the course of duty. The very name made my scalp prickle. Long ago, when I was a child, I tried to escape from the room if my parents made any reference to the hazardous day when they shepherded a pack of schoolchildren round Holyrood. When they came up to Edinburgh to see me, my mother had remarked when the itinerary was being planned, 'It's all right. We shan't mention Holyrood.'

The Old Town (I just called it Edinburgh) I had not yet ventured to explore beyond the section of the Royal Mile which took me from the castle to the Church of Scotland canteen at South Bridge. I was fascinated by the closes, but dared not venture down them. The fear was not physical: I was frightened of trespassing. *My* Scotland lay beyond those gaslit entries, and Time had not yet invited me in.

In the autumn I made a new acquaintance, an anglophobic Scots girl from Dalkeith. She had been an anti-aircraft gunner during the war, and rejoined the A.T.S. after a brief period of demobilisation. She felt for the Army as I did, that no other way of life suited her. We had in common other things besides – a rich vein of poetry and a heavily ironic sense of humour. We had shared a table in the mess or in the NAAFI several times when one day there occurred a typical small incident of the kind which shows up English people not to their advantage. I did not hear what was said, but when Betty and her companion rose silently and left the table, I followed. I found her in the ablutions, white-faced and unapproachable. When I asked what was the matter, she said softly, 'I hate the English.' Then, 'I'm sorry, Ada, but I do.' I felt obliged to apologise for my fellow-countrymen – but they had never been *my* countrymen, and I realised, helplessly, that I felt towards them precisely as she did. Suddenly she laughed and said, 'Och, you're a Scot, anyway!' I appreciated the recognition after so many years, and I reflected that my homeland's acceptance of me would have to take place in such unlikely surroundings as the camp ablutions.

I knew many Scots but this girl was different: she had not accepted centuries of English rule. We never discussed history, we felt it, and she belonged to my time of Scotland, pre-Union. This I sensed, though we never spoke of it. It was through her that Time invited me into the closes along the Royal Mile.

One evening we travelled into town together and shared a meal in the Church of Scotland canteen. It was a quiet place were they served well-cooked snack meals over which one could linger peacefully. I was supposed to be taking cultural exercise at some obscure cinema, but when my companion announced that she was going for a walk, I asked if I might accompany her. To ecounter someone who shared my predilection for prowling cold, dark, wet streets on a winter evening was an unbelievable stroke of good fortune. We set off along the High Street, where Betty was astonished to learn that I had never explored the closes. She had been reared in Scotland, accustomed to the common stair tradition. She led the way into the first, and thereafter I would not pass a single one of them. In the warren of gaslit courts and passages I found my Scotland. All it lacked was people – particular people, dressed differently from the few we passed, and I missed the noise of voices leaking from the windows of the tall houses.

The next of our walks took us further down the Royal Mile, into the Canongate. In White Horse Close, the largest and, at quarter past ten, the most heavily populated, I could have stayed for hours just observing the domestic night life of Scotland. Then, as we turned to leave, I panicked: I knew that somewhere in the dark, close by, was Holyrood. I fled back up that hill as if hell's minions were after me. I did not feel safe until I saw in the distance the lights of Princes Street. Safe from what, I could not say, except that Holyrood was linked in my mind with marriage and 'the English Princess'. Betty admitted to sharing my aversion to Holyrood, but for more obvious Scottish reasons. Which brought us to the subject of that royal wedding – now safely over, and I had contrived to miss the broadcast commentary. It should have ceased to worry me by this time, but there was now a royal honeymoon in progress and the presence in Scotland of a newly *married* English princess made me feel hunted, bleak and doomed. As I relieved my pent-up feelings on the subject, the princess in my mind was quite clear for a moment: a little girl, almost a child, solemn and dumpy. She bore no resemblance to King George's daughter.

One evening my strolling partner preferred to remain beside the NAAFI fire. It was a savagely cold night, and they all thought I was joking when I announced that I was going for a walk. Drawn to the closes, I walked up one and down the next, knowing my way by this time. I returned from my expedition full of excitement; alone, I had felt the atmosphere yet more acutely. I had half-expected to see in the gaslit courts 'the ghost of some old kilted laird', I said, slipping into the tartan '45 idiom of Scotland. But the next time I went walking the closes I went by choice alone, and I had started searching for another, older Scotland unknown to my English education.

The bus for Davidson's Mains departed from Waverley Bridge. From the bus-stop I could see the Cockburn Hotel, a building with crow-stepped gables and a single round tower. The hotel entrance was at the foot of this tower, and I took to describing it as 'the door which lets me in'. Semi-joking, I would say to my friends, 'I'm sure if I went to that door, it would be opened by a man in doublet and hosen, and I should find myself back in the sixteenth century.' I was quite specific about the period – the first decade of the sixteenth century, no later. I never put my fantasy to the test, knowing that such things do not happen, and yet in some way afraid that to me it might. Gradually, without realising it, I became obsessed by that door and would stand gazing at it – sometimes letting as many as three buses depart without me to prolong the sensation that just across the road was *home*. My mind still pictured vividly the welcome beyond such a door, in a world of dip-candles, people furred and velveted against the cold, and a smooth, strainless existence – materially at least – in a great household geared to anticipate my requirements. How much I missed that life I had never realised until I stood alone in the mist and the dark on Waverley Bridge, remembering it.

My evening walks had now become a melancholy search for a welcome lost behind the centuries. One evening I almost found it. From the Lawnmarket I observed a door, just within the close mouth, to be open, and I went gladly towards it with a fixed conviction that I was expected there to sup. I stood in the pool of light cast by the gas-lamp on a wall bracket, staring at the stone spiral stair beyond the door. And the miracle happened: there before me was my host, presenting the members of his household gathered to receive me. I saw him quite plainly, noting details like the balding scalp showing through the long, sparse hair as he dipped a knee – my first sight of any man was usually the crown of his head – and it took a yellowish, waxen cast in the light of the horn lantern which his servant held above him. He wore a furred gown of a brown colour with a trace of red in it, and a plain chain of gold rested on his shoulders. I knew what to expect – at the head of the stair would be his wife, all smiles and curtsies, and behind her the room filled with many richly dressed people, musicians waiting, and the faintly hollow sound made by pewter dishes. Even when the fleeting memory had gone, the warmth of welcome still hung on the frosted air, like a warm draught, in the sad, pale light of the deserted close. I tried to tell myself it was illusion, but I could not dispel the conviction that somewhere upon that stair my company was wanted. For a long time I stood by the open door, trying to bring myself to pull a bell – but which bell? And if I did pull it, how did I say to whomsoever appeared at the stair-head, 'Are you the person who is expecting me to supper?' This time I had been so close to finding my Scotland that I was crying when I left the close, the forlorn tears of a child deprived of a promised treat.

One Saturday afternoon, as it was turning dusk, Betty and I set off up Lothian Road on what was intended to be a pre-Christmas review of the shops. Instead, I saw a turning, King's Stables Road, which I had always wanted to explore, and that was the end of our shopping expedition. We walked through the Grassmarket and on, until in the darkness we had lost our way in a canyon of tall buildings. It was like no other part of Edinburgh I had seen. We were actually in the Cowgate, as I discovered when a woman set us on the right track for the Bridges. I was completely fascinated, with a heart-hugging 'this is me' feeling, as though the ground beneath the street identified my footfall. The next day I asked Betty, 'Where was that close with the tall, black-timbered houses?' She told me that we had entered no closes on the Cowgate – which, when I came to think of it, was correct. Then where had I seen that particular close? I decided it must be somewhere down the High Street.

On my next free evening I set out to find that close. I could clearly remember the tall, black, wooden houses painted with pitch, each with its zig-zag wooden stair climbing the outside wall. It had been extremely dark, there were no street lamps – only starlight, which gave poor illumination in the shadowed wynd about four feet wide. The path had been sticky to the feet, I remembered, an unpaved surface, overlooked by small, shuttered windows about eighteen inches square; I had heard voices behind them, a clamour of guttural Scots. It was so distinctive I knew I would have no difficulty in identifying it.

I searched all the length of the Royal Mile. Eventually I concluded that I must have missed the opening in the dark, and retraced my steps. A second search proved fruitless. I knew I had seen it on one of my outings, just recently. Was it last week? The week before? Anyway, I knew that I had seen it. I had no doubt whatever that a painstaking search would lead me to it again. Until I left Edinburgh I was to continue my search for that close.

I think it must have been the first time I felt a prickle of unease, because I knew I *had* to find it. I asked Betty and a few other people if they could locate it for me, but my description fitted no place in Edinburgh they knew. They asked was I not mistaken? I insisted that I could not be mistaken. I could *remember* the place.

I went on searching. I never found it.

5

IN MY SEARCH OF THE CLOSES I WAS SEEKING NOT GHOSTS BUT MY own reality. During the process I was rapidly becoming myself a ghost, as my solitary footsteps echoed through the gaslit courts and passages. Worse, the images stored in my brain had begun to introduce themselves at Broomfield. From my M.I. Room window I could see ships in the Forth heading for Rosyth Naval Dockyard. There were modern vessels, and it was impossible that I could have seen a huge, black-timbered sailing ship riding at anchor in the Forth: yet one morning I looked out of the M.I. Room window expecting to see just such a spectacle.

Once I had loved to walk back to camp over the hill, particularly at dusk when the lights of Kirkcaldy were visible on the far shore, low on the water. The nearness of Fife gave me a tremendous sense of warmth, as though its lands had in some way been kind to me. Why should Fife, known to me only as hills across the water, bring back to me such melancholy – and worse, the remembered happiness that is more sad? At times I would set out for the education hut next door, going the back way, and then I would pause in the fringe of trees, my purpose quite forgotten, staring across the water towards Fife – trying to capture and identify the ghost which troubled me.

One morning when we had no patients and the M.O. was sharing the warmth of the stove with me as we waited through his appointed hour, I told him suddenly that I was frightened. Through the window I could see the thin line of bared winter trees which covered the narrow strip between the M.I. Room and the shore, and the water of the Forth had flashed golden for a moment in the sun. I felt the surge of tears inside me. Tears for *what*? I told him I was going to die. He said, 'Magnolia, aren't we all?' with a sigh and a smile. He rose, patted my shoulder, and went off for his coffee with the senior commander. He was wise; he was elderly; and he had the subtle perfume of mint-fresh tweeds, washed hands and cleanliness of spirit. He always said the right thing at the right time. I went off to the NAAFI for one of their hot, mid-morning sausage-rolls.

My sense of impending doom caught up with me again before the day was over.

The worst feature of my predicament at this time was an acute and increasing sense of loneliness. It was a particular kind of loneliness which had nothing whatever to do with lack of friends; it was rather the

108

feeling that my friends, of whom I had many, were not the right people. I began haunting the strip of woodland and the sea-shore, unwilling to have company but grief-stricken to find myself alone. Whose company was I missing? Who were the people whom I expected to see busily at work beside the sea-shore, heaving timber – men in homespun jerkins and leather aprons? Sometimes they were so close to the surface of memory I could nearly put a face to them, at other times a name; once or twice I wondered whether I had spoken aloud, so real was the conviction that I had been engaged in conversation wih them.

One day I identified the nature of my loneliness. I was on the tram bringing back medical supplies from Strathearn Road, and as I passed the Links at Bruntsfield I realised that I had just seen a totally different view of the Forth – the one I had perceived the first time I travelled that route, but the picture was more vivid, now, more detailed. Open fields instead of houses sloping down to the Forth, with a clear view across the water to Fife and the hills to the north; on the grass were small fires burning, and hump-backed tents, and a busy multitude of men in motley apparel were engaged in cooking – breaking from their task to wave and shout and run towards me. . . . For a fraction of a second their cheers lingered in my head as I looked out of the window of the tram, then they faded. I recognised that what haunted me was not the presence of these people, but their *absence*.

These mental impressions, so real, so fleeting, did not in themselves worry me. To have them seemed entirely natural. I looked upon them as moments when I was intensely real to myself. What had begun to worry me were the increasing bouts of depression, of unreality, which I experienced during the time between. I had begun to live only for these moments, which was a bad sign.

Ironically, during this period I had more cause for personal satisfaction than I had known at any time in my life. Within a few weeks my military career would shape itself precisely as I wanted it: all I had to wait for was my posting to Buchanan Castle for my A.E.C. course. My colleague at Broomfield had already promised to give me, on demob, her khaki gabardine raincoat – no longer on issue, these garments were prized above pearls – adding, 'You won't even have to change the stripes.' I felt happier now about the prospect of staying at Broomfield for a while; the sergeants' mess would be a good deal more comfortable than my present quarters. I had never visualised myself as an N.C.O., but my three stripes would give me useful experience. My next step would be a commission – as originally intended. All Scotland lay before me. . . .

The only flaw was that it no longer seemed identifiable with *my* Scotland.

One day I listed my name upon morning sick-parade, presenting myself to the M.O. not as his assistant but as his patient. The M.O. knew me as a conscientious medical orderly, renowned as a bit of a character, with a sense of humour and a flair for handling people which he found extremely useful in the surgery. (He sometimes joked before a patient's entrance, 'Magnolia, is this one of yours or one of mine?') It came as a considerable surprise to him to learn that within my starched white overall I carried an intolerable burden of inexplicable misery. There was nothing, really, that I had to tell him except that I was suffering from appalling attacks of depression. He asked whether I had had similar bouts previously, and I replied that I had – but never so bad, or of such duration. At the end I said, 'I was wondering, would it help if I saw a psychiatrist?'

He looked astonished. 'Magnolia, you don't need a psychiatrist!'

When he had gone I reflected that he was probably right. Half an hour of the M.O.'s sympathy and common sense had restored my sense of proportion.

I should never have thought of a psychiatrist had it not been for a signboard at Strathearn Road C.R.S. which I saw whenever I went there for medical supplies. 'Psychiatric Department' caught my eye on the way to the dispensary. Once, while waiting for my order to be made up, it had struck me that it might be worth asking someone in the psychiatric department if they could recommend a cure for persistent depression.

After my talk with the M.O. I gave the matter no more thought until, a short while later, I found myself going down to the shore at dusk in the grip of hoplessness so acute that I seriously considered drowning myself. When this situation repeated itself a couple of days later, I decided it was time to tell the M.O. that my condition was deteriorating. I described my two adventures on the beach, and he said, deeply compassionate, 'Poor Magnolia, poor lassie. . . .' Whereupon I raised again the subject of seeing a psychiatrist.

At eighteen I believed that psychiatrists were endowed with a magic cure-all wand; they were the professionals appointed to deal with maladies like my melancholia. The M.O., older and wiser, said doubtfully, 'Well. . . . I can arrange an appointment for you, if you like,' then added intensely, 'but are you sure you want to see a psychiatrist, Magnolia? Do you realise what is involved? Personally, I don't think you need to be bothered with them.' I, thinking of death beyond that border of trees, said, 'Yes, I do want to see one.' Still he persisted, 'Are you *sure*?' I told him I was sure. He looked unhappy, and replied, 'Well, if you insist I can't stop you. You have a right to see a psychiatrist if you want to. But I think you would be wiser to go for your NAAFI break' – it was then 11 a.m. – 'and think about it. Sleep on it, Magnolia.'

I now had the bit between my teeth. If my visit to the psychiatrist did me no good, and it could do me no harm, I reflected, at least I would have tried it. The next day I told the M.O. firmly that I wished him to make the appointment. With a heavy sigh he agreed to do so.

I arrived at Strathearn Road to meet a pleasant man who spent quarter of an hour checking date of birth, etc., and asking what chiefly depressed me. In quarter of an hour I had just time to say that I was depressed. I was glad the session lasted no longer, because I had a truck waiting to take me and medical supplies back to camp. Restocking the M.I. Room cupboard was foremost in my mind at that moment.

I felt relief on escaping and as I put the new bottles and rolls of lint into the cupboard; but those trees beyond the window looked doom-laden. Melancholia returned.

My second psychiatrist was female, an agreeable person with an amazing hypnotic voice. Under its spell I was able to tell her of my acute sense of loneliness. When she had learned that I had many friends and no communication difficulties, she asked, did I feel unwanted? I said, 'Yes' – for unwanted approximated to my curious sense of being left-over.

She asked, 'Unwanted by whom?'

That was precisely what I wished to know.

'Is it your mother? Do you feel your mother doesn't love you?'

I cried, exasperated by this irrelevance, 'Of course my mother loves me! It has nothing to do with my family.'

'Then why do you feel unwanted?'

I replied truthfully, '*I don't know!*'

It never entered my head to tell her about my search of the closes, the door which eluded me, and the people amongst the trees who had always just gone when I became aware of their presence. I doubt whether I connected those things with my depressions; and even if I had I would never have mentioned them to this kind soul of twenty minutes' acqaintance who appeared to have some kind of fixation about mothers.

I reported back to the M.O. that I did not think that psychiatry was getting me very far. Like any other treatment, I had tried it, but it did not seem to work; I felt those twenty minutes could be put to better use. I had another appointment the following week, and I was resolved to tell the lady with the hypnotic voice that I was grateful for her trouble, and wished to terminate my visits. The M.O.'s face was worried, but I thought nothing of it at the time.

My third week's psychiatrist was yet another person. He arrived late, it was near his coffee time, and if he had asked whether I felt unwanted I might have retorted, 'You should know!' I felt the antagonism, mutual and immediate.

111

He asked whether I had an 'obsession'.

I thought carefully. An obsession sounded to me a bit unhealthy, so I said no. (My love for Scotland did not fit this category.)

'Is there anything in particular you like?'

I liked many things, so I took some while to think about it. Clothes, music, jewels, solitude, writing, sewing, painting, walking in stormy weather, winter tea by the fire with my parents when I came home from school. . . . These were too obvious, however; experience had now led me to conclude that psychiatrists preferred the obtuse. He had begun to show impatience. I was suddenly inspired by the sight of a sheet of paper on the table with doodlings upon it. I said helpfully, 'I like curves.'

His eyes lit up. 'What kind of curves?'

I said, 'Give me that piece of paper, and I'll show you.'

Rapidly I filled the page with my own doodles – thus ⌒ and thus ∽ and thus ℮ . He looked at it, his face expressionless. To fill the awkward silence I said, indicating the best of them, 'That's a good one.'

Momentarily joining in the spirit of the thing, he said, 'So is that,' pointing to another. Then he looked annoyed, and pushed aside the paper. 'Yes, well, never mind that now. Is there anything you dislike?'

He was pushed for time and pushing me accordingly. The list of my dislikes would have been as long, and as ordinary, as the catalogue of things I liked. Again I pondered.

'Is there anything you dislike physically?'

'Yes. I don't like cats brushing against my legs.'

He looked as though he could have hit me. 'Is there *nothing else?*'

I was about to say that I disliked sleeping with people, but I realised this statement was open to misinterpretation. So, more carefully, I specified, 'I don't like sleeping with my mother' – my mother being the only person with whom I had occasionally shared a bed during the war years when my father was on night-duty. She had a habit of rolling herself into a cocoon of bedclothes while we slept, so that I wakened up cold and uncovered. (I never thought to mention the earlier episode of the evacuee.)

At once he pounced. 'But you wouldn't mind sleeping with *your father?*'

I thought of my wholesome, ascetic father, and I looked at the two upper panes of the window, still blacked out, wondering how far that psychiatrist would travel through the glass if my clenched hand on my knee did not relax. I counted five, subduing the red mist which had begun to rise before my eyes, and then I snapped at him, '*Don't be disgusting!*'

His glance at me was savage: we had each other's measure now. Then he wrote swiftly on the page before him. With despair I realised that, whatever I said, he was likely to write, 'Says "no" means "yes".' He had to make me fit his theory.

Oh well, I would certainly not come to this place again. Then, to my horror and amazement, I heard him say that I would be appearing before a medical board which would consider my discharge from the Army.

I cried, flabbergasted, 'But I don't want to leave the Army! I'm due to go into the Educational Corps. . . .'

To which he snapped 'Oh, for goodness' sake make up your mind! If you wanted to continue your career, why did you come to see me?'

When I poured out my terrible tale to the M.O. he said unhappily, 'Magnolia, I did try to warn you.'

The sequel to that interview is curious. I went straight back to the M.I. Room and wrote the only complete poem I produced during my entire service life. It was a sonnet, which poured from me so fluently that I did not have to change more than two words. Its subject was the unused, unworn crown in Edinburgh Castle, of which I wrote with such love and terrible anger that my hand perspired upon the page. When that was out of my system a tremendous sense of achievement filled me, as though I had seen a purpose born out of my miseries, though what it was eluded me. I was full of optimism and confidence the next day.

During the week prior to my medical board I composed my statement: I would apologise to the board for wasting its time, and explain that I had done so under the impression that one visited a psychiatrist in the way one went to any other kind of medical specialist. I knew I could sort out the misunderstanding and that it would all be forgotten afterwards. In a relaxed, cheerful frame of mind I went off to Strathearn Road at the appointed hour.

The 'board' consisted of one – the character I had met the previous week. I began to say, 'There has been a mistake—' but he was not prepared to hear a word. He had recommended my discharge from the Army. It was all over in less than five minutes.

6

MY IMMEDIATE REACTION WAS SHOCKED DISBELIEF. (SO GREAT WAS the shock, it left me incontinent, a condition which was subsequently to require treatment.) At first I retained the conviction that common sense would prevail if I applied myself to fighting my sentence. I appealed to the M.O., the company officer and the senior commander, plying them with the questions I had intended to put to the medical board when I met it. What, I wanted to know, could anybody learn about the complex structure of the human personality within the space of twenty minutes? The three people whom I regarded as my friends were sympathetic but noncommittal; from their guarded faces I read that they, too, were under orders. There was no court of appeal higher than the psychiatrist.

When I learned this I stormed like the wrath of God round Broomfield. The Army had had its share of mad generals, but they at least had not operated behind a cover of medical philanthropy. I knew that I had brought the situation upon myself with my naïve belief that the purpose of psychiatry was merely to heal, and I had at last learned my lesson never to trust doors with labels on them – to this day even the humble word 'Enquiries' on a glass panel defines for me an area of high risk – but I felt that the entire destruction of my future was a high price to pay for my folly. In the privacy of the M.I. Room I unburdened myself powerfully to the M.O., who listened, his lips sealed by propriety. At the time I thought 'Et tu, Brute?' but years later I realised that possibly some of my views he shared. At the end he observed with a deep sigh, 'Well, Magnolia, perhaps you will be happier as a civilian,' and went away sadly for his morning coffee with the senior commander. I knew from his tone that he did not believe it. When he was gone, it occurred to me that his words were intended to cheer both of us.

I asked whether at some later date I would be able to rejoin the Service, and was told not. My discharge was final. To be prohibited from the Army and banished from Scotland was a sentence too heavy for my soul to bear. Unable to fight, my mind slid away into apathy and despair. I wondered if, unconsciously, I had willed my destruction. But why? I had no answer.

Like a condemned man awaiting execution, I decided that in the brief time left to me I would do some of the things in Edinburgh which I had promised myself 'one day' – take a walk to Cramond, and board the Granton tram.

I tried and failed several times to board the Granton tram, my nerve deserting me. Then, one day, I took a running jump on to it as it was rounding the corner into Hanover Street. I was all right when I reached the upper deck, and made for the front seat, suddenly filled with exhilaration as the tram clanked up to the ridge of George Street and I leaned forward urging a *horse* beneath me. I knew what I would see: marshland and teeming bird-life upon the scattered, small, pewter-coloured lochen . . . a mental image of a falcon loosed from my hand made me so happy that I laughed aloud, momentarily. Then all the joy was knocked out of me in an instant when I saw on the far side of the ridge a whole urban area reaching as far as the eye could

114

see – banks, shops, houses, streets. . . . Of my expected view nothing remained but the distant prospect of the Forth and the hills of Fife beyond it. I leaped from my seat and fled down the staircase to the platform, where the conductor asked me, smiling, 'Forgotten something?' I said yes, as I jumped off the tram.

My walk to Cramond was indirectly inspired by a question put to me in the NAAFI one evening: 'What will you do in Civvy Street, Magnolia?' I had gone to bed with this question still on my mind, and the following morning awakened with the thought that I must go to Cramond. That afternoon I locked the M.I. Room door behind me, leaving word with the hairdresser where I was going: for the first time I felt quite free, certain that on that day there would be no call on my services before the five o'clock treatment-parade. I had from two o'clock until four-thirty of a winter afternoon, crisp, clear and golden. I followed the path from my back door down through the trees to the promenade – then merely a concrete strip binding the shore, like the one at Rossall in the days of my childhood. Across the water the hills of Fife were calm and dear to me in the sunlight: I had known this view, it seemed to me, for ever. A few of the girls were doing P.T. on the grass between the trees, and I saw them with affection; this day they seemed real to me, as though they had taken the place of those people I could identify only by their absence. As I walked along the shore I remembered building a great ship . . . was it at Rossall? (No; that was nonsense; I must stop day-dreaming.) Civilian life had some things to recommend it. I would be free to exercise the dogs and horses. . . . I would wear a dark brown suit with yellow knitted woollen stockings to match a yellow knitted sweater. . . . (This thought was possibly the most curious of all, for I had a lifelong aversion to coloured knitted stockings.)

I came upon Cramond sooner than expected – I had not realised Broomfield was so near. A middle-aged man bade me the time of day, and I asked him questions about the extension of the harbour. We chatted for some while; I wanted to know about farmland in the area, for the name Cramond was linked in my mind with a *farm*. When we parted I made for the Cramond Inn where I intended to have tea. On the door I found a proclamation that the inn would be reopening on such a day to serve luncheons, teas and dinners. It was the notice that one saw everywhere in 1947, but the disappointment on this occasion stunned me. That the inn at *Cramond* could be closed to me was inconceivable. I actually hammered on the door but nobody came. I stood there thinking, 'I have come too early.' When that door opened, I would be gone from Scotland. I was crying when eventually I turned away.

My absent people were with me again as, following my instinct, I

115

took the inland route from the village. I walked some way towards the church before I realised that I could get lost among the unknown houses. Some women talking at a gate fell silent as I passed, and I crossed to ask them, was I on the right road for Davidson's Mains? They made quite a fuss of me, which, oddly, I expected. One of them finally elected to escort me part of the way. As I turned to wave in response to the group at the gate, I was mysteriously warmed by the thought, Somebody in Cramond still remembers me.

Later, in the mess for tea, I buttered my bread, saying, 'When I'm a civilian I shall have a marvellous time. I shall be able to get on with my writing – and I'll have time to exercise the dogs and horses.' My words came automatically, paying no account to the fact that my home had no dogs, no horses, and the farmland I was remembering had never been at Thornton Cleveleys.

Every minute now was precious. Each time I bandaged a wound or massaged an aching muscle, my hands gave each patient a final benediction. My place, I learned, would be taken by not one but three medical orderlies working in rota. (I had pressed the point many times that a conscientious orderly required a locum.) As I instructed my successors, I felt that their task would be easier than mine; but it would not, I felt, be so satisfying. The autonomy of my small kingdom had made worthwhile the anxiety it caused me. Some of my patients said openly that the M.I. Room would never be the same again – and I could believe them: Private Patterson and I, in our different ways, were unique people doing a unique job. The M.O. too, would miss me, I reflected sadly.

A calm fatality had now replaced my earlier bitterness. With hindsight came the feeling that I had always known it would end this way, with my banishment from Scotland. My brief residence there had always seemed too good to be true. Born in exile, exile was possibly the only relationship with Scotland that I fully comprehended. What to do with the rest of my life I had no idea.

My friend from Dalkeith invited me home to sup with her parents – a gesture long contemplated but delayed because of her father's antipathy towards English visitors. However, I was, she said, her mother's guest, and her father would probably go out for the evening. When I arrived the Scots ogre courteously shook my hand, then studied me cautiously from a distance. Something that I said in response to my hostess – I cannot remember what it was – caused him to warm to me so suddenly that Betty and her mother looked at each other in astonishment. Was I near enough to the fire? See, he would bring this chair over here – so. Within moments I was seated beside him at the fire, commandeered as *his* guest. Later, when asked by my hostess, was he going out, he said no. We talked with such animation that I missed my last bus back to Edinburgh.

They were delighted to have me stay overnight, and in the morning my host and I continued our discussion over porridge. The previous evening we had talked mainly about Army life – I was fascinated to meet someone who, in youth, had served with General Gordon at Khartoum – but over porridge our talk became political (which Betty had feared). She need not have worried. I shared totally his view that Scotland required independence – 'my' Scotland had never been otherwise. I was keenly interested to hear all I could learn about the present state of Scotland under the Union, and Betty had great difficulty prising me away to catch the early bus which would get us to the castle in time for the duty truck reclaiming telephonists from the night shift. (Living locally, she had a regular sleeping-out pass, which I did not.) As we ran from the house, my host said, 'Ye wull come back?'

Those words still rang in my ears as we boarded the bus. Passing through Dalkeith, this time in daylight, I knew the place; not as it was now, but as it had been. I had known the ground on my arrival the previous night, even though it was too dark to see where I was. It was to me no wonder that I had been welcome there.

Later, as we stood on the Castle Esplanade high above the city, waiting for the lorry to take us back to camp, the rising sun struck the hoar-frost on the roofs below. Heriot's green field appeared as though snow-covered like the Pentlands. Dazzled by the white and gold upon the black roof-tops, what I saw was a medieval city. Then it was gone. I was left only with the sensation that this castle-window view of winter-morning Edinburgh was known to me; I had seen it not once but scores of times. It was as familiar as my bedroom wall at home.

Later in the week Betty returned from a visit home, bringing messages from her parents, including her father's instruction that she was to take me to the house any time. She added, half incredulous, 'And that from *my father*!' It was bitter irony that acceptance of me came at the point when I was leaving Scotland.

In the NAAFI on the night before I left camp one final door admitted me – that of the recreation room which the Don Rs used as their snuggery. The infantry corporal had painted a mural there and, learning that I had never seen it, wished to show it to me. Entering from the dark at the back of the building, I blinked away the impression that I had entered *a castle guard-room*. Booted young men with pints of beer or tea beside them relaxed after their various missions across Scotland. Asked what I would have, I automatically chose ale – an extraordinary quirk in behaviour for one who disliked beer and rarely drank anything but tea or coffee. Later, a sing-song started, and I waited for my favourite 'We're no' awa' tae bide awa'' – by this time known indulgently as my 'national anthem'. When it came, my voice rose

117

louder, clearer, stronger than any, and with a Scots accent so broad that it fitted no region of Scotland in the year 1947. At the end, someone remarked, 'I didn't know you could sing like that, Magnolia.'

I replied, 'I can sing *that* song.'

On the day I left camp my departure passed almost unrecognised. I felt myself to be already a ghost as I passed the locked M.I. Room. In the mess I found luncheon disturbed by an emergency which had ended just before my arrival – one of the general orderlies had had an epileptic fit. I asked why nobody had called me, and was told that everyone had assumed that I had already left camp. Sick at heart, I ate alone, realising that the world could get along without me. Saying no goodbyes, I set off with my kit-bag and a large, square, cardboard box containing the overflow. Then fate took compassion on me. I had dreaded the long walk away from the life I loved, and my last sight of the camp from the hilltop, but I was to be spared backward glances: a motor-cycle stopped beside me. 'Want a lift, Magnolia?' It was the mechanic whose blood I had saved one action-packed morning. He was testing a machine he had been servicing. Pillion-riding was contrary to regulations, but we could stretch a point on the camp lane when a machine was 'in dock' and the rider was not a courier. He fixed my kit-bag somehow, balanced my box on the handlebars, and told me to hang on. So at least I *rode* out of the army, out of my Scotland – and a ghostly sense of triumph pursued me down the wind, as though it came back like an echo across wide centuries.

I was taking the night train and had asked all my friends to be at the station. As it turned out, those from Broomfield were on duty, and the Fairmilehead contingent mistook the date. (I discovered this later.) Only my Scots friend from Dalkeith was at the station. I had wanted a great send-off, with the words of 'We're no' awa'' ringing out on the platform as the train departed – a demonstration not intended to be dramatic, but I deeply required to hear voices proclaim their faith that I would return. Betty's last words were undemonstrative: 'Och, you'll be back. That's one thing certain.' As the train bore me away, I watched her thin, khaki-clad figure move amongst the trucks and mail-bags to see me to the last moment. Her face looked bleak in the dim gaslight, and the empty platform seemed indescribably forlorn. I expected grief in myself, but what I felt was Scotland's grief at losing me. I never saw her again to ask whether the desolation was something she felt: it could have been within my memory.

One person did sing my song. I went into the toilet where I stood rocking to the motion of the train as I sang 'I'm no awa' tae bide awa'' with the passion of a vow. Facing my reflection in the mirror, I saw a curious change come over it. My face looked older, narrower – a gaunt face; like mine, but masculine, and it seemed to have a gold circlet above it which flashed small points of sapphire. I took it to be an optical illusion caused by station lights shining through the ventilator. I examined the ventilator to make sure that it was so, but came away no wiser.

My mother had prepared the fatted calf for breakfast to cheer me. I managed two or three mouthfuls, then I burst into tears crying, 'I'm sorry – I'm sorry!' My mother asked, 'Would you prefer to go straight to bed?' I nodded and was led away. When I had undressed I was taken with a sudden notion: my greatcoat and cap I hung up behind my bedroom door like a battle standard. There they were to hang, a constant challenge, through all the years I was away in England.

CHAPTER FOUR

1

THREE DAYS AND NIGHTS I SLEPT AWAY OF MY UNWANTED NEW LIFE down in England. Roused with difficulty to take nourishment, I would slide back into slumber immediately afterwards with no awareness in my mind of anything but the greatcoat and cap hung behind the door. These items had assumed a personality of their own, as though the A.T.S. girl who had worn them had her abode within their folds: who it was sleeping within my body I had no idea.

My condition, unusual for an insomniac, worried my parents and on the fourth day my mother compelled me to rise, dress and go out shopping with her in the grey, cold, December afternoon. It was Saturday, and we set out late because I baulked at the prospect of meeting people who would tell me that I must be happy to be home for Christmas. I stood outside the shops while my mother conducted her business within, glad of the dim 'austerity' lighting which concealed my presence.

Then, on our way home, we passed the tailor's outfitters known to me since childhood, and in the window was a raincoat. I gripped my mother's arm in sudden excitement, and said, 'I want a *riding mac*.' It was the first sign of interest I had shown in anything since my return. The shops were closing and we were heavily laden; we agreed that I should come back first thing on Monday morning. We had gone fifty yards when my mother, seeing my face, said, 'Buy it now. Run back.'

Inside the shop that riding mac transformed me into a personality as crisp and sure as itself. The lady's model was slightly short for me – also, it lacked weight. I knew precisely how it ought to feel; very stiff and tough, like canvas, rigid about my waist and chest to give me protection. When I was shown the gentleman's version, it knew me like an old friend the minute I put it on. It was, needless to say, a great deal more expensive – in fact, it cost me the whole of my demobilisation dress allowance. My mother, usually a careful budgeter, applauded the extravagance; anything which produced in me the faintest trace of animation was an investment. I carried home my new identity wrapped in paper, and excitedly put it on to show my father. I actually insisted, like a child, on wearing it while I ate my tea! My mother was to say many times during the ensuing months, 'Thank God for that riding mac' – for to rise and wear it gave purpose to my otherwise empty days.

Apart from the raincoat, my purchase of civilian clothing proved extremely difficult. I had large quantities of clothing coupons but no idea of my sartorial identity. It was the first time I had ever been at a loss when buying – or making – clothes, but I simply could not imagine what I ought to look like. The mental picture, born on the way to Cramond, of myself in yellow sleeves and stockings had now gone. The only thing of which I was certain was colour: I wore black. (I had never owned any black clothes.) Black with white. Black with gold. Armed only with this slender clue to my identity, I made an unhappy foray in the January sales. Returning home with a load of sable attire, I set to work to make it fit me. While pinning and darting, I realised that my usually meticulous dress-sense had deserted me, but at least I would wear black. The colours black with white, black with gold, related me to Scotland.

I pined for Scotland every waking moment. It was a monumental grief, too great for tears. Nothing mattered to me after Scotland. My parents had asked was there *nothing* I wanted? Remembering, very dimly now, my walk to Cramond, I said, 'A horse and a dog. . . .' A horse and a dog had been my request every birthday and Christmas in my childhood, and I had long ago accepted the fact that I could have neither. Now, it appeared, I could have both. The horse would have to be hired, but at least I would ride; and I could own the dog. I asked, 'Even an Alsatian?' My mother gulped down her lifelong fear of dogs, and nodded. For her to make such a concession showed the depth of their concern for me. Yet I did nothing about either. The dream I had by Cramond, there so real to me, had no substance when transported to Thornton Cleveleys. My riding mac was possibly its closest substitute.

Always in times of stress I had consoled myself by writing. Or I would set my hands to work upon some creative occupation. I had never been known to sit doing nothing – until now. Left untended, I withdrew into silence and immobility. The efforts of my family and friends to interest me in something – anything – were tireless and unfruitful. I spent hours seated on the hard chair in my bedroom, its back to the window, my hands empty and my mind a total blank. I had slipped away so far that I was not even aware that my withdrawn state warranted anxiety.

By the end of February 1948 concern was mounting. One night my mother came to my bedside with three five-pound notes in her hand, and said, 'Now, child, listen: this is your birthday present and I want you to spend it on going back to Edinburgh.' Listlessly, I asked what was the use? She countered vigorously, 'Find somewhere to stay, and take a job there. I am offering you a chance to go back to Scotland.' But at the mention of 'a place to stay' there had come immediately to

121

my mind a picture of a tall stone tower. Only one place I knew resembled it: 'Can I stay at the Cockburn?'

It was not what my mother had intended, and, as she pointed out, on ten pounds my stay there would be brief – but I was obsessed with a memory of that door which, I still believed, would admit me back to my Scotland. So she booked me a room at the Cockburn.

I had broken my rule about allowing Time to be my host – and another, about pressing dreams like dried-out flowers between the pages of a book: I knew what I did. My arrival at the Cockburn was just as commonplace as I had known to expect in my wiser moments. That door, viewed dimly in the gaslight from the far side of the cobbled slope, led nowhere. My glimpse of the fifteenth – sixteen-century vanished once I came to close quarters with it. There was no man in doublet and hosen to admit me – in fact, no one admitted me, for the porter was elsewhere on my arrival. So I carried my own suitcases to the reception desk of a commercial hotel no better and no worse than good commercial hotels the world over. It was not my Scotland; it was not my time; it was nowhere. On the way up to my room I looked at the artificial flowers in the hall and wished that I could like them.

Instead of trying to go forward, to make new connections, I merely haunted the tracks of my old life trying to fit back into it. I went up to Fairmilehead two or three times, but as a civilian I had to be escorted into camp by an occupant who knew me. Gwen was on leave. For the rest, life had changed as it had changed for me, and we had nothing left in common. I tried Broomfield, where I was allowed to visit 'my' Sick Bay – something of myself still lingered there, faintly discernible. Nowhere else did I belong. Most of my old friends were gone, demobilised. My Scots friend from Dalkeith had been posted overseas (as she told me in a letter). In my civilian clothes I felt conspicuous and ill-at-ease in the NAAFI.

I hung on while the money lasted, trying everywhere to find my kindred. At the army study centre I clung to the few remaining A.E.C. friends who had belonged to the drama group – dragging them out to dine with me, conversationless, at the Cockburn. Everywhere it was the same; life had moved on, leaving me behind.

Worst was the castle, where I stood alone one evening upon the Esplanade, not daring to go nearer. It was outwith the tourist season and no member of the guard would give me admittance, much less a salute. My sense of belonging was quite gone. I felt suddenly horribly self-conscious standing where I could be seen by the sentries, wearing a *female* black suit.

I did not attempt to explore the closes of the Canongate. They belonged now exclusively to the real Edinburgh folk, amongst whom I came as a stranger. Also, dressed in my black I did not feel safe as I had felt in uniform. Safe from what is hard to say.

My visit was extended. Friends at home, desperately concerned about me, sent me a gift of money for 'more days in Scotland'. My mother urged me by phone to 'stay on and fight'. Perhaps had I known how to make a small life function in Scotland, I might still have found my door. I do not know. I did once mention in casual conversation at the study centre that I wondered if a university course in Edinburgh might be the answer, but I took the thought no further. (Edinburgh University never seemed real to me as did the name St Andrews.) I left until late my visit to Uncle Adam and Auntie Mamie, who said, 'You should have told us you were coming. We'd have given you the address of a friend of ours who keeps a boarding-house at Bruntsfield. You could have stayed longer and found yourself a job. Why did you waste your money at the Cockburn?'

Why indeed? – except for some kind of memory about a towered building of the fifteenth – sixteenth century which for me had represented 'home'. Inwardly I wept as the train bore me away down to England. Everyone had tried so hard to ensure that I stayed in Scotland, why had I myself been so lacking in initiative? Years later, with less money and but two friends there, I was to have no difficulty establishing myself in London.

It is useless to speculate how much my life would have been changed had I fought harder for my Scottish foothold in 1948: the ghost I carried knew of no future but death in England.

All that I had to show for my visit were two souvenirs – neither of immediate use to me, but each has a place in my tale. On my last evening at the study centre one of the company was demonstrating on the back of a cigarette packet the rival merits of two shades of brown ink made, respectively, by Stephenson and Waterman. My gaze was riveted by the sight of ink which *dried brown*. Long ago, at junior school, a stone container of ink prepared from powder had been rejected because its blue-black colour took on a brown tint when it dried. When all the inkwells were taken away to be washed and refilled with good ink, I had fought vainly to keep mine. That single exercise copied in brownish ink I had treasured for a long time, because it gave my writing the appearance of truly belonging to me. I had never during all the years between thought to enquire if anyone actually manufactured brown ink.

The other new idea came to me later that same evening in the tram on my way back from the Haymarket. Seated near me were two young men and a girl who carried fencing foils and masks. I shrank from the masks. In fact, I was repelled by everything about the trio, for they were English, armed, and I was not a swordsman. I felt vulnerable and self-conscious in my cloth coat – as a hedgehog or porcupine must feel

123

if caught by the enemy with its soft underbelly exposed. I made the resolution, seated in that tram, that I would learn to use a sword before our next hypothetical encounter. Long ago, as a child, I had boasted of my swordsmanship – until one terrible day when I tried fencing with a raspberry cane and a boy evacuee had routed me: it had never occurred to me that it was a skill I would need to *re-learn*.

The most important inspiration I brought back from Scotland had no obvious, single explanation: merely I wakened up with it on the morning after my return, having spent much of the night muffling my ghost-tears beneath the bedclothes. I came downstairs, astonishing my mother by my cheerfulness, to announce, 'I have just designed my tombstone.'

I made her sit down to listen while I described it. It was to be a huge marble catafalque, Renaissance-style, with my effigy upon it. The attitude of the effigy was unusual; it was to be a seated, life-size study of myself, perched with knees crossed on the edge of the tomb, head flung back, laughing. My mother, deeply shocked, exclaimed, 'Ada, you'll do no such thing!' I was astonished. 'It's blasphemous,' she said. It was my turn to be shocked – and, anyway, I reminded her, it was *my* tombstone. I wanted the effigy to represent me 'just as I am now' – aged nineteen – 'dressed in my riding mac'. At which I flung back my head, roaring with laughter in a way she had not heard since I left the Army. She still looked faintly disapproving, so I said, 'But don't you see the point? When they all think I'm dead, I shall be there sitting on my own tombstone, laughing! I think it's a glorious joke.'

During the next few days everyone had to listen to my description of the tombstone. It was my sole topic of conversation, the single thought which made me happy. My friends, humouring me (for they were as pleased as my mother to see me smile again) pointed out that such a monument would cost a lot of money.

I said, 'I know. I'll write a book to earn it.'

I was at work within twenty-four hours, my theme the day of a wedding unwanted by one of the protagonists. At forty pages a day, I had the rough draft completed inside seven weeks.

My mother, glad to see me occupied and happy, refrained from comment when after each meal I rushed back to my work with a zestful, 'Let's get on with the tombstone!' Once, she did murmur sadly that she wished my incentive had been less morbid. '*Morbid*?' I told her that, if other people worked to possess mink coats and Rolls-Royces, I saw no reason why I should not feel the same way about owning a tombstone. Then I added, 'Don't you see, this time they will know where I am buried.'

The words 'this time' slipped out without any conscious awareness of their implication. Gone were the days when I could be drawn into a discussion about the possibility of human recurrence. I had summed up my attitude to life on a recent occasion when asked to specify my idea of hell. I had replied promptly, 'My idea of hell would be to die and then discover there is reincarnation.' The saying had become a joke amongst my friends.

During my work upon the book I was having various kinds of investigation into the problem of my bladder, which had malfunctioned continuously since my sudden discharge from the Army. The cause had not been discovered and ultimately I was sent to a psychiatrist. He knew his brief – to discover why I leaked – and I agreed to the appointment to give his profession one more chance to convince me. I went prepared to meet the enemy, discovering instead a sensible, kindly character, who showed no morbid interest in my relationship with my parents but a keen one in my writing. He liked the design of my tombstone, too, and chuckled with me at the idea of my sitting on my own grave laughing. We never solved the mystery of my bladder, but he read my book – within ten days – and talked of nothing else during my last session with him. He was fascinated by the characters, whom he had obviously studied deeply, and told me my psychological perception was remarkable. He considered that the person I should see was a publisher, not a psychiatrist, and with the words, 'Keep at the writing; you have a great future,' he sent me on my way certified competent.

After two rejections, a third publisher liked *Amongst Those Present* well enough for acceptance to seem certain. The manuscript eventually came back to me with a sad letter saying that 'but for the paper shortage' they would indeed have published the book. This situation would change, they hoped, within the next twelve months; meanwhile, they felt it was unfair to retain my manuscript, thus preventing my sending it to another publisher whose paper stocks might be in a healthier condition. In view of the book's considerable merit, they suggested that, if I had not found an alternative publisher by the year 1949, I should re-submit it to them.

Perhaps I should have shown more patience, but I had lived with that damnable paper shortage for five years. Driven by a single motive, to have my effigy made 'as I am *now*' – just back from Scotland and before the riding mac wore out – I said to my mother, 'There must be a way to earn money which doesn't require so much paper.' Then, suddenly – 'I know! I'll write a play!'

I threw into a trunk the manuscript of *Amongst Those Present* – I never looked at it again – and, mounting my bicycle, I rode to Thornton Library where I filled my saddlebag and basket with all the plays I could obtain. During the next twelve months my father and I ran a ferry service between our house and the library, he slightly cross

125

because I purloined half his library tickets, but nevertheless obliged to respect the fearsome dedication of a student who in twelve weeks had digested Sophocles, Chekhov, Ibsen, all the sixteenth-century and Restoration dramatists, Noel Coward, Terence Rattigan, Emlyn Williams, Jan van Druten, Jean-Jacques Bernard, Jean-Paul Sartre, innumerable volumes of miscellaneous plays, and a refresher course in Shakespeare. Then I put the whole lot out of my mind, and set to work to construct within the proscenium arch a view of life which was my own.

I was never to acquire the tombstone, but as I fought back after each rebuff by the theatre I created inadvertently its substitute – a way of life.

After my inglorious return to Lancashire I had for a while avoided my old school friends. Then one day I bumped into Sheila at the tram stop, wearing a riding mac like my own, but lighter. She said 'Hello' as though nothing had happened since we said our traditional 'Farewell' on the tram the day she left school to be a bank clerk. She was on her way to the theatre with a mutual friend from our junior-school days and said, 'Come with us – oh, *do*!' in the way she had which made the most commonplace outing turn into a huge, hilarious adventure.

My theatre-going had been until that time occasional, sitting in the stalls or circle with my family, and it was Sheila and Josephine who introduced me to 'the gods', where I could see one play per week if willing to queue for backless seats with rock-hard upholstery.Thereafter, every Saturday I was to be found in the gallery of the Grand Theatre in Blackpool, viewing each new play on its trial performance before it went to the West End of London. In this my companions possibly found me rather a bore, for I studied each play as an exercise, not as entertainment.

The single advantage of having Blackpool in the vicinity was that during the winter months its theatres were on the touring list of every major ballet and opera company and most British orchestras. One booked weeks in advance, rarely missing a single performance, for these delights came to us after months of eager anticipation. (I am sure accessibility dulls the appetite, for when I lived in Leicester Square I never went to the theatre if I could avoid it.) When tours coincided, it was not unusual for us to be at the opera on Friday night, see the matinée of a play on Saturday, another opera on Saturday night, and hear an orchestral concert on Sunday evening.

When Sheila and Josephine wanted to join a local amateur dramatic society in the autumn, that, too, fitted my plans: I required to learn a great deal more about the practical side of drama. I was the one who suggested the fencing classes. Sheila never made a swordsman, but

126

Josephine stayed the course with me. It was a happy, hectic year during which hard work and active recreation kept at bay, as far as possible, my aching sense of loss for Scotland.

One night in April 1949 the three of us walked home as usual from rehearsal in Thornton. It was a clear, mild night and we were in high spirits. At the corner where I turned off into North Drive, we paused beneath the mercury-vapour lamps to discuss our plans for the weekend: the night was Thursday, I remember. Sheila said, 'I'll see you at the Grand on Saturday.' I replied that I would not be there that week because there was a film at the Odeon which my aunt particularly wanted me to see. Sheila said, 'Never mind. I'll see you sometime.'

Suddenly I saw her in isolation from her background. She was poised on one foot, the other leg swinging in the familiar stance I had known since childhood. She was clad in her white riding mac, with a black beret on her head and the blue light of the lamp shining on her dark hair. It was like looking at a cut-out from a photograph, of which I had time to study every detail in the moment of infinity in which I was suspended. When she waved her arm in the salute we had used since we were children – 'Farewell!' – I was already turning my back upon her.

As I walked away I had to press my hand against my cheek to stop my head turning for one more glimpse of her across the wasteland at the corner. I had stopped pretending at fifteen that I did not know, when I last saw my father's sister happily pregnant and carried for four days the knowledge that she would die in childbirth, but I still clung to my superstition that if I did not take a deliberate last look there was just a chance it might not happen.

Sheila died on the Sunday. The healthiest of us all, she had never missed a day's schooling through illness. Now she took pneumonia and it was all over in two days. Her family telephoned the news to me on Tuesday morning. At once I rushed to the house to do what I could, for she had been to me like a sister. We had always known, as children, this would happen: more than once she had remarked, 'I shall die young,' and I had told her, 'Yes, you will.'

Before I left the house I asked to see her. She lay stately and strangely magnificent in a formal, white satin shroud with a knotted silk cord round the waist. I found myself admiring it. Her mouth had settled slightly, giving her face an expression I did not recognise as Sheila's. Into my mind came an impudent thought that she was beside the coffin, inspecting the contents with her indignant, laughing, 'I don't look like *that*!' which had greeted so many of her photographs. Sheila could not be solemn if she tried. It was that which convinced me that, wherever *she* had gone, only the body was dead: had she been inside it, I would have recognised her still behind the sunken face.

127

She was buried in Thornton churchyard, across the road from the hall used by our dramatic society. After the funeral I took the short cut across the fields we had used on light evenings walking home from rehearsals. I was wearing my riding mac, and as I climbed over the stile I remembered the debates we had had about the rival merits of our respective macs. I had agreed that hers was more graceful, but mine, I said, would outlast hers.

When I reached home I took my grief upstairs to the typewriter and closed the door. I wanted Sheila's twenty years to be on record, so I waived my rule about writing only for the theatre. The book was autobiographical, the tale of youth in April and the springtime of two friends. I called it *The Daffodil Season*.

As a book it lacked the ironic observation and technical accomplishment of my last novel, but I sent it to a publisher. It came back with a gentle letter of rejection saying that 'apart from the paper shortage' the book fell into the awkward category between generations. I knew that; I knew also that with careful revision I could have cured its faults, but I was too close to be objective. I put away the manuscript, still in its corrugated-paper wrapping, and never looked at it again.

Josephine and I continued to attend rehearsals, fencing classes, concerts and the theatre, but the fun had gone with Sheila.

If asked, as writers sometimes are, who has most influenced my writing, I reply, 'Nobody. Except George Higgins.'

I had discovered at the age of fourteen that works of fiction read while I was writing tended to influence my style, so I stopped reading for relaxation. I had used music as a stimulant when working, but my response to music had always been over-emotional, and when purple passages began to appear in my writing I switched off the radio and thereafter worked in silence. Rightly or wrongly, I had to work in a vacuum and think for myself. By the age of nineteen austerity had proved its value: I could see and read hundreds of plays for their stagecraft without being influenced by their style or content.

When I wrote my first professional play in 1948 – professional in the sense that it was intended for professional production – I typed it beautifully in black and red on costly vellum paper. To hear how it played I enlisted the grammar school dramatic society to give it a reading, and made the cardinal error of reading one of the main parts myself – a mistake I spotted during my first speech when I found myself unable to listen and read simultaneously. A yet more vital discovery was that, while it is very nice to be a nineteen-year-old ex-pupil with a three-act play to one's credit, the calm of the school library was very far removed from the cut-and-thrust of the commercial theatre for which I was aiming. What I required was advice from

128

someone who really knew the theatre, so my parents advised, 'Why not show it to George Higgins?'

George was a friend of my father's through the historical society, in age half-way between our generations; a man of many parts, cast in the Renaissance mould, and impossible to pigeon-hole in our bureaucratic century. George was an enormous character with as many facets as a diamond: George in overalls and beret, clambering over roofs with his workmen; George, in the same overalls and beret, at the bottom of a trench digging for Roman paving – a quest which had occupied the Fylde Historical Society since my first 'dig' when I was seven. Amongst his many sidelines, George taught drama (loathing the word 'elocution') and bought, identified and sold (when he had lived with them) lost historic paintings. He was a splendid actor who refused to turn professional, and a potentially brilliant playwright whose vivid first scene of an unfinished, robust play set in the eighteenth century set my back teeth aching to have his skill. The absolute all-rounder, he spent many a Saturday watching Stanley Matthews from the terraces. Thickset, red-haired, uncompromising, George became my taskmaster. Remembering myself at nineteen years of age, I doubt whether any other human being but George would have accepted the task of moulding such intractable material.

Generously, I offered to let him read my play. (His initial reaction, I learned in after years, was, 'Oh Lord, not another!') He spent an hour on the phone with a scathing list of its faults, concluding, 'But let me see your next. That is, if you write another.' Years afterwards he admitted that his purpose had been to discourage me if he could; and if I could not be discouraged, then, eventually, I would make a playwright.

My second play was based on the Lancashire cotton famine of the 1860s. Since the age of ten I had promised my paternal grandmother that one day I would write a play about Lancashire's contribution to the abolition of slavery in America. She had passed on to me her mother's eye-witness account of the arrival in Darwen of the first load of American cotton after the four years of weaving surats and semi-starvation. Men, women and children poured out of their terraced houses to meet it at the station, where they removed the horse from the shafts of the dray, put ropes round it, and pulled it themselves in triumphal procession to the circus; there they stood round it, singing the Doxology. Given such a theme, nobody could fail.

There was no official history of the subject, so I went to Darwen to trace what I could of contemporary records. I stayed there several weeks, and having no under-the-counter relationship with local tobacconists (essential in 1948) I was reduced to smoking 'Pasha' cigarettes, which would have cured me of smoking had my research lasted but one week longer. My mind forever associates the death of

President Lincoln and poor-relief committee reports with the acrid taste of bad Egyptian tobacco.

When I returned, I set against the background of international politics the story of a fictitious Darwen family and their neighbours. I gave the play the title *Warp and Weft* and despatched it to George Higgins. He telephoned me in record time with a note of excitement in his voice which belied what he had to say in criticism. He offered no hope of success, but he did introduce the play, through friends of his, to a West End agent. It was well received (apparently with some surprise as the work of a nineteen-year-old) and regretfully declined because 'there is no market at all in the West End for plays with a North Country setting'.

By this time I had written my third play, '*The Devil's Children*', based on my knowledge of Richard, Joanna and John Plantagenet, and the third crusade. George warned me that historical plays were hard to sell, and asked, 'Can't you write something modern?' So I did, and George's single comment was 'Burn it!' I put it on the fire immediately. My next play was set in the future, following a global nuclear conflict; a small group of survivors establish themselves in the ruins of a fifteenth-century abbey, creating an ideal society which is ultimately destroyed by the rogue element we have with us always. I called it *So Runs the World Away*. This brought the first real tremor of reaction from the West End, but nothing came of it. Returning to the Plantagenet family I wrote *The Shadowed Star*, a sequel to *The Devil's Children*. George's verdict: 'You have certainly written a tragedy, but it's not the historians' view of King John.' (No, it was not; but any king had my sympathy who was placed under ban of excommunication by the Pope.) I intended one day to write *Eleanor of Aquitaine* but I knew by this time that George was right: there was no market for historical plays. (My record for arriving on the scene too early must be second to none!)

My first play, *The Man Who Came Too Soon*, had been impeded by the remoteness of its setting – Egypt 1300 B.C. – so I now redrafted it in an abstract version, eliminating Time, and retitled *The Empty Scabbard*. It was full of purple passages and George told me it was terrible. So, in retaliation, I wrote *Frontier Fragment*, so bleak in dialogue that George said, 'I didn't tell you to write in monosyllables.' While *Frontier Fragment* was being 'considered' in the West End – which meant, I knew, that it was lying in somebody's IN-tray collecting dust – I took a short holiday back to the fifteenth – sixteenth-century with *Florence, 1490*: this was pure self-indulgence, but once in a while I had to get 'home' to my period. I then made up for it by writing two modern plays in a style which later would have been termed 'black comedy'. They won from George no higher commendation than that my stagecraft was 'improving'.

What most impeded my career, I knew, was that I was a creator, not a salesman. I was always too busy writing my current play to spare time for its predecessor. Also, I had been too well brought up: I knew theatre directors and managers were, like myself, busy people, and I did not like to pester them with letters. When a script was returned to me (at my request) after a year with no tell-tale crease-mark on the cardboard cover, showing that it had never been opened, much less read, I took it as one of the trials of my profession. Some of my plays I never submitted anywhere, and the only people who saw them were George Higgins and my mother.

During what I considered to be my apprenticeship, my age was a worry to me. Youth was still unfashionable, and nobody other than the agent who read *Warp and Weft* knew that I had not yet attained my majority. As my twenty-first birthday approached and I had still not broken my way into the theatre, I grew increasingly anxious: I knew I died at forty.

In the amateur dramatic society I had progressed rapidly to playing leading parts. Flattering reports appeared in the local Press, but even without George's guidance ('Most of us can act brilliantly for four nights after six months' rehearsal!') and the diaries of James Agate, considered by George vital to my theatrical education, I should have found it difficult as the West End's most unwanted playwright to feel that I had charged the world with starlight after giving a good performance with the Windmill Players. Amateur acting was my recreation, never to be confused with the theatre, which was my profession. For this reason I never offered any of my scripts to amateurs – until one day I realised that our company held three of us capable of sustaining the leading roles in *The Devil's Children*. I submitted it to the play-selection committee, who rejected it on the chairman's casting vote. One of the objections, I learned later, raised by a lady member, was my use of the terrible word 'bastard' to describe the situation of a medieval king's illegitimate son. This did make me wonder, not for the first time, if Thornton Cleveleys and I had very much in common.

Rejected as a playwright by the West End *and* our local church hall, I felt by the age of twenty-one so soured that I refused to have a formal twenty-first birthday party. As I pointed out to my parents, what did I have to celebrate? At the last moment I relented, admitting four friends to share my gloom. My birthday fell on a Sunday so there were no postal deliveries, shops and restaurants were closed, and my mother had 'flu'. I could report nothing on the day I came of age but a lifetime of habitual failure and near misses.

In the autumn of 1950 I was rehearsing a dire, low comedy of the kind which had conditioned theatre managements to flinch at the words 'set in Lancashire'. However, that did not prevent my giving to the caricature role I played a dimension of real character. Others did the same, with the result that we brought the house down. I was outraged that a play which vulgarised my native county should play to packed houses when my own play, *Warp and Weft*, which celebrated its grandeur, should have nowhere even a hearing. Swallowing my pride after the rejection of *The Devil's Children* I made the gesture of offering the script of *Warp and Weft* to our dramatic society – and it was a gesture on my part, for I agreed with George that it was the best play I had ever written.

In December 1950 I was awakened by my father's voice ringing from the hall, 'Somebody has taken the Stone of Destiny from Westminster Abbey!' His excitement ill became an Englishman proud of his pre-Conquest Saxon lineage, but I suppose those red-haired Celtic genes hidden somewhere in our patronym had risen like a Lion Rampant to bite him. Within seconds I had hurtled from my bed and down the stairs, to stand at his shoulder perusing the report in the morning paper – barefoot, in my nightgown, oblivious of winter cold. It was the one great piece of news in my lifetime. I seized the paper when my father returned upstairs and, seated on the hall settee, I read that someone called Wendy Wood had run up the Lion Rampant outside her croft cottage, and I was beside myself with glee. All that day I was laughing – a curious laughter which welled up in the same way as the ghost-tears.

My head held a vivid mental picture of that fluttering, defiant Lion Rampant, and by evening the characters and situation for a new play had formed themselves crystal clear. It was to be set in a German-speaking, mid-European republic called Höffentlich where the ex-crown prince's expatriate Scots secretary uses the arrival of the tourist industry as a device to restore the monarchy. The scene of the play is the ramshackle royal hunting lodge now run, unsuccessfully, as a boarding-house by the impecunious ex-royal household.

My method when starting a new play was to draft a few preliminary notes – first the names of characters, then a groundplan of the set, and lastly a few sentences of plotline to define dramatic nuances. The groundplan at this stage required no detail, but from the first I was harassed by a suit of medieval armour which introduced itself, uninvited, on to the set and refused to go away. I shunted it from corner to corner, but it always made its way back, stubbornly, to its original position up-centre by the main entrance. It contributed nothing whatever to the action, but I seemed unable to write the play without it. I let it remain, intending when the play was completed to strike out the suit of armour, but it guessed what I was up to, and right at the very end it made itself indispensable by providing the prince with a sword. I knew when I was beaten, so I left it in.

All through the New Year 1951 and the writing of that play, *The View from Olympus*, I was happier that my parents had seen me since I left the Army. With the Stone of Destiny returned to Scotland, and my own contribution to the national cause cunningly concealed in a Ruritanian political satire, exile had ceased to pain me. I would willingly stay banished for a lifetime if my Scots could have a second chance.

Then came the news that the Stone, after being put on public display at Arbroath, had been seized and taken down to England. The play had reached the stage of being typed, and I fought on grimly, my fingers stabbing home a blow for Scotland on every key. The sound was like the rattle of gunfire in my father's den.

Then came a second major attack – this time on my genetic loyalty to my county. The Windmill Players rejected my cotton famine play. The combination of the two fired a depth-charge in my head. Suddenly I knew that my own victory was vital; somewhere I had to stand my ground and hold it. At ten o'clock at night I announced to my parents, 'I am tired of writing good plays which get nowhere. This time I am going to write a pot-boiler. And I shall start it now.' I stalked upstairs to the den, and closed the door behind me.

I was attempting something I had never tried before, to write for a particular market. It was to be a domestic, drawing-room comedy of the kind which I saw so often *en route* for the West End, lacking either great fault or great merit. All that mattered was to smash my way into the theatre. With not a whiff of inspiration in my mind, I sat staring at the first page of a new exercise-book. Obviously, the characters would be a family, and the scene some kind of living-room. Needing to start somewhere, I sketched the basic outline of the set. Immediately, in trudged that confounded suit of armour to take its place up-centre by the door. I could actually *see* it. It would not go away, so I had to write the play around it.

It had to be the kind of family which would keep a suit of late-fifteenth-century Milanese as a pet. So they grew up round it – a charming, talented, impecunious tribe of dilettanti, at their head a matriarch dedicated to amateur dramatics and her own current role as Lady Macbeth. A devious lady, holding creditors at bay by charm and dubious stratagems, she was determined to put at least one of her children on the stage. That this enabled me to have throughout the play a sprinkling of fifteenth – sixteenth-century costumes to keep the suit of armour company was incidental – as had been the same mixture of modern and historical dress when it featured in *The View from Olympus*.

133

I had the play written within a week, typed out by the end of the fortnight. For the first time in my career I had difficulty finding a title, and it was my father who finally suggested *Cardboard Castle*. When I showed it to George Higgins he said, 'Not one of your best, but it will sell.' George recommended it to the Jack Rose Repertory Company in Blackpool, who accepted it immediately for production in July of that year.

2

WHEN *Cardboard Castle* HAD BEEN ACCEPTED I DECIDED IT WAS time to take a holiday. I had been writing non-stop for three years. Leaving my parents to deal with the Press, I made my escape to France.

I sailed from Newhaven to have the longer crossing, and because the name 'Newhaven' meant something to me – although what, I had no idea, except that my mind associated it with shipbuilding. When I saw it receding from me across the water, I had some difficulty with ghost-tears – why, I could not imagine. It was, to my joy, a French boat, so I went below for luncheon to celebrate my freedom.

As soon as I sighted Dieppe I went native. It was the only time in my life when I was not harassed by Scotland. France does not play an active part in this story, but in Paris and Alsace I came alive with a *joie de vivre* which had nothing to do with duty. I had fallen in love with a country which I did not have upon my conscience. Staying with friends of whom only one member of the family spoke English, my still faintly archaic French was rapidly brought up to date during visits to family friends, Parisian milliners and Alsatian dressmakers. From students at the Sorbonne I learned the art of French philosophical debate. And I so charmed the president of the polling station in Belfort by my interest in the French elections that he apologised for being unable to supply me with a ballot paper. Later, in Paris, at 3 a.m. I sat with Gabrielle and Paul amongst the students in the Place de l'Opéra, listening to the election results on the loudspeaker with the enthusiasm of one who knew a little, cared deeply, but did not have the responsibility of being enfranchised. It was the only time in my life when I took a holiday.

It was more than a holiday; I did seriously contemplate making my home in France, which seemed to my exiled Scots eyes the only congenial place of banishment – and it is likely I would have done so had it not been for that play requiring my return to England. As the weeks passed there began arriving in Belfort and Paris urgent phone calls and telegrams from my parents who had upon their hands a repertory company and the local Press demanding to know the whereabouts of a lost playwright. The most curious was a cryptic

134

message from friends in Thornton, 'Has she gone missing with Burgess and Maclean?' – which puzzled me, for in Belfort I used newspapers mainly as insulation against the sun when sitting in the gardens.

I returned to reality with a vengeance. It was the playwright's responsibility to provide acting scripts and, as I could not afford to have them typed professionally, I did them myself, using carbons, in batches of five. In my innocence it never occurred to me to ensure that all the scripts tallied precisely in pagination. When I arrived for the first rehearsal on the Tuesday morning I was welcomed by the cast with a measure of respect for 'the writer' which pointed my professionalism. This warmth had waned considerably by mid-afternoon when we had still not completed the first read-through, having been held up on every page because the scripts had been typed in three unmatching editions. My heart bled for the actors, who in weekly rep had to act one play, rehearse a second, skim-read a third, and forget a fourth, all simultaneously; and it bled for myself a bit because I had typed all day and all night for a week to have those scripts delivered on time. When I reached home at four-thirty for my 'luncheon', nerve-shattered and exhausted, I screamed to my mother, 'I shall never write another play as long as I live!' My mother, who had been stalling the Press until I came, told me to be quick and eat my food because I had to telephone an interview – thus ending what might have been a promising attack of artistic temperament.

When I had dealt with the Press I went down the road to recount my ghastly experience to the scenic designer, who by a remarkable coincidence used the disused stables at the end of North Drive for her studio. Joan told me not to worry. The first read-through of any new play was a mess, she said (she had worked in the theatre in London), and it would teach me next time to make the pages synchronise! She was right; by the end of the week I had regained my lost popularity, and in their enthusiasm for the play the cast had agreed between themselves to redden their hair to match that of the matriarch, for they felt it was essentially a red-haired family. In those days copper bole was used, which left the scalp green, so this united impulse was generous in workers who had so little time for hair-washing.

For the Monday opening of the show my father brought me a rose from his school garden to wear upon my dress – and thus began a family tradition. Curiously, apart from that one detail I have almost no recollection whatever of my first First Night, which should have been my great occasion, and must depend upon old newspaper reports. They record that to repeated cries of 'Author! Author!' I took eight curtain calls with the company. They say, further, that I was very pleased, made a charming speech of thanks to the company – and that I would be present at the *News Chronicle* theatrical garden-party on the

Saturday of that week. When interviewed I appear to have shown warmth to all concerned, but took a clinically detached view of my own play which was, to me, merely one of many I had written and by no means the best. One reporter mentions that I admitted feeling a certain enjoyment when my autograph was requested, but even through this naïveté there filters a cold, world-weary indifference to the success for which I had worked so hard.

On three nights I noted to my satisfaction that we had 'House Full' boards ouside the theatre. I endured much anxiety, but I cannot remember being excited. As I remarked at the time, 'Yes, but it has come too late.'

I might have felt differently had *Warp and Weft* been the first of my plays to be performed. Into that I had poured all of me that was native to Lancashire. When the run of *Cardboard Castle* ended, I handed a script of *Warp and Weft* to Jack Rose, and thereafter came never a word. I was once more back in the doldrums, still writing, and my initial impact on the theatre lay behind me like a rocket which had soared off leaving only the stick.

Five more plays came from my pen. The account of my struggle as a playwright in the provinces trying to break into the West End theatre is typical of my profession, and largely irrelevant to my story; what is interesting is that during all this time of intense creative activity the ghosts in my head stayed quiet – or so I thought. In fact, a present-day survey of my writing of that period shows them to have been hard at work, as busy as I was, disguised as characters or plotlines in the plays which I regarded as fiction.

Within the space of four years I had written two books and fourteen plays. By this time I had established connections with the West End theatre, but what eluded me was the spark of luck which is required more, possibly, in the theatre than in any other field. Also, although writing was my career, I was never a careerist; I still lacked the diligence – or brazen effrontery – to push my plays once they had been written. The profusion of ideas kept me too busy; as one script left my typewriter, the next had already appeared as jotted notes in an exercise-book. As long as I kept writing, constantly, I did not feel the pain of my separation from Scotland.

For all that, my apprenticeship to my chosen craft had been undertaken seriously, and the continuous recognition within the profession of my 'great potential' had begun to irk me: a play must be *performed*. I had just about given up hope when, in 1952, a year to the day since the acceptance of *Cardboard Castle*, there came a phone call from Jack Rose, out of the blue, telling me that *Warp and Weft* would be presented at the Royal Pavilion. Characteristically, he grumbled at the cost of 'all those extras' for the crowd scene, which he said I could not have, and warned me that the production of my play would no doubt ruin him and the theatre, but he would put it on. . . .

I told him I would take care of 'the crowd of extras', for which I had made allowance when writing the play: all it needed was a gramophone record. I spent four pounds of my own money on hiring a professional recording team for (I think) half an hour. I borrowed, free of charge, the entire manpower of Thornton Senior School (Boys) where my father had once taught. I told them, briefly, the tremendous, terrible story of their own ancestors' decisive contribution to the outcome of the American Civil War (when my father heard about this he groaned, 'Oh, Ginger, why are you not a teacher?') and painted a quick, verbal picture of the arrival in Darwen of that first load of Georgian Bowed or Middling Orleans in May 1865. Then I divided my choir into three groups: those who cheered, those who cried 'T' cotton's come!' and those who began, raggedly at first, the singing of the Doxology, in which finally the entire company joined. It made a good record.

On the first night at the Royal Pavilion everyone who could be spared from other backstage duties rushed to make a 'crowd' seen in torchlight beyond the window and the open door. I myself had hurried backstage to help out, putting a heavy woollen shawl over my head and evening dress to stand in silhouette behind the window, an anonymous Lancashire millworker; there I was joined by stage-hands in their overalls. To my recorded background of schoolboy voices, we all sang — I could hear an electrician's voice up in the gantry — 'Praise God from Whom all blessings flow. . . .' As we sang, we all cried — real tears. I have never since known a first night like that; possibly I never shall.

As the curtains closed we all clung together, crying and hugging each other. From the auditorium there was first a great silence, then a storm of applause and cheering. As the actors lined up for the call, the noise from the audience was deafening. Then shouting began: 'Author! AUTHOR!' I was too dazed to go forward, oddly reluctant to be parted from my momentary role as a woman of Lancashire; then one of the stage-hands took the shawl from my head and members of the cast pulled me forward into the glare of the lights where I stood with my father's red rose pinned to my dress.

I looked out at the audience, half its members standing, many unashamedly clutching man-size white handkerchiefs, and in the light from the stage I saw rows of faces streaked with the shining lines of tears. My own cheeks wet, I made a gesture to embrace them all, for these were Lancashire's people, whose tale my genetic line carried; all I had done was to set it to paper in terms of theatre. I made a brave speech through my emotion of thanks to everyone — including carefully the assistant stage managers who, as well as acting, had worked between scenes making prop porridge: the only person I forgot to mention was the producer, William Brookfield. I herewith make amends.

I went home alone on the tram, glad to have no company. Like the cast, I was exhausted. But as I took my tram ticket and held it, I felt a curious sense of triumph: *Nobody on this tram knows who I am.* A young actor who had just played his first principal role in the play travelled with me a small part of the way, and I was glad of him because he was exhausted like myself, triumphant like myself, and silent.

There were guests at supper when I reached home. All had seen the play and were waiting to congratulate me. I stayed long enough to drink a glass of sherry, say 'thank you', then I wilted. My mother, reading the signs, whisked me away to bed where I slept for twelve solid hours. When I wakened she brought me a late breakfast and a heap of morning papers. Those which mentioned my play gave it enthusiastic notices.

For two days telegrams, flowers, letters were constantly arriving, and the telephone never stopped ringing with messages of congratulation and demands for Press interviews. There were 'House Full' boards outside the theatre for almost every performance. (At the opening night the designer and I had perched on bar-stools hurriedly put for us in a corner of the dress circle, because the box-office had accidentally sold our seats!) 'House Full' boards represented to me success: I had done my job, which was to entertain an audience.

In the August the Royal Pavilion put on a second production of *Cardboard Castle*. That also played to full houses. My pot-boiler was fun, but it was never in the same class as *Warp and Weft* – now filling seats at Ashton-under-Lyne. Preston Repertory Company chose *Warp and Weft* for production during Guild Week, in the forthcoming September. One of our small papers announced the event beneath the heading 'Local Playwright Honoured' – it was indeed an honour, and one which cannot be given to many playwrights, for Preston Guild, an ancient crafts' festival, occurs but four times in a century. In our part of the world it was customary to say when wanting to postpone an action, 'Ay, I will – come next Preston Guild!' and 'as rare as Preston Guild' was a comparative still heard among the old people. To have my play represent the craft of the dramatist at Preston Guild gave me considerable satisfaction.

Thereafter *Warp and Weft* became known as 'the Guild Play' and I as 'the Guild Dramatist'. There survives a Press cutting bearing the headline 'Guild triumph for girl dramatist' which gives me precedence – being local – over Diana Dors and Yolande Donlan. The opening sentence of the 'show column' runs, in heavy type: 'Twenty-three-year-old Cleveleys dramatist Ada F. Kay looks like being

138

famous.'

The next production of the play, also in September, was at the Royalty Theatre in Morecambe, during the same week that the Labour Party Conference was held there. I never knew whether, in fact, the two events were connected, but the Press carried the statement that *Warp and Weft* had been chosen to appeal to party delegates. As a Tory of Liberal tendencies, I was both amused and exasperated by the implication that I had written a 'socialist' play. My play dealt with a fight for human liberty conducted by *all classes* in nineteenth-century Lancashire. There were 'House Full' boards outside the Royalty Theatre in Morecambe on the night I went to see the show, and I was delighted with a tale told to me by the theatre commissionaire. He happened to be laughing with the box-office saleswoman as the audience filed out, and a woman, still weeping, had struck him with her handbag, declaring angrily, 'It's nothing to laugh about!' He had cherished the bruise to show me.

Laudatory comments by the Press and audiences passed above my head. I was immersed in theatre, and deeply worried by the enormous load of work I had created for the stage-management staff. During the first run of the play in Blackpool I had watched the juvenile leads, who had to double as A.S.M.s, rushing away to make pots of tea and bowls of steaming porridge between their appearances on stage in exacting roles. By the middle of the week I had volunteered to take over the porridge-making before I went on stage to take my nightly call as the author. (It was the only time within my experience when the author of the play was demanded by the audience every night; word had, presumably, circulated that I was in the theatre to help make up the 'crowd' at the end.) I had achieved historic realism with those meagre bowls of milkless porridge and pots of marjoram tea which were Lancashire's diet in the years 1861–5, but at terrible cost to my actors. I was asking too much of human beings who worked for £4. 10s. in weekly rep. I had realised that I had much to learn. So I asked Jack Rose if he would take me on as an assistant stage manager.

3

I ENTERED WITH ZEST INTO MY NEW ROLE – THE HECTIC, HARASSED life of an A.S.M. and small part player. By this time histrionic ambition had left me and, although I still enjoyed acting, it is the props I made or chased all over town which have stayed longer in my memory than the parts I played. Never had my talent for improvisation been put to better use. My most spectacular contribution, made when all other sources of supply had failed us, was the suggestion that we *sewed* a prop turkey (raw, dressed) from a discarded nylon underslip – once-white, now turkey-flesh coloured – stuffed with cotton-wool. We stitched a limb apiece between performances on the Saturday night, and I ran out to rouse a nearby butcher just at closing-time to draw me a diagram so that I assembled them correctly. Plays calling for impossible props were to me a challenge, and the constant exercise of my ingenuity gave me the sense of exhilaration I had not known since my Army days. To be a successful playwright was all very well, but I was never happier than when toiling in the ranks.

My new way of life caused dramatic changes in my personal appearance, largely by accident. I could not wear my spectacles on stage or during intervals when they would have smudged my make-up, so I began leaving them at home when I went to the theatre in the evening. I found I did not require them out of doors – and then one morning I forgot to take them to rehearsal and read my script unaided. On the way home I engaged my travelling companions in a sight-test, using distant tram indicators and the small print on tram tickets, thus discovering that my sight was as good as anybody's. When I reached home my mother greeted me, 'You forgot your glasses.' I replied, 'I know. And I'm never going to wear the blasted things again.'

To be rid of that detested facial encumbrance which I had worn since I was thirteen restored my lost self-confidence. It was not merely that they made me look plain and donnish, they gave me a terrible feeling of *defeat* which I had known ever since the ghost-sobs had greeted the news that I would have to wear them. Some obscure fear lurked in my head causing me to cower behind anything which shielded my eyes – I had had it at the fencing club when obliged to wear a mask. I would risk my eyes at the end of a blade any time in preference to seeing my opponent through the wire mesh of a visor. To fence unmasked was contrary to club rules, and it was that loathing of a grille across my eyes which caused me finally to leave the club and the one sport for which I had a natural talent.

My glasses were not the only unwanted attribute I shed during that period. Rushing to and from the theatre, the strenuous exercise and frequent lack of meals caused me to lose weight at the phenomenal rate of two to three pounds per day. Within a fortnight I had got rid of my puppy fat, built up during the years of wartime carbohydrate diet and post-war army rations.

My last problem was a hank of long, curling hair, which, worn in a bun or a coil, had never really suited me. In bed it looked marvellous plaited into two long, shining braids, but, as I lamented bitterly, 'What's the use of looking beautiful in bed?' When reported along the corridor this remark apparently caused great amusement in the male dressing-room, though I could not see why. My innocence had lasted rather a long while, but I had been immersed in playwriting when my contemporaries were making up their minds which of their fiancés to marry. Now, at last, I too had time for a boy-friend – at the age of twenty-three – and it was he who persuaded me to have my hair cut.

My session at the hairdresser's was a terrible ordeal, and I let out a cry when the first long, severed tress was laid upon the board beside me: it was beautiful hair and it had taken me ten years to grow it. But the new, shoulder-length, waved-and-set Kay reflected a personality of new dimensions. I *think* I was pleased.

On the day I had my hair cut we were all going to a party after the show. In Number One dressing-room I stood before the mirror in the dress made for the Preston Guild reception, considering myself. My gradual transformation had been openly discussed in the dressing-room, where one's looks were a professional asset (or not) and my new hairstyle had met with considerable approval. Then I said sadly, 'If only I had a figure to go with it. . . .' I had lived with my puppy fat for so long. Eileen said, 'I don't know why you worry. You have a perfect figure.'

I said, incredulous, '*Perfect? Mine?*'

Then I did some fast mental arithmetic – 37 – 23 – 37 – and at last the penny dropped. I stood staring at the beautiful girl in the mirror, all the right shape, size and colour, and thought in a strange, detached way, 'Is that *me*?' In other mirrors round the room I caught side reflections, and there was no doubt that this lovely apparition moved as I moved, smiled as I smiled. I was utterly amazed and quite enchanted by her. It was only when my eyes travelled to the hands included in the picture that I laughed inwardly at some obscure joke which I felt rather than thought: even the hands fitted. *My hands fitted.*

I threw back my head and laughed.

I had an acting part usually once a fortnight. When the cast-list appeared on the board at the end of the week I knew whether I would be working. The Christmas show was *When Knights Were Bold*, a comedy containing a dream sequence set in the fifteenth century. I was stricken to discover that my name was not on the list for that week. There was, however, room for extras with non-speaking parts in the medieval castle sequence, so I promptly volunteered to be an extra, free of charge, that week. Jack grumbled, 'What about the cost of hiring your costume?' I told him I could provide my own. He warned it was too late for my name to be included in the programme, but that, I told him, was an advantage as my costume was masculine.

Deliriously happy, I rushed home to make adjustments to my Hamlet costume. I discarded the cloak which I had worn for the fancy-dress dance at Fairmilehead, and I set to work to embellish the doublet. For my shoulders I made a new ornamental chain of brass curtain-rings grouped in trefoils, each surmounted by a pearl, and to this I added a large, pendant cross of rubies and double pearls. For my hand I fashioned a large cabouchon turquoise ring of moulded sealing-wax. To the skirt of the doublet I stitched some gold flowers taken from the heraldic costume worn by my aunt at a ball. The item on which I lavished most work was a belt, very broad and tight, of black felt stiffened with buckram, on which I stitched diamante and a looped chain of crystals set in silver. When I tried it on with the costume I felt at once its lack of *weight*. What I needed, I remembered suddenly, was a length of iron chain. Immediately I knew the very piece I wanted – it hung in the garage, nine inches long, and its last wearer had been a horse. (It was actually a curb chain, made of nickel, but I always thought of it as iron chain.) I could not bring myself to ask for it directly, it was too important, and I let my father offer me both gold and silver chain before I led him out to the garage to search for what I wanted there. When I had declined the offer of brass chain, I said, feigning sudden inspiration, 'What about this?' taking down the curb.

My father said, 'Ginger, you don't want *that*. After all the work you've put into that belt. If you don't want gold or silver, at least use brass.'

'No. I want *iron* chain. Please can I have this – *please*?' I clung to my prize, terrified he might say no.

He gave it to me with a shrug, baffled. As I left the garage, clutching it with terrible elation, my father's voice followed me, 'If you want my opinion, you'll just spoil the belt. . . .'

I replied, almost snapping at him, 'Don't you see, it's the *weight* I need' – and made off to my bedroom with my precious acquisition, my hands trembling with excitement.

I incorporated the chain into my belt as a sword hanger, empty, save for my dagger. I did not seem to want a sword – just the weight of iron at my hip. As soon as I fastened on the belt I knew it as an old friend. My costume was at last complete.

Knowing it might interest my grandfather, I told him that I had used the flowers from my aunt's costume upon my doublet, adding, 'Aren't they heavy? And haven't they kept their colour well all these years?' My grandfather replied with a brief glance from behind his newspaper, 'So they should. They're gold bullion.'

The doublet decorated with gold bullion I left in the theatre over the weekend, but the belt with its length of iron chain I carefully brought home with me. That belt was to travel with me to and from the show. When I put it round my waist I became *me*.

It was on the Monday afternoon at dress rehearsal that we began to have trouble with me. . . . At earlier rehearsals I had been more of a gap than a presence in the scene, for nothing was required of me but to stand on the castle ramparts with three others to make a noise of welcome as the hero entered. The others were characters in the play, I was just 'crowd'. On the Monday, when I appeared in costume, my presence dominated the stage from the moment the curtain opened on Act Two. I heard the producer call, 'Move upstage – upstage right! Further – *further!*' He was in despair and I was nearly off the stage altogether before my impact had been sufficiently subdued to make way for the hero.

All through that week's performance members of the audience were enquiring at the box-office who was 'the new actor' who had joined the company. I had acquired quite a following by the Saturday. There was nothing I could do to diminish my stage presence. I did not have it normally. The magnetism of the man in black came out of another century. An extraordinary fusion within my time-sense occurred during each performance of that play. As I stood on the ramparts of painted canvas with their topping of cotton-wool snow, waiting for the signal from the gantry – 'Stand by!' – I *knew* that out beyond that curtain lay the fifteenth – sixteenth-century. Even though I could hear the coughing and rustling of the audience, I yet remained convinced that when the tabs parted I should see beyond the footlights the landscape of my Scotland. Each time the miracle failed to happen, and each pain was so keen that my voice cracked when I began the cheering.

There was one other moment in the play when reality was not entirely real. I had a later entrance, just a few lines before that of the villain of the piece. He was clad in plate armour (tin, with chainmail made of knitted string covered with aluminium paint). Waiting in the wings on the first night I saw him loom suddenly above me as he appeared round the corner of the staircase, and I let out a yell of terror. This became a company joke, and I laughed with them; but the terror persisted every time I encountered that armoured figure in the wings. Crowded close upon me in a small space, I knew he came to kill me.

During that week there revived the two old, clear memories which I carried all my life . . . that of being a small child lifted to stand on the chair by His Grace my father . . . and the other memory of myself, as a boy of fourteen, clad in scarlet with a gold chain about my shoulders, riding at the head of a small cavalcade out through a castle gate, somewhere, into something. . . .

When the curtain closed on the last night of *When Knights Were Bold*, I was inconsolable. Until the end I believed that *one night* the miracle would happen and I should see the world that in some way was trapped inside my head. The miracle had not happened, and I was no wiser than before.

My melancholy lasted from Christmas into 1953 when, on Easter

143

Saturday morning, I walked into the sea from the sand and marram grass at Rossall Beach to drown myself.

4

I WAS SAVED FROM DROWNING BY TWO MEN FROM A CAR PARKED BETWEEN the sand dunes where I had not seen it. When I was taken home, a sodden bundle, and handed over to my mother, my last words to my departing rescuer were an anguished, 'I'm so sorry about your shoes.' Even in the water my concern had been for his shoes, nothing else: sodden shoes were some kind of nightmare at the back of my head. I was not at all grateful for being salvaged.

Everywhere I met the question 'Why?' – impossible to answer. I had at the time everything to live for. *Warp and Weft* was scheduled for production at the Oldham Rep at the end of April; at Morecambe the presentation of my two plays had given me introduction to the company as an actress; I had for the first time in my life fifty pounds in the bank, earned in royalties; most exciting of all, I had just heard that my untried play *The View from Olympus* had found favour with the B.B.C. Drama Department (Television) who were intending its production. I had now acclimatised myself to the new me, discovering that to be glamorous is quite exciting. I was actually waiting for the call to go to Morecambe for my first important acting role when I took my unpremeditated step into the ocean.

I cannot recommend suicide. The depression which precedes it is as nothing compared with that which follows the attempt. I had been agnostic if not atheist for some while prior to my act of self-destruction, but what I encountered in the sea that morning was a tyranny imposed by *self*: there is no prospect so terrible as the discovery that there is no one to blame, no hell to fear, but self.

I was still in this state of total dejection when the call came for me to go to Morecambe for rehearsal. I accepted the part because in a world where all is desolation it is better to be active than idle. For this piece of initiative I was rewarded by a miracle – but I had to work extremely hard to earn it. There was a man in the company towards whom, at first sight, I was drawn by the most powerful attraction I had ever felt. It was primarily spiritual, an affinity between two human beings who saw in each other a reflection of themselves. He knew what it was like to be me, and gained my confidence as no one else had ever done. I poured out my troubles, not realising that I was imposing my distress on him. He flared in rage, revealing my selfishness.

For three days and nights I undertook the hardest exercise of my life, to pin a bright smile on my face for the sake of other people. I wore it like a mask, my facial muscles nearly cracking with the effort. On the fourth night, in the theatrical digs where I stayed, I was lying in my bed when the amazing truth dawned on me that happiness is not a privilege but an obligation owed to God and man. At that, there came over me an ecstasy which I had never known before and may in this life never know again. The walls of my small room faded, and I did actually hear the sound of many bells and the multitude of voices proclaiming their joy because, as I described it afterwards, 'Ada Kay has come to join us.' I was never to look back thereafter; after years of praying to an empty sky – and latterly not praying at all – I have ever since been aware of an immense, immediate listening when I put up a prayer.

The following morning I made a pilgrimage to the ancient, tiny church at Heysham high upon the cliff edge. There I sat in solitude, looking down through the low window upon the sea below me. I felt serenity of spirit such as I had not known since the days when I used to sit thus alone in the ruins of Fountains Abbey.

I was never by nature a public worshipper – other than during communion; I preferred at any time to sit in an empty church listening to the silence. That for me had been the great attraction of Fountains Abbey where I used to stay with friends on the estate during the time when the scarcity of petrol kept most cars off the road, and I had the ruins entirely to myself on most evenings. I would stay until it was quite dark, walking in the derelict monastery or sitting still beneath the broken filigree of the east window in the Chapel of Nine Altars.

Because I knew the ruins so well it came as a considerable surprise to me one evening to find a high, locked room which I had overlooked. It was the abbot's dormitory, used as a store by the stonemasons, which possibly explained why I had never explored to the top of that flight of stone stairs. Before me was a door which had, on this night, a broken panel, and beyond it I saw in the twilight leaking through the window a room filled with timber and rubble. . . . *I belonged in that room.*

I tugged at the door, but it was unyielding. I had to make do with pressing my face to the aperture to obtain just the smell of that chamber, the musty odour of ancient ecclesiastical masonry, unbearably familiar. I wanted in that moment to be rid of my life which denied me access to that room. If only I could have been left there, undisturbed, for ever. Outside the locked door my ghost-sobs were more a whimper, falling away into the twilight quiet.

Our friends had left Fountains Abbey shortly afterwards, so I never went there again, and my calm I had left behind at the door of the abbot's dormitory.

Now something of that peace returned as I sat in the church at Heysham looking down upon the waves and seagulls.

My happiness at Morecambe lasted that single summer. I knew not

145

to expect more. Deep spiritual affinity between two people does not necessarily lead to mundane happy endings – indeed, it can be a barrier. I learned to appreciate every moment while it lasted – and learned never to keep souvenirs of happy evenings. (I had a great throwing-out of my life's collection when I went home.) I brought new rules into my life, such as weekly attendance at early communion, and daily study of Thomas à Kempis's *Of the Imitation of Christ* which were to be a source of strength to me through the years that were to follow. The single great attainment at Morecambe was spiritual serenity: I had now not only endurance, but *hope* – which, I had always said previously, was 'the one thing I was born without'.

I brought back from Morecambe one other new habit which belongs to a different context.

I was there at the time of the coronation. Coronations were something I avoided, and I managed to concentrate on the new play I was writing all through the ceremony broadcast on television in the public room which I had usually to myself. This I had to do, to tether my thoughts to the immediate present for my head held too many images relating to a crown. I thought I had been successful until I awakened next day convinced that I had just seen a document awaiting my signature on which the newly dried ink was *brown*. After rehearsal, in the afternoon when I was free, my feet carried me involuntarily to the nearest stationer's shop where I made enquiries about the brown ink of which I had first heard in Edinburgh. Only Waterman now made it. I purchased a bottle, and filled my pen. I wrote my signature and sat gazing at it spellbound. It was the first time that my writing had ever looked as though it *belonged to me*.

In the autumn I was once more back in Cleveleys. I was soon at work upon a new play but I missed the comradeship of the dressing-room. During the next six months my career as a writer fell once more into the doldrums, a situation familar but now more frustrating after my year's spectacular success. Due to a change of management in the B.B.C., the pending production of *The View from Olympus* remained pending – until eventually the script was returned to me. I was angry at this rejection of my play written, covertly, for Scotland. At the same time my statement of Lancastrian independence, *Warp and Weft*, came back from French's who declined to publish because they doubted the authenticity of my nineteenth-century dialect. In fact, my father, who was an authority on the subject, had vetted my script from the beginning; he had been fascinated by my ear for the dialect but irritated by my spelling of it. He said it was 'foreign'. (Neither of us realised that, due to the similarity between the two tongues, my mind had lapsed frequently into Middle Scots.) This, however, had been corrected, and I was furious to learn of the rejection of the play, roaring my wrath about 'my ane tangue' with all my non-Lancastrian gutturals blasting.

For the second time a blow at Scotland and at Lancashire arriving simultaneously roused me like a demon to fight back – but this time I took war into the camp of the enemy.

CHAPTER FIVE

1

I WENT DOWN TO LONDON ON 30 JUNE 1954, WITH TEN POUNDS IN CASH, TWO suitcases and a partial eclipse of the sun to bear me company. Of the last I had an excellent view from the carriage window, taking it as an omen for my venture. I had left home suddenly with the pronouncement, 'Either I shall be back in a week or I shall not come back at all.'

I had made no plans other than to book an hotel room for a few days and announce my impending arrival to a friend who had blazed the trail and said he would instruct me. I was arriving in London with less money and fewer friends than I had in Edinburgh at the time of my ill-conceived expedition of 1948, but my attitude of mind was entirely different: I came to conquer London.

Within two days I had bespoken a bed-sitting-room in Belsize Park and enlisted at a secretarial agency as a temporary typist. My room was not immediately available, so for the first three weeks I remained at the hotel, where I made the acquaintance of an African prince in London on official business. He had a sense of humour like my own, and we took stately strolls in Kensington Gardens where our vividly contrast-ing presences, his towering dark and mine red-gold, caused heads to turn among our fellow promenaders. When he left he took away a photograph of me and gave me his personal telephone extension number written on the back of his card which bore the address 'The Royal Palace'. I took it as a matter of course that my first new friend in London should be a visiting foreign potentate, but my friends said no; most people met clerks or cab-drivers.

I had never lived in a bed-sitting-room before, and my awareness of so many strangers living boxed-in lives beneath the same roof was an acute reminder of the loneliness of London. When, after three days, I found myself darting back into my room if I heard a footstep on the stair, I decided I would have to combat the tyranny before my northern friendliness was quenched by it; so I went on to the landing to waylay the first person who appeared with an invitation to take tea with me, and within a week I knew all the occupants of the three upper floors.

Learning to live with other people was not difficult; learning to live with myself required greater effort. To begin each day entirely alone, combating the depression which came to me naturally without the added stimuli of poverty, grim offices and crowded tube trains, tested my resilience. I formed the habit of reading a chapter of Thomas à

Kempis each morning, and, on bad days, submitting myself to a rigorous catechism:

'You are not blind, are you?' (No)
'You do not lack a limb?' (No)
'You are not ugly?' (No)
'You are not mentally defective?' (No)
'Then what the hell have you to complain about?' (Nothing)

After that I washed myself and dressed, then cooked and ate my breakfast of bacon scraps bought cheaply. By the time I reached my ghastly office I could cope with anything.

I had retained my habit of going to mid-week communion formed during the hard days after I left Morecambe, and during my first week's office-job in Oxford Street I had discovered that St Giles' Church held a mid-week communion at lunchtime. I never spoke to anyone there, but I felt a tremendous kinship with this island of men and women of all ages, who had, like myself, crept out from their offices to meditate for half an hour on matters other than sales charts and what-was-on-the-telly. It was like being a member of a resistance movement.

I never learned to use my elbows, knees and teeth as others did when boarding buses. After several days of being permanently at the head of queues which trampled me down, I decided to use another form of transport. The advantage of the Underground, for me, was that I was put aboard the train by the impetus of the crowd surging in behind me, and thus reached home. Consequently, I never did see much of London above ground for all the years I lived there.

The few weeks I worked as holiday relief for a shipping company in the City I was happy. On those summer mornings, early, I was entranced by the tall, dark buildings of Lombard and Leadenhall Streets through which the sun barely penetrated, with their great, gilt bank-signs, and the fluttering, bell-shaped, cotton dresses of the girls hurrying to work – like a handful of flowers cast down from the high window-boxes. There was one street to which I was particularly drawn, and strolled there several times during my lunch-hour before I looked to see its name – Cheapside. Having read Dekker's *The Shoemaker's Holiday*, the name brought a smile, though that did not entirely account for my feeling that the ground there knew me. I felt close to myself, a curious but warming sensation.

Some weeks later I was crossing Smith Square on my way to visit a new acquaintance when I was halted by the sight of a bombed Restoration church. The tower held my attention – the tower with the clock still intact, its hands possibly recording the moment when the bomb fell. I stood in the quiet of the evening, staring for a long time at the tower, thinking of *my head*. Churches destroyed during the blitz were still a feature of London in 1954, and thereafter, whenever I saw one with the tower standing, I stopped to look at it, still trying to figure out why a burnt-out church tower reminded me of *my head*.

The best offices, usually in the City, required temporary staff only for a short period in the summer. In winter good jobs were almost non-existent and, work being scarce, one was glad to get anything which paid for rent and minimal nourishment. It was then we were sent to firms where working conditions were so bad that it was obvious why they could not keep permanent staff. If approached on the very first morning by the personnel officer offering regular employment, one knew to expect the worst – and was never disappointed! My experience of these clerical hell-holes left me with an abiding horror of certain areas of London – mainly in the west and south-west – which no subsequent affluence could dispel.

When working in the West End my favourite lunchtime refuge was the British Museum. Just to stand looking at the Mildenhall Treasure gave me the feeling that my stale cheese sandwiches washed down by cloakroom tap-water had been a banquet. And I am sure nobody can better appreciate the absorbed Hellenic sunlight in the Elgin Marbles than a temporary typist whose shoes are lined with newspaper to keep out frozen snow. On days when the Egyptian Gallery was open, I never failed to visit my friend Arthur (a name I chose at random). He was a small, wizened creature with dabs of grey wool still adhering to his scalp, naturally mummified by pre-dynastic sand burial, and he lay curled inside an open stone coffin not his own and several sizes too large for him. I knew how he felt to be exhibited dead before all these people, and he seemed to know how I felt, standing there beside him.

The advantages of this precarious, impecunious and frequently depressing way of life were independence and shorter working hours. No London firm owned my services. If affronted I had the right to take my coat and leave at a moment's notice. This I never did, but to know that I could put me above the tyranny of departmental petty godlings. Our relationship with the agency was a fluid understanding of liege-lines and tripwires; we cherished its reputation and it gave us protection. On Fridays, mustering in its office at Notting Hill to collect our wage packets, we resembled a band of mercenary soldiers reporting back our week's adventures on many fronts. I enjoyed the camaraderie of those weekly half-hours.

Household economy was learned the hard way, in one week, when I spent my first pay-packet on a salami, olives, poppy-seed bread, camembert and a box of Sobranie cigarettes: I enjoyed my Friday evening supper – then awoke to the fact, on Saturday morning, that, when the rent was paid, my washing taken to the launderette and money put aside for the week's train fares, there were but three shillings for the gas and nothing to eat for the next six days but bread and dripping. By the following Friday the technique of husbandry had been mastered.

I had left home with no knowledge of cookery apart from one hideous year of domestic science at school. During what should have been my experimental years, wartime rationing had prohibited my helping in the kitchen except as a scullion. I learned to make pastry from the directions on the back of a flour bag, and everything else was done by instinct. By the end of two years I could cook pigeon pie with four vegetables, and a pudding, in a dutch oven, or veal escalope Holstein for three people on two gas-rings. (At one point I even wrote the cookery articles in the house magazine of an organisation which employed me as a temporary typist.)

My bed-sitting-room in Belsize Park Gardens was one of eighteen in a happy house. On the ground floor was a curved door set into a convex wall, and the resident behind that 'tower' door was a Mr P. A. Stewart. I became fascinated by the door and the unknown Mr Stewart who lived behind it. I knew most of the people in the house by this time, and I asked Molly, my next-door neighbour, which was Mr Stewart. She described a slim, dark young man, an architect, but I had seen no one who fitted her description. Then, one morning, when obliged to go to the ground-floor lavatory because the one upstairs was occupied, I crossed the hall just as the tower door opened and there emerged a dark young man carrying a briefcase. We smiled and exchanged 'Good morning.' At our third meeting we talked so long in the hall that he cautiously invited me into his room for cocoa.

It was the beginning of a relationship which would eventually take precedence over all others. I would cook a meal in my room for the two of us on most nights of the week (shared expenses) and afterwards Peter would go away to work at his drawing-board. One most important thing we understood about each other as creative people was that architecture and writing came first. Saturday evening was the exception, when I prepared a special meal and he provided a bottle of wine over which we talked late into the night. It was a good relationship and in the process of cultivating it I nearly, but not quite, forgot my purpose in coming to London.

During the year 1954–5 I was not writing. This worried me a great deal, for the whole purpose of my garret-starving existence had been to acquire those few precious hours of additional working-time in the evenings. Instead, I found that living at subsistence level and the daily battle with rush-hour crowds left me too limp when I reached home to be creative. New varieties of ill-health were a feature of my London life – asthma, which I had not known previously; tonsilitis in winter;

151

and then acute exhaustion which left me leaning against walls wondering how on earth I would get home. I could never afford to take a day off, for I was paid by the hour, and when an attack of tonsilitis more ferocious than usual laid me up for a fortnight with no money I decided grimly that, as I was doing no writing, the best thing was to take a permanent job. To my mind this savoured of capitulation, but my resolution had weakened in the process of becoming 'a Londoner'.

At the Labour Exchange my qualifications were too high, so I was sent to the Appointments Office. There I found they had a problem with writers who, although professional, were not necessarily graduates. By this time I had begun to see why my father had said, 'Ginger, you will regret not having a professional qualification.' However, there was at the Appointments Office a remarkable lady who specialised in finding square holes for square pegs. We called her Min, and Min's brief but enormous contribution to my life covered many areas, a fact not apparent to me when I knew her. She was like a boundary stone – once past Min and the entire scene changed.

One day Min phoned to ask, 'Can you write a play in a month?'

It transpired that an eye-maker, on the eve of his winter holiday, had come to the Appointments Office seeking someone who, for a fee of £20, would man his consulting-rooms for a month while he was away. I told Min it sounded like my idea of heaven.

So I moved into Woburn Square as an eye-maker's locum, my duties being to answer telephones, doorbells, correspondence and generally reassure the patients until my employer's return. I loved the few people whom I met in Woburn Square – they all seemed gentle and civilised after the hard-pushing multitude I met on trains. Also, I loved the eyes. To work in a room that was simply littered with eyes, so many jewels of the soul, was to me absolute heaven. Unexpectedly, however, they proved a deterrent to many friends who had planned to call upon me there, and thus provided me with a great deal more time for writing than I would otherwise have had.

I sat in the Art Nouveau consulting-rooms in a blissful solitude far removed from the tyranny of trains and departmental demi-gods with grammatical problems. From my table I looked out upon the winter-bared trees, and, on one occasion, watched the courtship and copulation of two pigeons – so eloquently male and female in their respective attitudes that I could have written every word of dialogue that passed between them.

On my way to and from Woburn Square I passed a bombed house. The façade of the ground floor was intact, even to the letter-box and the number on the fire-blistered door. The neatly boarded windows when seen at dusk seemed merely to be shuttered, and my fancy created behind them the living presence of firelight and winter family tea served in the drawing-room. It was when I lifted my eyes that the illusion was dramatically shattered by the sight of the open sky and a fringe of grass and willow-herb growing where the upper floors should have been. There tugged at my mind the beginnings of a new play. I was not ready to write it yet, but I was overjoyed to find my creative imagination functioning again after twelve sterile months.

A short while before Min's vital phone call my agent had told me that B.B.C. North Region was holding a radio play competition, but at the time my confidence as a writer was at its lowest ebb and I did not feel equal to the challenge. Now, in the peace of Woburn Square, I decided that I would have to win that competition. The rules required either the author or the theme to be north country. I qualified on the first count, but it seemed to me that if I was to write a play out of Lancashire there was but one subject I could choose – the cotton famine, our county's great fight for the liberty of man against the power politics and foreign policy of London. I had never written a radio play, but I took up my pen and *listened*. . . . I heard the early morning clatter of clogs as they reached me faintly from the streets, in my early childhood, whenever I stayed at my grandparents' house in Darwen. And I heard again the strong resonance of voices from nineteenth-century Lancashire. . . .

I wrote the theme of *Warp and Weft* in terms of sound, and I gave it the new title *Red Rose for Ransom*.

As I walked home on the last night of my month in Woburn Square, I stopped outside the blistered door of the bombed house to say, 'Thank you.'

It was twelve months before I learned, in March 1956, that mine was one of the three prize-winning plays selected out of 960 entries. The news came as a relief, but it was no more than I had expected: I had written my play to be a winner, otherwise I would not have entered the competition.

Colin Shaw's production of *Red Rose for Ransom* was broadcast on 5 April 1956. Transmitted from the Manchester studios, the winning plays were confined to the North Regional Programme. I heard my play heavily overlaid with atmospheric noises as Peter and I sat with our ears pressed, literally, to the radio in his bed-sitting-room in Belsize Park.

The play contest had been given much publicity but it did not much alter my life-style: I went on typing invoices. (It galled me to see myself described in one Press report as 'a London typist'!) Then, in the summer of 1956, the secretarial agency sent me to work for the British Olympic Appeals Fund. The words 'Olympic Games' occurring constantly in the letters I was typing revived an idea for a play which had been in my mind since childhood, when I discovered in an old pocket encyclopaedia this reference to the battle of Thermopylae:

Thermopylae. Here, 480 B.C., Leonidas, at the head of 300 Spartans and 700 Thespians, withstood the whole force of the Persians for three days. The enemy being secretly guided to the rear of the Greeks, the latter, hemmed in between two assailants, perished gloriously, all but one man who was held in dishonour for his flight.

Over the years, unconsciously, my mind changed that last sentence to: ' . . . perished gloriously, except for one man who returned to bear witness.' The predicament of the one man, who came back to describe a battle which no one else could remember, haunted me. When I was thirteen I read Herodotus to learn more about him. Then I made the discovery that there were in fact two Spartans who survived the battle of Thermopylae – Aristodemus (presumably the one referred to in the extract I have quoted), and another, Pantites, who was despatched as a messenger by Leonidas just before the battle. Pantites became the hero of my play, although in changed circumstances; my soldier, engaged in the battle, was rendered unconscious and then, coming to his senses when all was over, returned to Sparta to report for further duty – and it is there, on his homeward journey from the battlefield, that my play begins.

The shape of the play had been in my mind for years – indeed, I still had part of the opening scene on paper, just as I had written it when I was about fourteen. What prevented my completing it was that I simply did not know how to conclude it: Herodotus had claimed that Pantites hanged himself, but that seemed to me a negative climax. Now, I decided to embark upon the theme as a play for radio, and leave the ending to write itself when I reached it – which is precisely what happened, and the dénouement startled me as much as it was to startle subsequent audiences. I had the entire play written within ten days, working at night, and the manuscript typed by the end of the month. Then I sent it off to Colin Shaw who had produced *Red Rose for Ransom*. It was accepted immediately for transmission in December 1956.

I had just posted the script of *The Man from Thermopylae* when, in October, I was commissioned to write a television version of *Red Rose for Ransom*. I went north to plan the script with its producer, Vivien Daniels. Staying with my parents, I had just a week in which to write it – one week's unemployment being the most I could afford. The munificent down-payment of £42 could not be given to me until I had a television draft to show. I was tired after writing *The Man from Thermopylae* at night and typing Olympic Appeals letters during the day, and the prospect of learning how to write for a new medium within seven days was somewhat daunting; however, I had not been a professional all those years for nothing, and by pounding my typewriter round the clock I managed to complete the script before returning to London.

At the end of November I was approached by B.B.C. Television in London to write two scripts for the *Grove Family* series. To me just then anything for which I would get paid was my style of writing. I went to Lime Grove studios to meet the editor and the producer, obliged to confess that I had never seen an instalment of the *Grove Family*. (I had rarely seen television!) I was given an armful of *Grove* scripts, back numbers, and went away to study the genealogy of the characters. At the end of my day's typing I read, thought and dreamed *Grove Family*, and within ten days I was able to submit two plotlines which were acceptable. For each twenty-minute play I would receive £52, thus enabling me to take time off from the secretarial work and write during the day. Having no access to television in my bed-sitting-room, I watched the transmission of my first television playlet in the viewing room at Lime Grove studios.

Meanwhile, I had received another, more important invitation from Shepherd's Bush – to join the central script section of the B.B.C. (Television), a team consisting of eleven men, at a salary of £1060 per annum. I sat in Donald Wilson's office at the television centre, wearing my last remaining good suit, and said that I would think about it. Donald asked what I was earning in my present capacity, and I replied, 'Five pounds ten a week.' (I had just had a rise of five shillings.) Donald said, 'Well, a thousand a year is preferable, isn't it?' I agreed that it was, but I was primarily concerned about my future as a freelance playwright working for the live theatre. I was not sure whether I wanted to become a television staff writer. The trial contract period was three months; I was not committing myself to lifelong union with the B.B.C. in London; all the same. . . . I went away to think it over.

On 8 December I was in Leeds for the rehearsal and recording of *The Man from Thermopylae* with a cast whose names are now theatrical history. Alec Clunes, Carleton Hobbs, Lionel Jeffries, James Scott, Geoffrey Segal. . . . By coincidence, Colin Shaw had just returned from Greece where he had been making a documentary which included Thermopylae. He had brought back with him a recording of Macedonian pipe music, which I had specified in the script but with small hope that it could be supplied: to have the real thing, recorded in Greece, was a magical happening in accordance with much else that characterised that first production of the play.

I stayed with the play until its final recording. Producers, actors, technical staff – all of us loved it, and to the canteen staff and the

155

porters it had become 'our play'. The effects-department boys created everything from the noise of an obvious 'all-purpose gadget' (described in my lines) to the more lyrical sound of the approaching circus. I shall never forget that small cavalcade, hooves clip-clopping, bells jingling, as it came out of the morning with an air from Macedonia played on the pipes – an image in sound so sharp and clear that I could *see* the landscape of Greece as it had been upon some long ago morning.

During my stay in Leeds I talked to Alec Clunes as to a father confessor. I told him of the post offered to me by the B.B.C., and his advice was, 'Don't take it. Stay original. Leave the office work to someone else. You could be the young white hope of the British theatre – you must know that. If you go into the B.B.C. we may never hear of you again.'

I had a shrewd suspicion he was right. But it was now winter and the summer run of happy offices had ended; we were back to the Dickensian atmosphere of windows that did not open, doors admitting draughts, dust-covered ledgers, frozen snow, and me with my nose pressed (figuratively) to the windows of restaurants where I could not afford to eat at lunchtime. I was sick to my soul of doing a boring job for £5 10s a week, and I felt I could not face another winter of icy pavements, cheese sandwiches and poverty. I went to tell Donald Wilson that I would accept the appointment as scriptwriter/adaptor. And I have joked for twenty years that I must be the oldest young white hope of the British theatre still in circulation.

2

The Man from Thermopylae WAS BROADCAST ON 14 DECEMBER 1956. The reaction of the listeners was immediate, some reaching for their pens to write to me before their radio sets had cooled. The letters came from a complete cross-section of the public, and were to continue in a steady stream for many months to come.

My duties at the B.B.C. were scheduled to start on 15 December, and I was still dizzy from the previous night's congratulatory phone calls when I presented myself at Donald Wilson's office as one of the two new members of the central script section. My fellow recruit was Frank Baker, and we were put to share a secretary and a minute office in one of three carvans in the television centre car-park. The new centre had not then been completed, and builders' materials and workmen were much in evidence, giving the whole place a stimulating, experimental atmosphere which ideally suited me and no doubt permeated our work.

Before I left Donald's office I was handed my first assignment in a manner reminiscent of my initiation as an army medical orderly.

156

Donald asked, 'Have you read *Villette*?' I replied that it was one of my favourites. 'Good,' said Donald, 'I want you to adapt it for television in six parts.'

Within two days I had received my second instruction. I was to watch a certain programme, then telephone the producer to offer him my services as a play doctor. It was a tall order for someone with my limited experience of television and my terror of telephones – communication for me depends on seeing the eyes. However, when I had seen the programme I sat down at my desk, drew a deep breath and, with a hand which, literally, dripped with nervous perspiration, reached for the telephone. My voice conveyed nothing of the strain I suffered – which possibly was a pity, because only the hard, competent side of my nature came through, which is not the most lovable. However, I was not employed to be lovable, and every week thereafter I corrected like a schoolmaster the next script of the series. It was certainly no diplomatic triumph – I learned later that the producer concerned referred to me as 'that terrible woman from the B.B.C.' – but I was always grateful to Donald for throwing me in at the deep end. After that I could use the telephone to tackle anyone about anything.

With my long-term project *Villette* I had no difficulty dramatically in making the six-episode break-down; it was when I came to make a start on the actual script that I found myself in the wilderness. When writing for the stage I had always placed myself 'out front', viewing the action, and bereft of the proscenium arch I had no way of locating characters. Having rarely watched television except on the studio floor I was shortly to be chased up firmly by the B.B.C. for not owning a set. I spent three terrible weeks in what seemed to be a mêlée of cameras and dramatis personae, trying to discover the fixed point of the action. On the tenth day I was so desperate I told Donald that television drama was beyond me and asked could I be released from my three months' trial contract? He advised me to persevere – which I did, and one blissful afternoon, in the midst of episode three, I suddenly saw drama through the 'camera eye' of one person in the audience. I had learned to think through a camera lens, and I shouted aloud in triumph. From that point I was firmly in control.

Months later, during the actual run of *Villette*, I deeply appreciated the comment of Peter Black – with Maurice Wiggin one of the two critics then in circulation who actually knew something about the problems of studio floorspace and transmitting 'live'. He wrote:

On B.B.C. TV *Villette* continues to work its magic. Having at last caught up with Charlotte Brontë's book, I salute Ada F. Kay on a remarkable feat of distillation. In terms of problems faced and con-

157

quered, I suspect that none of the B.B.C.'s adaptations from classics has been more successful.

Television drama in the 1950s was transmitted live. Actors had to run from one set to another pursued by a retinue of wardrobe and make-up staff who might have to recostume and age them by ten years in some corner amongst cables and scenery supports. The writer's job was to provide cover during this obstacle race by creating a scene to engage cameras and boom upon a third set, which not only gave the artists time to change but also contributed to the dramatic structure of the play. One could not dissolve from one scene to a successive scene using the same set and the same faces. The use of filmed sequences was heavily discouraged; it was costly, but – worse – the difference in texture between studio shots and telecine showed on the screen. In place of film one used dramatic ingenuity, devising miracles in the form of montage, so that a hand holding a fan, a whisper between couples, a single swirling skirt could collectively build up the atmosphere of a great ball. When advising authors new to television (one of my official tasks), I used to say that it should be possible to create for the small screen the chariot race from *Ben Hur* using three revolving wheels, puffs of dust, a superimposed sound-track, and cross-cutting at an increasing tempo.

The announcement of pending arrival of coloured television – made at a meeting of technicians which included our script team – filled me with apprehension. I pointed out at a subsequent script meeting that one of our main problems would be to allow for costume changes; in black and white a few, small, altered details in dress gave the illusion of an entire change, but in colour this would be impossible. I was assured that by the time the colour process had been adopted, 'something would have been invented' to take care of such problems – which, of course, was to happen with the arrival of all the recording devices which contribute to the presentation of television drama as it is today.

Our work was not recorded and no trace of it today survives – even our scripts, I suspect, were long ago destroyed to make room for the work of new writers. For all that, I think we who served in the Old Brigade of the 1950s had one enormous advantage over our successors; we were experimenting in a medium still comparatively new, due to the interruption of the war years, and every problem tackled was an adventure. Once, I was given to adapt for television an old radio play of the middle twenties, and I, who had grown up with radio, was curiously moved to see in the script a dramatic instruction which was purely visual. I exclaimed to my colleagues, 'See, here's somebody who had our problem! We're the interim men who span the period between changing styles of warfare.'

158

Our small unit had all the characteristics – including eccentricity of dress (except in my own case, for I was female) – of a front-line army patrol, left much to its own device provided it achieved results. One of our main functions was to do a rescue operation wherever one of us was needed, either in one of the various departments at the centre or at studios in the regions. Due to the lack of suitable office accommodation at that period, we were allowed to work at home provided we were on immediate call. From the caravans we were moved out to a converted factory in the dark hinterland of Shepherd's Bush which we shared with Music Department and Religious Broadcasting. I termed us 'the outpost men'.

We worked always at top pressure. (A colleague once observed, 'When I'm told a script isn't urgent, I put it to the back of the pile, and by the time I get to it it *is* urgent.') The casualty rate due to overwork was at one time so high that I ventured to ask at our fortnightly script meeting whether a period of 'hospital time' could be written into our contract. Sick-leave was granted readily enough when we showed signs of failing, but, dedicated to our task, we did not ourselves always recognise when we needed it. Personally, I loved the atmosphere of perpetual urgency, my temperament responding to it. Eveything was urgent – even our short bursts of recreation, when a few of us chanced to meet on the same day in our offices and we all repaired to the local pub for an hour's session before hurtling home to resume our labours.

Our local was in Woodstock Grove, its name The Duke of Edinburgh. We were well known to the locals, who watched our plays and told us with engaging frankness what they thought of them. They made no pretence to know ought of technical matters, but they knew real drama from false and I valued their opinions. Talking to them, I invented the initials P.D.V. – Poor Dim Viewer – whom I kept in mind when I was writing. He was, in fact, anything but dim, and I worked on the assumption that I was myself the P.D.V. We had to work *up* to our audience, not down to it.

The only time the unit assembled in full force was at our fortnightly, Thursday script meetings where attendance was compulsory. There we gave a progress report upon our individual labours. These meetings, essentially business-like, were occasionally enlivened by dialogue so sparkling that I wished many times it could have been taped. Like gentlemen of fortune, we owed allegiance only to our work, through Donald and Michael Barry; the Corporation had our services, but it never owned us. It was to my mind an ideal arrangement. Not only was I working full-time as a writer, and for adequate remuneration, I was also a member of a team – and one which I loved and respected.

We had all established reputations before we came into television, either in the theatre or film world, so that we were grounded in drama

159

before we picked up television technique. Later, the new boys arrived who had not been so long-seasoned, and sometimes they shocked us with enquiries about dramatic strategy which we had known so long we had forgotten the rules we now applied unconsciously. (I once observed to Frank Baker, 'Thank God when I was young youth was unfashionable!' – the first time I had thought in those terms.) Pretension was discouraged. Only once did I engage in conversation about art in the abstract – with Frank Baker, who shared my horror of attaching grandiose labels to what was merely our job – and it was memorable for its depth of true feeling. Otherwise, discussion was of practicalities; size of studio, number of sets, and which cameras were available. A dishevelled figre bursting through a doorway, slurping tea-cup in hand, with some dire problem which others might have encountered was greeted with a mixture of practical suggestions and the type of hearty cruelty which sends a man back to pick up his fallen grenades.

The team had been hand-picked by Donald so that each of us could take over another's work at a moment's notice. We learned to pick up each other's creative thread so that no joints showed. Because we could, when required, think alike, we frequently felt with the same harmony. So closely knit, we responded in unison to any personal crisis affecting one of us. The death of a father or a wife evoked an immediate reaction; wasting no time on words, we all swung into positive action. When my turn came, it was the problem of 'Ada's wedding'.

In the beginning, Peter and I had not intended marriage, but throughout the hard times when he was qualifying as an architect and I was typing in those dreary offices we had become the mainstay of each other's life. When he proposed marriage and I accepted, we were as happy as two people can be at such a time. I realised that it would entail my settling in the south, but through Peter I had gradually come to regard London as home. All I asked was that I would not, when I died, be buried there. It was the promise I had already exacted from my mother, that if I died in London I would be taken north for burial – threatening, 'If you let me be buried in the south of England, I shall walk up the Great North Road in my shroud!' (Why I should specify, not once but several times, the Great North Road, which as I well knew was not the route to Lancashire, is a riddle I leave with my reader.)

I was to marry a Scot, albeit not a native. Born and educated in England, my Stewart fiancé had not at that time visited Scotland – an omission he hastened to repair before marrying me. With a friend he set out in September 1956 for a tour of Scotland. I felt it was right that his expedition should be undertaken without me, but when the time

160

came for their departure I found it unbearable to see them set off for my country leaving me in the south – so I arranged to go as near to the Border as my state of exile would allow, to my parents in Lancashire. Peter and John would visit us on their return journey down the west coast. Although our engagement was not yet official, my father realised that his daughter was being courted, and I had to stand a good many teasing references to 'Young Lochinvar coming out of the West.'

Young Lochinvar duly arrived, bringing me a gift. Before departing for Scotland he had asked me what I wanted, and I had specified 'a piece of heather from the Pentlands' to replace the sprig, now but a bare stem, which I had worn since 1947 inside a locket. I had been terribly disappointed to learn, by telephone, that my request had been impossible to meet, because it was the only reminder of Scotland that I truly wanted. As he put a parcel into my hands my happy, smiling, unofficially betrothed said that he hoped I would see the point of the tartan (it was hunting Stewart), a loving small joke which was lost on me.

I remember standing in the dining-room, frozen-faced, watched by four pairs of eyes as I slowly unwrapped it. Inside was a soldier doll with its eyes closed. It was to be years before I realised that its container represented a sentry box – what *I* saw was a dead Scots soldier lying in an open coffin. The walls of the room closed in upon me and there seemed to be years of silence before I wetted my lips to shape the words, 'Thank you.' Then, to everyone's embarrassment and consternation, I ran from the room clutching the ghastly object and raced upstairs. Safe in my bedroom, I thrust it to the back of a drawer and frantically buried it beneath layers of clothes, hearing as I did so the crescendo of my hoarse weeping.

After a while my mother came to find me. To get me downstairs, she bade me help her with the supper. In the kitchen she rebuked me, 'Your face! I have never felt so sorry for anyone as I did for Peter. He has come all this way, bringing a present to please you. Yes – *I* know you don't like souvenir dolls, but *he* didn't—' Then she broke off, realising that the tears gushing out of me were of the wrong kind to be caused by anything so small as a gift which I did not like. Dismayed, baffled, compassionate, she asked, 'Oh, *what is it, child*?' trying to put an arm about me as I sat on the kitchen stool, rocking in my alien anguish. The tears did not switch off as abruptly as usual, and I was still weeping when I said, 'Mother, he's asked me to marry him, and I've said yes. But I can't marry him *now*.'

My mother's perplexity showed in her face, but she knew after twenty-seven years' experience that there were areas of my psyche best left unexplored. Her obvious, safe course was to recall me to my sense of duty to others, a plea which never failed. 'Ada, we have guests. Now wipe your face. Take the cheese and biscuits to the table. Say thank you to Peter, and apologise to them all for having left the room so abruptly. We are not having supper spoiled. Ada, *do you hear me?*' I always heard her when she spoke in that voice. Dumbly I nodded, grateful to obey, not to have to think about it and, head high, tears dried, I went into the dining-room with the cheese and biscuits. Forcing a pasteboard smile, I thanked Peter for the doll and apologised for having 'to rush off to the loo'. I knew that none of them believed me – how could they, when even I was aware of the dead and empty eyes above my smile. ('Oh God, she's caught your dead look,' my mother once said of a portrait drawn of me at the age of twenty-two.)

Next morning I waved off Young Lochinvar and John, returning to London myself on the following day. But the coffined doll I left in Lancashire, buried at the back of the drawer. It was never mentioned again and only by putting the episode out of my mind could I resume my previous, happy relationship with Peter. On subsequent visits to my parents, if ever I disinterred the doll by accident I would immediately re-bury it. Strangely, I could not dispose of it because it was identified with myself.

In the December of 1956 we once again went north to ask my father's consent to the marriage, intending the journey to be one which we would remember for a lifetime. It was – though not in the way envisaged. We travelled through the worst fog that the guard on the train could recall in all his experience. We were two hours late at Crewe where a mechanical fault delayed us further. My beloved and I sat in the dining-car and ordered another brandy to sustain our prenuptial mood – but supplies of alcohol had run out. We had instead more coffee – then supplies of coffee failed. Five hours later the train chugged faintly on its way to Preston. When the heating system broke down, Peter remarked morosely that the next thing to go would be the lights.

Our teeth were chattering as we pulled into Preston, but of course our connection had long since departed so we had to go on to Blackpool where the Central Station was closed and all taxis had disappeared for the night. Young Lochinvar and his intended bride finally reached Thornton Cleveleys on the 7.30 a.m. workmen's tram. At 8.30 a.m. we collapsed at the parental door with the suitcases we had carried from the distant tram stop. As I blearily helped my mother to fry bacon, instead of steak, and swapped the cheese-board for a dish of marmalade, I left my betrothed and my father together in the dining-room. I half expected that by this time my fiancé would have changed his mind, and if my father had said no to a suitor who had kept him up all night I could not have blamed him. However, all parties were happy, and we celebrated the betrothal with an untimely glass of sherry before breakfast and Peter's departure home to Jersey to acquaint his parents with the news.

As my mother and I trudged through a candle-yellow fog to procure the last of the Christmas Eve shopping, she said, 'I do hope Peter's all right.' We learned later that his flight was grounded at Ringway Airport and he spent Christmas night marooned in Manchester! That he still wanted to marry me after these misadventures shows the stamina of our affections.

Sometime in March 1957, on a cold day which should have been spring, we set out upon one of our day-excursions which were invariably smitten by disaster. We had made a late start and our destination was decided for us by a railway timetable. We took the train to Dover. For me the horror began somewhere in Kent where the train paused briefly in a cutting between green-smeared white chalk walls. I began to shiver as an icy chill pervaded my body and my holiday spirits were snuffed out, leaving intolerable depression in their wake. (Afterwards, I came to describe this particular sensation as 'the smell of grave-damp in the bones of my soul'.) I broke off our conversation and sat silent. The sun was shining outside the carriage window, but it was grey and cold to me. Farther along the track we passed whitish piles of soil on the embankment. I cried with sudden revulsion, 'I hate Kent! How can anything grow in soil like that?' Peter looked at me in surprise. I gestured towards the banks. 'Look at it! – like piles of road chippings left by untidy workmen. I loathe chalk soil. It's so *dead*.' Then I was shaken with violent sobbing.

At first Peter tried to laugh me out of it. Then he became angry with me for spoiling our day. He could not fathom what was the matter with me: nor could I. When he suddenly drew my attention to Canterbury cathedral in the distance, bathed in sunlight, I said, 'How lovely!' Then I came back to the point: 'You won't let them bury me in southern England, will you?' He was so taken aback he almost laughed. He gave me his promise and added that I did pick some odd subjects for conversation. I dashed away my tears, trying to smile, but I kept to my theme, hard and determined: I told him that unless I could be *certain* that I would go back north for burial in good, black, peat soil, I would call off our marriage. He humoured me, saying that I could leave instructions in my will, and if it mattered so much he would leave instructions in his will that, if he died before me, I was to be parcelled up and sent back to Scotland; would that do?

I nodded, speechless – so happy and grateful that my tears splashed on his hand.

He was accustomed by this time to my foibles: that we had ranged against us enormous, unknown problems of which these were simply warning signals was something to which we never gave a thought. Young and in love, why should we?

3

THE FIRST SIGN OF REAL TROUBLE APPEARED WHEN WE WERE PLANNING the date of our marriage. In the beginning I had a happy, hazy notion that our wedding would be in October, followed by the honeymoon in Finland we had discussed during the early days of our betrothal. Mine had to be an October wedding – I had always said that – because October was my happy month, marking my regeneration after the August to September cycle of depression which I had now come to identify as my 'dying time'.

When my fiancé mentioned one evening the likelihood of an August marriage, I fled to my room in panic. Thereafter he had the greatest difficulty in pinning me down to any discussion of our wedding plans. With parents and friends constantly reminding me that churches, hotels and honeymoons have to be booked well in advance, I charged ahead with my work at the B.B.C. using that as my excuse to postpone thinking about my wedding.

One night Peter waylaid me in his room, closed the door firmly, and said that we were going to fix the date of our marriage that night. We had already, he pointed out, lost our chance of going to Finland due to my dilatory approach and at the current rate of progress there would be no wedding unless we moved fast. I said, 'October.' I begged for October, and was told that October was out of the question. We had to find a date which fitted both our work schedules, for architects' contracts, like television programmes, are planned a long way ahead. A comparison of our respective diaries revealed that we had but two dates available to us, and both were in August.

I pleaded 'Not August! Please, not August!'

He asked what was wrong with August?

I told him, 'It won't work. An August wedding *doesn't work!*'

My visible dread caused my fiancé to pause. He had by this time lost his initial scepticism towards my 'hunches', for he had seen so many of them proved true. The purely practical problem remained, however, that if we did not wed in the August we could not be married at all that year with time available for a honeymoon which fitted in with Peter's annual holiday. He pointed out that the important thing was to get married. Did it matter which month of the year?

His rejoinder made it difficult for me to argue. I could not tell him why I saw an August marriage as being doomed, for I did not myself know why. Yet the association of the words 'marriage' and 'August' flashed red warning signals in my head like a traffic indicator. It is extremely difficult for a rational person to present a groundless argument – I tried and failed. By this time Peter was growing angry and threatening to call the whole thing off. I was sorry for him, and guilty because I felt that I was being difficult. In the end I mouthed my acceptance of the date 31 August.

Restored to good humour, my betrothed began making plans with all the eagerness of a happy potential bridegroom. I sat deep in my chair, icy-cold and all but silent, nodding at appropriate intervals. Noticing my lack of response, he reminded me that it was our wedding and asked me not to look so sad about it. I did my best to smile. Later, when I left his room, I asked one final time, 'Is there no way it could be October?' At this he began to show exasperation, and I went up to my room quietly, leaving him at the door with a flat, hopeless, 'I know it can't work.'

That discussion marked the end of my joy in the marriage. Until that time I had accepted cheerfully the fact that marrying Peter entailed my living in London for a large part of my life. Now all that changed. A chain of ideas formed in my head: August – marriage – *alliance with England*. I seemed no longer to be marrying a husband but a *place*. We would be buying a house in London where our children would be born and reared. I wanted children, but not *English*-thinking children. There was fixed in my mind a certainty that any child born of me and London-orientated constituted a danger to Scotland.

I told myself that, if I ignored them, these ridiculous anxieties would go away, as they had come, of their own accord.

The wedding had to be in London for the sake of convenience, and my parents were anxiously awaiting my visit to Lancashire to discuss the arrangements. My mother became concerned as time passed and I showed no initiative. It was true that I was heavily laden with work – my adaptation of *Villette* was scheduled to begin transmission in July – but most people (even in the central script section) can find time to get married if they try. I did not wish to discuss it. I had grown terrified of 'all those people' gathered to see my nuptials – I could see them at night, in pictures before my eyes when I was trying to get to sleep, or they populated dreams – enormous crowds of people gathered in the streets and at upper windows, all jostling to catch a glimpse of me because it was *their day*; not mine.

After one such terrible night I awoke with an idea fixed in my head which seemed to offer the only hope of success. If the two of us, with two witnesses, could go informally into a church early one morning to be married privately, I believed that we could save the situation. I hurried up to Lancashire with the new idea.

It met with no favour. I was the only nubile female which either side had produced, so I had to let them see me as a bride. I could not even plead that I disliked ceremony and dressing up, for that was not true and everyone knew it. I was no modest violet, and they had all been

165

expecting me to want festivities so lavish that I would need to be told to trim my guest-list by at least a thousand. I hoped fleetingly that I might find an ally in my father, on the grounds that it is usually the men who prefer unobtrusive weddings, and I tried to confide my fears in the privacy of his den. But what, truly, had I to tell him? His answer was that my mother would be disappointed if I did not have a proper wedding.

I returned from Lancashire having secured only a compromise – the assurance that the guest-list would be limited to members of the family. Throughout the entire debate I had not once asserted my will in the formidable way for which I was renowned. I accepted this doomed August marriage *as though it had already happened*, and I assumed that I was merely seeing the future.

Had there been opportunity for quiet reflection I might have seen what I was doing, but in my action-packed job at the B.B.C. and the turmoil of city life there was neither the time nor the quiet in which to think. Also, I was in London, in an environment where I no longer heeded the inward promptings which had always, until now, shaped my destiny. Now I was trying to rationalise everything in the urban way, and viewed at that level my fiancé was eligible and I loved him. We had lived in close association for three years, so neither of us was taking a leap into the dark. *I had no grounds for panic.* Yet as the wedding drew nearer I grew more despondent and apprehensive.

Then fate introduced a digression – whether to help or hinder, I cannot say. One afternoon during the production of *Villette* I was required to write some extra lines of covering dialogue for a lengthy costume change, and instead of returning to my remote office, I was offered by the producer a spare room in the television centre. I found it occupied by an assistant floor manager typing prop lists. As he made to depart I recognised him as a fellow actor from Morecambe. During the ensuing glad exchange of news he said, 'Do you know that Leonard is in London . . .?' giving me the name of the production in which he was participating. The upshot of all this was that I spent a terrible afternoon wondering whether I ought to see my old friend, and finally, when I had poured out my troubles to one of my colleagues, he swept me off to the theatre that evening to see the show and meet my friend afterwards. The three of us went out together for a drink, and, though conversation was general, the spiritual link remained as ever.

I went home in a cab alone, wondering how to tell Peter we must stop the marriage. His tower room showed a chink of light when I entered the hall, so I tapped on the door to be greeted with huge relief and the demand to know where I had been.

I sat on his bed and said, 'Look, I can't marry you.'

Having heard me say this before, he was about to brush it aside when he realised that this time my voice held a more determined note, so he asked me what had happened.

I told him of my meeting that evening – he knew the important role Leonard had played in my life. As we talked, I realised that the threat of 'the other man' was something he could appreciate; unlike my usual reasons for panic, this one had identifiable substance. My fiancé began to look worried. Then, as he pressed for more detail, I was obliged to confess that the question of 'the other man' had not really arisen. At this his face cleared, as he saw no real obstacle to our marriage. For me it was different: I had just seen quite plainly that in my current state of turmoil I was unwise to think of marrying anybody. I asked if we could postpone the wedding for six months. He asked how we could possibly do that.

The church had been bespoken, the hotel booked for the reception and the invitations had gone out. Wedding plans can be cancelled in an emergency, given good reason, but mine was not; also, we had an additional commitment. For the first year of our marriage we were renting a flat in Leicester Square belonging to a friend of mine who was going on a long visit to the United States. I had agreed to move into the flat before Diana left, so that she could instruct me in the idiosyncracies of the property before her departure – which meant that I had to be there three weeks in residence so that my banns could be called as a spinster in the parish of St Martin-in-the-Fields as required by law. I had already given a month's notice to our landlord in Belsize Park, and my successor was waiting to move into my bed-sitting-room when I vacated it at the end of that very week. I began to realise how deeply I was trapped.

I never really had a chance to talk again with my fiancé. I removed from Belsize Park two or three days later, hoping that when I moved into the new flat I would see the marriage in perspective. Instead, I took the nightmare with me. The conviction that I was making a disastrous mistake was balanced all the time by the extraordinary certainty that it had to happen. It has to be remembered that my fiancé's name was Stewart. I knew it as my name. I had always known it as my name. Beyond that point reasoning failed me.

My efforts to escape provoked Peter to say one night (when we had an hour to ourselves) that if I could look him in the eyes and say that I did not love him, he would let me go. I looked him in the eyes, and cried, 'But I do love you!' So he told me that there was nothing to worry about, was there? – and took me in his arms. I can remember staring over his shoulder, devoid utterly of hope, and saying soothingly, 'No, of course not. . . .'

My nuptial problem had by this time overflowed on to everyone, and even the studios were filled with it. As we neared the end of July my desperation became so apparent that the leading actress in *Villette* said during camera rehearsal, 'I have borrowed a villa in the South of France for a holiday at the end of *Villette*. If you want to get out of the marriage you can come to France with me.' At the mention of France a sudden, remembered flame of hope leaped in me, and I cried, 'Do you mean it?' She said, 'Of course.' But by the end of rehearsal I had to tell her, 'I've promised to marry my fiancé. I can't let him down.' She left the option open, but I knew I would not go.

It was this terrible sense of duty – to my fiancé, to my family, to everyone expecting the marriage – which held me to the end. I was *conditioned* to accept my role as the reluctant protagonist: I had lived all my life in the shadow of 'that marriage with England'.

We still had a terrible job to get me to the altar. That I had even a wedding dress was due entirely to my matron of honour, who, with ten days to go, frog-marched me round the West End in search of my trousseau. In the first shop I asked for 'something suitable to wear at a wedding'. Joan looked daggers at me and hissed, 'You might at least mention that you are the *bride*.'

In the end she did the talking, and I stayed mute. I refused to go near the bridal-wear departments. Eventually I was shown an elegant, ballet-length gown of pearl satin banded with oyster-coloured lace – it was so much like me that I would have bought it in any case; it had just arrived from Paris, and had not yet been priced. As the saleswoman went away to discover the cost, I said to Joan – for the first time with some animation – 'It will make a marvellous cocktail dress afterwards.' To which she replied, 'Let's get you married in it first, shall we?' We bought the rest of my trousseau in two hours. The item I liked best was a raincoat which my fiancé described as looking 'like an army great coat' and made me take back to the shop.

The friend who owned the flat had now departed to America, and it was Molly, my bed-sitting neighbour from Belsize Park, who was appointed to guard me overnight and ensure that I did actually reach the church. At 8 a.m. she came in with a cup of tea for me, and began to pack my clothes. She admonished me, 'You can't go on your honeymoon with that old handbag! You must have a new one. I'll see what I can do at Swan & Edgar's.' Before she left she poured me a large glass of sherry and said, 'Drink that! And promise me you'll still be here when I come back, because I gave my word to your mother and to Peter that I'd see you reached that wedding.'

I drank half a bottle of Dry Fly sherry while Molly dressed me. Then, all but hat and veil, I was shepherded into the taxi. My parents were staying at the hotel in Belsize Park where the reception was to be. Molly's task was to deliver me there, and then she was free to go home to the West Country for the weekend.

We sat through a series of traffic jams all the way to the hotel. Each time the taxi stopped people on the pavement waved to me. I raised my hand and bowed in response – I seemed to *expect* this would happen. Then, at some point, I realised there was something curious about the reception and said to Molly, 'Why are they waving? It's not a bridal car and I'm not dressed in white.' Molly, her eyes on her watch, said grimly, 'They probably think you need cheering up!'

In one traffic jam at Camden Town we stopped for a long time outside the Underground station. Molly must have read my eye, because she caught my hem and said, 'You can't jump now, you'll be run over.' Just for a moment my mind held a map of the Underground, as seen in the carriages, and the name 'King's Cross' leaped out of my memory. A train from King's Cross. . . . Molly released her hold when the taxi began to move.

My parents' suite at the hotel contained a great mirror above the fireplace. I stood before it gazing into the deadest eyes I ever saw. My long-ago school friend, Amy, moved across to me to arrange my hat and veil – and suddenly I broke down and cried to my mother and my father, to Amy, to everyone, 'Please stop it! Stop this wedding. It can't work. I know it can't!' And the tears rolled down my beautifully made-up face.

There was silence. I looked round the battery of eyes of people who had known me for a lifetime, all staring and uncomfortable, all compassionate, but I saw no flicker of help to save me anywhere.

My mother said, 'Oh dear, and I did so want to be the mother of a happy bride' – which caused me to screech at her, *'Whose wedding is this?'* Brought back to her duty, she recalled me, more quietly, to mine. 'Ada, you can't let Peter down in front of all these people. Give it six months and if it doesn't work, you can get a divorce.' This from my mother who was happily married and did not believe in divorce was astonishing: what she did not know, in her sweet ignorance, was that divorce takes far longer than does the ceremony of marriage.

I arrived at the church, and there is somewhere a photograph of me being assisted from the carriage by my father, and my face behind the short, oyster-coloured veil is so serenely beautiful that I can scarcely believe that it was myself upon that hellish day. My cascade of orchids to match my dress had been mounted on skeleton leaves the colour of oyster-shell: when I saw it, I asked my mother to take it home to put on Sheila's grave. To me a wedding and a grave belonged together.

At the church door I learned that the organist had gone missing on a train in Wales, and had telegraphed his apology for being late. The vicar said we would give him half an hour, and then, if necessary, proceed without him. So our guests sat in their pews like dried-out ducks, while I was escorted to the rectory to await events. On my way round the corner of the church, I came face to face with my bridegroom and his best man — and I screamed and fled as my intended husband, all smiles, jokingly declared that surely I was not superstitious. Normally I am not, but I had doubts aplenty without a surfeit of bad omens in addition.

In the rectory my father and the vicar discovered a mutual interest in ecclesiastical photography, so the two of them went away to look at some photographs in the vicar's study. Warded only by my matron of honour, I sat stately in the drawing-room, my eyes on the french windows and beyond them the narrow strip of churchyard bounded only by a low wall. . . . Joan, desperate to obey the call of nature, bent her eye upon me, saying, 'Ada, I'll have to find the bathroom. Promise me you won't run away while I'm gone. *Promise me*.' Like a fool, I gave my promise, but what else could I do with her in her predicament?

As a last, cruel irony, as I sat with the unlocked french window before me, I saw beyond that low wall a cruising taxi for hire. Three times he circled the church, passing that window. . . . And there was in me a leaping instinct to run out through the rectory window, hitch my skirt to vault that wall, and get into the taxi. Asked, 'Where to?' I would have been nonplussed, except for an urge to say 'King's Cross Station. And hurry.' Home to liberty! — but where was home to a fugitive in oyster-lace-banded pearl satin with a shower bouquet of orchids? I had been south so long I had forgotten my orientation. All I could remember was that life began at King's Cross. But I had no money on me. (A bridegroom at least has trouser pockets, which may explain why traditionally more grooms than brides fail to arrive at the altar.) Anyway, I had given Joan my solemn promise. . . .

I was still in my chair, hope now dead, when she opened the door with a fervent, 'Thank God you're still here!' She confessed she had been afraid of returning to find me gone. I told her that I would have been gone, but for my promise.

The organist returned from Wales with ten minutes to spare. Had he been late *efficiently* there could have been a crisis in the programme sufficient to allow me to have hysterics, a nervous breakdown, anything to save me from that marriage with England. As it was, I walked up the aisle on my father's arm with an expression on my face which caused my husband to reproach me at the end of the day with having walked to the altar looking as though I were going to the execution block.

I stood at the altar rail repeating 'till death us do part' with eyes upcast and a frantic inward cry, 'Please God, pay no attention to this vow, because I cannot mean it . . .!' Then a cold ring slipped over my knuckle.

In the vestry I caused consternation by signing the register in my

170

maiden name. Treating the error lightly, I said, 'Oh sorry! I must have thought I was signing a cheque' – a silly explanation, but it was the only one which came to me. The signature was crossed out, and I wrote carefully Ada Florence Stewart, the initial F shaping itself like a J as it had done ever since my return from Scotland in 1947.

I got through the reception, being charming where required. I left with my hair uncovered, full of brandy and champagne, knowing that the awfulness could not be real and that tomorrow I would awaken.

For our honeymoon we were going to Paris. Realising at the last minute that we were too tired to travel, a friend booked an overnight room for us at the Black Swan in Thames Ditton. We arrived at Thames Ditton to find no transport available. Together we lugged two suitcases from the station to the inn, where late booking had caused us to be given a remote chamber in the medieval part of the building. I was too tired to eat and crawled to my bed asking Peter to order for me some hot milk. Sleepily, I heard him in the distance speaking to a waitress, and the firm use of the words 'for my wife' brought a pang of warmth, the first I had felt that day. He dined alone, I drank the milk and fell asleep, exhausted, still believing that it was all a bad dream and that in the morning I would awaken.

Alas, for once I had disobeyed my instinct, and I wakened in the grey light of that first September day to realise that I was *married*. I wished I could have touched my husband's hand for reassurance, but we had separate beds due to the shortage of accommodation. I saw the outline of his slumbering form in the light of dawn, and he seemed very far away. I wept softly in the quiet.

For a moment I had some kind of recollection of another marriage, but long ago, when I had felt like this. . . . But I knew that was impossible.

4

THROUGHOUT ALL THESE EVENTS *The Man from Thermopylae* kept pace with me like my own shadow. In March 1957 it was transmitted on Radio Free Europe to Czechoslovakia. In May it was repeated by the B.B.C. On 7 November it was broadcast in Germany, preceded by a four-minute introductory talk by the author which was taped and sent to Hamburg. (My extraneous German qualification had outlet!) In January 1958 it was broadcast a second time in Germany; in March it was heard in Canada; in April repeated yet again in Germany. It went on the air in the Netherlands; in Norway; in South Africa and Australia. For the French production, to conform with French broadcasting requirements, I became a member of Le Société des Ecrivants et d'Auteurs Dramatiques. (One of my B.B.C. colleagues, also a member of the Société, thought we two should have some kind of order ribbon to wear at script meetings.) *The Man from Thermopylae* had done rather well for itself, in addition bringing me, by letter, many friends in all parts of the world.

My cotton famine television play, *Red Rose for Ransom*, had fared less happily. Constructed originally for a seventy-five-minute slot, allowing time for captions, the theme could be accommodated. (I used to observe bitterly of Programme Planning Department, 'It wouldn't matter what you wrote, if it ran exact to a second they'd call you a genius.') On the night my play was scheduled for transmission, the Queen was addressing a regimental dinner. The length of royal speeches being more elastic, my play was dropped from schedule on the eve of production. I spat blood. The seventy-five-minute series then ended, and I was asked to cut back my play to sixty minutes. This would entail eliminating all the light relief, leaving nothing but stark tragedy. However, as there was no plan to restore a seventy-five-minute series within the foreseeable future, I cut the play, and it was scheduled for transmission in the sixty-minute series. When I learned, subsequently, that the seventy-five-minute slot *would* be reintroduced, I could not face the task of 'writing in' fifteen minutes' worth of new material, my original text having gone into the wastepaper basket. So I let it remain at sixty. On 12 August 1958 *Red Rose for Ransom* finally reached the screen.

Back streets of Darwen still extant were photographed for use by the scenic designers, and two ancient Blackburn gaslamps of the period were 'brought out of retirement' (to quote the Press). When I saw the set in the Manchester studios, even I who knew the tricks of the trade in creating atmosphere had the sense that I was back in the real streets of Darwen in the 1860s when hunger stalked the cobbles. For the interval music Ewan McColl recorded an unaccompanied rendering of 'The Four-loom Weaver', a song written during the famine years. The cadaverous faces, the melancholy clip-clop of clogs on cobbles, and the lone voice of the proud craftsman singing of his plight as an unemployed recipient of poor relief contributed realism beyond my expectations.

It was savagely mauled by the Press for its 'unrelieved gloom' and 'lack of light relief'. One does not write explanatory letters to newspapers about those lost fifteen minutes; but what I had to say in private about regimental dinners and programme planners remains unprintable. To my comfort, I had a considerable number of sympathetically angry letters criticising the critics, some from notable members of my own profession; in the theatre abuse is an occupational hazard one learns to live with.

*

If one has to live in London, one may as well live at its heart. Our furnished flat was five floors up, commanding a view of bird migration from the roof of the English National Gallery. I did not watch television unless I had to; my favourite viewing was from our living-room window whence could be obtained a glimpse of almost every historic landmark in London. My classic scoop was the sight of a cub-mistress leading her pack along Irving Street in search of a suitable restaurant: all I saw of them was a gyrating motion of circular cub hats looking so much like the dancing coolie-mushrooms in the film *Fantasia* that my shrieks of joy brought my husband rushing to the window. Our part of the parish of St Martin-in-the-Fields consisted of about one hundred residents, tucked away in eyries and tunnels where nobody suspected our existence. Most of us knew each other, either through professional connections or because we met on Saturday afternoons when shopping in New Row, which we had to ourselves when the office workers had returned to their suburbs, a perfect village high street. The shops were small family businesses, some kept by people who had retained their native accent like the Welsh brothers who had the dairy. There was even a small shop which, in the village tradition, appeared to stock everything from fly-papers to reels of Sylko. When meeting one's neighbours, usual topics of conversation were pigeons, garbage-collection, late-night revellers, milk pinched from the doorstep, and derelict lift-shafts. I have never lived in a village more parochial than Leicester Square. Going to early Sunday communion at St Martin's, I passed a totally deserted Trafalgar Square to join our 8 a.m. score of local communicants. On my way back, I collected Sunday papers from the news vendor on the corner and enquired about his family. Anything which happened as far away as Tottenham Court Road or the Embankment was 'foreign affairs' to us.

My memories of life in Leicester Square are mixed; great gaiety, much stress. Stress predominates. My husband's parents left Jersey, coming to stay with us until they found a flat in town. The apartment was too small to accommodate four people when two of us required working space, so I worked in the living-room at night when everyone had gone to bed. No sooner had the in-laws moved out than Diana announced her return from America earlier than planned. We went out house-hunting.

Friends of mine found us a furnished flat in St George's Square S.W.1., to which we moved in the summer of 1958. 'My' Dorothy, whom Diana had engaged for me at Leicester Square before I was married, came with me. My domestic life depended entirely on Dorothy. She cleaned for me, sewed for me, watered my plants, did the ironing, shopped for me, and took my letters to post. She could be

173

relied upon to plan a menu at short notice, choose wines and, when necessary, cook and serve it. She dressed me, mothered me, scolded me and put me to bed when I was ill. From the first my husband referred to her as 'your Dorothy'; she treated us both with equal firmness and respect, but I was 'her' Mrs Stewart.

Peter and I, tied by our work, never had time for illness. One teatime he came home early, and became quite savage when I pointed out that he had flu. I knew better than to argue. A few minutes later I heard a firm, 'Now Mr Stewart . . .' and to my surprise, when I went into the bedroom, I found Peter, red-faced with fury, sitting up in bed. Cosseted with hot-water bottles and suitable potions, he roundly cursed 'my' Dorothy. I burst out laughing and fled. Dorothy was in the kitchen, cooking. She said, 'Mrs Stewart, I don't like that cough of yours. . . .' I protested that it was nothing, and I had to finish a script. Five minutes later I was tucked in bed beside my husband with my allotment of medicaments and hot-water bottles. We fumed together as Dorothy departed with a stern, 'And let me catch *neither* of you getting out of bed.' Even when the final door-slam announced her departure back to her wee flat in the City, neither of us dared move. We laughed for half an hour at our mutual plight, but move from that bed we dare not until Dorothy authorised our release.

My husband and I were at our happiest when both of us were on 'night shift'. He working at his drawing-board, I in another room busy at my typewriter, we each seemed to sense when the other needed a break for tea or coffee. One of us would steal softly to the kitchen to make it, and then enter with the steaming cups saying, 'Feel like a break?' We gave ourselves ten or twenty minutes, during which conversation was a delicate concerto upon quality in art, or moral philosophy, beautifully controlled by both of us so that neither lost the thread of the work that he or she was doing. . . . It was the closest working harmony I had ever shared with anyone. Temporary occupants of the flat upstairs, from America, designated us 'the working Stewarts'. The 'working Stewarts' were, alas, working themselves into the ground and out of a marriage.

The first real break in my health occurred at a most inopportune time. I had suddenly had an inspiration to write a play conceived purely in terms of television. It was a pattern of overlapping human lives, their dialogue, present and past history, linked only by the eye of the camera and an eavesdropping microphone. It was highly experimental for those days and its potential was immediately recognised, even before I had the rough draft completed.

The producer and I had to decide whether we should take advantage of a time-slot available at Bristol (the smallest studio with the least up-to-date equipment) with a camera team well known to us, or wait for the largest studio (H) at Lime Grove and risk missing the camera team we wanted. It was a script requiring ample floor space for camera manoeuvres and the most modern equipment, but everything ultimately depended upon the collaboration of the technicians. We might wait years for a large studio and a camera team so enthusiastic to become available simultaneously. Remembering the fiasco of my two-year wait for *Red Rose for Ransom* to reach the screen, I declared that I would risk my luck at Bristol. I said I would have the script ready in time.

I worked for five consecutive days and four nights, then I broke down. I laid the mass of script on the producer's desk and said, 'Can you hack it out of this? My doctor has ordered me off for three weeks' rest.'

The technique I was applying required the writer to stay on the job to the last moment for the sake of the cameramen. That we had committed ourselves to produce the play in a studio with limited resources would not have mattered if I had been there to amend the script where necessary to match the producer's requirements. That the play reached the screen at all was a miracle, but I was left haunted by the feeling that I had failed everyone at the critical moment. *No Through Line* was, in fact, moderately successful, but it could have been sensational had my own physical resources lasted out.

I never properly recovered after that experience.

In March 1959, when I was thirty, *The Man from Thermopylae* was presented in a festival of contemporary drama at the state theatre in Rheydt, Germany. The adaptation from radio to stage was made by the German producer. I tried hard to get to Germany to see it, but I was too busy and too ill. The theatre sent me a set of superb photographs and the programme. My theme had been treated as I intended, linking past with present in terms of human responsibility: an illustration of an ancient Spartan helmet inside the programme, and on its cover the photograph of an anonymous German schoolboy weighed down beneath a soldier's uniform and greatcoat, his face blubbering child's tears. Beneath was the caption: *Ein Dokument aus dem zweiten Weltkrieg: wird der Sechzehnjährige jemals vergessen können?* (A document of the Second World War: will the sixteen-year-old ever be able to forget?)

Looking at the eyes I wondered, 'Which battlefield is he still seeing?' I kept the programme near me, feeling an extraordinary affinity with that sixteen-year-old forced to become a man before his time. He seemed to be trying to tell me something about *myself*, but I was not sure what. Those days so many things disturbed me for reasons I could not pin down. Everything seemed to be more difficult since I became Ada F. Stewart, that initial F more like a J than ever. Furthermore,

175

now that my name actually was Stewart, I insisted more desperately upon being styled Miss Kay. For some complex, contradictory reason, the survival of my relationship with my husband depended upon my not using the name Stewart. I was safer as Ada F. Kay, author of *The Man from Thermopylae* – the soldier condemned by the gods to return to life bearing the memory of the battlefield where he had 'died'.

5

AT THE BEGINNING OF 1959 MY COLLEAGUE AND STABLE-MATE Frank Baker left the central script section for a three-month sabbatical and a new member of the team arrived to share my office. Alistair was to spend six months with us before being posted to Glasgow. He had travelled widely, but the strong Scots voice of the Lothians and the dour humour had not left him. Usually I worked at home so that whoever shared my office had it mostly to himself, but the impact of that Scots presence in the room disturbed in me awareness of another reality, far from London, now all but forgotten. He was the Scot homeward bound, the man who took the night train out from King's Cross Station.

My own contract was due to expire in the July, after which, as a freelance on a B.B.C. writer's contract (which guaranteed four commissioned plays per year), I should be free to go where I pleased. The thought of this freedom frightened me. For as long as I was required to attend script meetings at Shepherd's Bush, London had a hold on me – and so had my marriage.

My husband's roots in London were taking hold more deeply just as mine were breaking. He was going into private practice in 1959, and we were planning to buy a house in Hampstead for which all the real enthusiasm came from his side, not mine. I wanted a home of my own, but not in the south of England. I pretended enthusiasm and feigned disappointment on two occasions when attempts at purchase failed, but inwardly I felt each time a sense of reprieve. I did not even go to look at the properties, though I would be paying the mortgage deposit from my royalties. I was tired of life in furnished flats – I felt that renting a flat was economic nonsense – but as long as I owned no abiding mansion in the south of England I still belonged to the north. My link with the north provided my sole guarantee that when I died my body would go there for burial. Peter's pre-nuptial promises were all very well, but London-born children could not be relied upon to understand how deeply it mattered to me. I made no will to safeguard my remains, for I had always known that the disposal of my body was in the hands of other people.

On a day whe a Birmingham producer (with whom I had worked but never met) stalked through the building to discover whether 'that elusive woman Ada F. Kay really did exist' the two of us went to The Duke of Edinburgh for a noggin. Within minutes there arrived Alistair with *his* current producer, down from Glasgow, and for the first time since 1947 I heard the perfect, clipped English of a native Gaelic speaker. The sound of those two different Scots voices talking in The Duke of Edinburgh brought alive in me the awareness of Scotland which the years in London had almost, but never quite, obliterated.

Some days later, when working at home, I was seized by a sudden impulse to go to Shepherd's Bush, though there was nothing there requiring my attention. I called on the boys, dictated a couple of letters, then, as I was leaving, I went back to my office to pick up a script and this time found Alistair at his desk, sighing over a script he was to do for Glasgow. He asked, 'How's your Gaelic?' I went to peer over his shoulder. My Gaelic consisted of a few words acquired during my army days, but the sight of those few phrases scattered through the text brought back the memory of a spoken language that *I had once known*. The play was about fishing boats. It was all so much my world that the next day I suggested to Alistair that we swapped scripts – he could have *French Without Tears* in exchange for the Scottish play, subject to official approval. The exchange was duly made, and I set to work upon the play for Glasgow. Then came the day when my secretary booked my flight to Renfrew.

Peter and I had both worked hard the night before I left for Glasgow. Since I was travelling, I took an hour's sleep and he took turn of duty to waken me at the appointed time and cook my breakfast. I do not think we had ever had a domestic interlude more harmonious. I had never travelled by air before whereas he was accustomed to it and, having bestowed appropriate advice, he went to make me a second cup of coffee. I can remember sitting painting my nails in the drawing-room, while he was busy in the kitchen, and thinking, I am never coming back, with a terrible mixture of elation and guilt – guilt because I could not tell him what I was thinking.

As the plane lifted into the clouds above Heathrow Airport, I can remember all my ties and worries falling from me. Above the clouds, I looked down on those ephemeral fields of snow and thought how irrelevant was England below me. As we touched down at Renfrew I felt the final bump of Scots ground beneath me and put a hand across my mouth to stop the other self who wanted to cry and sing and shout with exultation. On the bus to Glasgow I stared out at the grey streets with their Scots names above shop windows, and not just one but *every* door seemed to open to me as I passed.

I worked on the script in Glasgow – a challenge to any adaptor transferring it to television – and stayed so long that there came a laconic message from Shepherd's Bush to ask if I had 'gone missing in the Celtic twilight'. On the night before I left for London I was taken through to Edinburgh to present my adaptation to the author of the play for her approval. As we drove over the Dean Bridge into Edinburgh I saw in the late afternoon sunlight the curving bow of the back of Ainslie Terrace above the froth of green trees edging the Water of Leith, and something crashed awake in my head – so I snapped at my companion, who was speaking, 'Oh, do be quiet a minute!' I was watching the sun on stone, as I had remembered it across a dozen years' exile, and some huge part of me was crying with inward astonishment, 'What on earth am *I* doing, living in the south of England?'

I went back to London armed with the courage to be brutal and knowing how I intended to break the news – as gently as I could, in the evening when we had finished dinner. But I had to leave a suitcase at the flat before continuing in my taxi to Shepherd's Bush, and I walked into the drawing-room to find my husband there, when I had expected him to be at his office. He was engrossed in calculations, and he leaped to his feet when I entered the room with the glad news that we had at last acquired our own house. I had no other way to say it then but to blurt out, 'I'm sorry – but I'm leaving you.'

I had formed while in Glasgow an attachment to a Scot and in explanation I made a good deal of this, for I had now recognised that, whereas my husband could understand that I might choose to leave him for another man, he could not comprehend why I should leave him for another *country*. I had him convinced initially, and then as we talked the thinness of my ground became apparent. The attachment offered no future – just the reverse, in fact, for it would have to be severed to enable me to go to Scotland. And I was going to Edinburgh where I knew nobody, not to Glasgow where I now had friends. At the end of a long and painful discussion, involving much love on both sides, my husband demanded to know the *real* reason for my decision. At which I broke down and out came the truth. I told him, 'Scotland to you is just a place for holidays. I have to live there *as an Edinburgh ratepayer.*'

It was a curious statement, but the passion with which I voiced it left my husband with no answer.

I was by this time very near to a breakdown, and our local G. P. suggested that I should see a psychiatrist. The suggestion gave added stimulus to my sense of self-preservation: that psychiatrist who had long ago invalided me out of the Army and banished me from Scotland had, unwittingly, done me a good turn – by identifying *the enemy*. If the English got me they would keep me hanging about in hospitals until my homing instinct was dead. On my next visit to Glasgow my

178

resolution to return to Scotland had been made. I heard myself saying in a voice quite unlike my own, 'If I stay in London, within two years I shall be dead in a lunatic asylum and they will bury me in a chalk soil grave in Kent.' These words, more cryptic than I realised, became a constant refrain in my head, and I repeated them to my husband when I returned to London. At the end of another heart-breaking discussion he concluded by saying that he could fight me but he could not fight the Sight.

Then I set to work with demonic possession to wreck the relationship with the man in Glasgow so that no human relationship stood in the path of my return to Scotland. My third and last visit to Glasgow was for camera rehearsal and transmission. I can remember leaving Glasgow in the gentle rain of a dull June morning. I stood looking at the grey stone backs of the houses, banded by trees, and thought, 'This is *my* country'. It had not been a happy visit, but it defined with certainty what I wanted: Scotland mattered to me more than any human being.

Emotional strain, anxiety and overwork had crippled me; also, the distress of living with a husband whom I was about to leave had taken toll of both of us. We had never loved more deeply than during those weeks of upheaval and anguish, and this intensity of feeling tempted us at times to consider making one more attempt to stay together. For my husband's sake as well as for my own I needed a few days' peace and recuperation in some place free of strain, so that I could think. Where to go was the problem.

As before in times of crisis, Leonard's name appeared upon a theatre programme. I had written to him in Stratford-on-Avon between trips to Scotland, and what I wrote to him I cannot remember, but I have his reply which arrived just as I was leaving for camera rehearsal in Glasgow. It opens 'What can I say? What am I supposed to do? Should I answer your letter? – *I* don't know. It sits on my desk day after day, saying "Do *something* with me". . . .' I wrote a note, 'Can I come to stay!' and the reply was a telephone call giving me the train time, telling me where to find the key – he would himself be out, but the tea-tray would be waiting. My husband packed me off with his blessing.

I stayed a week, and wrote a play by an open window through which the summer breeze fluttered from the river. I rarely met my host, and we had little to say. He served breakfast tea, while I in return cooked the occasional meal when he ate at home. I loved him best when he was out, and left me all his personality in the beautifully appointed surroundings: I think he loved me most when he was absent, securely knowing that his house was filled by someone who created there. It was as it had been at Morecambe. Like two monks we stole softly through each other's lives, unmolested. There is a Persian proverb, 'Before you love, learn to walk over snow leaving no footprint.' Possibly this sums up our relationship.

In that lovely great room, at the open window, watching the swans on the water below me, I wrote within one week the play that had its beginnings all those years ago outside the bombed-out house near Woburn Square. It concerned a young man whose memory lacks chronology, a lonely old lady who had been his family's neighbour on the night the bomb fell, and a young girl in the street who was an actress-typist new to London. By the end of the play the three stranded human beings have come together to create a united, real life for each other. I called it *A Question of Time*.

I returned to London and increasing pressures caused by the urgent need to get planning permission for the house in Hampstead. Peter had originally intended to convert the two upper floors for our use as a maisonette, but if he were to go there alone he would occupy the smaller basement apartment. I was in no state to make a decision about anything – a fact obvious to our local doctor, who, believing that I was just another upset housewife, recommended that I should consider going into St Thomas's Hospital. I fled to friends in Brighton.

My troubled nights were filled with dreams about an open coffin in a madhouse, but the promptings next day were to buy a cabin-trunk in which I could transport home to Scotland my mortal effects. On this theme I wrote a sensible letter to my husband, confirming our agreement that I was going to recover my health in Scotland, returning after six months. He wrote in reply that he thought the cabin-trunk an excellent notion. He understood that they designed them now so that one could pack one's clothes in one side and sleep in the other – on wheels too!

This plan to return after a period of six months was a fabrication to help both of us. My conscious mind wanted to believe it – during the day it seemed quite credible; it was only in the small hours that my nocturnal self, scribbling fragments of verse, truly knew its own fears and intentions. I detested Brighton, despite the welcome I always received there, and my verse bitterly compares the softness of the South Downs with the harsh, rugged moorland of my birthplace. Again it is those white chalk walls, green-smeared, which command my loathing, where I am *unburied*.

I returned to London at the end of July to keep an appointment with my doctor. Again St Thomas's was mentioned. Too ill to argue, I said I would 'think about it' and made a further appointment to see him. As I walked home from the surgery I did wonder for a moment whether a period of care in a place away from all my anxieties might not be the answer – asylum (why have they abolished that good word?) was truly what I needed for a while. . . . Then I remembered what had happened in the Army when I made the mistake of thinking that psychiatry was intended to help people, and rejected the idea. I do not usually break appointments without notification, but I decided this was once when it was justified: I meant to be on that train out of King's Cross on the day I was supposed to see my general practitioner.

I had one huge anxiety holding me back and later the same day I broke down in Donald's office at Shepherd's Bush; my whole life's crisis revolved around a monumental problem: how was I to take my new Standard Adler typewriter to Scotland? Donald said, 'Take it back to the shop and trade it in for a portable.' I can remember staring at him through my tears, astonished that life could be so simple. The huge cloud lifted: I could leave London. The next day I exchanged my typewriter. I was now free to work in Scotland. The next move was to buy a cabin-trunk from Selfridges. I chose the coffin-sized model, like a medieval chest, in dark blue and gold. As I saw it being loaded into my taxi I suddenly felt that there should be two of them. I left the taxi waiting while I ran back into the store to buy a second trunk exactly resembling the first. Equipped with twin coffins and a portable writing machine, I saw clearly my homeward road to Scotland.

As Peter and I packed our possessions in the flat that had been meant to save our marriage, we worked out a meticulously loving distribution of household items. Neither said, 'I want that,' but instead, 'I know that should be yours, do have it.' We hugged and packed and kissed and wept together. Then, when finally the bed-linen had been shared between us into two separate piles, we found high on the top shelf a square tin box. We were baffled a moment, then remembered it was the top tier of our wedding cake, preserved with brandy, which we had set aside for the christening of the first baby. We both broke down. Silently we hugged the tin, and each other, crying. I said, 'Peter, what can we do with it?' With sudden inspiration, he said, we should give it to Dorothy. The next day 'our' Dorothy tucked the cake-tin beneath her arm, knowing all it meant to us, and said, 'Yes, Mrs Stewart, now don't you worry. I'll think of you both when I'm eating it.'

Peter saw me off in the taxi from St George's Square. He had to go to his office, and, anyway, we had agreed that neither of us could stand a parting at the station.

I had departed on schedule. On the day I should have seen my G. P. to discuss going into St Thomas's I was travelling northward, free of psychiatric menace and that marriage with England.

I had a first-class compartment to myself, and sat with my eyes glued to the window as the lush grass of the south of England gave way to the thin, spikey moorland turf of the north. I can remember ignoring the tea-call of the dining-car attendant, not wanting him to see my tears.

I was watching the railway embankment. Through the moorland

181

grass I saw fronds of bracken like the irregular line of a rough marching army with its banners. And I vowed aloud: 'I will never go south again as long as I live. I swear it. *I swear it*.' And some kind of triumph mixed with tragedy filled the compartment as I cried tears too deep to have real sound – like the rustle of a robe down all the corridors of time I could remember.

CHAPTER SIX

1

MY RETURN JOURNEY WAS MADE IN TWO STAGES, ALLOWING FOR A WEEK'S recuperation with friends in Yorkshire. Whilst there I ricked my back and was immobilised. An osteopath laboured to make me travel-worthy, and as soon as I was able to stand I insisted on continuing my journey, saying I would 'get to Scotland if I have to travel flat on my back in the luggage van'. A friend of the family returning to Edinburgh University after the vacation was appointed my bodyguard. Her main duty was to ensure that I had a seat on the train and spent the hour we had to wait in Newcastle stretched on a bench in the ladies' room. Her task should have been easy, for in my determination to reach Edinburgh I had obeyed the osteopath's advice to the letter, spending many boring hours supine on the drawing-room carpet. We had, however, reckoned without the 'black sweater'.

The 'black sweater' was the name of convenience I had given to an unidentifiable black, or black and white, garment which, I was convinced, had to be taken from England back to Scotland with me. It was not in my possession and I had to find it. The result was a futile search of the shops in Brighouse where I began by asking for 'a black sweater' which became successively a black shirt, tunic, overall-thing — until finally, distressed and agitated, I would leave the shop without making a purchase. As a customer who usually knew precisely what I wanted when buying clothes, this behaviour was out of character.

My ensuing incapacity had ended my search for the 'black sweater', we thought. Then, on the train, when I had far more important matters to occupy my attention — my future in Scotland being one of them — I talked of nothing but the 'black sweater' I had been unable to find. In the end, to pacify me, my companion mentioned reluctantly that there was a branch of Marks & Spencer quite near to the station in Newcastle. At once I was elated: where else but in *Newcastle* would I find the mysterious garment I sought?

Quite apart from the explicit instructions to rest my back and my own considerable pain, it has been my lifelong rule never to leave a station between trains. Yet here I was, with agonised back and very little time to spare, embarking on a shopping expedition in Newcastle for a garment which I did not, at practical level, require.

In the store I began, as before, by asking for 'a black sweater', working my way through to 'a garment of black and white squares'. In the end the saleswoman asked did I know what I wanted? I was so convinced that they would have in Newcastle that elusive garment that I could not believe her when she failed to produce it. I would have missed that vital train to Edinburgh but for my companion's reminder that we had to hurry. I left the shop in great distress. I was still worrying about the 'black sweater' when we reached the Border – and then my anxiety ceased and I did not mention it again.

When we arrived at Waverley Station Geraldine, my companion, said as we were parting, she to go to her digs and I to my hotel, 'I'll meet you tomorrow and we'll look in the shops on Princes Street for your sweater.' I looked at her blankly for a moment, then replied, astonishingly, 'Oh, it doesn't really matter. It's not important.'

Back in Scotland, I did not give another thought to the 'black sweater' until 1966.

I arrived in Edinburgh in October 1959 with the means to buy a house. That I did not go immediately to Uncle Adam and Auntie Mamie who could have advised me on house purchase was possibly my greatest mistake, but there lay a ghost between us – that of an eighteen-year-old A.T.S. girl who had haunted Edinburgh's gaslit closes. If she now existed anywhere at all it was in the folds of the old army greatcoat which my mother, at my behest, had dusted and moth-proofed for all of a dozen years. A successful playwright of thirty, elegant in a black suit, I had no wish to be encumbered with ghosts.

Edinburgh, too, had changed; the trams were gone, as were most of the gas-lamps. The alterations saddened me, but they served to separate me even further from my army past. Learning to find my way by the bus-routes made it seem like a city new to me. Also, my territorial boundaries were different; as once I had gravitated towards the south side, never venturing beyond the ridge of George Street, now I confined myself to the Georgian New Town.

I did not choose to live in the New Town, it chose me – through a newspaper advertisement, when I was looking for a bed-sitter to serve me while house-hunting. As soon as I entered the house in Great King Street I knew it meant to have me. I paid a month's rent for a small room on the top floor, and, after a flying visit to my parents, came back to find my two trunks occupying the middle of the floor like a medieval tomb, surmounted by the flowers wired by my husband to greet me on arrival. I cried, 'My trunks have *arrived*!' in a tone which must have made my landlords think I viewed it as a miracle.

Had I been free from that moment – just for a week! – to begin my house-hunting, much would have been handled differently: instead, I arrived to find that the producer of my play *A Question of Time* had

184

been trying to reach me by telephone all day. The message I had left at Shepherd's Bush had not reached him, and, obliged to go ahead with the casting, he had omitted to call upon the services of the actor for whom that particular play had been written. I flew down to London next day. My new-found health dropped from me like a cloak, and I behaved for the first time like a 'difficult' playwright. I stayed with my husband while I was there, at the flat of friends with whom he was living temporarily, and for the sake of us all I had to resume the pretence that I would eventually be returning. By the time I got back to Edinburgh nothing any more was as simple as it had been.

My renewed sense of divided loyalties would not have interfered with my plans had I been able to view the purchase of a house in Edinburgh merely as an investment. I did not, however, come to Scotland to exploit its resources. I came back to serve the country, by living in it. Either I must own and inhabit my plot of Scots earth, or I must be there a pilgrim. No compromise was possible. To own a house in Edinburgh and spend six months of the year with my husband in London would have put me in the category of an absentee landlord. Whilst there remained the slightest chance of my returning to my husband I could not properly settle in Edinburgh. So I hung on to my house-money, waiting.

At this time my financial future was assured. I could sell as many plays as I could write. If I wanted a bank loan, I could have it. In 1959 I could have bought the entire house in Great King Street.

And in a disastrous kind of way I did. . . .

The house fascinated me from the beginning. A shabby shell containing fine antiques, it reeked of dynasty. My involvement began, as it usually does, in a small way. By the end of six months I was acting Mother Superior with my copy of Thomas à Kempis at the ready, on call to deal with illness, heartbreak and the sporadic outbursts of tribal warfare which occur in any community.

At first the smallness of my room did not matter, for I had meant it never to be more than temporary accommodation. Then came a time when accumulating commissions turned it into my working area, and I found myself hemmed in by piles of typescript. I asked my landlords for a larger room. They took me to a door on the first floor which I had identified as 'mine' since the first day I entered the house.

The room itself had not been decorated since the turn of the century when the great mirror above the marble fireplace had been screwed to the wall over the white, watered-silk wallpaper. What drew me immediately was the view from the tall window – green gardens latticed by stone walls, formed into a quadrangle by the towering 'Edinburgh backs' as I called them, of the adjoining streets. I had the double-bed removed and a divan-bed substituted; I demanded sud-

185

denly an old print I had seen on the landing – of sea dashing against rocks, with a plummeting seagull at its focal point – which I hung above the bed. On a stately walnut commode I set a huge vase of eucalyptus leaves. Then I went down to spend Christmas with my husband in his new house.

By the time the eucalyptus leaves had died in late January 1960 I knew the extent of the household's economic plight. The place was run on the lines of a monastic hospice, and nobody was evicted for non-payment of rent. Meanwhile, bills had to be paid. The gas-meters were emptied on the day the electricity bill arrived, and the gas bill was paid with money intended for the mortgage. I got us all out of the immediate difficulty by paying my rent three months in advance, which, of course, though I did not realise it, eliminated me as a source of revenue for the next quarter. So when the next crisis arrived I paid more rent in advance.

That was the point where I should have rushed out to view property for sale in Edinburgh, but I was gripped in the spell of the dynastic myth I had uncovered, which had moved me deeply, and I, too, required an emotional link with the phantom family which, with myself as matriarch and catalyst, was rapidly becoming a reality. It counter-balanced my ties with London.

My neglected great room became a source of concern to me: I felt I owed it restoration. Discussing the matter with my neighbour, Joe, with whom I shared a kitchen, I managed to talk both of us into a terrible zest for redecoration. In a community like ours, where the accident-prone rallied together for survival, the normal barriers between landlord and tenant did not exist, and when I suggested to the cousins that Joe and I should employ a firm of decorators to beautify our respective dwelling areas, they agreed, albeit it with misgiving. They were afraid not of me but for me, and tried to explain that my money was at risk. I assured them they need have no fear; I could always earn more money.

It was the first home I had made, and I lavished upon it all the love, money and time which I had been aching to give Scotland since birth. Stripped and redecorated, the room was magnificent; shining new curtains framed the view of green gardens and stone walls. Turning my hand to carpentry, I designed and made a storage unit for clothes which left the visitor unaware that my drawing-room was also a bedroom. Towards the same end I designed and made all the soft furnishings. The next step was to send to Lancashire for the Italian inlaid Amboyna table which had been my grandfather's gift to me when I came of age – a treasure which I had made sure never went to London – and other inherited pieces. The Amboyna table had always a fateful influence, for it needed a *palazzo*, and I was one person who, in

186

Scotland, required no encouragement in that direction. Palace-building had seized me like a fever. Once the table was installed, nothing less than a fitted dove-grey carpet would content me and, because the floorboards were bad (a common hazard in New Town houses), beneath it I had put down inch-thick rubber underlay which, I said, would 'last me a lifetime'. My landlords, hopping with fright, kept trying to tell me that the entire house might have to be evacuated within a month, but I paid no heed: I was a builder on the grand scale, determined that my work should last forever.

It was Joe who got the message: his paint was scarcely dry when he announced his imminent departure, warning me to do the same before I discovered that I had nailed my colours to a sinking vessel.

I could not now be parted from my room, so beautiful that my friends asked sometimes just to sit in it to absorb the serenity of its atmosphere. When Joe left I took over the entire first floor, paying rent months – later, years – in advance for it, as the economic structure of the household crumbled gently beneath me. By the time I saw my folly I was too heavily committed to withdraw, even had I wanted to.

Having spent the money intended for my house, I set to work to earn more, accepting an invitation from Ted Willis to write a play for ITV. It was now March, and I finished the script during a non-stop stint of four days and three nights, while the magnificent flowers, which had been Joe's birthday present to me, swiftly carbonised in the fumes of nicotine and the oil heater bought to boost the gas-fire in my acre of freezing grandeur.

I had left the B.B.C. on the usual terms accorded to those who had done their stint in the front line as staff-writers – the offer of a writer's contract. All I had to do when I reached Edinburgh was to submit four play-synopses, have them accepted, and receive a down-payment which would keep me comfortably for six months while I wrote the plays; their completion would secure my income for the rest of that year while leaving me free to undertake other commissions. It was an ideal arrangement, but when I reached Scotland some kind of mental blockage inhibited me from signing any contract with London. I made the excuse that I had no ideas, yet I managed very well to think up plotlines when writing for ITV as a freelance.

Writing and furnishing occupied so much of my time that I had no social life outside the house. When I first returned in the October of 1959 I had been determined to take up fencing again. While looking for a fencing club to join, my eye fell upon a newspaper item: 'Gaelic classes'. Enrolment was that very night, and I nearly ran to the university building to ensure that I was in time. My studies were erratic, for my best writing time was the evening; I missed most of the classes, but I worked hard at home and my kindly Gaelic tutor corrected my exercises by post. In written Gaelic I raced ahead, sometimes outpacing the class, but on the few occasions when I put in an appearance I found myself unable to respond by mouth and ear. There was nothing surprising in that, for written and spoken Gaelic are very different – and, as with most languages, to acquire the ear is not immediate. There was, however, an additional factor: I had alienated myself from the language by learning the written form, which *in my head* did not exist. One evening, when pottering in the kitchen with my mind half upon the food I was preparing and half upon the play I had to write, I became aware of a discussion on the radio about land reclamation. I listened with much interest, and it came as a considerable shock to hear at the end an announcer speak in *English*. I simply had not realised that I had been listening to a programme in Gaelic. The next time I switched on, deliberately, a Gaelic programme expecting, excitedly, to understand it, I found it incomprehensible except for the occasional word. On a subsequent occasion – again in the kitchen, with my hands busy drying dishes and my mind elsewhere – I found myself singing. . . . The song expressed the wish to be buried upon a certain island where the winds would never waken me. As I straightened up from the kitchen cupboard, holding a plate, I heard my own voice singing and the song was in *Gaelic*. The moment I realised that, a flood of consciousness stopped the singing. All that remained was the tune, which was to haunt me for several years, until 1966, when suddenly it vanished. I never heard the tune sung anywhere, nor did I find its words on any of the sheets we sang in Gaelic class. It was a very old song, that I knew, but whence it came I had no idea. These two experiences were unrelated to my Gaelic studies. During lessons on the few times I attended the simplest question would cause me to panic and reply in French or German. It is possible that an obscure fear inhibited my attendance at classes, a need not to know too well a language hidden – so fluently! – in some recess of unconscious memory.

As in 1947, I saw little of Edinburgh deliberately. To be there was enough. However, during the autumn and winter of 1960 I made a point of breaking from work every afternoon to take a brisk walk. My route never varied: up to Princes Street, up the Mound, through Ramsay Gardens to the Castle Esplanade. I never looked towards the Forth, my favourite view in 1947; now I always crossed to the south side, whence I could survey the Old Town and the far profile of the Pentlands. Looking across the old town I saw 'my Scotland'. I allowed myself ten minutes there, but sometimes I would look at my watch to be astonished by the discovery that an hour or more had passed whilst I had been watching the light play upon cloud, mist and smoke, above a city so lovingly remembered. Once, on a morning when we had snow, I

188

had raced up to the Esplanade before I took the airport bus from George Street terminal. The smoke-blackened houses on and below Johnson Terrace, each capped with its roof of snow, made me think I saw a medieval city. I was still musing on this when I boarded the plane at Turnhouse, and I mentioned to a fellow passenger that I 'half-expected to touch down in the fifteenth – sixteenth-century'. I said the same later in the day to my agent, as I sat in her office, adding the regret that 'it had not happened'. She had loved my description of 'medieval snow-covered Edinburgh'.

Until this time work had been going well. Now suddenly my luck began to desert me. The long tale of scripts that were commissioned, paid for and then never used is a saga told in the correspondence of that year. There was nothing wrong with the scripts; I merely had the misfortune to become involved with programmes which for some reason or another were abandoned. Alistair reminded me that, when I had time to spare from my upholstery, I had promised to write 'that play for Scotland'. Using a plot supplied to me by a friend, and a title ('*Hills Beyond the Smoke*') inspired by my view from the Castle Esplanade, I quickly completed the synopsis. When I came to write the actual play I found that I could not write dialogue in the modern Midlothian idiom – it did not sound to me now like *Scots*. (I had in the past written Scots characters into my plays, and adapted Scottish plays without any difficulty.) I attributed my deficiency to lack of experience – I had lived in Edinburgh but a year – but this explanation did not tally with my record for picking up accents so quickly that accidental mimicry was a frequent cause of embarrassment. In the end the whole play had to be written in formal English, almost archaic, and presented to my Glasgow colleague for translation.

This play marked the point where I began to have difficulty in writing modern English, as my colleague caustically observed when changing some of my lines. It was also the first play into which I introduced a minor character who was a Scottish Nationalist. I could not follow it immediately with another Scottish play, for the B.B.C. schedule of plays from Scotland was full for that year, and nobody knew what would be the position for Scottish plays in the foreseeable future, but I was warned that the outlook was grim. Even had I wanted to write a play set in southern England, always sure of a market, I had begun to lose touch with southern current affairs. I had felt the first nip in the air of the great freeze-out of Scottish writers which would characterise the 1960s.

I was determined to hold my ground; to stay in Scotland was more important than my career. I must find another medium of expression – the theatre. I had in fact never ceased writing stage-plays, even during my time with the B.B.C., but the slowness of getting them

189

into production compared with the ease of selling work to television had caused me to shelve them as soon as they were written. The play I had been wanting to write since 1956 was, of course, the stage version of *The Man from Thermopylae* in which I could explore the theme more thoroughly than radio time had allowed. I threw myself into the task with enormous vigour, my intense concentration keeping at bay the economic worries which I hoped the writing of the play might resolve. At last I was writing the full play about the soldier who 'sees with the eyes of the dead'. The sole survivor of a battle which nobody else had lived to remember seemed to be the only character through whom I could breathe and think and feel clearly. My curious new linguistic difficulty presented no problem to me here, for the play required the formal, non-colloquial style in which I had begun to speak as well as write.

I had at this time no contact whatever with the Scottish theatre, and it was through Joe the introduction was made. He attended mass at St Mary's Cathedral in Broughton Street (known to me in Army days) where Moray Maclaren and his wife, Lennox Milne, were his fellow worshippers. A new project had just been launched, the Mercat Theatre Trust, to sponsor any new play based on Christian principles. The Greek gods in my play were on the right side, whatever their denomination. I took the completed script one afternoon to Lennox Milne, thereby, unknowingly, making a connection which would profoundly affect the future pattern of my life in Scotland. The play was received enthusiastically by the Mercat Theatre Trust who passed it on to Moultrie Kelsall at the Gateway Theatre. I knew from experience that it took a great deal of time for a stage play to be accepted and produced, so I put the matter out of my head while I concentrated upon more immediate problems, such as supporting the roof above our heads.

I now had to face the fact that Scotland offered no future to a television writer. To stay, I must find an alternative means of livelihood. I began to search the advertisement pages of *The Scotsman* and almost the first to take my eye was a vacancy in the B.B.C. for an information officer for Scotland. Immediately I identified it as 'my' job. I had been born with Scotland in my head, and the title 'Information Officer for Scotland' seemed to fit me in the way that the words 'Scottish Command' had fitted me those long years earlier. I sent for the application forms, which I completed and despatched, and it was only then that the scale of my temerity became apparent to me. That I should feel myself qualified to speak for Scotland after a residence in the country of only twenty-five months (including my nine months with the Army) did not appear strange to me at the time: what did worry me, however, was my total ignorance of Scottish history. I

190

had about a fortnight in which to repair the omission. Hurriedly I wrote to my Gaelic tutor a request for bibliographical advice. By return of post he sent me two books, Agnes Mure Mackenzie's *The Kingdom of Scotland* and H. V. Morton's *In Search of Scotland*. I was delighted with the first, but the sight of the second book filled me with precisely the same immediate revulsion I had experienced years earlier at school when I was handed the book which turned out to be *Marmion*. I never opened *In Search of Scotland*. It became the book I buried beneath piles of other books, hidden in a drawer, put anywhere to keep it out of sight.

By contrast, I romped through Agnes Mure Mackenzie's history as gleefully as if I had been reading an old, lost diary of my own. Parts of Scotland's early history seemed dimly familiar, as though at some time I had learned it before. This, I knew, was impossible: one has to be born in England to know how thoroughly the history of Scotland is omitted from one's education. Intellectually I knew nothing about the Stewart Jameses except that the sixth of them had become our James I of England, so presumably there had been five others preceding him. So for the first time I met James IV, discovering with a shock that he had died at Flodden.

Flodden. . . . All my life it had been the one battle about which I did not want to know. Even the name sent shivers down my spine.

This king who died there seemed to be a nice fellow, to me a person totally comprehensible. I was a shade surprised that an historian who knew him as well as did, obviously, Agnes Mure Mackenzie should fail to grasp that this 'highland policy' was part of a three-stage programme, and that he died at the end of phase two – with the third part still in his head. And surely she ought to have seen the purpose of the building of the ship *The Great Michael*? Curled up in my dark blue velvet chair, I muttered, 'Yes. . . .' 'Of course!' 'Naturally. . . .' 'No, that's wrong.' 'Yes, but. . . .' I was pleased, and a little amused, to see what she had made of him. At the mention of Henry VIII's accession to the throne of England the red mist began to rise before my eyes. A landscape radiant with achievement had darkened on that day young Tudor became Scotland's regal neighbour. My hatred welled up, sending the blood pounding through my head. There was great bitterness – and pain, too, for it should not have happened; any of it. I knew all the rest of the story. Memory could fill the gaps left in the summary account. And thus we came to Flodden. . . .

Her chapter ends:

James was given no grave: no man knows where he lies today. His people refused to believe that he was dead, though his body in fact was found and borne to Henry. They said he had but gone to Jerusalem, and would ride home once more to be their friend and leader: but the years passed, and he never came again.

It was the 'he never came again' which shocked me. There came from me a great cry, '*It's not true!*' and I bowed my head into the book as the terrible weeping came upon me.

I never learned the rest of Scotland's history. Oh, I read it, but it never seemed real to me. For me reality stopped in 1513. Mary Stuart and the Young Pretender were like fictitious characters, existing in another dimension, as far away from me as used to be the tartan souvenirs that repelled me in my childhood.

I installed the last of my meticulously chosen domestic ornaments on the day the crash came which my landlords had warned me to expect. I had just three weeks in which to find another home for myself and my furniture, and my money was all gone which I had intended for a house. The cousins escorted me all over the New Town to find a suitable flat, but I was desolate and past responding. I was incapable of making any kind of practical plans, for fatalism had overtaken me in the way it had done in 1947: Time's door had closed upon me, and circumstance would once more bear me away down to England.

I stitched the great Amboyna table in blankets and canvas, and stood incredulously watching the removal men crate my china and take up the grey carpet. On that very morning there had arrived by post a twenty-fluid-ounce bottle of brown ink ordered direct from Waterman's which, still in its unopened package, went into store with my furniture. My personal possessions I loaded into my two trunks and sent them by taxi to the house of acquaintances who had undertaken to accommodate them temporarily. Then I was left with my suitcases, at the telephone kiosk on the corner of the street, dialling the number of my husband's house in London. I said that I had nowhere to go and he told me to come home.

It was too late to book a flight, and the quantity of luggage decided me to go this time by rail. It was the first time I had ever travelled by train on the east coast route *to* England via Berwick and Newcastle. I could come up to Scotland that way, but I had never dared to face the journey in the opposite direction. I had no idea why; I said it was the fear of 'losing Scotland' if I took that route. This time I had no choice. I travelled in a third-class compartment, packed four to each side, and I kept my eyes upon the luggage-rack opposite me for all of the eight hours. Just once I mouthed a polite reply to the woman seated beside me, otherwise I sat entombed in a silence as terrible as it was contagious. My mind had died. All that remained was a body borne down to England.

192

My husband's warm welcome met with a flood of ghost-tears and the request, 'Please can I go to bed?' I took my sleeping-pills and went to sleep *for ever*. When I wakened, I took more pills to put myself back to sleep. It was the same pattern which had characterised my behaviour just after I left Scotland in 1947, but now I had sleeping-pills to prolong the slumber. Once by husband, exasperated by my doped condition (the misuse of sleeping-pills was totally out of character), slapped my face to rouse me. I began to howl. He, thinking I was going into hysterics, slapped harder. I howled louder. Finally, he fled before those howls, demanding consideration for the neighbours. I did think of the neighbours, and the only one whose wavelength I shared at that moment was the neurotic dog next door, locked out from nine till five, an aimless, sad, unloved and unlovable beast which defeated even my attempts to befriend it; on that morning I heard an echo to my howls, and realised suddenly that my animal cries and his were almost identical.

I forced myself to go out, do the household shopping and prepare an elaborate evening meal. During the next weeks I fought my way back to the surface by trying to please my husband, cooking, cleaning and making new lampshades: I was 'playing at house' almost like a child. I assumed gaiety like a cloak and, wearing it, remustered our old friends and some new ones. In no time at all I was surrounded by what my husband had once termed my people, the enclave which he once had cursed and now welcomed. One of our new friends observed, 'The marvellous thing about you two is that you never admit defeat. Most people whine about their broken marriage.' He was right: we kept up the gaiety until the very end.

I had never properly unpacked since my arrival in London. It gave me the feeling that my stay was temporary, and that I would return to Scotland. Also, there was another reason: in one of my suitcases were two books, those lent me by my Gaelic tutor, which I had not had time to post back to him in the turmoil of leaving Great King Street. I had intended posting them from London, but he had told me to keep them. I was happy to have the Agnes Mure Mackenzie in my case, I liked to see its bright, heraldic dustjacket when I opened the lid, though I never took it out to read it. The H. V. Morton remained a nightmare to me. Wrapped in my underclothes, it lay buried beneath the rest of the case's contents – then, when I was in a hurry, it would rise, uncovered, to the surface, and I would set to work frantically to re-bury it.

Then, one day, came word that my play *Hills Beyond the Smoke* was about to go into production in the Glasgow studios. I packed a single bag and headed north, straight through to Glasgow. I was there for camera rehearsal and transmission, staying at the hotel I had used when I was working in Glasgow for the B.B.C. For those two days I came alive, but they were a tiny island in an ocean of desolation. The play was a great success, but it led nowhere; when the current run of plays ended, there would be no more Scottish drama going out from Glasgow.

In Edinburgh were my two trunks which by this time had, understandably, outstayed their welcome. On the day after the transmission of the play I went through from Glasgow to deal with them. By a happy coincidence, my French tutor from schooldays and his family were staying at the Grosvenor Hotel in Edinburgh, so I joined them there overnight which gave me a temporary sense of belonging. When they had left, I set to work in my hotel room to re-pack the two trunks, separating all the important personal possessions into one, and into the other putting those items which I did not immediately need – my patchwork dressing-gown with the fleur-de-lis, my fencing foil, and the green velvet theatre coat which I had bought on Princes Street the first week of my return to Edinburgh. I took the second trunk to be stored in the Maclarens' basement, and Lennox hung my theatre coat in her wardrobe. All my jewellery, silver toilet articles, fine clothes, play-scripts and personal papers – including my passport and birth certificate – I put into the main trunk to go down to London.

Unable to face again the journey by rail via Berwick and Newcastle, I despatched my trunk by rail and booked my own transport by air. As I delivered the trunk to Waverley Station I was asked did I wish to insure it? I said no. If I lost that trunk, I said, no money on earth could compensate. And the horrible thing was that I knew it would go missing. As I watched it being lifted from the wooden grille and borne away to the back premises, I knew that I would never see it arrive in London.

My presentiment proved correct. The trunk containing everything I knew as 'me' failed to arrive in Hampstead. No enquiries could trace it. A search of King's Cross Station conducted by my friends failed to discover any trace of it. Meanwhile, I was stripped of all my jewellery other than my silver bracelet, and all my clothes except the suit in which I had travelled – and it was now high summer in Hampstead; I had to borrow clothes or buy oddments in the summer sales to tide me over. The worst loss, professionally, was that of my scripts and papers; the most painful, my passport and birth certificate. I kept saying, 'Now I know what it is like to be a stateless person.'

I had no sense of location or identity, and now began a terrible period of flight between the two remaining places where my few scraps of possessions gave me a temporary sense of belonging – my husband's house, and that of my parents in Lancashire. Once, I rushed off from Hampstead at lunchtime, leaving a note, to be met by my parents at

Blackpool Central Station. As soon as I saw them I burst into tears, with the words 'I shouldn't have left Peter!' The next day they put me back into the train for London. It reached the stage where the only place where I felt secure was in a railway carriage. What brought my desolate daundering to an end was the basic hard fact that I could no longer afford train fares.

Marooned in London, and bereft of country, house, possessions and identity, I began to slide into a state of complete withdrawal. My husband and our friends were kind and for their sakes I would make an effort to respond, but if for a moment my attention wandered from what I was doing and saying, my personality fell apart revealing a hollow filled with grief which was all that remained of me. There were large parts of each day when I sat in unbroken silence, immobile, the person whose identity had gome missing somewhere in England. On one such day my husband, driven desperate by my unseeing eyes and idle hands, thrust at me a drawing-board, paper, pencil, rubber and a box of pastels. Reminding me that I had won the senor art prize at school, he ordered me to *draw*.

I had never used pastel. I had not touched a drawing-pencil for seventeen years. I took the paper and drew the first subject that came into my head – a dead, decapitated tree with lopped-off branches, standing in a desert of dried mud shards glistening with salt, and with shadows beneath their curled edges. . . . Beside the first tree appeared a second; whereas the first thrust down its roots towards a water-hole it could not quite reach, the other had been headless, dried out and dead for aeons. I worked at the pencil drawing for two hours, totally engrossed, and when it was completed I showed it to my husband. He looked up from his own drawing-table, where he had been detailing an elevation, and exclaimed that he did not realise I could draw like that.

That drawing brought me back to life. I rushed out to buy pastel paper, an additional green crayon, and some *tortillons*, and then spent an exciting day working out for myself a method of blending the colour into the paper with a *tortillon* to produce a sculptured effect. I worked constantly on the same theme, a pair of dead trees in a wilderness of dried mud, grappling their roots, the one to draw life from the water, the other to bury itself. Anyone who visited the house was called instantly to see my drawings, and the subject of 'Ada's trees' became a main topic of our Hampstead conversation. I mentioned the tree drawings in every letter I wrote at that time, making a joke about my 'obscene trees'.

My use of the words 'obscene trees' puzzled my friends, who considered my sculptured tree-trunks beautiful. So they were. It was, I discovered, only to my eyes that they bore, when finished, a terrible resemblance to muscular *human* trunks, decapitated and demanding

195

burial.

To the friends who had wanted the drawings, I gave them when the time came for me to leave London.

My call home to Scotland came on a postcard, out of the blue, a few lines telling me that the Gateway Theatre Company planned to present *The Man from Thermopylae* in the autumn. My cry of gratitude to heaven must have shown my husband more clearly than anything that our interlude of compatibility did not constitute sufficient grounds for the resumption of the marriage. Now he was glad for my sake that Time had re-admitted me to Scotland.

I had nowhere to stay in Edinburgh, a problem resolved for me by Moray and Lennox Maclaren who booked a bed-sitting-room for me in the house of friends of theirs. When my unknown landlady wrote to describe the apartment, the house and the nearest shopping centre, Tollcross, I could not place the locality. All that mattered was that it was in Edinburgh, and I flew home, clutching all the way that vital postcard from the Gateway.

At the air-terminal I said to the cab-driver, 'Leamington Terrace. I don't know where it is.' As we passed the Castle to my left and swung into Lothian Road, I had a hazy sense of recollection. It was dark and, the trams being gone, I did not immediately identify the route, but I knew it as the right one. As we reached the Links at Bruntsfield possibly there stirred in my head the ghost of a girl who came with an army ('I shall live here one day,' I had said in 1947), but it was not of those days I was thinking as the taxi turned off to the right. I was remembering a *welcome*, of many hands reaching up to touch my cloak and stirrup . . . and the shouting of men who came running from their campfires. . . . And then immediately before me was the open door of my new home, and I was being welcomed back into the twentieth century to a huge fire, cups of tea, and the warmth of the family.

2

MY THIRD RETURN TO SCOTLAND WAS LIKE NEITHER OF THE two preceding attempts to settle. I seemed to have arrived back into the midst of an enormous rescue operation mounted on my behalf. The loss of the trunk which in London I accepted fatalistically was judged to be a monstrous affront by my friends in Scotland. Moray Maclaren packed me off at once to put the matter in the hands of his lawyer. Meanwhile, everyone was trying to replenish my wardrobe, lend or give me jewels, provide me with a host of new friends. On the first Saturday after my arrival at the Hellers' (Martin, my landlord, was to play Iolaus in the play) I was whisked away to a party, the first of the Saturday gatherings which opened for me the door into almost every field of Scotland's activities. The welcome surrounding me had a perceptible double-dimension: as though 'all of me came alive simultaneously' I would have said in 1947, although I did not seem able to remember as I shopped by Leamington Terrace that I was on the ground traversed by tram those years ago.

The production of *The Man from Thermopylae* at the Gateway was (apart from the German production) the first stage presentation of a play of mine since *Warp and Weft* in Lancashire a decade earlier. Due to my straitened circumstances the two events bore a strange resemblance: once more I found myself typing twenty-five scripts in batches of four; once more my spine was playing me up, and for part of the time I typed standing at the tallboy between visits to an Edinburgh osteopath. My beautiful clothes had gone, and I was back to the old routine of trying to look magnificent upon a shoestring budget.

The first night was to be a gala occasion. My parents sent me the money to buy a dress, and then I set to work to make a necklace to replace my lost jewels. I had done this kind of work before, threading thousands of minute metal coloured beads upon copper wire and twisting it into filigree patterns, but wire of the right gauge was no longer obtainable: the electrician next door to the theatre searched everywhere for suitable wire, and between the theatre and the house the elaborate, glittering collar of pearl drops and bronze beads became known as 'the crown jewels'. I worked on the crown jewels at night when I had typed scripts through the day. Everyone helped to dress me, Sadie Aitkin offering me the use of an evening coat from the theatre wardrobe, and somehow the costume for the playwright became as important as costumes for the cast. In the end I wore over my black velvet dress and the crown jewels the green velvet theatre coat which in Lennox Milne's wardrobe had survived the holocaust. (Nobody pointed out to me until years later that this coat was an almost exact replica of a medieval man's surcoat.)

Nothing which could help to make the play a success had been omitted. Magnus Magnusson had shown an excerpt from the play in his weekly television arts programme. Publicity had included the usual interviews with the author which appeared in Scottish newspapers. Evening dress was *de rigeur* for an audience invited to a buffet reception. The most important person there, for me professionally, was Jerry Devine who, on a visit from America, had come to see the show with a view to buying the option for production on Broadway.

I followed my own order of priorities. The electrician from next door and his mates had kept a bar-stool waiting for me in the pub beside the theatre. I left the reception to take my drink with them, for without that quest for wire there would have been no crown jewels: I nearly missed the opening of the play as I sat listening to what the locals on Leith

Walk had to say about the plight of Scotland. Back in the theatre, I sat alone until the designer came to join me in the suffering which is the lot of playwrights and designers on a first night. In the interval I spoke briefly to my parents, and then did my gracious best to be nervelessly conversational during the formal presentation of those who wished to meet the author. Back to my seat, and then, in the second interval, I got down to what the theatre is all about – the play, which I discussed in hard, professional terms with Jerry Devine, who, to my great joy, loved it. Disaster struck in the third act, and the designer and I gripped hands in sympathetic agony when his rocks failed to descend at the critical moment and Tom Fleming temporarily went missing during an elaborate costume change designed for the more-than-mortal. The supernatural storm did last for eternity so far as we were concerned, cowering in the stalls with heads bowed in prayer for poor Tom, as lightning flashed and thunder rolled, and I, all too human, wet my knickers!

The next day in the newspapers I read the reviews of a new play by a *Scottish* playwright.

My husband came up to see the play on the Saturday. We met in the oyster bar of the Café Royal before the show and after it returned to my bed-sitting-room where we talked through the night. Both of us faced now the fact that 'marriage with England' had ended. The next morning, a Sunday, he wanted to go for a walk. Within easy reach were the Pentlands. Until this time I had never ventured to the site of the camp at Fairmilehead, fearing that it might be overspread by bungalows and new roads – but now I felt a terrible compulsion to take my husband to the place where I had been a soldier in the years before we met. I went, dreading what I should find there, but by a miracle nobody yet had built upon that plot of W.D. ground. The camp had vanished, but there remained concrete patches in the grass to remind me where had been the mess, the cookhouse, the NAAFI and the A.T.S. billets. I stood at the gate surveying the grass-grown foundations of what had been the nissen hut, and I cried, 'Do you see that bit there, four bed-widths from the end? *I slept there.*'

My husband proclaimed, with his short, quick, apologetic bark of laughter, that they would mark it with a plaque! There came from me a peal of merriment which held a ring of triumph, and we sat down on a seat near the sealed army gate, which once had been my entrance, to smoke a companionable cigarette. I regretted nothing in that moment.

My links with that other army life were closer than I realised sometimes. When I had been needing evening shoes, Joyce Heller had suggested I should first try the Lotus seconds shop at Church Hill. Her direction had been, 'Turn right at the end of Leamington Terrace, then follow the road up the hill.' When she added, 'You know Church Hill?'

I had at the time professed ignorance. In patches my memory had gone, as the trams were gone, of an A.T.S. girl heading back to Fairmilehead, and the sudden 'this-is-me' lurch of recollection at an older memory of a metallic something on the wind, no longer there.

But a sense of place remained; and when I found the shoe-shop I felt again 'this is me'. Quiet, gentle women were on duty, and I felt compulsively drawn to those racks and heaps of shoes. *A heap of shoes* . . . a heap of shoes upon a hillside . . . what on earth was I remembering? For a moment there had been people, many people, and it was raining, and their feet churned the moorland grass to mud. . . . As soon as I had straightened up from the heap of shoes to focus my mind on the recollection, it was gone. But in the quiet of the shop I sorted the shoes as I searched for what I wanted, pairing them together so that each shoe on the floor stood neatly below its partner on the rack above it. This was to become a therapeutic exercise to which I resorted whenever my life without that trunk became intolerable.

After my first visit to the Lotus shop on Church Hill I became a compulsive shoe-collector – and this was very strange, for until that time I had hated buying shoes, and when I had found a pair which I could wear with comfort and elegance I would wear them until they fell to pieces. Now, my shoe-buying at Church Hill became obsessional. Knowing that I had no money to spare, Joyce would cry, 'Oh, not again!' as I came home laden, sometimes with as many as four pairs at a time. I had the excuse that I was replacing those lost in the trunk, but that I knew was not my real motive: I bought those shoes because they were in a *heap*, and the nameless Scots who had tried them on were very dear to me. In my compassion I would have bought the entire stock, had I been able to afford it. Once, when picking shoes from the rack I saw below them my own feet encased in laminated metal shoes riveted at the edge; when I looked again the armoured feet were gone.

Jerry Devine stayed in Edinburgh for a fortnight, working with me to re-shape the play for the benefit of an American audience. It was a period of tremendous intellectual excitement, and the stimulus kept me going through the next half year while I worked upon the play. The purchase of the option gave me twelve months' income during the desperately straitened circumstances in which I was living. Into the new version of *The Man from Thermopylae* crept many new lines depicting an awareness of the posthumous state greatly intensified. I was supposed to be looking forward to going to America, but I dreaded New York, even for the purpose of seeing my play there. I made no effort to replace my lost passport, for I had come to believe that identity itself had gone missing with the trunk.

As the months passed the distress of my loss did not lessen but intensified. The worst was the missing birth certificate. I became obsessed with the idea that the lack of it actually *showed*. I began to walk on the shadowed side of the street, afraid of being pointed out as the-stranger-who-has-no-birth-certificate. One day in the bright spring sunlight I stopped in the street, overcome by tears, and fled back to my room where I closed the curtains so that nobody could see me. When Joyce came to see what was the matter, I remembered suddenly a tale I had read as a child about 'The Man Who Had No Shadow' – he having sold it to the devil for a bag of gold – and I told her, 'I feel life the man who had no shadow. I have no *birth certificate*!' and I broke down into the hoarse, hopeless ghost-weeping.

During the lawyer's fight for compensation from British Rail, we had won to my cause a railway official named Mr Collins who made it his business not merely to negotiate compensation but actually to mount a tremendous search for the trunk. His faith in its ultimate recovery never weakened. However, after fourteen months, when all effort to trace it had failed, British Rail agreed to pay in full the claim for compensation. On the day the cheque arrived it was a warm, clear, summer afternoon and the visit to the bank gave me a reason for venturing out to take the air. I intended to go from the bank up the hill to comfort myself amid the piles of shoes, but for some instinctive reason, which I did not understand, I turned the other way, heading for home as quickly as possible. As I put my key in the door I could hear the telephone ringing. The call was for me: it was Mr Collins announcing 'We have found the trunk.'

It had lain for fourteen months at King's Cross Station. I ran through the house shouting the glad tidings. By five o'clock, the time the trunk was due to be delivered by a triumphant Mr Collins, there had assembled in my room a fair number of people eager to behold the miracle. The only sympathiser absent was Judy, the eleven-year-old daughter of the family who had rushed in from school so many times to ask, 'Any news of the trunk?' She had never tired of hearing me list its contents. Judy that evening was at a guide meeting.

Promptly at five o'clock Mr Collins and the trunk arrived, and I poured for us all a minute trickle of whisky from the small bottle which was all I could afford. We toasted the trunk, then I knelt down beside it, unlocked the heavy brass hasps and flung back the lid. In a state bordering on ecstasy I plunged my arms into the chest and pulled out my cherished possessions, identifying each one with a cry of joy, and scattering them around me. Mr Collins waited to make sure that nothing was missing, then departed. When everyone else had gone, Joyce said, 'It's a good thing Judy's not here.' I looked at her surprised. She said, worried 'You don't know what she's expecting!' Suddenly I realised what I had done: in Judy's mind I had unintentionally created a veritable treasure chest. Joyce said, 'I'll fend her off just now. Don't

200

let her see that stuff until it's been cleaned and sorted.'

Suddenly I saw what she – and presumably the others – had seen, a trunk full of crumpled clothing. What I had remembered and described were the garments as they had looked on me when last I had worn them. Now, after fourteen months' unplanned storage, the best of them looked fit only for a jumble sale. The treasure in the chest, for me, was my *identity*.

When I repaid the compensation to British Rail my lawyer negotiated for a smaller sum to pay for restoration, and during the next fortnight I ferried armfuls of garments to and from the cleaners. Hanging in the wardrobe, they looked well enough to satisfy me and Judy's mother, but they still bore little resemblance to the limitless splendour now exisiting in Judy's imagination. However, not for nothing had her mother and I both worked in the theatre. . . .

I set to work to wash and iron my forty-odd scarves of many colours, intending to create a spectacle for Judy. But it was not Judy I had in mind that summer evening at the ironing-board when I looked at the wet streamers of coloured silk and thought of a *battlefield*. It was gone in a flash, but I was left holding the iron, my arms goose-pimpled, as I wept over the saddest sight on earth, a heap of sodden bands and squares of colour beside the ironing-board. I was filled with an agony of loneliness and desolation. I did not recognise – as I might have done in 1947 – that those people had been present again whom I recognised only by their absence.

I gritted my teeth and forced myself to work on the task which I felt to be beyond my strength. Then, as each scarf left the board crisp, fresh and colourful, my spirits lifted. I laid them over the clothes' horse to air where they hung like banners. This time I did not put them into a bag or a box in my lifelong fashion, but set them out in regimented rows, flat in a drawer, so that each could be instantly identified. It gave me a huge happiness, there in the twilight, to see the coloured pennants assembling. When the drawer was filled I called Joyce in to view it. She admitted that anyone who owned so many scarves measured up to Judy's expectation of unlimited grandeur! However, to my eye one thing was lacking: the display required, I said, 'some kind of crowning glory'. Then, inspired, I raked out of my oddments box a length of diamante which I had used in rep. Twisted round a spray of waxed orchids, and set inside a round, transparent box supplied by Joyce, it created a child's vision of all the world's great social evenings packaged small enough to hold. We laid it on top of the rainbow of scarves, and Joyce and I agreed that we had created the impression of 'everything plus the crown jewels'.

The stratagem worked. Led on a conducted tour which began with tweed and ended with silk, Judy expressed herself satisfied; but it was the scarf drawer which invoked the greatest response. The episode was to give me subsequently an idea for a play.

It gave me something more. That drawer filled with orderly ranks of colour, topped with the preposterous plastic box of glitter, was never dismantled. It was to remain a feature of my life from that day forward. I knew what it had done for Judy; what it had done for me I was not to discover until many years later. . . .

3

DURING THE TIME THE TRUNK WAS MISSING THE SATURDAY PARTIES had been the bright spot in my week. Their inner corps was artistic, medical, legal, but anyone passing through Edinburgh who knew of their existence had only to contact a member of the circle, ask 'Where is it being held tonight?' and arrive at the given address armed with a bottle of wine. Included, apart from ourselves and personal friends of the hosts', were members of foreign cultural missions, delegates to conferences, and, indeed, just about anyone of any creed, class, colour or profession who might be interesting and interested. There was no telling who might be seated at one's side, conversing in which language. I loved those gatherings because they were *my* Scotland – no longer remote to me beyond a medieval portcullis, but live and immediate within a contemporary Scottish living-room.

It was at one such party, not long after the return of the trunk, that Alec Reid tried to tell me about an item of historical interest just up the road from where I was staying: I was not truthfully interested. I had just embarked on a modern, homely, television play by way of respite from dramatic happenings in ancient Sparta, and historic monuments were the last thing I wanted to discuss. A lively debate going on just behind Alec drowned his voice. He was telling me about the 'bore-stane'. In my English-educated ignorance I had no idea what was a bore-stone, but I gathered from a few words which reached me that it was the stone in which a battle standard was set at the time of a mustering. At this point I grew restive and cast envious glances towards the rival group whose conversation was drowning ours. All I could hear of Alec's discourse were a few isolated words – 'burgh muir . . .' 'mustering . . .' then the name 'Flodden'. That was the point when I became intensely irritated, cross with Alec for spoiling my evening with a load of history when I had come decked-out in my favourite full-skirted dress with dangling earrings and stiletto heels, pretty as paint and knowing it. Normally I enjoyed talking to Alec and I felt guilty for feeling this way about him, so I tried to make amends by shouting above the noise, 'Where did you say it was?'

202

'Just up the road from where you stay. You know Church Hill? You should take a walk to see it.'

'I will,' I said, meaning to do nothing of the sort. As I rose to leave him, urgently now, I found myself standing feet apart in a strong, unfeminine stance, and I felt the wide, stiff belt of my dress containing me like armour. The next moment I had tucked myself on the floor within the protective circle of people arguing about life today. Spreading my skirt, fluttering my eye-lashes, I pulled out all the stops in the *femme fatale* act which was my usual contribution to the evening. It was the role expected of me on Saturdays, and I played it with zest for the amusement of all. On this night I overplayed, knowingly, conscious all the time of my dangling earrings which gave me reassurance.

I worked hard and played hard, the only way to keep at bay the economic terrors now engulfing me. The year's option on *The Man from Thermopylae* had ended, and with it the regular monthly supply of dollars. Bills for storage of my furniture depleted my now small resources: hard times were becoming a permanent state. One consolation, however, was a return of my proficiency in writing, and the new television play was going well. I had not submitted a synopsis for commission, so financially it was a gamble, but I was enormously cheered to find myself once more writing with all my old professionalism. Between work, worries, and the Saturday parties, I was anchored firmly in the present, which made the more startling an incident which occurred during the writing of that play.

A friend from the Saturday gatherings had taken me out for a drink at the Abbotsford. There we encountered a man introduced to me as Sunny—a small, neat fellow in his fifties with a square head and thinning hair. The three of us left the pub together to call upon another friend, and the conversation between Sunny and myself became isolated from the rest.

He wanted to talk about writing and the theatre. I wanted to talk about the Army, for I had identified the man immediately as an ex-regular, which, it transpired, he was. He had just been telling me of his meeting with Vivien Leigh and his correspondence with Siegfried Sassoon when he suddenly flashed at me the question, 'What was Richard the Lion Heart to you?'

I gasped, and asked, *How did you know?*—meaning, how did he know that when I was nineteen I had written a play about Richard, Joanna and John Plantagenet. Sunny replied, 'I just wondered. . . .' I told him briefly about the play, then led the conversation back to the Army. I was referring to my experience with the A.T.S. and assumed that he was speaking from similar recent context; the Army being the ageless institution it is, it was in no way surprising to find ourselves discussing the advantage of the legion over the phalanx – although the phalanx, I said, was best for 'green men'. Then I went on to mention the cavalry deterrent of crossed spars with a sharpened timber resting in the crutch – which he had last seen used at Waterloo, though I remembered it from an earlier time and the name I used was older French than his. Then again he interpolated a sudden exclamation, 'Of course! They were the ones with red hair. Your hair was black.' I tugged my short red locks and snapped, 'Of course my hair was black!' He was being as tiresome as people who squeal at me, 'Oh, you're left-handed!'

Then I clutched at him. 'I remember you,' I said, 'wearing mail and some kind of leather jerkin. You had a square steel bonnet on your head with a kind of red braid inlaid down the back, or it may have been a strip of enamel inlay. You are standing on the foreshore with your back to the sea, and the waves are lapping nearly to your heels. You are very angry about something.'

He laughed. 'I wouldn't be surprised at that.'

The sudden, clear picture excited yet perturbed me. Just then sandwiches appeared, the conversation became general, and any questions I might have asked were lost. Shortly afterwards we departed, with some distance to walk to the parked car which was taking us home. Crossing Charlotte Square we fell in step together, automatically. We had walked like this before – across a camp ground. Out of the dark, the man marching at my side said suddenly, 'Of course! You were a *man*. That's what has been confusing me.' I retorted, 'Well, of course I was a man! What did you expect?'

'Of course I was a man. What did you expect?' I heard my own voice say it, and I knew it to be absolutely true: the swish of my several petticoats and the click of my high heels did not seem incongruous to me, merely making me want to laugh at some uproarious cosmic joke. In the car he tried to take my hand, as many men did, but this was plain ridiculous. I said, 'Oh, not you, for God's sake! *You* should know better!' He laughed and clipped back at me, 'You can't blame a soldier for trying.' I replied, 'No, I don't. But damn it, man, I was *your commanding officer*!' It was the plain truth, and our chorus of merriment from the back seat was impossible to share with our friends in the front who could hardly be expected to see a joke which spanned several centuries.

When I reached home, automatically I began to prepare myself for bed, but my mind, stimulated by the extraordinary encounter, could not be dragged away from the subject. Scraps of words came into my head, and a name – Thaler – Thailer – Tahler – I could not visualise the word, but its sound rang through my head, a heavy guttural no longer spoken. Jehann Thaler had been his name. He was Flemish.

More broken words came into my head – Flemish? – or old German? I was no longer sure, for the next clear name was Nuremberg. The man I knew as Thaler seemed to be connected with Nuremberg. I scribbled down his name on the back of my cigarette box. (I always bought cigarettes in boxes of fifty because it saved me fiddling with small packets when I was working.) Then I wrote Nuremberg – but my hand instinctively spelled it Nürnberg, which was the way I thought it. So he was *German*. And so, presumably, was I. Munich was the next word, which my hand set down as München. München, I felt, related to me. Who on earth was I?

Then came into my head a conviction that Thaler had been my father's quarter-master serjeant-at-arms who had accompanied me to the wars when I was eighteen, young, green and scared of making a fool of myself. This I was sure was right, wherever it fitted.

We had mentioned the Third Crusade, therefore it was to that period I related the subsequent happenings in my head. What I was now remembering was my own voice roaring across a chaotic camp-site for 'Thaler!' – the man who dealt with everything when I was harassed to death by too many people, my indispensable right-hand man.

As I took off my high-heeled shoes and crossed to the cupboard to put them away, I was still trying to remember who I had been. The name München fitted somewhere. . . . Then suddenly I had it: whoever held Munich of the Emperor was my father. This, I decided firmly, was the point at which I would leave the subject and go to my bed. As I sat drinking my hot milk I told myself that, whatever it was, it was better forgotten.

I was due to finish my television play the next day, and most writers would agree that when one is nearing the climax of a play concentration is at its most intense. I had joked many times that at that stage of my writing the house could burn down and I would not notice until my wax earplugs melted. Nothing foreign enters my mind. I was typing like a maniac, entirely absorbed, but, to my absolute fury, a whole collection of old German words tumbled into my mind every time I paused to fit carbons. To accommodate this tiresome phenomenon I put beside my typewriter the empty cigarette box from the previous evening and my pen, so that whenever a word came into my head I jotted it down automatically so that I could forget about it. In that fashion I approached the last page of the play.

It was then I had to rush away to the lavatory, and I had no sooner left my typewriter than a mass of medieval images poured into my mind. As I sat on the pedestal I screamed in exasperation at the toilet roll, '*Who was I?*' I did not even want to know, but there was something in my head determined to get out. A name surfaced – it sounded like Aileg. To appease my overactive unconscious so that my conscious

205

mind could get back to work, I accepted the name Aileg – Aileg von München. Whether Aileg von München had been a factual person or a fictitious one I did not care, and I had no intention of wasting time trying to find out. All I wanted was to get back to the play.

Then, as I came striding from the bathroom, my pace lengthened in sheer anger, I happened to glance down and saw with startling clarity *a black on white linen surcoat* worn over armour. It was gone in a flash, and in a downward glimpse of one's own chest it is not easy to make out detail, but the squared line of black on white is unmistakable. This experience totally unnerved me, for it was the last thing I could have expected.

Why *black* on white?

I had to fight my way through the last page of the play, and then I turned to deal with the ghosts in my head. It was fourteen years since I did the research for my play about Coeur de Lion and I tried to recall what I had read about the insignia of the Third Crusade. The English had worn green crosses on their surcoats. The French were red. Then I remembered: the German followers of Barbarossa wore black crosses! This startled me. Had my mind gone a-roving wishfully with Coeur de Lion's crusaders I might have imagined a green surcoat, but I would never in a thousand years have pictured myself as one of Barbarossa's men! This seemed curiously to corroborate a tale which by this time I preferred to treat as fiction.

Fiction or not, my playwright's mind seized at once upon a new way to present *The Devil's Children*. I could use the hypothetical Aileg von München as an introductory character in the play. Within an hour I had composed a powerful, new dramatic framework in which to set the theme of Richard's battle with his soul, and *The Devil's Children* – still one of my favourite plays – began to look as though it had a future.

I did not write it. The black and white surcoat put me off. As a writer I could devise a splendid tale of the young German knight, his veteran henchman and their fortunes interwoven with those of the English king – all the stuff which had filled my head for twenty-four hours could be comfortably suspended between fact and fiction. But not that surcoat. *I* had worn that black and white surcoat, glimpsed briefly coming from the bathroom, and into plays I did not put *myself*.

At the next Saturday party I was full of this weird story. It was the detail about the surcoat which I continually stressed. I wanted them to tell me it was nonsense. Some of them did. Others questioned me more closely. I went on and on about it, inwardly screaming to have someone persuade me to my own satisfaction that my pretty, high-heeled self was Ada F. Kay, playwright, suffering from too much imagination. But I went home knowing that I had made no mistake about that black and white surcoat.

206

From Sunny I received a poem, inspired by our encounter. It had been written in the formal, courtly style of a man dedicating a poem to a woman, but it recorded his amusement at my reaction to our meeting. Did I not know, he asked, that man had many lives? When I read it, I slammed it down with a quotation, aloud, from Browning, one which had imprinted itself firmly on my mind at school: 'Man has but one life and one death, one heaven and one hell.' I never acknowledged the poem, and I hoped not to meet the man again; but I kept for a long while the cigarette box scribbled with the words in old German. The memories I tossed into the mental rag-bag that stored all the irrelevant, unidentified pictures which had been in my head for as long as I could remember. The only one I put away carefully folded was the black and white surcoat: that, ominous now, lingered in my room at Leamington Terrace.

And I did not want to know about it.

I was Ada F. Kay in the year 1962; occupation, playwright; gender, female. *I did not believe in reincarnation.* I pulled down the shutters and I closed off half my mind.

The new television play written on speculation failed to find a market with the B.B.C. and I sent it nowhere else. To have another stage play presented in Scotland was my ambition, a modern Scots play. Using the theme of the lost trunk, I set the action in my own immediate locality of Bruntsfield – and made an interesting discovery: whereas formerly, in Great King Street, I had been too timorous to venture into Midlothian dialogue, here in Leamington Terrace I had complete command of accent and idiom from any part of Scotland. What set out to be a play about shattered illusion became an essay in verbal communication. I had the characters voice identical phrases to illustrate their lack of communication, and then at the end I had the Lewisman launch into a spate of Gaelic to convince the lady from America that he was a foreigner. With no thought of being 'national-istic' I had begun to fight for an old Scots culture against a world that could not see its value.

During July, August and September of 1962 I worked feverishly upon *The Trunk*. I worked without food or sleep, desperate to complete the play before I died. This sense of impending death which came with summer was nothing new – I had had it all my life – but some years it was worse than others, and that year it was particularly bad.

Nothing ailed me. To work such hours without food or sleep required the stamina of an ox. Also, it required dedication, which I had, for this play was being written *for Scotland*. All the work I did now had to be for Scotland; the old incentives of money and success had ceased to matter. Here was an astonishing change of attitude towards my work, for when in the 1950s there had been much talk about the playwright's 'commitment' I had quipped to my B.B.C. colleagues, 'The only thing to which I am committed is hard work.'

I worked at night when the rest of the world was sleeping, taking a short rest during the day. The ground floor of the house was shared by other nocturnal workers, a university lecturer, and a student and his fiancée. We four had adopted a way of life akin to that of monks in their cells; it was an extension of the way my husband and I had worked together. Nobody interrupted anyone else's work. Notes slipped silently beneath doors announced when coffee or cocoa would be available for those who wanted it. Softly, so as not to awaken the rest of the household, we would forgather in one room or another for a short break; sometimes talking of many matters, at other times sitting, cup in hand, quite silent. Occasional guests came to join us.

My room at this time had become a spiritual surgery. I joked, 'I'm sure there is a neon sign above my door which reads "Those with problems, apply within."' My window, at the front of the house, showed a light until daybreak and it held an irresistible attraction for strangers in agony. My copy of Thomas à Kempis was by my hand night and day, and when answers were needed to desperate questions there rose a ritualistic chorus, 'Let's see what Thomas has to say about it!'

During this period I became intensely telepathic, to the extent that my friends complained that telephoning me was a waste of money. When callers were heading for my door I knew precisely when to stop work, remove my earplugs and sit waiting for the doorbell. On one occasion, when deep in concentration, I was prompted suddenly to put on the coffee and set three cups. The doorbell rang just as the coffee was ready, and I said to my two friends on the doorstep, 'You're spot on time.' In answer to their astounded, *'How did you know?'* I explained, 'Well, you were just leaving the Bruntsfield, and you suddenly said "Let's see if Ada's at home." Actually, you had intended going home, so there was a bit of a discussion about it.' That was precisely what had happened. My two friends were physicists and wanted to examine the phenomenon. I dismissed the matter with a brief 'I'm used to it.' As long as I had removed my earplugs in time to hear the doorbell, I was not really interested in whys and hows and wherefores.

Telepathy and foreknowledge of others' deaths I had lived with, off and on, for a lifetime. What was new to me during this period was an extraordinary sense that the walls surrounding me were not entirely real. I said frequently that my room was open to infinity upon all sides, and I made use in the play of 'walls of glass' both figurative and real. On occasions I would lift my head suddenly from my typewriter to answer questions put to me by people who were not there. Once, I was astonished by the presence of the *room*. I had just glimpsed the Forth in the distance, reflecting sunlight, as though I had been in the open air.

The sense of impending death was more definite, and it never left me. I had put into the play a line – given to the elderly Lewisman – 'As I grow old, the curtain between life and death is so fragile that I am sure I could put through it my hand and touch a shoulder on the other side.' This speech was pure Ada F. Kay 1962. I could feel death like a wall growing ever closer – on my left. I kept saying that death was just here, by my left cheek, and it was so close that I was sure I could put my hand through it.

At one of our evening coffee sessions I made pencil sketches of them all – Jim in his chair; Barbara curled up with a book; Ian and Denis playing chess. It was the first drawing I had done since leaving London. When I returned to my room I began to compose a picture. It was pure allegory, as I knew at the time, and, unlike the individual sketches, had no artistic merit. It was more like the drawing of a child, or of a late medieval painter, proliferating in limned happenings. The page was divided down the middle by a stone wall, reaching to infinity. On one side was living land where grew flowers and leaves: on the other was a barren wilderness of dried mud-shards, with rank upon rank of decapitated trees standing like soldiers. In the wall was a gate, guarded by two black-winged angels. At the foot of the gate, on the living side, sat the figures of Barbara and Ian playing chess; seated at the foot of the wall, watching them, was Jim. My own figure I drew seated on top of the wall, head turned to look back into the wilderness as I watched for 'the next man in'.

I wrote a fragment of verse upon the same theme, calling it 'The Song of the Night Wanderers' but it was never finished. Then I used the idea for a novel which opened 'There is always one who sees. . . .' Several pages were written before I dismissed it as 'pretentious'. Having no esoteric learning, I was unaware that the interlude passages, the only parts which really interested me, described higher planes of consciousness recognisable to the initiated.

These artistic and literary experiments were to me a waste of time. I had to obey the compulsion to set them to paper, but once compulsion had been recognised it went away leaving me to get on with my work. My growing concern was to finish the play in the short time I had left. Death at my left hand had come so close that I could feel it clammy, like a wall of damp stone.

At the beginning of October I was nearing the end of the play. Then, to my annoyance, my watch and my alarm clock broke down simultaneously. I could not spare the time or money to have them repaired – and, anyway, I had the feeling that my need for any sort of time-keeping instrument would not last much longer. Meanwhile, I borrowed from Jim, my neighbour, his alarm clock during the day and his watch at night. Before I retired at 7.30 a.m. for a few hours' rest I would hand in the watch and take in its place the alarm clock. This Box and Cox arrangement was now almost the only contact I had with any of my neighbours.

One night in mid-October (the date may have been the 25th, but of that I am not certain) at about 11 p.m., I knocked on Jim's door to make a somewhat unusual request. I explained that I was reaching the end of the play, and reckoned that I would have it finished by about five o'clock in the morning. What concerned me was the closeness of death: the presence, which had been about four inches from the left side of my head, had now moved in so close that I could feel it brushing my cheek. I made it clear that I was not certain I would die, but the chance was fifty-fifty. My intention was to work to the end of the play, then I would put Jim's watch on the hall table for him to find in the morning. I would then put the 'Sleeping – Do Not Disturb' notice on my door, which was customary when I retired after an all-night working session. Usually, I woke at noon, drank my coffee, then removed the notice. I told Jim that if the notice was still on my door when he returned at his usual hour of 5.30 p.m. he could take it as indication that something was amiss. ('You will know that I have not quite made it' were the words I used.) In which case I wanted him to open my unlocked door, and 'deal in whatever way is necessary'. He would find on my table several packages and documents, all labelled, and I wanted him to see that the various instructions reached the people for whom they were intended.

I could have expected him to say, 'Of course you'll be alive tomorrow,' for he was agnostic, a scientist, and he took many of my ideas with a liberal dash of salt. Or he might have tried to humour me. He did neither of these things. He simply nodded, took careful note of my instructions, and agreed to do what I asked. As I left his door, he said, 'Good luck, Ada.'

I went back to my room and found the roughly scribbled 'will' which I had written and friends had witnessed some days previously. I then wrote a note, asking my B.B.C. colleague Alistair to complete the text of the play from the rough draft I had compiled. Swiftly, I scribbled another note asking Ian, whom I had already consulted in the matter, to burn any writings other than play scripts which he might find anywhere in the room. None of these directives contained farewell messages; they were simply a precaution taken by a practical person. No thought of suicide was in my head, so I had no cause to leave explanatory notes for anyone. As I had said to Jim, I hoped that none

210

of my precautions would be necessary, but I was obliged to take them 'just in case'.

I dealt swiftly with these items of business, then took up my pen to complete the play. For that script I had reverted to my old system of writing the rough draft in long-hand, a practice I had discontinued when I joined the B.B.C. Blank pages filled rapidly with dialogue in that long-familiar brown ink. I had now reached the last drops in my bottle, and when I refilled my pen I can remember wondering whether it would last long enough to finish the play.

The climax of the third act was the arrival of the lost trunk and the child's disillusionment on finding that it held not the treasure she had imagined but what she described as 'Just a lot of *old clothes!*' I ended it on a note of hope, using the device of the sparkling diamante I had shown Judy, but in the play the diamante had become a crown – a battered, old, theatrical tiara. I had taxed my strength to the utmost by the time I had brought forth that crown out of my trunk.

There is always an exhilaration and a sadness when one reaches the end of a play; relief because the task is almost finished and regret because the characters with whom one has lived for so long go on their way, leaving the writer alone. This one play was different from the others I had written because I knew that, when the characters made their exit, their author might go with them.

Truly, it was irrelevant to me what happened. I felt only a faint apprehension because my world might be a different world by morning, but that prospect faces everyone at some time, be it on the eve of battle or the threshold of an operating theatre. The one certainty that life allows us is the knowledge that some time, in some way, we shall die. It seemed to me a terribly familiar situation, novel at that moment only because I was thirty-three years out of practice. I would have liked to finish off the play myself but, if it was not to be, I had completed the rough draft and Alistair, perhaps, would finish it for me. The rest of my worldly affairs were in order.

I heated a cup of hot milk and contemplated two sleeping-pills, my normal dose. I pondered whether the sedative would top the fifty-fifty chance of survival, and finally decided to take them: my future, or lack of it, depended on something a great deal more powerful than two capsules of sodium amytal.

I prepared myself for bed, then drank my hot milk, having taken special care that it did not boil over to leave a messy stove behind me if I died. Kneeling beside my bed I 'commended myself to God' – the phrase used in all the best fairy stories of my childhood – then I lay down, resigned to whatever lay ahead of me.

The last sound I heard was the marching of many feet – heard so clearly that I roused myself to momentary consciousness to listen to their tramp, tramp, tramp. . . . So many, and there was a great field darkened by the column of a marching army. . . . Conscious, I smiled as I recognised the thud . . . thud . . . thud of my own heartbeats. I lost the image, and slept.

At noon of the next day I wakened. I was in the bed-sitting-room in Leamington Terrace, and the damp presence from beside my left cheek had gone completely. I surfaced from sleep with the thought, 'Good gracious, *I made it!*' and a tremendous sense of triumph and relief. I was totally a different person. With great cheerfulness and a zest for living, I scrambled out of bed to light the gas-fire and make my first cup of coffee.

What happened during that night is still to me a mystery.

4

WHEN I CAME TO THE END OF THE BROWN INK IN THE SMALL CONTAINER I used when travelling, I sent to Waterman's for a further twenty-ounce bottle to replace the one which had gone into storage with my furniture. On 8 November my cheque was returned with a letter informing me that their stock of brown ink was exhausted.

I sat staring at the letter as though it had brought tidings of death. When brown ink went off the market I had been assured by Waterman's that supplies would still be available direct from the manufacturers; that they were simply disposing of old stock had not occurred to me, for I had inferred from their letter that a limited quantity was still being made. I wrote frantically to the firm, asking could they make up for me a quantity as a special order, or alternatively supply me with a recipe for making my own brown ink. When my letter remained unanswered I resorted to purchasing a number of inks in various colours, hoping that by mixing them I could – as with water colour – obtain a tolerable shade of brown. The experiment was a failure, and I was left to face a future bereft of brown ink until such time as my furniture came out of storage.

I had never asked myself why brown ink was so important to me. When it was remarked upon, I always explained that 'when I am writing thirty pages at a time I find brown ink less trying to the eyes', but I never said that I used brown ink because I liked it. My compulsion always to explain away its use should have warned me that I was possibly covering up some deeper motive which I did not wish to know. The brown ink, in fact, had been a link in my chain of continuity – as I realised, now it was broken.

The trouble with black ink was that it dried grey. For a spell I tried indian ink, but that clogged my fountain pen. In an effort to reconcile myself to grey ink, I bought grey paper, discarding the parchment colour I had always used, and left the ink to dry instead of blotting it – but it bore no relation whatever to me. All my writing during the period 1962–6 gave me the impression that it was done by another hand.

The end of the brown ink in 1962 coincided with a proliferation of nocturnal verse writing.

My serious efforts to write poetry ceased at the age of twenty-one when I realised that I could never write a sonnet as well as William Shakespeare. By setting my criterion so high I spared myself a lot of heart break and the world a lot of third-rate verse. Since that time, no longer obliged to take my own poetry seriously, I had occasionally written humorous verse to amuse my friends or, more often, used the blank-verse form to jot down my inward reflections which did not have a place in my professional writing.

When I came to live in Leamington Terrace there was a noticeable increase in the quantity of these jottings. Ideas totally unconnected with the play I was writing would invade my mind when I was at work, distracting me to the point of exasperation. To get rid of them I seized the nearest sheet of paper – or even inverted the exercise-book in which I was writing, to use a back page – scribbled them out of my mind, and then forgot about them. Their destination was the waste paper basket, but all too often my filing system consisted of layers of daily correspondence interleaved with vital pages of manuscript, and, as the poems were usually written on the back of an item more important, a good deal of this verse became more immortal than I had intended. The twin themes which recur persistently are dead men's hands and the skeletal form of trees in winter.

In 1962 I began to write a great deal of verse in semi-conscious moments. Awaking in the night to obey the call of nature, I would go suddenly to the table, scribble over several pages, and return to my bed. Or, returning exhausted in the small hours from one of the Saturday gatherings, I would find myself compelled to write a poem before retiring. Or when my sleeping-pills had begun to work, I would be struck by some thought which had to be set on paper. In the morning these pages were normally pushed, unread, beneath the litter of papers on my table. My fully conscious self had no interest in looking to see what I had written.

The most extraordinary feature of these discarded poems is that almost every one of them is meticulously dated. This trait becomes more curious when it is set beside another habit, developing at this period, of heading my personal letters 'Monday 11 a.m.' or 'Sunday afternoon' with no reference to month or year. Odder still, in every one of the undated letters there is inserted somewhere, quite naturally in a sentence, a reference to the year of my age. Why did my semi-conscious mind wish to record so carefully what were my inward thoughts at a certain moment of my life, and why did my fully-conscious, letter-writing mind date my world according to the years of my age instead of a calendar?

Reading the fragments of verse these years later, I am able to see plainly why my conscious mind at that time wished to have nothing to do with them, for every one of them is trying to tell me something which I was fighting to reject. I shall quote just one, totally unedited, written in the fateful October of that year 1962, which illustrates my state of mind at that time:

> I am endowed with death.
> Across my day the hairline cracks
> Encroach as softly as the sun at noon
> Tips from its zenith one hint down.
>
> No malady wastes visibly my bones;
> All spent of morrows that I shall not see,
> Led by a hope which is the ruse of time
> To keep me venturing on,
> Yet see beyond the face that other face
> Set free.
>
> So moves a pen . . . (supple of grasp,
> These dead men's fingers, mine!)
> — Scribbling novelties which were age-old
> When penned by me in Achelon.
>
> Here, in the moment of restatement
> I may surely claim the privilege
> To think that I am me, and for a moment *am*.
>
> The voice beyond the voice beyond the voice
> Ipse eternal, is not deceived in thinking
> That this beating heart cages reality;
> Nor are the eyes within too much confounded
> By the image of a rose, hung on its bones
> By dead men's dreams, for dead men's hope
> To muse upon.
>
> Hung on its bones by dead men's dreams,
> *This* is illusion, that I am fathered
> And fathering of man, mortal posterity.
> Truth is: I am and was brother to me in Achelon.

214

I am, shall be, to me by friend, here
And hereafter. Freed of death, in unity,
Amused, we from our quietude shall dream
Again a whim of flesh upon a bone, and say,
'Humanity passed here. . . .

Plans for the American production of *The Man from Thermopylae* had
to be abandoned: at the time of the Cuban crisis it was unlikely that a
play which viewed war through the cynical eyes of a 'dead' soldier
would draw enthusiastic New York audiences. I threw myself into the
revision of *The Trunk*, which henceforward I retitled *The Year of Mrs
Hannibal*. The Scottish theatre was my last remaining hope – if hope it
could be called – for there was no opening in television in Scotland.
Two or three times I had travelled through to Glasgow to remind the
Corporation that I was still alive, but the B.B.C. in Glasgow had
worries of its own.

My few journeys to and from Glasgow were marked by nothing
more important than a curious phenomenon which occurred upon the
train. I always sat upon the left side of the carriage, and at a certain
point where the train stopped I saw close to me a board which read
Linlithgow. Just for a second I felt the terrible surge of spirit which once
had filled me when, as a small child, I had seen the Stirling Castle
poster. I was not interested in the view, just in that strip of platform and
the magic word Linlithgow which made my stomach lurch because it
spelled for me *my* Scotland. I said once to Joyce Heller, 'I shouldn't
mind going to live in Linlithgow.' She observed, 'Yes, it's a nice town.'
I confessed that, actually, I had not seen it, but its station platform
made me think of *home*.

On my return from Glasgow I was each time immersed in the
evening paper. My destination was Haymarket Station, Edinburgh. As
the train began to slow down, I sensed that I was nearing home, folded
away my newspaper, put on my gloves and picked up my briefcase to
leave the train. Expecting to see the sign Haymarket, I was startled to
see the name Linlithgow. Feeling an utter fool, I returned to my seat,
wondering how I could thus have misjudged the distance I had
travelled. When I had done the same thing three times, I made a joke
about it to the Hellers. It never happened at any other station – only
Linlithgow.

As a playwright desperate to earn a living, I should have been on that
train more often going to Glasgow, establishing wider connections
with the television world. B.B.C. television drama transmitted from
Glasgow had all but ceased under the stranglehold of Shepherd's Bush.
One day my old stable-mate, Alistair, came through from Glasgow to
see me for the last time: his position as script editor had been one of the

posts swept away by the new regime, and he was going back to London. His anger was directed against me, provoked by my determination to fight on in Edinburgh. He told me that I was 'a bloody good writer destroying yourself for the sake of – what is it, Ada? – some kind of lunatic dream about Scotland. Well, *I* won't! I'm going back to London where I can get paid good money for script-writing. And if you have any kind of sense, you'll do the same.' I stood my ground and told him I was staying. He poured out a torrent of Scots rage against 'this——country!' I knew precisely what he was feeling, and I let him rage. He shouted at me from the door, 'You'll ruin yourself! Why? Why? Is this bloody country worth it?' I shouted back at him, 'I'm *staying*. One of us must stay.' The last look we exchanged was one of mutual compassion; his final words were flat and resigned: 'I think you're mad . . . but if that's the way you feel about it. . . .'

When Alistair had gone I beat my fists upon the table, calling down damnation upon those who ruled us from London. I had not done that before.

I had met them everywhere, in trains and aeroplanes, expatriate Scots whose jobs had died on them due to London-orientated administration. Alistair's departure had merely brought home to me more plainly what I knew from my own experience, that Scotland held no future for a writer. And if a writer, technically a free agent, could not earn a living in Scotland, what hope had the rest of the population?

My own fight for survival had become for me Scotland's fight for survival. The plight of its people was the source of my inspiration: not heroic tragedy, just the small stuff of families torn apart, people uprooted whose dream had been to rear their children and be buried in the small towns were they were born. My synopses sent to Glasgow were returned. There was no Scottish television drama now; just a few slots available in London drama schedules, which had been filled for the current year . . . and I thought to myself, Yes; and not one of them will be allowed to make a statement about human life in Scotland as it is lived *today*.

I had meant it when I told Alistair that I would stay to fight for Scotland no matter what it cost me, but I had come to dread the morning mail, bringing its load of bills for storage of my furniture, reminders about my bank overdraft and letters of rejection from my old colleagues at the B.B.C. Nobody worked harder to achieve so little and each morning's failure became a terror which I took to bed with me at night.

Bad days though they were, I let nothing quench my gaity: I wore it like a flag. Come the day of the Saturday party, wherever it was held, I would be dressed and ready when transport arrived, complete with my bottle of wine and my extra box of fifty cigarettes. (I was always lavish

216

with cigarettes and impecuniosity could not change the habit.) I never wore the same clothes for consecutive parties, and my extensive wardrobe, changed around with scarves and jewels worn differently, made it a question of interest what I would be wearing. I had to make the most of being a bonny, well-dressed woman of thirty-three, for it was all I had left.

The Saturday parties remained my sole recreation. I never took a holiday. It had been remarked that, for one who had sacrificed both personal and professional success in order to gain a foothold in Scotland, I took surprisingly little interest in seeing the country; for all that I saw of the landscape beyond my typewriter, it was said, I might as well have stayed in London. It was impossible to explain that my chair at the typewriter in a room in Leamington Terrace was my Scotland. In good time, if I waited patiently, Time would invite me out into a wider field; some personal connection, or a duty, would take me to the Highlands, Islands and the Borders, where I would be not a visitor floating upon the surface of reality, but an accepted member of the living, working community.

It was at one of the Saturday gatherings that I met Kathleen McLellan, the wife of Robert McLellan the playwright, over from Arran. As soon as we met I had the premonition that 'Time would let me in'. During the party she introduced me to another guest, Ian Hamilton. I hailed him, 'So you are the man who took the Stone of Destiny!' and told him how the deed had affected me, down in Lancashire, those long years ago. He, upon introduction, had hailed me, 'So you are the author of *The Man from Thermopylae!*' and told me how profoundly he, as an advocate, had been stirred by a statement in the play on the theme of justice. For much of the evening we held a duologue of mutual admiration, only slightly marred by the fact that I was sick and tired of being the author of *Thermopylae* – I had written other plays! – and he was sick and tired of being The Man Who Took the Stone of Destiny. At the end of the evening the three of us were driven home together, and Kathleen, who shared my Lancastrian origin, said to me in the car as we were parting, 'Do you like Lancashire hot-pot?' And when I replied that I did, she continued, 'Then would you like to eat some with us on Arran next weekend?' Time had let me in. Her letter containing travelling instructions reached me a couple of days later, and included the observation – 'This maybe foolish, and maybe even rather cheeky, but I had a hunch you were in some sort of inner distress, and if you are – which I hope you aren't! – you'll find Arran very healing.' (Had it begun to show, I wondered, the bleak despair behind the mask I wore for parties?)

The next weekend, following Kathleen's instructions, I took the train to Glasgow, and thence to Fairlie. Along the route landscapes that I knew kept flashing by me. It was a grey, misty day with a raw wind sawing off my ears as I boarded the vessel bound for Arran. Weather regardless, I stood alone upon the boat-deck, watching for my first sight of the Islands.

It was not my first sight – as I realised when, through the mist, I saw looming the blue-grey shapes of the two Cumbraes and the long, humped line of Bute. The Clyde Estuary was momentarily as familiar as the ferry crossing to Knott End in my native Lancashire. I had sailed here many times; not even the mist could blanket my awareness. Only the retinue of tall ships and of people was missing, and the swarm of small boats approaching as near as they dared to satisfy their curiosity. But their absence carried physical reality, as though I saw the holes they had made in Time's wall. . . .

My spirit soared to meet the seagulls and the wind bore away my tears. Happiness had left a salt taste to my lips, for my last visit to the Islands had been *so long ago*. So long. . . .

Scotland had a place for me still on Arran. My visit coincided with a meeting of the Arran Parents' Association fighting for the upgrading of Lamlash School so that the island's children would no longer have to go to Bute or to the mainland for their secondary education. There was little I could do to help but pay my subscription and cheer when I read their correspondence in *The Scotsman*. Not a parent, nor ·an islander, it was astonishing how passionately I cared about the future of the island children: I had forgotten the ambition that once I had to found a university upon Iona.

Apart from my long winter visits to Arran, I rarely now left Edinburgh even to see my parents. My journeys to London, so necessary to me professionally, had ceased. It was not merely that I could not afford the expense of travelling, I hated leaving Scotland even for a short while. To be absent seemed to me like dereliction of duty.

At this time, the beginning of May 1963, began the pattern of arrested menstruation which was to become part of the process of memory recall during the years that followed. My experience of that particular female phenomenon had been erratic from the beginning. I was simply not good at it. From the age of thirteen it had been to me an alien manifestation and I was amazed that women could take it in their stride as natural. To me it was the most unnatural occurrence imaginable, and when I had other matters on my mind it became the most expendable item in my programme. Unfortunately, it was, however, a biological feature whose malfunctioning affected the clarity of my thinking processes – and with those I had enough trouble at this time without further interference.

My problem in the past had been over-frequent menstruation, a condition which had already taken me to the hospital where there was found to be no organic disorder. Now I was at my doctor's surgery to report a reversed pattern of symptoms. I asked him whether this could be the beginning of the menopause? He asked, 'How old are you?' I told him, 'Thirty-four,' at which he laughed, 'You're but a lassie yet!' I asked what was the earliest menopause he had encountered, and he replied, 'Thirty-five, but that was exceptional.' I went home reflecting that my menstrual system had never been anything but exceptional. However, I had no other menopausal symptoms, and my distressed way of life would have made any female's biological system rebel.

Recent news from my husband had not cheered me. The break up of 'the marriage with England' had set in train a pattern of events affecting others besides ourselves. This added greatly to my distress, for it revived old memories for which I could not account of the severance of a 'marriage alliance with England' which had brought some kind of tragedy to Scotland. I was hounded by a sense of guilt – guilt for what? – which tore my psyche to ribbons.

Both personally and professionally I was a worn-out shell by the time I received a phone call to say that *The Man from Thermopylae* was planned for West End production. I liked the sound of both partners in the enterprise, with one of whom I established immediately that deep rapport which does not happen often in a lifetime. The sound of the Kentucky drawl upon the telephone became a lifeline in my wasteland existence. When I was asked to go to London to do some more work on the script (reshaping the American version for English consumption), the voice enquired where did I normally stay when in London? I replied that in the past I had stayed with my husband, but that just at present relations between us were not too good – whereupon I was promptly offered hospitality, which I accepted.

When I arrived at the flat in Shepherd Market I was told, 'The first thing you want to see is your room,' and was escorted to it. Everything that was silver, exquisite and necessary to my comfort awaited me. I exclaimed, 'But this *is* my room!' to receive the reply, 'It was intended to be.' (In fact, it had been created for me.) 'And the next thing,' said my host, when I had cast my gloves and jacket, 'is a drink. Come along.' And by the touch of a finger he led me into the drawing-room. There I came face to face with it: above one of the two beautiful, oval, Regency mirrors there was set a diadem, made of paste stones set in base metal, shrieking its incongruity.

I did not know him well enough to ask what it was doing there. His partner, who called later to meet me, had no such inhibitions. It turned out to be a souvenir of their previous show, and my host that morning upon a whim had set it above the mirror. He did not require telling that its dominating presence spoiled the room, but he said he meant to leave

219

it there a while. Asked for my opinion, I was non-commital: I could not explain that to my eyes it represented stark tragedy. Whose tragedy I did not know. I was repelled and fascinated by it.

I was marvellously cherished during those days when I worked in my right-royally appointed bedroom-study. My favourite cameo brooch, with its pin that broke on the morning I was setting out for London, was taken instantly to a jeweller for repair. When I snapped one of the slender straps of my favourite high-heeled sandals (bought on Church Hill) it was taken promptly, not once but three times, to a cobbler for stitching. When I required paper handkerchiefs (colour and size unspecified) he gave me first a box of small pink tissues; then, as I said involuntarily, 'Oh, but – I always—' he produced from behind his back a box of male-size white ones. He had purchased first the kind I ought to want, but his real hunch had been the right one. One day, when my brain was so bleak, befogged and empty that I wilted at my typewriter, a hand appeared suddenly over my left shoulder containing a silver vase of roses which was set behind my typewriter with the words, 'I felt you needed them.' I was cherished because I was 'the Author at work on the Play' (said my host); also, I was a badly damaged human being.

It was he who persuaded me to telephone my husband. In consequence Peter and I met in one of our old haunts and resumed communication. My host stayed out late that night, but he left the tray of decanters and glasses in the drawing-room for me to entertain my husband in my area of neutrality. Peter, however, declined the invitation, for which I was not sorry; I valued my stronghold free of disruptive emotions. He saw me to the door at the foot of the stair, then waited until I switched on the light to signal my safe arrival on the floor above. I watched from the window as he waved and then walked away across the courtyard.

Swift as light, Barnet, my good angel, returned to ask, 'How did it go?' and we had a drink together as I told him it went well; then I was packed off to my bed to be fresh for work upon the play in the morning.

While Barnet was in the house the presence of the diamante diadem did not too much worry me. I took care that when I walked from my room into the drawing-room or across to the dining-room I never allowed my reflection to fall upon the mirror beneath it. Then he had to go away for a weekend house-party and I was left alone. He had furnished me with everything I required to stand a siege, together with the telephone number of the house where he was staying so that I could reach him in emergency. As it was, he telephoned me each evening to make sure that all was well with me and to enquire about the progress of the play.

Actually, things were far from well, and progress on the play was minimal. I had assured him that I was safe, well and working. What I

220

could not say to anyone alive was that I was being drawn into that mirror which had a diadem above it. I went many times to look into the mirror, anxious to see myself as I knew me, but each time at the last moment I dodged the encounter. I was afraid that I would see my face in some way changed; or that I might see just a head-shaped hole where my face ought to be. Also, some old instinct knew not to see my own face beneath a crown: it had been a private rule of mine.

I could not work upon *Thermopylae* although desperately I tried. Instead, I wrote pages of verse, which took me nowhere, about an empty diadem above a mirror. It began: 'Alas, poor wraith, so to display man's nakedness on view. . . .' Seated in the chair beneath the mirror, where I could not see the diadem above me, I grew into the thing; it disturbed me less to feel its presence than to see it – indeed, I found it comforting, strangely familiar – inevitable – that glittering circlet suspended over my head. It was the pages of unfinished lines, constantly repeating, 'Alas, poor wraith . . .' which harassed and haunted me. I was thus seated when Barnet's key turned in the lock. Swiftly I concealed my pages of uncompleted verse within the script of *Thermopylae*. I think he was disappointed that I had done so little work, and I felt guilty because his great kindness had been so ill rewarded. I had meant to have the play nearly finished by his return. Also, I was guilty because of the pages of scribbled lines that I did not want him – want anyone! – to see: I was weighed down by my secret.

With Barnet back in the flat I finished the play in a matter of days. When I flew back to Edinburgh I had in a briefcase the London West End script . . . plus, unseen, hidden pages of secret verse describing the plight of a man beneath a diadem who had not been given proper burial. And with me came anger, huge anger for a diadem now *empty*, and in a strange way I knew at last what I was really for.

5

I HAD BEEN BORN WITH THE CONCEPT OF SCOTLAND AS A SOVEREIGN nation so there had never been a time when I was not a nationalist. It had taken me some while to discover how far nationhood had been eroded since my time, but the image in my head stayed clear as flame through all the vicissitudes besetting my process of discovery. When I came to live upon the ground I knew as Bruntsfield I was seized with a compulsion to recruit for Scotland. In the beginning, I do not think I was fully aware of what was happening; naturally hospitable, I gave coffee and an attentive ear to everyone who rang the doorbell, acquiring thereby confirmation of my own findings, namely, that life gets harder the further one moves from London. I knew my subject in hard contemporary terms by the time I began, in 1963, to point out to my various callers that the root cause of all our ills was maladministration from Westminster.

I had never been interested in politics, only in statecraft; the latter is, however, too often absent from government to allow most voters the chance of electing a parliamentary candidate on that ground, so my choice fell where it fitted. In Lancashire I had voted Conservative, even though my plays caused socialists to acclaim me as one of themselves. I was naturally apolitical; a determined fighter for individual human liberty, and a believer in the usefulness of law and order. When I went to London I voted there once as a Conservative, in Belsize Park. In the election of 1959 I did not vote at all because I was in process of removing to Edinburgh, a coincidence which spared me the dilemma of casting my vote in the constituency of Westminster, where, even by that time, I had realised it would be of no help whatever to Scotland.

In Leamington Terrace, during a municipal election, I allowed a Liberal poster to be displayed in my bed-sitting-room window, and I even went so far as to accept an application form for membership of the Liberal Party – although I never signed it. As the parliamentary election approached, I became that rogue creature the floating voter, holding strong views which benefit no official candidate. In Scotland I saw the Conservative Party as the Unionist Party, for which it was impossible to vote. I could not vote Labour, being too much of a realist, and anyway, socialism was only another name for Unionism in Scotland. There was no third candidate.

My electoral responsibility is something I hold dear as my life, for it shapes the future of a nation. To be a floating voter on the eve of a general election worried me profoundly.

My problem was resolved for me, in an odd way, when I was down in Lancashire. A Conservative lady canvasser called one evening when both my parents were out. I was in the throes of writing at the time, and, as I did not reside in the constituency, I felt disinclined to be drawn into its politics. I explained that I was a visitor, and my parents were not in the house. She then asked me what were their politics. I replied, politely, that if she wished an answer to that question her best policy was to call again and ask *them*. She snapped at me, 'But surely you must know?' By this time my hackles were rising. I said, still amiably, that, even if I did know how my parents voted, it was not for me to say.

She was persistent, asking me what were my own politics. I told her that I did not think that mattered; that as I did not reside in the district the local constituency affairs were not really my business. At this she gibed, 'I suppose you are one of those people who do not care about politics?' (She was not a very good canvasser.) By this time I was wearing the taut, sweet, dangerous smile which should have been a warning. In a tone to match it, I replied that I did indeed care very much how I cast my vote. She turned to go, and I heard my voice follow her, ringing clearly through the night air: 'And if you really want to know what I am – I live in Scotland, and I am a Scottish Nationalist.' She froze, eyes wide and mouth open; then she hurriedly clanged the iron gates and fled in terror.

I closed the door with exquisite satisfaction and leaned against it, laughing. Then suddenly I realised what I had just said, and my laughter switched off. I sat down on the stairs, shattered. My mind had been made up for me by a voice from within, and I was as astounded by my answer as the lady canvasser. I knew of the existence of the Scottish National Party, but I was too busy writing plays, too busy recruiting knife-grinders, rag-collectors and gypsies selling lace to give a name to the cause in which I laboured. All I cared about was the welfare of *my* Scots.

And there from a doorway in North Drive, Thornton Cleveleys, Lancashire, a voice had committed me to something I had never before defined in terms of politics. I made myself a cup of tea, as treatment for shock, which I drank seated on the stairs. Then I went back to my father's den where I was writing, pausing at the door to reflect that at least I was no longer a floating voter.

In the constituency of Edinburgh South there was no Scottish National Party candidate: Labour or Conservative were alternatives. On the morning of election day, I was feeling very ill, and it was raining. My spine was giving me trouble and my head was just a brainless fug. I dressed with much difficulty, and set out in the rain, limping wearily down to the polling station. Joyce said as I set out, 'And remember it's *Darroch* School,' because I had consistently made the mistake of calling it Boroughmuir, which was the other one. I had even asked her was she *sure* that Boroughmuir was not my polling station, so firmly was the name fixed in my head.

I had set out knowing what I meant to do, yet it seemed a futile gesture. Then, as I crossed the threshold of the polling station, I took on another personality: I came to challenge England's despots, and from the way I handed over my polling card it could have been they who were behind the table facing me. The classroom to which I was directed I found empty save for the two presiding officers, towards whom I directed a smile which stopped before it reached my eyes. In the booth I ignored the official pencil on its string and took out my fountain pen. As I set to work on my ballot paper I heard the stillness behind me, for it was apparent that I was writing words, not putting my docile cross beside either of the candidates' names. The two men started a false, impromptu conversation to cover my activities. I wrote

223

across the sheet, 'A plague on both your houses. Scotland needs Home Rule.' Then I folded it across, twice, to make a sharply pointed missile which I shot into the ballot box; I gave its lid a firm slap with my hand, a sealing gesture. I sensed the empty classroom shiver as though caught in the blast of an explosion – or was it my inward vision seeing moorland and water when there were no walls upon the Burgh Muir of Edinburgh? I know that in that second I felt enormous power surge through and from me. I bade the officials a ringing 'Good morning' and departed.

Once outside the polling station, again I wilted. I was just the battered Scot who got beaten everywhere; the body with a twisted spine and the head with a fog inside it and a depression so deep that no meteorologist could have charted it. And it was raining. . . . Normally I like rain, but on that morning it spelled for me annihilation.

I thought as I trudged back, what had I achieved for my pains? Who cared about spoiled ballot papers? I knew from my father, who had been presiding officer so many times at his own school, that nothing was to be gained by spoiling, intentionally or otherwise, one's ballot paper. I made myself a cup of cocoa and went to bed to rest my back. Still, I had done my duty. To abstain from voting would have been a negative gesture: at least I had made the effort to cancel out one vote for Westminster.

It was not until some weeks later that I met Wendy Wood for the first time, and during the course of general conversation I mentioned my lone, fruitless gesture. Then I learned that I was not alone: the number of individuals who had made their protest in the same way was sufficient to be taken seriously. Those ballot papers bearing our Scots messages had made, I learned, an impressive pile.

I was elated to hear that I had not limped through the rain upon the Burgh Muir for nothing.

6

THE REASON I MET WENDY WOOD HAD NOTHING WHATEVER TO DO with politics. We were introduced at the preview of an exhibition of paintings by Kathleen Wylie, a recent addition to my circle of friends. Wendy knew of me as the author of *The Man from Thermopylae*; I knew of her for her patriotic activities, and it came as a surprise to me to learn that she was herself an artist. We took to each other immediately, and for the rest of the morning we discussed painting, drama and the arts in general.

My drawing phase had ceased on my return to Scotland in 1961, as though I no longer required it. Then, one evening, at the beginning of

1963, when I had completed work on the script of *Thermopylae* for the West End, I found the ending of the play lingering in my head: 'When you are tired and crammed with years, I will not let them send the grey old ferryman to summon you. I will come myself, in the guise you best knew me, and we will set out together upon the road as in some morning from a memory.' I felt compelled to take out the new box of pastels (a gift from one of our circle in Hampstead) and draw the 'afterwards'.

I drew a long road, a hot, white road in Greece, with cliffs on either side, leading upward towards Mount Olympus encircled by its diadem of cloud – and beyond the cloud a Doric portal opened upon a colonnaded flight of steps reaching to infinity. The colouring and perspective of my landscape were so successful that, knowing pastel cannot be erased, it was with trepidation I set to work upon the two figures. Viewed from the rear, they had tremendous animation if no great technical merit. The soldier in his red cloak and the old beggar clad in a ragged blue mantle walked well together, their penultimate destination clear ahead of them.

I could have left it thus, but my mind knew that somewhere I must include a tree, struggling for life in the arid terrain. It had to be an indigenous tree, an olive, growing high upon a ledge, surviving there by sheer determination. I had never seen an olive tree. Then it turned out that Leslie, a temporary resident upon the ground floor, had whilst in Greece made a sketch of an olive tree so ancient that he felt compelled to record it: he had been fascinated by the new green leaves springing from a trunk so gnarled and senile. It had the look of a crippled ancient whose wits and will had defied whatever death had intended. It had every aspect I wanted – indeed, the rough ink sketch excited me so much that Leslie gave it to me. Working from it, I included in my composition a tiny speck of vegetation set high amongst the surrealistic rocks; it looked scarcely bigger than a weed, but there was no mistaking the tree which was one half dead, one half living.

It was a picture full of light and optimism, so serene that I left it lying in my room where I could see it. It was admired by my friends, of whom only one ventured a criticism: 'But your landscape has no shadows.' The remark startled me. I had never thought of adding shadows. I replied, 'But that landscape doesn't have shadows.' My critic (a physicist) insisted: 'But there must be a source of light. Where is the sun?' I explained: 'It doesn't have a sun. The whole place is made of *light*.'

Then I realised that my dead-tree drawings did not have shadows either.

As my circumstances and my health worsened I used the drawing of that radiant landscape to cheer myself. I needed it. My brain was beclouded most weeks of the month. My depressions were abysmal. Joyce came in one morning with the milk to find me huddled in the chair with the morning's mail laid out before me: of six letters received, one contained a stern letter about arrears of payment on storage of my furniture; another, a stiff reminder about my overdraft; a third announced that the Arts Council (despite my known record as a dramatist) had decided against awarding me the bursary for which I had been recommended; the fourth contained the rejection of a play synopsis; the fifth was a negative reply to a job for which I had applied; and the sixth broke the news of the death of my friend in Brighouse. Joyce stamped her foot by the fireplace, and said, 'Oh *honestly*! It shouldn't happen to a dog! Let me make you a cup of coffee.'

I had not failed for lack of effort. *The Year of Mrs Hannibal* had been condensed further by rewriting and sent to the B.B.C. in Glasgow where it had, initially, a good reception. Then came the news that Glasgow studios had been taken over for the (English) Classics series, so 'local' (i.e. Scottish) drama was restricted to one opt-out play per year. It was hoped the situation would improve by 1966.

1966! It was now 1963 and sometimes I had to eat – also, I was in arrears with my rent, which worried me, although Joyce and Martin knew that I would clear my back rent 'when something good happened to me'. The only prospect I had was the elusive West End production of *Thermopylae* and I knew never to attach hope to anything in the theatre. My life as a writer seemed to have ceased utterly. The world held nothing for me to do. Then I remembered my dead-tree drawings. Once before they had saved me.

I borrowed from the children a toy blackboard and easel which I set upon the table in my room. Purchasing three sheets of pastel paper, blue, green and grey, I set to work upon the green sheet. Having bestowed my original dead-tree drawings upon friends in London, I had to recreate them from memory. This time, to improve the composition, I took both trunks straight up to the edge of the paper, losing their heads above the top of it. In all other respects, I could have sworn, the drawings were identical.

It was not until years later when I sent for my first tree drawing to be photographed that I discovered one vital difference. In the London drawing it had been the tree in the background which tried vainly to draw life from the water-hole; in the Edinburgh drawing made in 1963 the dead tree trying to come to life had moved in to the foreground.

I had originally made the drawing for my neighbour, Jim: in my own eyes even occupational therapy had to be justified by pleasing someone other than myself, otherwise I was just a time-waster. When it was completed I could not bring myself to part with it immediately. The shadowless, infinite landscape was so peaceful, I wanted it near me; so I pinned it temporarily on the wall of my room.

It was the start of another compulsive drawing phase. The second was on a sheet of dark blue paper, a line of four ghost-white trees upon the edge of a river flowing to eternity. The trees, as before, were decapitated by the edge of the paper, and of their severed branches nothing remained but the stumps. The water of the river was calm, tideless and held no reflections. (This feature had nothing to do with deficient draughtsmanship: one of my favourite exercises in youth had been to draw light reflections in a glass of clear water.) This time I did include the sun, but it was the heavy, dark red sun of winter, huge and low upon the skyline, giving neither light nor heat: it was the sun remembered from my childhood on the Fylde coast, late on winter afternoons, which as it sank took down with it all my hope of life. Leslie wanted this drawing when I could bear to part with it.

Drawing number three was dashed off in a hurry because I hated it. On the grey paper I drew a strip of city street wet with rain. On it were reflected the colours of neon signs, and it bore the criss-crossed tracks of car tyres. Beside it ran a line of paving stones, marked with muddy footprints. On the right was a suggestion of dark bushes, caged alive behind iron railings. In the foreground could be seen the trunks of two urban trees, branches lopped, headless, but where my other trees had shown a will to win in the vigour of their downthrusting roots, these trees were confined to the dimension of a circular hole in the pavement. It summed up everything that I had ever felt about London. This drawing too had its admirers, one anxious to claim it, but I would not let it go: secured by drawing-pins to the wall above my bed, it had its place in my ever-increasing gallery.

By this time I had begun to wonder if this neglected talent of mine could, with practice, earn me a living. Kathleen had said she would come to view my pictures, and afterwards take me out 'to Newhaven or somewhere' for a drink and a sandwich – like everyone else, she was appalled that I so seldom left my room and the ever-closed curtains which had now become vital to my security. She herself made a living by combining the verbal and the graphic arts, and when she came she said that she saw no reason why I should not do the same. This cheered me. She then proposed that we should go to Newhaven for some fresh air, and a bar snack at the Old Chain Pier. Newhaven was one of her own favourite haunts and she was astonished that I had never been there.

I felt exhilarated on the bus ride to Newhaven, and in the pub when chatting to the landlady and the locals from the fish dock. They seemed particularly warm towards me, which, I realised, I expected them to be – in Newhaven. My head was clear and I felt relaxed and happy in their company. Once we left the pub and walked towards the harbour, I changed completely: my head clouded and ghost-tears gathered behind my eyes ready for a downpour. My distress was so apparent that my companion agreed that we should take the first bus home. Unable to endure the wait near the harbour for the bus, I found a small shop open – it was early-closing day – where I purchased shampoo and cigarettes, enjoying momentarily a warmth of welcome in the shop, which, again, I expected. When the bus came I could not get out of Newhaven fast enough. Afterwards, I found that I had no memory whatever of the place, save for the interior of the pub where I had drunk half a pint of Guinness, and the small shop where I bought the shampoo. Newhaven did not exist for me otherwise.

Encouraged by Kathleen's opinion that my work would sell if my technique developed at the present rate, I went to purchase further stocks of paper. The colour of the paper, I knew by this time, decided my choice of crayon – and, therefore, in a way, ultimately my subject. The sheets I selected were green, brown, grey, blue, and a parchment colour – then, on a whim, I included a sheet of black and one of terracotta. Why I had taken the last I had no idea.

Following my visit to Newhaven I was seized with inspiration for a new picture. My urge was in fact a craving, to draw the keel and ribs of an ancient, great ship wrecked in a limitless expanse of desert. I was somehow frightened of that one. I made small pencil sketches of the keel, and talked of it a great deal, but I seemed unable to start the picture. I did not know why. I believed it was because I might find myself incompetent to draw the ship in the right perspective – which, truly, was nonsense for someone who had once won the school art prize on the strength (I had joked) of my ability to draw fan-vaulting. I put off tackling that ship.

Meanwhile, I worked upon a seascape; a reach of sand from which the tide had long ago receded. A line of wooden groynes reached to infinity, with two leaden, shining pools of water, one each side of it, left by the ebbing sea. (Flo, who came to clean my room, loved this one.) What I had captured was the atmosphere of Rossall Beach in my childhood, but what came into my mind was *Newhaven*; Newhaven, not as I had recently seen and forgotten it, but as the-place-with-no-name where the keel of my great ship had been laid. . . .

My inability to draw that great, dead ship was now blocking my head, like a physical lump behind my eyes and nostrils. Had the difficulty been merely technical, I could have gone to Newhaven – or, for that matter, to Granton, Leith or Cramond – to sketch an actual boat, but I was profoundly shy of visiting any of the Forth harbours. I had thus far stayed clear of them.

In desperation I reverted to tree-drawing, though I knew that I had now outgrown that subject. This time it was a whole army of trees entangling with each other. This picture gave me a waking nightmare: I was trapped by those roots and branches, so like limbs, fighting in mud. . . . I sent for Joyce, who found me in a state of acute distress, still struggling to complete the picture. She advised me to leave it, but I felt I must go on; I had to master it. I was screaming in near dementia by the time she managed to drag me away next door for a cup of tea.

The next day I set to work on the drawing of that ship beached upon the sands of time. I knew by now that I had to get it out of my system. To obtain the angle of the bow timbers I resorted to the old technique used in my architectural drawing: I drew a rectangular box, and within it laid the keel of my ship. I completed the entire hull, then cut away all substance save the spine and ribs. The sketch was a success. For the actual drawing I chose the terracotta sheet of paper, the one I considered expendable if my draughtsmanship failed me. It was, in fact, precisely the right colour on which to draw desert sand in evening light, a point which, for all I know, I might unconsciously have anticipated when buying it.

Within a morning I had drawn the ruined hulk in the centre of my paper – grey-white ribs protruding from the sand. It could have been the ribs of a human skeleton – of the parenthesis I was aware when drawing it. Then I seized all the magenta, pink, and crimson crayons that I never used, slashing into them the even darker hollows of umber, indigo and purple, and the white highlights touched with a glint of gold. These were not my colours, but they grew out of the terracotta paper. They were the evening-light colours of a high ridge of sand reaching to infinity, and on it lay the bones of my great ship, bleached by time and forgotten by the water which long ago had washed up and left her there.

The tension in my head eased after the ship had been given life on paper: I had no compulsion to complete the battling tree-root drawing, now abandoned as my only failure.

Art was my sole interest during June and July. Kathleen was about to enter her paintings for the Women Artists Exhibition at the Royal Scottish Academy and suddenly suggested that I should submit two of my drawings. We had less than two days before the closing date for entries and decided to send the dead ship and the seascape resembling Rossall – this last choice dictated by the fact that if we trimmed it at the sides it would just fit an empty vertical frame she had!

At her studio in the New Town we did the fastest job of mounting and framing that I have ever known. I had not yet applied a fixative to the drawings – it had not mattered when they were pinned to the walls of my room – and my obsession had been simply to keep working at my easel. Neither of us had time to run out to buy fixative. The alternative would have been a window mount to lift the glass clear of the pastel, but she had none of the right size and time was, again, the vital factor. In the end we had to put the pastels directly behind the glass, in frames still tacky from their application of grey base-coat the night before. With my innate perfectionism, I shuddered at the thought of entering my work so crudely presented, but there was in me a terrifying compulsion to see my great ship go into the contest before 5 p.m. on submission day. Kathleen's collection of paintings was held back to wait for mine, and I finally waved her off in the loaded car at twenty to five. Then I paced the floor, wringing my hands and praying she would get through the traffic to the Academy. I was in a terrible state when she returned with the cheerful announcement that she had beaten the deadline in 'ample time' – 'ample time' being a margin of ten minutes. My incredulous, tearful relief amused her: I had remained convinced throughout that my ship *would not arrive on time*.

I had come temporarily alive during that battle against the clock to despatch my great ship and the sandscape of Rossall/Newhaven. It had been an enjoyable, frantic afternoon. She had made the suggestion as we worked that it might do me good to go to stay with herself and her son: there was no lack of life in her world of energetic, organised chaos. I said that I would think it over.

All my friends at this time were trying to prise me out of my retreat where I lived surrounded by my drawings and closed curtains. Ian Hamilton phoned one night at 10 p.m. with an invitation to go to a party aboard a fishing boat at Newhaven. As it happened, I had done sufficient sailing in my youth to know that nocturnal gatherings in the fo'c'sle do not necessarily mean an introduction to the white slave traffic. All the same, it was a wet, dark, windy night, and nobody but a lunatic would have agreed to go, for his assurance that he would meet me at the gates of the fish dock allowed a vast margin of error. It was a day when I had been too ill and depressed even to draw and I no longer cared what happened to me. Now suddenly, at the mention of Newhaven and a boat, I felt a surge of excitement: I had to go. As instructed, I called a taxi; then quickly I put on my heaviest sweater and a leather coat. When the doorbell rang I gave one last look at the mirror and saw a pair of glittering eyes challenge me.

Out in the wind and wet a huge exhilaration seized me. The cab-driver was plainly worried by my direction 'To the gate of Newhaven fish dock,' and, appointing himself my bodyguard, insisted he should wait to make sure my friend was there to meet me. We stopped in a pool of blackness. 'Well, this is the fish dock,' he said, 'Are you sure . . .?' I was sure of nothing, except that in Newhaven no harm could come to *me*. I stepped out of the cab and the salt wind and small rain slapped at my face. This was my kind of weather, my kind of salt-wind-fishy smell; my remembered world. Then a voice spoke from the dark, 'I'm here.

It's Ian.' The cab-driver was relieved, but he still looked apprehensive as he drove away.

I let Ian guide me past the sheds, but once out into the open I cast off his helping hand. Who was he, or anyone, to tell me my way at *Newhaven*? He was afraid that in the darkness I might step off the edge into the water. I roared at him, 'I can see the water!' and went striding ahead at a furious pace. All I required was the name of the boat, and her position. I allowed him to point out to me her riding lights and the vertical iron ladder nearest to her mooring. I looked down at the oily, black water, the smudge of a bobbing deck against the jetty wall, and judged carefully my distance. A ray of light shone from the fo'c'sle as a figure appeared on deck to help me down. Above the wind I shouted at the pair of them, 'I can get down myself! Do you think this is the first time I've climbed a rat-rail?' I grabbled the iron staple, swung myself over, and went sure-footed down the ladder, arriving safely on deck at the order, 'Now – jump!' I was in a rage at being treated like a landlubber and a woman. 'Don't teach me about boats!' I shouted through the wind as I nipped smartly below to find myself the cosiest corner in the cabin.

When we had sat some while over drinks, Ian disappeared. Expecting his return, it was very late indeed before I realised that I had been shanghaied. There was a spare bunk for which the crew supplied a blanket, and I lay down in my clothes, listening to the slap of the waves beside my head. As I dozed off to sleep the name 'Newhaven' rolled round in my mind. . . . Why did I associate it with the flat thistle called sea-holly which grew on the sand dunes of Rossall in my child-hood . . .?

The next day I was back at work at my easel, drawing the only *living* thing I knew – a huge, medieval tomb, burst open by a strong sapling, this time complete with its head and branches covered with meticu-lously drawn spring-green leaves. It was a sycamore, and its five-pointed leaves when drawn edge-on in perspective, as two of them were, had the formation of hands – my hands. I had been drawing my hands either consciously, or, as now, unconsciously for a lifetime.

I called in Joyce to see it, and she said in tones of heartfelt relief, 'Well, at least, thank the Lord, it has some *leaves*!'

When she had gone I looked at the tombstone burst open by the tree – it was, technically, the best pastel I had done – and then suddenly I set to work, fully knowing that I was destroying the composition, filling in all the surrounding space with rank upon rank of smaller headstones in perfect formation. I had reverted to my childhood graveyard drawing and my terror of the solitary grave. When all the tombstones were assembled, I was happy; I had spoiled my picture, but I was happy.

Later in the day I called Joyce to see the finished work. When I asked would she stay for coffee, she said she had to go. Then, at the door, she said suddenly, 'I'm sorry, Ada, I can't stand this room any more. It's all those drawings. They give me the *creeps*.' She shuddered visibly. 'I haven't liked to tell you, but that's why I never stay for coffee. I know they're good, and other people like them, but . . . urgh!'

I was astonished. I had noticed that latterly she came to my room less frequently and declined tea or coffee, but I had assumed it was because she was busy. It had never occurred to me that my drawings worried her: to me they were so peaceful. However, we were both glad that she had brought the matter into the open, and we discussed our varying reactions. I was curious to know why my pictures repelled her, but she could not tell me. At the door, as she was leaving, she said, 'I don't know what it is about them, but. . . . Can't you draw something *living* for a change?'

I took out the brown sheet of paper, pinned it to my board and tried to think of something 'living'. What came out of khaki-coloured paper? I snatched up a handful of crayons in brilliant heraldic colours and made down the middle of the page a vertical diagram of the 'ribbon rule', which had been one of my favourite doodles during art lessons. Like the rest, it reached to infinity, and each wave of the 'flag' I infilled with a different colour. At the end I felt something was missing – then I realised what it was: using a black and a white crayon, I superimposed two lines weaving their way forward with the rest. My personal colours: black and white.

When I showed it to Joyce she agreed it was not one of my best, but 'at least it has some colour'. She said the two weaving lines of black and white reminded her of the diagrams in the *Radio Times* illustrating Victor Sylvester's dancing programmes. We both laughed, and that particular drawing became known as 'Victor Sylvester'.

A visit by the McLellans reminded me of Arran. Also, I wanted to draw a 'healthy' picture for Joyce's sake. On a sheet of dove-grey paper I recreated a view I had watched so often from my favourite perch on the rocks above High Corrie. I had noted the dark 'ropes' in the water made by the clashing of currents, and these were faithfully reproduced. I drew on memory for the distant outline of the Clyde coast. Above it was a skyscape of evening cloud; the pinks and gold of the sun now vanished beyond Goat Fell, bands of colour reflected in the sea in a crab-shape formation.

Technically by far the most accomplished of my pastels, it was to my mind the least interesting. An evening sky which took its orientation from sun, moon and stars I could see any time by opening my curtains; what I needed to draw were the inward landscapes where light formed substance, and the ghosts haunting me identified themselves.

My two pictures sent to the Women Artists Exhibition were rejected by the selection committee. As a beginner with – at that time – but seven pastel drawings to my name, I had not held high expectations. The two framed pictures went back to Kathleen's studio where, eventually, one of them sold for ten pounds.

By this time I had reached the sheet of black paper and the last of my energy. I pinned it to the board and looked at it for a day, trying to visualise what came out of *black*.

What came out of black was an army. It was an abstract, composed of verticals, horizontals and blobs, with patches of colour between, representing battle standards and small pennants. It was an infinite column of men, with spears and helmets, the front rank fully armoured in pale steels, grey, square-shouldered, and those behind represented by the brownish smears of leather jerkins. Reds were the colours of the first block, a deep crimson, then bright yellow; there was blue, then we came to green; away at the tail the banners were lost behind the wall of tall spears. The light shone upon them, stiff beams like a searchlight, from the cumulus and nimbus of a storm-piled sky. The light beams worried me because they lacked *blue*, and they were so solid: but they had been solid, and I wondered how on earth to deal with a blue cast of light which had been present for a moment over the entire column, so that it registered upon my memory. I never completed that army; I drew the front section, and the rear, but when I reached the contingent of green banners I left a gap. The drawing stayed on my easel uncompleted.

Then suddenly, some nights later, I went berserk, tearing up all my drawings. They were too personal to be allowed to live. The two which had been framed and rejected by the Academy were saved because they were with Kathleen. The four ghost trees with the deep red sun escaped because Leslie had begged to have it. The army which marched out of the black sheet of paper I put carefully aside. The rest I destroyed as quickly as I could rip them to pieces. When Joyce found me I was huddled in my bed, saying, 'Look what I've done.'

It was September. When Kathleen suggested I went to stay with her and Brian in the New Town, I packed my bags in a matter of hours and fled the Burgh Muir of Edinburgh. But the most precious object I took with me was the technically poor, uncompleted drawing on black paper of an army marching beneath its spears and battle standards.

7

WHEN I WENT TO LIVE IN PITT STREET I DID NONE OF THE things which we had planned. With the resources of Kathleen's studio available to me I should have been at my drawing-board immediately, but I never touched pencil or pastel once my drawing bout had stopped. Worse, I did not resume my writing either. I had nothing left to say. Selecting words had become a difficulty even in everyday speech, and my vocabulary had curiously dwindled. All I could do was cook and, as Kathleen still had a market for her work where I had none, I channelled the last of my intellectual energy into devising palatable, inexpensive dishes dubbed by me 'boyfilla' to satisfy the healthy appetite of a teenage son.

We were all going through the hard times which recur in the lives of those who make art their profession, and by pooling our resources and ingenuity we managed to derive amusement from our mutual predicament, but my own mask of gaiety slipped more frequently now, showing the grey face behind. There were times when I crept to my bedroom in tears because I was unable to communicate to this vigorous, extroverted household that I was simply too ill to reach out to people. Adding to my depression was the proximity of Great King Street and the lost splendour I had created there: I would go out of the way to avoid seeing the house where my disasters had begun. In fact, I was to discover years later, the New Town was always to blight my health and fortune: it did not exist in my head except as marshland, so that there I was never more than half alive. Now, as before, the Old Town became an area I rarely visited.

Nevertheless, from the depths I made a superhuman effort to reinstate myself as one of the world's successful people. I saw that the B.B.C. Television Studios in Glasgow were advertising for a costume supervisor, and, having the necessary qualification, I applied for the post and reached the short leet. Enormously cheered by this first small success, I went through to Glasgow for the interview. I had just the money for my train fare plus thirty shillings for emergencies, but morale was high. I was wearing a green tapestry dress and my green velvet coat, an outfit which I knew suited me. I was smiling as the train passed through Linlithgow.

In the familiar building in Queen Margaret Drive my spirits were buoyant and my head quite clear. I knew the job was mine; as I sat waiting near the reception desk I slipped back so naturally into the easy relationship with hall porters which is a characteristic of the Corporation. Then I was escorted to the boardroom and everything changed. I recognised it later as the very room I had once used briefly to make some script alterations when I was a staff-adaptor – but on this day I found it in use truly as a boardroom. I had the shock of my life when I saw at the far end of the room a line of people seated behind a table, and a vast expanse of floor to be crossed with all their eyes upon me. Normally this would not have daunted me, for I tend to specialise in

234

powerful entrances, but the people I saw *belonged to the wrong period.* Or I did.

I had lost my verbal competence, and I used entire sentences to replace an adjective or preposition gone suddenly when it was required. Some members of the board were known to me as one-time colleagues but now there lay between us a great unease. The chill was on my side because I could not reach these people. I sat stiffly on my chair, throughout the entire interview morbidly conscious of my clothes. I felt horribly overdressed (which I was not). I realised I should not have worn my heavy, gold shoulder chain. . . . . I was wearing no gold shoulder chain (I did not own one!) and the only visible item of jewellery was the smoked-cairngorm ring I wore always. When asked how I would set about obtaining costumes for a show – a question presenting no difficulties for anyone who has worked on stage-management in weekly rep – I gave answers which created the impression that my specific subject was medieval history. Inside I was screaming to tell them that the wrong person had arrived today; it was the other one of me which had, confidently, applied for the job of costume supervisor.

I left knowing I had failed the interview. Afterwards, waiting for the train at Queen Street Station, I fell into conversation, with no difficulty, with a woman whose 'braid Scots' conveyed to me entirely the vital points which her own inarticulacy failed to render. Her plight sounded worse than mine, so I took her for a cup of tea and left with her the thirty shillings emergency money. I could deal with Scotland's problems.

In February 1964 I was homeless. Kathleen was letting her flat and I could not afford to take it. There was nowhere my body could drift except down to England. Helpless and hopeless, I went to my parents, leaving my two trunks with the Hellers.

Seen from the train, trees made skeletal by winter compelled me to take out pen and paper. My lines of verse in grey ink, barely decipherable and almost incoherent, filled two pages; only their attempted theme is plain – dead men's bones returning to life, as the trees will regain life by reclothing themselves. Afterwards I could make no sense of what I had written.

My behaviour when I reached Lancashire was of a pattern with that of 1947 and 1961: the sense of being dead, and the need to lose in sleep the identity I wore in Scotland. When I revived I tried to create a new, small, temporary world in England.

One evening I suggested taking a walk with my parents, something which I had not done since my childhood. As though attempting to recapture my identity of that period, I insisted we should take the route which once had been the farm lane past our house. All trace of fields and woods had vanished, lost beneath bungalows and concrete; even to my parents, who lived there, the extent of despoliation came as a shock. (When I had suggested 'a walk in the fields' my mother had said, 'But there are no fields now.') The by-product of this walk was first a short story called 'The Lane' and then a series of articles about pollution of the earth by motorways, cars, and overpopulation. They were very long, their scope enormous, and I knew that nobody would want to print them. A decade later pollution would be a leading topic.

My mother had nursed me back to health physically, and my clouded brain had cleared sufficiently for me to write again; what nothing could cure was my sense of exile. One day there arrived for me a mass of flowers bearing the card, 'Nymph in thy orisons be all my sins remembered,' followed by a phone call at noon from Ian Hamilton, who had traced me via the telephone directory. I sobbed with joy to hear a Scots voice calling me from Edinburgh; for a moment I felt the elation which had filled me those long years before in that same hallway when I had shouted with joy at the removal of the Stone of Destiny from Westminster Abbey.

By the end of April I was huddled in my bed, too ill to rise and almost speechless. My mother came to my bedside as once before. 'Now listen, child. I have phoned the McLellans on Arran. We have to get you back to Scotland.' I wailed, 'But what can I do when I get there?' She said, 'You'll find the way. But you are dying here. I can see that. We have to get you home to Scotland.'

By the next day, resurrected, I was on the train to Edinburgh with my hand luggage. I went straight to Leamington Terrace to be united with my twin trunks, and the Hellers accommodated me overnight. The next day I went through to Fairlie and sailed for Arran where I stayed for a fortnight, recuperating. Then it was my mother's turn to be ill, and I went back down to Lancashire. The terrible daundering of the displaced person had begun again. But my mother had tremendous resources and she rallied from her sick-bed to pack me off once more back to Scotland.

In a desperate bid to find my way out of the wilderness, I went straight from the station to a friend of mine in Leith who, an unpractising spaewife, had the Sight more acutely than I did. When it came to the point, I was too much afraid of what she might see for me, so I did not ask her. However, she gave me a bed for the night and the next morning I made my way up to Leamington Terrace. As I left the bus at Bruntsfield my spirits lifted: I knew I had come back to fight.

The Hellers had visiting relations, but they could continue to store my trunks, and another friend had a spare bedroom for me. This friend, like myself, had a problem, though hers was alcoholic, so we pooled our worries. She had resourcefulness which currently I lacked and under her influence I fought to make a mundane stand for survival. I did what I had done long ago in London: I signed on at a secretarial agency in May of that year as a typist. In the Edinburgh offices where I was sent to work I tried to stay anonymous, but the worry plagued me that I would be discovered – as occasionally happened – as the author of *The Man from Thermopylae*, and then I would have to explain why I was typing for my living. I was terrified of being recognised 'in the ranks' in a way that I had never felt in London.

Insecurity was everywhere. When I came home I never knew whether I would open the door to be greeted by the smell of cooking or find that my key would not turn in the lock because my friend had had a lapse. It was my turn to show initiative, and one desperate Saturday afternoon I phoned the alcoholic unit at the Royal City Hospital – I, who dreaded telephones! – and said from a public call box, 'Look, a friend of mine has an alcoholic problem. I have her here now, beside me, stone cold sober and wanting help. What can you do about it?' I was told there was nothing to be done on Saturday afternoons. I persisted: it had taken me weeks to persuade her to ask for professional help, and I was not going to be thwarted now by bureaucracy. At this point I was put through to the duty doctor, who, sympathetically, explained that the hospital could do nothing until she had made an application through her G.P.

I kept her off alcohol for three weeks by feeding her cautious doses of a sedative prescribed for me – which I knew was wrong but it seemed I had to stand in for the health service – with cooking and sewing as occupational therapy. We were both elated by our victory. She had not a great deal of success when she applied to her doctor, so I went to see him myself, very determined. When formalities had been completed, I accompanied her to the hospital she so much dreaded – and I sat on the lawn, while she was interviewed, looking towards the building which housed the severely disturbed patients. Sitting there, I thought what a narrow dividing line there was between them and myself – but I was still on my side of it. That day I was very much on my side of it, for I was back at the only job I really knew, which was fighting to keep others fighting.

A week later, when I had handed over my responsibility for others, I simply fell to pieces.

I was back on ground which knew me and I could not remember my own identity. Flashes of some kind of memory kept blurring present thought, but they were gone too quickly to be recognised. All I could remember were what seemed like blank patches in my head. Some of this horror had crept into the letter which my mother answered: 'Do you realise just *how big* a battle you have won? Never mind about forgetting who you are. Remember who you are, and what you still will do. . . .'

It was true, I was fighting a tremendous battle to return to the world as one of its active, unfamous members, but I had begun to feel now the odds were stacked against me.

Then came an old friend from Leamington Terrace days, Richard, whose ability to make practical plans I had always envied. I said, 'Help me to find a place with *my own front door*. Otherwise, I shall be dead in hospital.' He drove me round many houses in answer to advertisements. Just one of them tempted me – at Church Hill – but it did not have a front door which was mine exclusively. He suggested I should advertise 'flat wanted' but by this time I was too ill to deal even with such a simple message, so he composed and inserted the advertisement for me. In reply I received three letters, one of which I answered. I went to see the flat in Steel's Place which I felt immediately was home for me. Apparently my gentle landlady had similar thoughts, because of three potential tenants I was, she felt, the one who needed it.

I moved into Steel's Place on 15 August 1964. On the first night of my arrival I held the Saturday party in my house.

What had drawn me to the flat was a small bed-closet leading from the bedroom. Here at last was a place to house my twin trunks out of sight: to bury my trunks was something I had been trying to do ever since I first brought them up to Scotland. I told my landlady, 'This will be my dressing-room' – then I confessed I had 'enough shoes to equip an army' and she offered to have a shoe-rack installed for me.

The only thing about the flat which I hated was a mirror facing the front door as I entered, so I buried the mirror with the trunks out of sight in the dressing-room. I disliked the mirror because I was not sure that it was my face I had seen reflected when I came through the door.

I was back home safe and sound upon the Burgh Muir of Edinburgh.

It was to be several years before I realised that the chemist round the corner, where I took my prescriptions, had the pestle-and-mortar sign which marked for me, in 1947, the this-is-me place, where, I had said blithely then, I shall come to live one day.

CHAPTER SEVEN

1

I OPENED WIDE THE CURTAINS AND BEGAN MY NEW LIFE BATHED IN
sunshine as I sat peacefully trundling my ancient sewing-machine at
the window facing towards the Braid Hills and the Pentlands. I could
not see them, for tenements obscured the view, but all the time I was
aware of their closeness just as I had been when encamped with the
Army at Fairmilehead.

When my mother asked me did I still want my army greatcoat – she
had read that A.T.S. khaki uniform was hard to obtain for amateur
theatricals – she met this time no storm of ghost-tears. I said, 'Let it
go.'

I had been at Steel's Place less than a month when there came a call
for me to go down to Northumberland for a reason which went back
rather a long way. . . .

In the 1950s, when the Korean War threatened to become a nuclear
confrontation between East and West, I had been struck suddenly with
the theme for a novel set in the garrison town of Borcovicus on the
Roman Wall, during the last year of the Roman occupation before the
legions were called home to fight for Rome itself. What fascinated me
was the similarity between their time and our own. It was to be a story
about soldiers, the outpost men, fighting a continuous battle against
the guerrilla enemy, the rain, and the fading daylight of Northumberland. I had done most of the research, but I could not begin
writing until I had actually seen the Wall. At any time during the
ensuing thirteen years I could have made time to pay that visit, but I
never did. I had discovered so many reasons for not going to
Northumberland – always berating Providence for preventing me –
that my unwritten Roman Army novel had become like a longstanding
symptom about which friends occasionally enquired with no expectation of improvement.

Then, in December 1963, during a chance discussion about Roman
remains, I happened to mention the unwritten novel, and one person
present, the ever-resourceful Richard, at once took up the challenge
and before I realised what was happening had organised an expedition
to the Wall. Checking his diary, he asked, 'Will September suit you?'
That was the first time I realised that I was terrified of going to
Northumberland.

However, September was a fine long time away and we could all be dead by Christmas, so I said yes, hoping I had heard the last of it. I had not reckoned with the fact that notes made in diaries are apt to be remembered (my father had bestowed on me a diary every Christmas in the faint hope that he could train me to use it) and it came as a considerable shock when Richard's letter reached me in August 1964, announcing that he would meet me with the van at Carlisle station. He had even supplied me with the time of the train from Edinburgh. Too late to extricate myself, I wrote to say that I would meet him in Carlisle.

As I was doing no other work, I should have been, and was, extremely grateful to Richard for reviving my interest in the Roman army novel; furthermore, I told myself, two days pottering amongst Roman remains would be a pleasant and healthful break. And I was travelling to Carlisle, a route I never minded. So I talked myself out of my dread only to have it replaced by a dense, foggy feeling in my head and a sense of fatalism: it was now my dying time, and an appointment in Northumberland had the ring of inevitability.

On the morning of the day before I left, I went into the art shop round the corner to buy some writing paper, and saw on the counter before me a slab of soft, grey clay. My fingers itched to feel it. There were other customers before me, and while I waited I eyed that lump of grey mud with a covetousness which sent me nigh demented. I left the shop and did one or two other messages, but all the time my mind was on that clay. When I returned to the flat I was unable to concentrate on my preparations for the morrow, being entirely obsessed with the *feel* of grey mud. . . . Grey mud churned on a hillside. . . .

In the end, just before the shop closed for lunch, I raced down the stairs determined to have and to hold that block of clay. I was astonished to find that it cost only five shillings, for to me it was worth *my life*. This thought actually came clear to my mind, that I would 'give my life to hold it'. Hugging my precious burden, I raced upstairs to the flat, barely containing my patience long enough to remove my coat and spread a newspaper to make a working surface before I ripped off the plastic envelope and dug out a handful of clay like one possessed. I had done no sculpture since childhood, and I had no notion of what I would model, but the moment I touched it I knew what I must make before starting on my journey to Northumberland: a female torso.

I had only a matter of hours in which to study anatomy, so I whipped off my clothes to examine the curve of my own spine – described by a dressmaker as 'a dancer's back' – intending to make that the main feature. Hurriedly dressing, I rushed back to work on the clay. The entire afternoon, evening and night passed without my noticing. I ceased neither for food nor rest – nor to make preparation for my journey. I had to turn that piece of grey mud into a female essence. To the slim line of my own back I added proportions of breast and thigh heavier than my own – she had to be all *woman*. The neck I smoothed gently where the head had been severed, and the seat of the limbs I treated in the same way. It was merely a living, human, ultra-female trunk.

It was finished at five o'clock in the morning and I left it to dry out on the table whilst I hurriedly threw some clothes together for my journey and made breakfast, my first meal for twenty-four hours.

In the train I slept most of the way to Carlisle, and I felt a bit guilty to meet Richard at the station with the words 'I'm sorry, but I've been up all night.' After all his trouble it was mean, I felt, to arrive for the expedition too tired to make the most of it, but my priority had been to mould the clay torso, an impulse I could not justify.

The opening sentence, 'It was raining on the road from Corstopitum to the Wall,' has been a joke between us ever since. We reached Housesteads (Borcovicus) in the late afternoon when it was turning dusk, and blown, stinging rain all but blinded us. He was sorry about the weather (taking personal responsibility for it) but I was delighted. I shouted against the wind, 'It would have been wrong for me to see this country in any other kind of weather.' Wet, hard Northumberland looked exactly as I had expected.

I could not have had a better guide. He took me to every part of the Wall I needed to know, himself tactfully withdrawing to a distance so that I could get the feel of it in solitude. He had calculated which museums would be most useful to me, eliminating those which gave more general information of the kind I had already. It was for my purpose a superbly planned tour, and one which I enjoyed but for a terrible, underlying agitation which lasted until the car turned home for Scotland; once safely past Coldstream I relaxed. My dread of going into Northumberland had been real; those excuses I had made in the past had been manufactured for a purpose. Once we had crossed the Border back into Scotland I became an amiable companion, pottering with enthusiasm round any interesting church upon our route.

The small clay torso had dried out when I returned, and I hugged it with joy, setting it on the sideboard. The next day I started work on the Roman Army novel. All the main characters were by this time delineated clearly in my mind, and I sustained the narrative for four chapters. 'It was raining on the road from Corstopitum to the Wall. . . .' And there I was to leave my centurions, with the baggage train, alert for enemy raiders, moving up towards the front in the late, wet, Northumbrian autumn afternoon.

November was for me a very important month. The reason should have been the presentation of *Thermopylae* in Ipswich, but of that my

241

mind was barely conscious: far more important to me was an invitation from Wendy Wood to attend the Scottish Pariots' St Andrew's Day dinner.

The West End production of *The Man from Thermopylae* had fallen through, due to the same kind of ill-luck which had beset the plans for Broadway. Ipswich was suggested for a pre-London try-out. From the beginning, I had been under pressure to change the title as it was felt that the name Thermopylae daunted potential audiences. This view had been expressed on earlier occasions, but I had always maintained that it was senseless to change the name of a play so well known on radio – and, anyway, I felt that this play had no possible title but the one I had given it. During the time I had been ill my argumentative force had weakened; also, after the failure of the play to reach either Broadway or the West End, I had almost ceased to care what it was called – or thought I had.

Whenever I tried to work out another title the tension in my head became so bad that I had to abandon the task. Only one came easily, from the beginning – *March Home Tomorrow*. It was a good title, but I was frantic not to use it. It happened to be derived from a book which my father brought home from the library when I was in my late teens or early twenties. Its subject was the Crusades – which Crusade I do not remember, because I never read the book. What fascinated me was its title: *Ride Home Tomorrow*. From Jerusalem. I would pick up the book whenever I was alone with it, not to read but to hold in my hands. I just liked living with it upon the bookshelf, a point to which my eye travelled when I came into the room. I felt bereft when it was gone, as though a tiny glimmer of light had died upon me.

March Home Tomorrow was, despite my reluctance to use it, the only alternative title for the play, and it was under that name that *The Man from Thermopylae* was presented at Ipswich in November 1964.

I travelled down to Ipswich by an extraordinary overnight train direct from Edinburgh. Alec Reid had used it when a play of his was done at Ipswich. I remarked that obviously it existed only to convey playwrights to Ipswich and actors to the Edinburgh Festival. Aboard it, however, I discovered that most of the passengers were army personnel going to Colchester. As we travelled through the long night, stopping at many stations, I thought what a great number of weary Roman miles my centurion Tarquinius must have ridden on his way up from southern England to Borcovicus. . . .

March Home Tomorrow never reached the West End. I was not sorry. I changed the title back to *The Man from Thermopylae* after the Ipswich run ended.

London seemed an aimless, a decaying, place on the day I spent there. Suffolk had been real; after it, Oxford Street had the air of an

242

amusement arcade. I could not have borne it now to have my play go on in London. I caught the night train from King's Cross back to Edinburgh.

I had never been so acutely aware of the *foreignness* of London. I was separated from it now not merely by geographical difference but by a wall of time, centuries thick, which lay between me and my connections there; I could feel it in my head.

Where I belonged was at the Scottish Patriots' St Andrew's Dinner; as a guest, I sat amongst the speakers at the head table. On loan for the evening was an historical exhibit, the Chancellor's Chair from the Scottish Parliament last used in 1707. By chance my place at table was directly facing it across a narrow neck of the room, and my eyes were fixed upon it for a great deal of the evening: I found that I was willing that empty chair to come back into service.

I did not go to the dinner pretending to be a Scot – on the contrary, I wished it known that I was Lancastrian by birth, for I had to win acceptance under my own true colours or not at all. At the end of the night I took away with me the small card bearing my name, with its attached shred of tartan ribbon, which had marked my place at table. It was contrary to my strict rule, observed since 1953, never to keep souvenirs of happy evenings, but this was different, being a trophy. It represented for me one more step in my long march home.

The small female clay torso had been much admired. Several people had tried to buy or beg her from me, but I would not part with her for anything. I had designed one other clay figure after my return from Northumberland, during the second week in September, which I had modelled roughly in miniature. It was Hans Andersen's little mermaid, at the point of dying: lying prone on a rock, with her right arm and her tail already merging into the ridges of stone and her hair blending back into the salt sea-water. She has raised her left arm, vainly to defend herself against the lancing spray. Her breasts are small, her physical body almost gone.

I never made the final sculpture of the mermaid, though a sculptor who had approved the earlier torso volunteered to wash the clay for me, told me how to hollow the rocks, and promised to have it fired. I never bothered. My compulsion to work in clay had gone as strangely as it had come.

The tiny, dried-out model was left lying awhile on the sideboard beside my place-card from the St Andrew's dinner, until I put the latter away safely into my drawer filled with immediate things. The clay figure lay in the open until her upraised arm was broken, then it went away into the cupboard where I kept old scripts and bits and pieces of my life that I would resume 'one day'.

243

ON 1 JANUARY 1965 I SAT DOWN TO WRITE THE SYNOPSIS OF A trilogy for television. It was to be the only play about a woman that I ever wrote, its title *Against the Wind*.

My next positive action, as soon as offices resumed work after the holiday, was to order the installation of a telephone in my name. I was still not a ratepayer, but I would become an Edinburgh telephone subscriber, the nearest I could achieve to my original ambition. One cannot, yet, become formally a naturalised Scots citizen, but I was heading in the right direction.

Within that same first week of January, out of the blue, I received a letter on Gateway Theatre paper with an enclosure from the Edinburgh International Festival announcing that my play *The Man from Thermopylae* would be presented in the Festival programme of 1965.

I cannot remember being excited. I perused the letters with my morning coffee, calculating that their contents might usefully serve to speed the installation of my telephone in an area where the waiting-list was at that time a long one.

What chiefly impeded my process of naturalisation was that marriage with England. I had now lived in Scotland for more than five years and my husband and I had not cohabited since 1961, but as long as I remained his lawful wife I was officially of English domicile. Therefore, when my husband telephoned one evening to suggest we should begin divorce proceedings, I readily agreed. He would sue me for desertion and I would not defend the case. It would entail further delay, but we agreed that the important thing was to end our marriage with a statement of truth. I could not allow some irrelevant Miss X to be introduced upon the scene in order to hasten the dissolution of my tie with England, nor did my husband suggest it. I knew that being cited as the guilty party would disqualify me from taking communion in the Church of England, and that was to me a major sacrifice. I had not checked my facts on this point, nor have I ever done so: I recognised in my own mind that the severance of the marriage alliance with England brought automatic excommunication. It was something I was inwardly conditioned to accept – the price to be paid for becoming a free Scot.

Against the Wind was, at this stage, being written on speculation. The Festival production of *Thermopylae* was still nine months away. Meanwhile, I had to eat and pay rent. I was at this time being intermittently financed by family and friends, a situation justified only by the massive labour upon the synopsis which occupied me day and night. I was desperate to *earn* money.

Then, in February, an old friend and colleague at Broadcasting House, Manchester asked me if I would be interested in writing a documentary about Mrs Gaskell to be broadcast on the centenary of her death. I promptly said yes, although I had never read more of her writing than a few pages of *Cranford* as a child. (I had an inbuilt aversion to authors styled 'Mrs'.) However, if Mrs Gaskell could earn for me an honest fee in hard cash as the subject of a B.B.C. documentary, I was prepared to do my best by her. I went straight to the public library, asking them to procure for me all the available writings of Mrs Gaskell. As soon as the huge synopsis of the trilogy *Against the Wind* had been completed and despatched to my agent, I made amends for my lifelong neglect of Elizabeth Cleghorn Gaskell, consuming each of her books as it came from the library. I read her biography but no books of literary criticism, having an aversion to meeting authors second-hand. Her own letters were my chief source of reference, particularly those to Charles Henry Norton, which intrigued me by her contemporary observation upon the effect of the Lancashire cotton famine. I became fascinated by her personality and the development of her work. This was the first documentary I had written, so I had to learn quickly by trial and error; at the second attempt I produced the right format and received the first half of my fee.

In March I had a further commission from Broadcasting House, Manchester, to distil Bill Norton's *One Small Boy* into four twenty-minute readings for radio. The amount of hard work and professional skill required to abridge an author's work so that it fits precisely his intention *and* programme planners' requirements is a test of one's own ability as a writer. To be reminded of this after my years in the wilderness gave me enormous satisfaction: there was life in the old horse yet.

Then the trilogy *Against the Wind* was accepted by B.B.C. Television on condition that I boiled it down to make one play. The editor, James Brabazon, came up to see me and we duly thrashed it out between us, then I began rewriting the condensed synopsis. It was strange to be in the reversed role of a freelance author working with a staff editor, but it brought a transfusion of new life into my failing bloodstream.

With so much work upon my hands, my working day occupied twenty hours out of twenty-four; I had to make the most of every minute when my head was functioning clearly, for I never knew how long this clarity would last. Twice, in dire emergency, my doctor had prescribed a German hormonal pill to restore menstruation, but during the four days I waited for it to take effect the blockage in my head was so terrible and my depression so extreme that I did not ask for the remedy if it could be avoided. Actually, I was more ill than I dared confess to anyone: there were days when I lay in a darkened room, unable to feed myself because I could not relate a cup to a saucer. I was fortunate in having a kind landlady who gave me absolute privacy and independence, and a doctor who believed that my own intelligence would solve the problem.

It seemed as though I was indeed in the process of resolving it, with my luck turning and my earning capacity restored. 1965 looked like being my good year. Then on 27 April my parents came to Edinburgh on holiday, and two days after their arrival my father was rushed into the Royal Infirmary as an emergency case.

They were staying not with me but at an hotel in the New Town so as not to hinder my work; my flat had but one bedroom and the other room was also my study. On the day they came to visit me my mother had been stricken at the sight of my living conditions. The neat, wee flat in which I had at first shown so much pride had deteriorated past recognition. Dust and piles of manuscript lay matted together in the living-room. My kitchen floor was filthy, and every horizontal surface littered with dirty dishes. The bedroom was spread with clothing and jewellery like a jumble stall before the sorting starts. The dressing-room my landlady had had fitted to my specification had become a lumber closet in which I buried those two trunks. The living-room curtains were closed against the sunlight and the houses across the street. My mother knew that I concentrated better behind closed curtains, but the volume of dust in their folds revealed how long it was since they had last been opened.

It had been a wretched tea-party, my parents knowing there was something desperately wrong when a person as habitually clean as myself could create, and live in, such squalor. The chaos they found in Steel's Place had appalled them.

And now here I was, within forty-eight hours, hurtling to the Royal Infirmary on the bus. My head was so bad that I had had great difficulty dressing myself. My palms left sticky patches of sweat on my hand bag when I removed my gloves to smoke a cigarette. Yet a part of my brain stayed ice-cold and clear as I journeyed to the hospital to see my father. Death and dealing with hospitals seemed, peculiarly, my job.

We found my father in a state of concern because the pain was in his abdomen and the hospital's interest was focused on his chest. I roared, *This will not do*! I shall speak to the Ward Sister. Where is she?' My head suddenly as clear as glass, I was terrifying. My parents besought me not to make a fuss: they had seen me before in odd moments when I literally towered with wrath, but never like this. I compromised by agreeing to speak *very gently* to the nearest person clad in uniform of sufficiently high rank.

Back at Steel's Place I wrote lucid prose through the night, but I

246

could barely fumble together my nocturnal cup of salted milk. It was as though a powerful intellect at work on a high level could not bend itself to mundane tasks.

The next day my father was operated upon for obstruction of the bowel; the cancer of the lung, of which we did not know, would wait until another day.

When I went to see him he had tubes draining or feeding every part of him. This should not have affected me – I had been an army medical orderly – but I stood aghast beside his bed. The tube through the nostril horrified me most: it put me in mind of the embalmer's process. My mother said, 'Ada, sit down,' for I had gone very white. A nurse brought me a glass of water, and my father smiled through his tubes, taking my hand to reassure me. As one unaccustomed to being daunted by the sight of anything, I was furious with myself for my sudden weakness. I knew that my father would be all right – his time of dying was not yet; his discomfort would pass, and he was in good hands. It was not my father's state which had shocked me: what had flashed into my mind had to do with a dead body, and the dead body was not *his*.

During the ensuing four weeks of my father's convalescence I visited him less than half a dozen times. I had on hand five pieces of work, all urgent. Also, I was myself very ill, and trying to work through it. My instinct told me that he had not long to live, and that I had lost my only chance of visiting him 'just round the corner' in Scotland. I wept because some kind of blight lay upon my relationship with my parents; always duty intervened, duty to my work, duty to Scotland; it had been so from the beginning.

I did manage to join them in their hotel for dinner on the first night after he came out of hospital. Then we had coffee with the proprietor and his daughter who had acted *in loco patris et filiae* during the time I had been so useless. I can remember fumbling with my cup as awkwardly as I did with my words. My mother explained on my behalf that I was not well, that I was overworked, and I listened to what I had asked her to say with but the bleakest hope that these kind people would understand that my silence was not due to lack of courtesy or gladness that my father was alive. . . . I just felt that one half of me was dead.

The next day my pent-up menstrual cycle started, and I was brisk, crisp and clear-headed. My parents were driven away in their own car back to Lancashire, and I with my new clear head resumed work on *Against the Wind* and *Mrs Gaskell*.

On 8 July divorce papers were served on me. I wrote to the court in England a letter which I hoped would clarify and speed the issue, stating simply that no marriage is perfect, and that both of us had tried to make it work to the best of our ability. (I learned afterwards that my letter had roused comment because of its fairness and lucidity, so there was no sign of mental blockage there.) The divorce hearing lasted about five minutes, as I learned from my husband, who telephoned me when the petition had been granted. Other than his phone call, I never received any formal word that my marriage had ended, save a crudely coloured blue and yellow leaflet from the Ministry of Pensions and National Insurance emblazoned with the words 'For Divorced Women.' I was so angry I tore it into four pieces, unread, and cast it to the floor where it lay until next day when someone picked it up for me and put it into the wastepaper basket. With a gesture of disgust, I demanded, 'Isn't that typical of *England*!'

We had been married for eight years and had lived in separate countries for six of them; but it was an acute pang to know that our legal relationship had ended. I had achieved what I wanted, Scottish domicile, but with it came a sense of apprehension, the feeling that I was now alone to battle against. . . . Some kind of memory stirred, but I could not identify it.

I spent the month of August divided between my typewriter and my sewing-machine. My gowns for the Festival were important. I had a seventeenth-century Florentine pendant of coral and kingfisher feathers set in gold, and I bought yards of kingfisher-blue wild silk and coral-coloured lining – a gift from my ex-husband to make a coat and dress to match the pendant. I was still at the sewing-machine when the Edinburgh International Festival started. (My mother had joked for a lifetime that I pulled out tacking stitches while I was running to catch a train.)

At the end of August there was reviewed in *The Scotsman* a book by two academic Americans upon that eternal subject, the Brontës. The review included a reference to the 'quarrel' between Mrs Gaskell and Mr Brontë after the publication of Elizabeth Gaskell's *Life of Charlotte Brontë*. I had never written a letter to a newspaper before, but it so happened that I had been living for five months with Mrs Gaskell, her biography of Charlotte Brontë and all her published letters. There had in fact been no quarrel between Mrs Gaskell and Mr Brontë, and some defensive instinct on behalf of these two people I had come to know was roused by this travesty. I had other things to do, but I could not let an untruth go unchallenged. The exchange was brief, courteous on both sides, and I won it.

This small victory gave me a sense of exhilaration out of all proportion to the achievement. At that time my name was appearing on bill hoardings along Princes Street in company with William Shakespeare, George Bernard Shaw and James Baldwin, and I had lived with the sight of it in the official Festival programme for several

248

months, but none of this gave me the extraordinary excitement that I experienced when I saw my name printed twice in the correspondence columns of *The Scotsman*. Playwriting had disciplined me to suspend personal bias when writing: henceforward I would let *my own voice* speak out in Scotland. A new personality was emerging.

At the last moment I decided to wear for the opening night not the new outfit I had made but my old, green, dinner gown dyed black. For it I bought a stark white stole, cast to cover my throat and hang in streamers behind me. Long black gloves, each wrist bound by a gold bracelet, the great cameo brooch pinned in the centre of my chest, and tiny gold sandals completed the picture. As I entered the theatre I was greeted by a party of friends from the Saturday gatherings as 'the Lady from Thermopylae' – as one of them put it, 'You look as if you have come straight from the Spartan battle line.' One of them presented to me a rose, which I held all the evening, cupping its fragrance to my nostrils instead of a cigarette. I did not smoke the entire night; I could not bring myself to use cigarettes, which were an anachronism.

This strange suspension of a normal practice was not the only difference in me. Days later I was still hearing from close personal friends who had been present in the stalls but had not dared to speak to me. Astonished, I asked why. Nobody could define precisely why they had found me so unapproachable.

The Edinburgh *Evening News* ran an arts column on Saturdays written by Alec Reid, which had contained an excellent article about me. It was headed, using my own words, 'Playwriting is a Skilled Job – Like Plumbing'. Centered between the columns was my photograph, the one I used always for publicity purposes; I liked it for its combination of glamour and intelligence, useful in one who is a playwright *and* a woman. I had heard it described as 'haunting' and 'enigmatic', which had made me laugh, for there is nothing enigmatic about oneself (I had said).

To sit poring some minutes over a good review of a play is not unnatural, but personal interviews are another matter; usually, I check for errors – this had none – and then put aside the paper. On this occasion I sat for a long time staring at my photograph. It was not narcissism: I found reassurance in that picture of my face. It was my face *as I knew it*, set in the context of an article about play-writing.

As my parents could not obtain the Edinburgh *Evening News* locally, I cut out the article to send to them.

It was not until 1972, when sorting the mass of material on which to base the chronology of this book, that I discovered on the reverse side of the cutting, behind my photograph, a feature entitled 'Could James Have Won At Flodden?'

3

THE DOPPEL-GÄNGER MADE ITS APPEARANCE IN MY WRITING late that same September. In my synopsis of *Against the Wind* the chief character, Cassandra, did not have an *alter ego*, and the device I was now using in the script was directly inspired by an experience of my own relating to the dressing-gown which hung behind my bedroom door.

It was a striking gown which I had designed and made when I was twenty-three, of dark and light patchwork squares alternating, the dark ones bearing an appliquéd motif – the fleur-de-lis. The fleur-de-lis had always held deep personal significance for me which had nothing whatever to do with France. Why the lilies were to my mind at once both personal and *Scottish* was something I could not have explained. With its high gorget collar to protect my throat, fitted bodice and sweeping skirt, the gown was designed for elegance, warmth and comfort; the fact that I had created a medieval robe was first pointed out to me by others. The discovery peculiarly embarrassed me, and I had to make a joke of it, thereafter saying whenever the gown was admired, 'When I'm wearing this thing I always feel my conversation should begin, "My lords of England and of Burgundy . . ."' – but I never said that I felt like the King of *France* in it.

By 1965 it had outlived three new linings, and the dry-cleaners knew it well enough to respect my wish not to have it returned each time with the pinned apology, 'Owing to the fragility of the garment. . . .' It had reached the state most happily described as venerable. More than once it had gone into the rag-bag only to be retrieved when the cold weather set in. It was the gown in which I became completely myself. I had discovered that when my head clouded to put on the gown partially restored my faculties, and I had worn it almost constantly during 1964–5. I even began to spread it over my bed at night (as I had done years before with my army greatcoat) for the sake of some kind of spiritual solace it gave me. During the summer months of 1965, it hung in its usual place behind my bedroom door, casting its reflection into the wardrobe mirror, and it was then that I began to see it differently.

Due to the style it required to be hung on a coat-hanger, its bodice fastened, the firm shoulders and high neckline suggesting a wearer. Suspended thus, I had seen it for years and thought nothing of it, but in the August or September of 1965 I became aware of a confrontation between that garment and myself: hanging behind the bedroom door it had a terrible presence of its own. I would awaken in the small hours, my eye falling upon its reflection in the mirror, and increasingly I had the feeling that we were twin entites, that gown and I. When I lay in bed it was my other majestic self which hung behind the door; when I put it on it became just 'old faithful', the garment I wore while lighting the coal fire on winter mornings.

This sense of separation into two identities gave me the idea I used in the play, of having Cassandra confronted and haunted by a harsh *alter ego* who always wore the dressing-gown suspended behind her bedroom door. The gown I described in the text was a hooded cassock, for, though I felt that a robe like my own would have been more impressive, it would have torn away part of my own identity to have my square-patched fleur-de-lis worn by a character in a play. When James, my script-editor, expressed his approval of the new dramatic device, I told him its origin and even managed to joke about the experience.

In fact, the situation had begun to defeat even my jocularity. I was growing into the gown. These days, when I caught a glimpse of myself wearing it, the presence it bestowed on me came from *within*. I had clothed myself in my own image, but *whose* image? When I crossed the darkened hall my reflection was caught in the wardrobe mirror; seen beyond the darkness of the bedroom, my silhouette against the light from the living-room was like an apparition from another century. My characteristic reaction would have been to joke about it ('I have just seen Banquo's ghost again!' I would have said to anyone present in the house) but I did not: the medieval figure standing in the open doorway, with the light behind him, wore no smile. We would stare at each other, I racking my brains to recover something which I ought to have known; his face showing my bafflement, as though wondering how to tell me. When this happened I would approach the reflection, pressing my face to the glass, eyes to eyes: the cold surface reminded me that what I saw was myself, but it gave no real reassurance. It was strange to be baffled by the enigma of one's own eyes. I began demanding aloud, '*Who are you?*' Who was I, this man inside a medieval long robe?

In December 1965 I was making plans to remove to the closes of the High Street known as the Royal Mile. The renovation of some of the old property was a Corporation project which had begun with the restoration of White Horse Close in the Canongate. My friends, knowing of my concern to house my furniture, had advocated in unison, 'White Horse Close! That's the place for you.' I had objected, 'But that's by *Holyrood*. I couldn't bear to live down there.' My horror of Holyrood had remained as acute as ever: if driven in a car I begged not to be taken on the road which cut across a corner of the park, and I had an inward warning-system second to none when it came to ducking my head to avoid any view in Edinburgh which contained the palace and abbey. I was still under the impression, after six years in Edinburgh, that the Abbey of Holyrood was intact.

251

The renovated Customs House in Chessels Court, however, was a different matter. When I saw the photograph of it in *The Scotsman*, I knew at once it was the place for me. The building included a round tower with a door at its base, which made me feel at once that this was *my* Edinburgh.

On the first viewing day I went to see the flats. It was a wet afternoon, and my Corporation guide apologised for the deep mud and debris through which we picked our way, explaining that the court would be paved by the time the residents moved in. I laughed, 'Don't worry, I'm used to it!' Just for a second I had been exquisitely happy because the builders' debris with its distinctive odour and the nearness of the Canongate had given me a momentary, crystal-clear memory of somewhere that was home. Then, trying to cross a puddle, I became aware of a *skirt*. Startled, I wondered what had become of the leaping black legs, like a male ballet dancer's, which I *used* to see when I looked down. Oddly embarrassed by my skirt – I felt that my guide expected me to be athletic and apparelled differently – I said, 'Forgive my being so slow. It's this silly tight skirt. I should have worn something different today. I hate straight skirts.' (Actually, it was my favourite tan suit that I was wearing.)

Skirt regardless, when I discovered that the two-apartment flats were in the tower of the building, I rapidly outpaced my guide in my eagerness to enter that door. Once inside, an odd thing happened: I who had never in my days feared burglars, dark roads or similar perils, became acutely security-conscious. I liked the first flat, but it was for me too vulnerable. The second was more easily defensible, but had less character. When we climbed to the top floor real fear took hold of me. It crossed my mind that I would be cut off from the world up there. Seeing the small gallery to the right of the front door, I thought how easy it would be for an assassin to hide there when he had rung the doorbell. (Yet how many times had I, living alone, opened the door at any hour with no thought for my personal safety?)

Once inside the flat this anxiety immediately left me. Ahead of me was yet another narrow flight of stairs, and the moment I saw that feature I knew I was home. Barely able to conceal my impatience, I toured the main area of the flat before I ran upstairs to the attic. Flinging wide the door, I proclaimed, 'This will be my work-room!' knowing I could step from it on to the ramparts, always my favourite thinking place. I crossed to open the window on to the roof, but my guide said she doubted whether the room had access to the roof. I cried, 'But it *must* have!' and we spent some while examining the window before I could be convinced otherwise. I was utterly baffled: if this was my home, there *had* to be a door opening from my turret work-room on to the roof-walk as I remembered it. I suggested that roof access

252

might have been removed during restoration, and I made another detailed inspection of the window to see if I could find traces of alteration. My guide conceded that might have been the case, but she really did not know. With no evidence, I expressed my firm conviction that it was so. The constant signals from my brain about a roof-walk had to be explained away somehow.

However, it was certainly my flat. I came bounding down the stairs from the attic, chattering eagerly about it. Working in that upper room I knew my head would be clear and vigorous, as it used to be. As we were leaving, I saw the cul-de-sac balcony on the *left* side of the door, and exclaimed, 'I could put plants there, like a garden!' Actually, what I had just seen was the strategic advantage afforded to a defender of that door who was ambidextrous with weapons.

I was astounded to receive formal notice that my offer for the flat in Chessels Court had been rejected by the Corporation. My connection with that tower room was so obvious that I could not understand how anyone could fail to see that it was mine.

By the middle of January 1966 I had decided to write a play about James, IV, King of Scots. Precisely when or how the idea first consciously entered my mind I cannot be certain, but my reasons for choosing the theme seemed to me entirely practical. I had been sickened by the fact that, although Edinburgh welcomed my play set in ancient Sparta, nobody wanted from me a play about modern Scotland. I had begun to see, like other Scots playwrights before me, that Scotland's voice existed only in the past. Robert McLellan wrote of Mary or James VI or used the eighteenth-century voice of Scotland. Sidney Goodsir Smith had evoked the Wallace. None of these was my period. My feeling was always for that span of about forty years covering the last three decades of the fifteenth century and the first decade of the sixteenth. By a useful coincidence, it was also Scotland's period of greatness when James IV was king. Here was the ideal person to voice my own feelings about Scotland.

The play was just evolving when I received news that my father had cancer of the lung. I wrote him a letter, which finally I decided not to send – on the eve of yet another operation he might not be cheered by my loving effort to prepare him for death. My father had cancer, but I had something else: 'to know that there is this dark, alien life-form at work within *oneself*. . . .' It continues: 'I don't know how you feel about death. It is something of which I am more conscious – I confess this rather sadly at thirty-seven – than I am of life: or should I put it, that I am always baffled by the fact that I cannot feel the flesh for the consciousness of *bones* inside it.'

I watched those bones, my bones, night and day. They were trying to tell me something, I knew it now, if I could but read the message.

Work upon the new Scottish historical play was delayed during February and March while I gave priority to family matters, but the period is marked by an extraordinary energy emanating from me. When I visited my father in Lancashire I took down with me from Edinburgh the unaccountable feeling, intensely real, that the welfare of hospital inmates was my personal responsibility. In the ward I made scathing comments upon what I considered to be the hospital's inadequacies. I went further, observing that I was far from satisfied with the progress of surgery and that it was time the entire subject was opened to reappraisal. I spoke with the absolute authority of one empowered to change the system.

This aspect of King James's work – his founding of the first faculty of medicine at Aberdeen and the establishment of a school of anatomy for surgeons in Edinburgh – was to be excluded from my play. At that time I did not, intellectually, know about it. I was planning to use James as a character solely to express my own feelings about Scotland's place in the world.

When I returned to the play the stress symptoms which arose to impede my work I attributed to natural anxiety about my father. Yet whereas I had to some extent been able to switch off personal feeling during *Mrs Gaskell*, *Against the Wind* and other recent writing, I found that work on the play about James intensely aggravated the symptoms. I began to have increasing difficulty in relating mundane activities to my writing. It was as though the two parts of me had separate existences.

From the beginning this one play presented me with problems unlike any I had met before. Never had my approach to a theme been so subjective. I began not by delineating character, always previously my starting point, but by analysing my own reasons for writing it! What emerged was a curious document, almost a letter, written out of the sixteenth century for the benefit of men of the twentieth who would have to deal once more with Scotland *as a sovereign nation*.

Four hundred and fifty-three years later, I was bent over my typewriter filling pages with the explanation of events which led finally to Flodden. Here I was depending chiefly upon information which came from *within*: I had attempted to re-read Agnes Mure Mackenzie's summary of those events in *The Kingdom of Scotland* but I had to put aside the book because where once it had enlightened, now it merely confused me.

My lack of research was unprecedented. I tried to go about it in my usual methodical fashion, beginning in the public library, where I picked from the Scottish section a small book dealing with the Flodden campaign. I took to the book immediately. Its facts were correct – I knew that – and its opinions I greeted with immediate warmth. I exclaimed as I closed the book, 'splendid fellow!' – meaning the author. Yet when I tried to read it a second time I met the same phenomenon which prevented my re-reading Agnes Mure Mackenzie – the pages became a mere jumble of words. This I blamed on my diminished faculties, but when I came to pick up the evening paper I had no trouble reading that; and later I could sit at my typewriter filling sheet after sheet with James's own thoughts about his world of 1511, cross-related to my feelings about Scotland in the present century.

My inability to disentangle James's thinking from my own was becoming a major problem. To relate him to *history* I needed to read about him objectively. From the library I brought the only biography there available, R. L. Mackie's study of James IV. On the first page I saw mentioned the month of his birth – March: James was, like myself, a Piscean. I seized upon this fact with enormous relief, and said aloud, 'So *that*'s why I know the way his mind works!' As I read on through Mackie I became increasingly confused and angry. The author inferred from known facts a mass of material which I knew was *not true*. Also, what seemed to me incredible was the quantity of information which was lacking. In response to implied neglect of the Highlands I shouted aloud, 'Do these people not realise that we had pestilence in Edinburgh that summer?' His dismissal of my ship *The Great Michael* as a mere toy built for prestigious purposes roused me to such fury that I hurled the book across the room: did he not *know* it had been designed as a floating fortress to sail up the Thames Estaury to blast Henry Tudor's palace at Greenwich? (In fairness, no other historian appeared to know this, either.) When it came to foreign policy, I nearly gave up trying to read the book at all, for the account bore no connection with the pattern of attitudes and events *as I knew them*. The author's most serious mistake was to assume that the word crusade meant to James IV what it had meant to Coeur de Lion, whereas I knew that the word had changed its connotation by that time and its closest parallel today would be NATO. Our reason for wanting to take Jerusalem was strategic: if we hit the Turk in the solar plexus he would loosen the grip on eastern Europe which was threatening the whole of Christendom by my time.

I had flung down the book many times before I reached the end of it; never, I felt, had a biographer known so little about the man he purported to describe! My practical mind revolted at Mackie's picture of the Scots king as a deluded romantic, out of touch with his own time and dreaming himself back into the world of knights and Saracens – or, worse, King Arthur. (King Arthur, forsooth! I paced the room roaring, 'Romantic rubbish!') Other minor details irked me. The author made too much of contemporary references to the king kissing the queen and all her ladies. Had it not dawned on him that it was my way to kiss all if I kissed one, so that none should feel slighted? More than a courtesy, it was a good way to ensure harmony at court and thereby keep treachery out of it. (I still did the same today when taking my leave after the Saturday-night parties.)

I cannot remember ever stopping to wonder why I used the pronouns 'he' and 'I' interchangeably. Nor why I should seem to know a great deal more than I had found anywhere written about James, Scotland and Christendom, in that order.

Greatly as I disliked Mackie's book, for practical purposes I tried a second time to read it. It proved impossible, for the same reason which had prevented my re-reading the two previous books; this time, however, it was worse, for the print itself blotted out before my eyes. I went to the mirror and screamed at my head for being so obtuse. Then, opening the pages at random, I found, to my relief, some passages which I could read without difficulty. By Henryson and Dunbar, they were in Middle Scots. I read them aloud, with tremendous joy, as though reunited with old friends. Mackie's commentary in English between the excerpts was just so much foreign language to me.

I finally abandoned reference books, using only the knowledge stored within me. Here I met, when writing, the other difficulty: I could write with brilliant clarity of people and events seen through James's eyes for a few sentences or a paragraph, then an interpolation by Ada F. Kay relating to Scottish current affairs would spoil yet another attempt to produce a straightforward synopsis. Or I could write of Henry VIII with anger still boiling from the battlefield; then the skilled playwright, accustomed to balancing all arguments for the sake of dramatic structure, would put out those pages later as biased.

Amongst the many spoiled pages there is one synopsis completed almost to my satisfaction which confines itself, for once, to sixteenth-century matters. At the end it is spoiled by this extraordinary personal message which I added in an almost semi-conscious state, after taking my sleeping pills, just before I went to bed: 'God bless you, dear James, wherever you lie. And if you are in a position to drop hints to a fellow Piscean and encourage a jaded fellow idealist, either in spirit, or by remote control influence of some kind – I don't know if it's possible after all this long time – will you do it, please, sir. . . .?'

That this invocation was entirely superfluous I might have recognised had I at any time taken the portraits illustrating Mackie's book to compare with my own face in the mirror.

I had never seen a portrait of James until I beheld the cover of Mackie's biography which featured the drawing of the king made by Jacques le Boucq. I did not then know that it is today usually identified as 'the portrait with the unfinished hands': my own immediate reaction when I saw it was a pained, 'I do wish he had paid attention when I told him about drawing my thumb from the *wrist*. . . .' When I looked inside the book, there, of course, was van Muyten's copy of the portrait with the falcon, which misrepresents the nose (easily done, for I have one nostril wider than the other: at a certain angle this gives a false impression of an aquiline nose, an error occuring not only in van Muyten's portrait but also in a modern photograph taken by my father). Van Muyten's, however, makes a superb representation of the hands; the great, square span between thumb and forefinger, the second long phalange, the slim, pointed forefinger. . . . It was, however, the le Boucq drawing with the spoiled hands which I saw every day lying upon the arm of the settee near my typewriter. Those hands alienated me; le Boucq had made a thorough mess of them, not only distorting the bone structure but also padding them with too much flesh. The face was well drawn, the nose excellent with its retroussé tip at the end of the straight bridge, and the wide space between the eyes, but it was the *hands* which chiefly I noticed, being so concerned with my own working at the typewriter. Watching them tap the keys – the great, square span between thumb and forefinger, the long second phalange, the slim, pointed forefinger and the absence of padding between skin and bone – I paused many times, wondering where I had seen these hands of mine before. *Recently*.

I did not look to the portraits for information. I had no need. All my inspiration came from the mirror, to which I was drawn constantly to read the information supplied in James's eyes.

4

MY BATTLE WITH THE JAMES SYNOPSIS COINCIDED WITH A GENERAL election campaign, and for the first time there was a Scottish National Party candidate in my own constituency. My brand of nationalism was apolitical, as I told the S.N.P. canvasser who called on me, but they could be certain of my vote. I had waited a lifetime for this opportunity. On polling day, 31 March, I had 'flu, so I asked for official transport to take me to the polling station. The sole passenger in a dormobile, I sat up high beside the driver, my jubilant spirits concealing a temperature of 102°. Responsive to my enthusiasm, the driver gave me his own lapel button as a souvenir, with its attached strip of white, blue and magenta ribbon. Deeply moved to be given his colours, I stood afterwards in my living-room holding them a long while in my hands before I laid them reverently in the drawer beside the card which had marked my place at the Patriots' St Andrew's dinner.

My work on the James synopsis seemed a trifle easier after that – for

257

a while; as though, having cast my vote in the twentieth century, I was free to write from the sixteenth without so many modern interpolations. In all other respects my problems with the play remained as great as ever, increasing the more I worked on it.

Nowhere in dramatic terms could I isolate the character of James himself. My play, in fact, took place *in the mind of James*. No matter how I tried, I could not see him outwardly as a physical personality. This non-existence of James nonplussed me. All my professional life, my skill in finding live people behind Time's dusty pages had been my most valuable and most highly acclaimed asset. (The documentary about Mrs Gaskell had been a great success.) The method I used was simple: never to invent, never to hold preconceived opinions; first to study everything written by and about them – also, portraits where extant – then to wait for the personality to emerge voluntarily. It had always worked. Even the minor characters dismissed by history in a couple of sentences would, as the events of their times unfolded, appear diffidently at my elbow to explain how *they* had felt. In the case of King James, for the first and only time, my main character failed to materialise as a person separate from my typewriter. I could type out his thoughts, a liberty I had taken with no other person, but, physically, for me, he had no presence.

In my effort to find him I sat staring at the portraits in Mackie's book, trying to see in them the virile Scots king who had charmed not only the ladies but an entire nation. I found nothing. My response was void. The total absence of reaction in myself was as worrying as the absence of James. As a woman writing of a man who shared my every thought, I should by this time have been half in love with the fellow: such feeling never entered my mind. I once cried aloud in my despair, 'I'd know more about him by looking at his skeleton!'

Many people, I had now learned (curiously, to my surprise), had written plays or novels round James IV, apparently with no difficulty. I had no recourse to such works of fiction because their existence embarrassed, even repelled, me. On hearsay, I formed the impression that James was usually regarded as a romantic figure. The romantic aspect of James did not exist for me: what I loved was his foreign policy.

In the beginning I had had no such difficulty with his contemporaries. Pope Julius II, King Louis XII, King Ferdinand and Queen Isabella, the Emperor Maximilian and the two Tudor Henries – all had come alive in the usual way when I started the work. Now even they had begun to fade as I worked inside the mind of James, unable any longer to see these people through history's eyes.

A further difficulty was my inability to translate the synopsis into dramatic scenes. I knew what Scotland was like at the end of the fifteenth century – I could see it! – but I could not stop the moving camera in my head for long enough to plot the location of the opening scene.

Then one day I received help from an unexpected quarter. I had been on my knees scrubbing our section of the common stair when my next-door neighbour passed me with a jocular, masculine, 'Doing your duty?' My reply had been a resounding 'Yes!' and a burst of hearty, deep-throated laughter. The idea of *me* doing my Scots duty on my knees, armed with a scrubbing-brush and pail, seemed to my James-mind hilarious!

Returning with my pail, I closed the door and, electrified with a sudden thought exclaimed, 'Why not?' The common stair, that institution peculiarly Scottish, had in Edinburgh a tradition which went back five hundred years. Why not begin my play upon the common stair? I loved the stair tradition, as he had loved it, the king who built Holyrood Palace and took his unescorted strolls among the stair-heid folk of Edinburgh. That was where my play began, not in the palaces or noble houses, but on the stair-heid.

I was confirmed in this idea when, that evening, my neighbour from the other side arrived at my door bearing the stair card. I knew about stair cards, and I had been disappointed to find that in Steel's Place we did not appear to have one. However, there was a small, dark passage beneath the stair-well which led, I now learned, to the drying green, also our common responsibility. Miss Welsh handed me the card with a slight air of apology but I took it from her with a huge cry of joy. I said, 'But this is a piece of *history*!' and, ghost-tears threatening, hugged it to me as the passport back to *my* Scotland.

'This must have a special place. I know!' and, kicking off my shoes, I climbed on to the settee and hung the card from an empty picture-hook on the wall where it reflected in the mirror above the fireplace, so that when I sat on the settee, my 'thinking place', I had it both before and behind me.

Later that same evening I had no more difficulty locating the play's opening scene. It began in a vennel of tall, black, timber houses, very narrow, where the stair had been a zig-zag ladder outside the dwellings. (I even knew the feel of those wooden stairs – walking past, I had severely bumped my head on one of them on a·dark, wet, windy night.) And I could still hear the voices of the householders arguing and laughing behind the tiny, unglazed, shuttered windows, so close that I could have joined their conversation.

Elated, I broke from my work to take a cup of coffee, and while I drank it I took down the card to examine it more closely. On the front was printed IT IS YOUR TURN TO SWEEP AND CLEAN. . . . The Common Back Passage – the latter pencilled in. Turning it over,

259

voraciously I read the information printed on the back of the card (issued on request by the Department of Health in the City Chambers) and laughed delightedly that modern bureaucracy had picked up the good idea of our fifteenth – sixteenth-century stair matrons . . . for there had flashed across my mind a strong, clear memory of a token carved of bone suspended by a thong of leather from a heavy iron nail set in a wall, the purpose of which had been explained to me those long, long years ago . . . and I was moved to see that the words 'between the hours of sunrise and sunset' were still used to fix the period of duty.

Immediately my synopsis came to life, with the stair-heid women gossiping on that August morning when the clash of bells proclaims the king's marriage at Holyrood to the pudgy English princess of thirteen years; and there it would end, in September ten years later, amidst pestilence and desperate anxiety as the women wait for news of their men 'a' gane awa' wi' Hiamie', unable to believe that Scotland's great army lies dead and broken with its king on Branxton Moor in Northumberland – Flodden to history.

My hands busy at my typewriter, I saw Scotland's stair folk as *he* knew them. Then, reversing the process, I eavesdropped upon their conversation, trying to form through the eyes of his female subjects a picture of the popular, handsome bachelor king who was the public presence of James. It was, I reflected at the time, a 'gey complicated way' to approach my subject, but as long as it worked I had no reason to query why the writing of this play had to be so different from all others. The ruse succeeded up to a point; where it failed was in parts of the play where James himself appeared in the company of other people, and there my mind was in James's head where it could not, simultaneously, use arguments emanating from other heads, as it must do in order to write drama. However, to have seen James at all from outside – even at second-hand – was more than I had achieved previously. That night when I retired to bed I told my reflection in the mirror, 'We're winning!'

The next day, armed with scrubbing-brush and mop-bucket, I drew back the bolts on that secretive, dark door beneath the stair which had fascinated me since my arrival, and found beyond it a piece of greensward bounded by a stone wall. When I had done my duty by the back passage, I felt at liberty to use the drying green, and within minutes I was out there in the spring sunlight using it for the only purpose I understood – practising lunging with my foil against a wall. It was the first time for years that I had felt compelled to exercise my sword arm. Afterwards, with enormous zest, I returned to work on the synopsis.

I was loth to pass on the stair card. A bit guiltily, I kept it longer than my allotted task required. I would look up from my typewriter to give it a salute from time to time: hung on the wall it had become my battle standard. The next time it came round to me, I banished my conscience and kept it with me until I had completed the synopsis.

In March 1966 I had blasted off to the B.B.C. and to the theatre at Pitlochry scripts of *The Year of Mrs Hannibal*, together with the suggestion that the only place to locate Scotland's future was in the past, and would they be interested in a play about James IV? The reply from Pitlochry was that Kenneth Ireland looked forward to reading *Mrs Hannibal* but was dubious about commissioning an historical play. The Senior Drama Producer at Broadcasting House, Glasgow, looked forward to reading *Mrs Hannibal* and was most interested in the idea for the James IV play, but there was no money available for such projects. (In Scotland, there would not be!)

Having completed a presentable synopsis, I sifted from the spoiled pages my declaration of purpose in writing the play, which I intended to include with the synopsis. (My reason for writing a play had never appeared relevant before.) I quote this document because it shows my feeling, unsupported by contemporary evidence, that nationalism was, in 1966, a cause already all but won.

This is the outline of a play I want to write now, and urgently, because of its relevance to present-day issues. Nationalism has come suddenly to the forefront in much of our current thinking – and come so suddenly that the time is with us already when one has to start asking, 'Yes: and then what?' In the fight of any nation for its independence, the immediacy of the goal (for those who believe in it) coupled with its lunacy (for those who do not) leave little opportunity for clear thinking about the destiny which lies ahead. So it is that when victory is won, and banners hang in a fallen wind, idealism is replaced by a void, in which the disbanding army becomes disgruntled knots of humanity looting the field for whatever can be used to enrich their own small ends. Chaos is not the prerogative of the African nations.

This play makes no attempt to ask hot political questions or supply cool analytical answers. Even less is it a rallying cry to encourage the Scots and down the English; Bruce and Wallace are the men for that job, not James IV. No; the Scotland of James IV is important to us because it had all the topographical features of the nationalists' dream come true. It is, in fact, a glimpse of the future projected from a mirror at our back.

History is an arras woven of human values; all the playwright has to do is to select his piece of it and snip off the loose threads. If there is any truth at all in the picture he presents, that truth is always

261

relevant, and the audience will pick it out. That is the only message to be looked for in the play *O Flodden Field.*

From this it can be seen that from the beginning my hero was not James, but Scotland.

Then, to allay the fear of cost-conscious producers, I added a second note:

PRODUCTION COSTS

In its own interest it is best for this play to be viewed as a low-budget job. With its action ranging across the courts and embassies of Renaissance Europe, any sign of the lavish hand in either writing or production will be to its detriment. The personalities and motives of the period are colourful enough; any further identification in visual terms should be an absolute working minimum – heraldic devices on mobile flats to confirm location, and one throne to serve everybody, recognisable as the stage-prop it is. Disregard for the outward show of office leaves us free to study the nature of these men who played at kings.

Their list of titles is imposing but the actual cast list is not great. Diplomacy in Renaissance Europe was plotted in a small closet, two heads together, three at most, in night-caps and boudoir robes; the formal reception of ambassadors in court dress was a show put on for the benefit of people who are no longer with us, either as characters in the play or as members of our audience. Even Pope Julius, when we meet him, will have left his diadem at home – a gesture in keeping with the role for which he cast himself.

The common stair of the sixteenth-century is a rickety structure of wood – the bare skeleton of the institution it will have grown to be by the time it reaches us. More a glorified external stepladder, connecting several doors. We never see inside the houses; the stair-heid is where the gossip of history is held.

As for the battle on Branxton Hill that we call Flodden. . . . Dramatically, the less we see of this the better. We shall see James before he goes into battle, and we shall see his body after it; we know without being told what happened in between. The only 'furniture' required to set a battlefield is the heap of slain, and there cannot have been much else left at Flodden. It is in this heap of slain that the body of the Scottish king is found, stripped by the looters of all but its bloodsoaked shirt. Like the embassies and palaces, the battlefield must be reduced to its basic visual essentials.

What we are searching for inside the costumes are the men themselves, and inside the men the motives and the values they held.

262

These two notes reveal little trace of the agonising conflict within the mind of the writer working at this time on split levels of consciousness. There is a trace of awkwardness in my use of English; and there are small, anachronistic errors – the references to courts and embassies (sic) and the use of Branxton *Hill* qualified 'that we call Flodden' – which show a mind confused by its task of thinking directly out of two different centuries.

When I had sent away the James synopsis, my link with common stair tradition, past and present, prompted me to use it as· the background for a modern television series. I collected information from my neighbours about the contemporary practice of common ownership of property. The very stair itself became a dramatic character. There could be no shortage of material for weekly episodes when the mere matter of replacing three roof-tiles required agreement between so many parties – and that over and beyond the human interest of birth, marriage and death in the numerous households. The more I thought about it, the more obvious it became that not only the James play but also *Scotland*, for me, began and ended on the common stair, rooted in an urban tradition which went back five hundred years. I had found, at last, my identifiable, contemporary locale. It would be my answer to the television penchant for bonny-mock-Scotland, and its opposite, the glaring, go-ahead new town with its range of stage-Scots accents, that non-place on the Scottish landscape which might as well be Slough. (I had refused on principle to contribute to a series which I dubbed 'Craig Compound'.)

I knew it was no use sending the idea to the B.B.C. in Glasgow whose quota of English-approved programmes filled the schedule for a considerable time to come. As the B.B.C. serials editor directed operations from Shepherd's Bush, I sent it straight to him, hoping thus to blast a way through the air of vassaldom which overhung Broadcasting House, Glasgow. It was returned to me. The idea had roused interest, but it was felt to have no immediate relevance. That is to say, no relevance to England: human life was universal only if it happened in London, Birmingham or Liverpool.

An obvious market from the beginning was, of course, Scottish Television, but it was a company with which I had no dealings for a very curious reason: STV used as its trademark the Lion Rampant, which I took as a piece of personal effrontery! When someone suggested my sending it to James Buchan of Grampian Television, then a relatively new company, I posted it at once.

June of 1966 was a bad month. I was waiting for someone to commission the James play, but was too terrified to go ahead and write it. The heap of spoiled manuscript lay beside my typewriter, rapidly becoming buried beneath layers of correspondence. I had begun to worry about my hands as I watched them at work: were they in fact *my* hands? I had never been sure since they took control of my typewriter to type out the thoughts of five hundred years ago. Mackie's book had lain too long on the settee and, though it had now returned to the library, I could not forget the misdrawn hands on the dust-jacket which had given me too much and yet too little information. At the back of my mind lurked an awareness of some clue I had missed because my muddled brain had failed to comprehend what it was seeing.

I was ill, exhausted with my current battles; I rarely left the house if it could be avoided. However, at the end of June I had to make a sortie down to Tollcross to Blyth's sale to buy up the remaining stocks of my favourite foundation garment, now a discontinued line. Like the cessation of brown ink supplies, this news had dejected me: I did not know how I could continue to function as a woman without that delicate cuirass-style garment sprung with steel encasing my body. (The fact that my muscles required no reinforcement had been pointed out to me, but I had worn that style of corslet since 1959 because *it felt like me*.) While in Blyth's I saw on sale heavy-weight black tights of the kind which had become fashionable of late – a fashion I had heartily deplored, as, crossing my nylon-clad ankles, I had remarked, 'Well, for those who *want* to look like cart-horses. . . .' I now rushed excitedly to buy a pair: what had come into my head was a memory of a pair of leaping, black-clad legs – my own.

The next thing I must buy was a sweater – the 'black sweater'. That mysterious garment had become clearly identified in my mind for the first time since my search for it in Newcastle. It was not a sweater to be worn with a skirt, but a tunic to be worn over tights. In the hosiery shop near Blyth's I had the choice of two sweaters in the sale window: one was woollen, my size; the second was nylon and much too big for me. It was the latter I chose. When the saleswoman tried to persuade me otherwise, I described exactly how I wanted to wear it. 'A long, black tunic to wear over tights' – there was no longer any doubt in my mind.

Reaching home in a fever of excitement, I tore off my clothes to try on the new outfit. The tights were a disappointment, being too thin for my purpose, but they would go beneath another pair, and I wrote off at once to the theatrical suppliers in London for a pair of 'extra-heavy black nylon tights without feet' as advertised in *The Stage*. For two days I chafed with impatience and when the precious parcel arrived on the early delivery I whooped with joy and rushed to put on the new ensemble without even waiting for my morning coffee. In the mirror stood a black-clad figure whom I knew as *me*. It was the modern, streamlined female version of the fifteenth-century gentleman in *When Knights Were Bold*. Its great advantage over my Hamlet costume was that I could wear it without needing an excuse.

264

I wore it for the first time that same evening, for the Saturday party, with the addition of a gold belt, gold earrings and the gold-laced walking-shoes which had been my most important find in the Lotus shop at Church Hill – the nearest I came to finding the laminated metal footwear which had dogged my memory. The overall effect was described by my friends as 'stunning', a style more often seen in glossy magazines than in real life. Peculiarly, by the end of the evening the decorative female image had begun to irritate me. I became so embarrassed by the earrings I took them off and put them into my bag. Within a fortnight the gold shoes, too, would disappear, to be replaced by a pair of plain black suede casuals. I was stripping back to the essentials.

My depression during that month of June had been phenomenal even by my standards. It reached its climax a week after my first appearance in the tunic and tights. That morning my dead eyes in the mirror held no hope of life for me and when the telephone rang with the usual invitation to the party I required much persuasion. Afterwards, I cursed my compliance, for this was once, I knew, when it was impossible to don the party-smile I had worn like a mask for three years. Like an automaton I ironed the dress of starched black and white striped cotton and the many petticoats I wore beneath it. Labouring to dress myself, I added my gold bracelets, belt, and the gold locket (still containing its shred of Pentland heather from 1947) which I wore pinned like a fob. I can remember thinking as I faced the wardrobe mirror that I was looking at somebody I could barely recognise as myself. 'Pretty as paint,' flashed the thought, 'and so feminine' – then I roared at the image in the glass, 'Damned liar! But you can get out there and let other people enjoy the sight of you.'

When transport arrived I wondered whether my friends calling for me could see the despair behind my gaiety. My head felt raw inside, as though constant tugging at the tangle of my thoughts had abraded the brain tissue. How I would make conversation during the evening ahead of me, I had no idea. Our host was not a regular member of the Saturday gathering and the party was being held in a Gothic mansion which, as I approached it in the summer-evening light, seemed both to augment and alleviate my distress. I had the sensation that I was walking out of my life entirely. Like a starched, crisp, black and white ghost I entered the company. My instinct was to turn back before I was obliged to speak, but a glass was put into my hand and I found myself being introduced to the only guest who was a stranger to me. A colleague of our host's, he had come with the intention of taking a sociable glass of wine and leaving early. At it turned out, we were to be the last to leave, having spent the entire evening talking.

We talked of history, of teaching, of fighting behind enemy lines, of the Himalayas, and lock-picking (lawfully, during the war). I had no experience of picking locks, but I was a past master in the art of flushing antique lavatory tanks, each with its idiosyncracy: at first meeting, I could sense through the links of chain its response to my fingers. The required skill is the same. I said, without the faintest hope that this particular feat would mean anything to anyone who had not experienced London bed-sitter life of the 1950s, 'I can even crack the Original Burlington.' To my astonishment, he knew at once my rating. 'Can you now?' He was impressed. He then suggested that I might find interesting the unique, nameless model which he had discovered in our host's cloackroom. I went off to see it, and returned wearing the smile of the victor. 'Flushed it at first try,' I said. At the end of the evening I had to ask again his name – it was Lawrence: names seemed irrelevant in the profound relationship between two experts capable of cracking the Original Burlington.

I had made a new friend at a critical time when worse puzzles lay ahead of me.

July brought the news that Grampian liked *The Common Stair* but could not yet afford to mount a serial. It was suggested that we review the situation again in a year's time. I put away the pages of the synopsis in my 'burial cupboard'. Its place had been taken by the common stair of 1511 in the steep wynd of tall, dark, timber houses – the Edinburgh close for which I had searched vainly in 1947.

I had to work on something. Although Scottish stage drama was a lost cause, with theatres and critics publicly bemoaning the dearth of Scottish drama while Scottish playwrights had no market for their plays, I took out one of my early scripts and set to work rewriting it: *The View from Olympus*, inspired by the removal of the Stone of Destiny in 1951. The idea of reviving this play came to me while I was working on the James synopsis, the two for some reason being linked naturally in my mind.

In *The View from Olympus* I saw an alternative way to present Scotland's predicament in order to make it palatable to theatre managements. Scotland's identity remained camouflaged behind the name Höffentlich, and the central idea was still the same – the postponed revolution at last happening in consequence of dressing up an ex-potential king to promote the tourist industry – but the humour in the new play had the bite which was lacking in the earlier version. What began as farce ended on the brink of tragedy – or salvation. Its purpose was to take the joke out of Scottish nationalism. I renamed the play *Message to Mittelplatz*.

I never got rid of that suit of Milanese armour. It crept stealthily forward into the plot, until at the end its cuirass clad the king. *Message to Mittelplatz* said everything I felt about the plight and needs of

Scotland. How faithfully it depicted a metamorphosis overtaking its author was something I failed to perceive.

On 1 August I learned through my parents that my *mentor dramatis*, George Higgins, was in hospital. I began to write to him a letter, which was never posted for I realised when writing it that it would arrive too late. When my mother telephoned to say that George had died, I put away my articulate, vigorous, uncompleted letter in the cupboard with my dead things. Of the crumbling clay mermaid little remained to distinguish her outline from the rock into which she merged; I had no reason to keep her, yet I could not bear to throw her away. She was falling to fragments in the dust of that undisturbed cupboard; I left her there in peace.

I, too, was dying. Dying of August. . . . I had ceased to eat.There was food in my cupboard, but I let it mould there until I threw it away. I recalled the words of a man I had once met on a train who had been a prisoner-of-war of the Japanese: 'You could always recognise the ones who were going to die. They stopped eating.' I realised what was happening but I could not take food to save myself. At the critical point there arrived, out of the blue, the daughter of an old friend with whom I had lost touch for years; she cooked me a meal and blackmailed me into eating it by refusing to touch her own until I ate mine. Because she was young and healthily hungry, I felt sorry for her and complied. That meal cooked by Sally marked a turning point.

On 15 August I was back at my typewriter, clad like a warrior in the black tights and tunic, pounding out a letter to *The Scotsman*. Its subject was our new civic theatre at the Lyceum which had taken over from the Gateway. *The Man from Thermopylae* had been the last production ever to be staged at the Gateway, and like everyone who had loved the small theatre in Elm Row I had kept my eye upon the progress of its successor. By August 1966 the Lyceum was in a bad way, and I sent the suggestion that, instead of spending £2,000 on a full-page advertisement telling us that it was our theatre, they could less expensively 'paper the house' with an invited audience picked at random, with a pin, of Edinburgh ratepayers. I advised that each invitation be signed personally by the Lord Provost, and that formal dress be the order of the day even for the poorest householder. It was one way I knew to convince citizens that it was their theatre. My letter was given what the theatre terms 'star billing' – it was first in the columns, its message condensed to make a sub-heading: 'New-Type Guest List for Civic Theatre.'

My new source of energy seemed directly related to my clothes: I now wore the black tights and tunic when working, and the ornamental gold belt had been replaced by one of plain brown leather.

To MEET STRANGERS WHO SEEM FAMILIAR IS AN EXPERIENCE common to most people. To have two such meetings within a fortnight is unusual, but it can happen; one does not, however, usually react to it in the profound way that I did in September 1966. Each meeting was like a small wedge driven into the ever-widening fissure in my personality.

The first was on an evening which I knew simply as 'this Friday'. I had been in a deep depression all the week and it was with the greatest difficulty that I dressed becomingly to visit new friends introduced to me by Lawrence. I was seated in the chair beside the fire when the son of the house, aged nineteen, came into the living room from the kitchen. At the sight of him I gave a brisk, gay greeting to conceal my turmoil of emotions. I felt immediately drawn towards the young man for reasons which had much to do with the fact that he was male and I was female, but there was something more: I was filled with a surge of pride in him which was *paternal*. Yet there was something more again: when he came through that door I knew at once 'my time is over'. Tomorrow was already upon me, the time when I was dead. As we chatted merrily together, I felt that the pretty lady in brown with matching violet-coloured pearls and eyeshadow who sat in my chair was already a ghost.

The evening which I knew simply as 'this Friday' was years later identified as 9 September – Flodden Day.

Throughout the ensuing week my head was terrible; I belonged nowhere and could do nothing. I was lying on the sofa when Wendy phoned to ask if I would join a group of people going to East Saltoun to commemorate the 250th anniversary of the death of Andrew Fletcher. In my English-educated ignorance I knew nothing of Fletcher of Saltoun, and my mind was too confused to take in what Wendy was telling me. All I had left was my duty to Scotland, and, however ill I might be, that afternoon an opportunity to perform it.

On that day, 15 September, I groped through the litter of clothes in my bedroom to find my tan suit, suitable for the occasion. Arriving early, I found two other people assembled in Wendy's drawing-room, one a man of about my own age, wearing a kilt in the graceful, unselfconscious way of those who wear it daily. I knew this man. In fact, we had not met before, and, when he was introduced to me as Dr Stevenson just home from Malawi, I was glad, really, that I had worn my tan suit – whereas, a moment earlier, I had been wondering what he would make of me now, clad in a skirt, and wishing I had followed my instinctive desire to put on my tunic and tights.

We travelled in the same car to East Saltoun, and in general conversation I managed to assimilate a few facts about Andrew Fletcher – namely, that he had resisted the Act of Union of 1707 (I had great difficulty learning any Scottish history which happened after 1513; it remained for me curiously two-dimensional). However, I was struck with a tremendous regard for this staunch anti-Unionist when I learned that he had said, 'Give us the poets. Anyone can make the laws.' There was a man who would have understood the purpose of my scripts!

In the kirkyard my new acquaintance played the pipes as a dozen of us gathered to make a photographic multitude for the Press. (It is difficult to muster a crowd for an anniversary which falls mid-week.) Watching him, I thought how brave he was to put himself in a position so conspicuous; I felt grateful and *proud of him.*

Afterwards, he and I went off separately to explore the kirk, meeting by chance at the rear door of the church. I desperately wanted to get inside, but the door was locked. I became terribly agitated as we stood outside the locked church, beseeching him to wrestle with the door handle. We walked together round the building seeking another entrance, but both doors were locked. I was nearly crying when our tour brought us back to the same unyielding door. At this point I began to feel the grave-damp surrounding me like my own minuscule haar – felt it so acutely that I quickly walked away before my companion became infected by it. I hated to leave him, but as I crossed the kirkyard, picking my way between the tombstones, I reflected that I had acted correctly: I must not cast my shadow over him a second time.

Standing beside the waiting cars my head became a blank, and I had the utmost difficulty in finding words to string together as conversation. I then noticed that Dr Stevenson was missing. At this, icy panic filled me. We were now piling into the cars, but I could not be persuaded to take my seat; I stood holding the open door, desperate with anxiety for him. Then, with a relief so great it made me catch my breath, I saw him approaching across the graveyard. He quickened his step, and I saw him stumble slightly over a hidden stone. This made me want to laugh, for the graceful figure was suddenly *coltish.* How well I knew that adolescent stumble! – and knew, also, to guard against rushing forward, for he had hated my being over-solicitous.

A few moments later Dr Stevenson had tucked himself neatly and swiftly into the car behind us, and our small convoy moved away.

The two of us stayed longer than the rest at Wendy's. It was early evening when we set off together from the gate, to part company at the bus-stop. On leaving me he gave me the title of a book he had mentioned, written on a piece of scrap-paper. When I reached home I found his name and address rubber-stamped on the back of it. I put it away carefully in my drawer. Life would change now, I reflected. There were two of us together on the war-path.

In a fashion, life did change slightly for the better at the end of September. James Brabazon came up to Edinburgh on B.B.C. business, and when we met I told him about the James play I wanted to write. He had mentioned that he was editing a television series of plays about the six wives of Henry VIII, and while I was rattling off my résumé of the dynastic policy of Christendom prior to 1513, he suddenly interpolated, '*You* are the person to write about Anne Boleyn.' I snapped back, 'Of course I am!' I knew the political evolution of sixteenth-century Europe as no one else could: I had helped to shape it!

The new commission I undertook in my customary fashion, going to the library armed with my B.B.C. permit enabling me to borrow books on long lease. Every volume immediately available on the subject of Henry VIII I scooped from the shelves – except one, which I rejected because, as I opened it, my eye fell, fleetingly, upon a reference to the body of James IV. I had closed it again before the words I glimpsed could reach my brain, and pushed it back quickly on to the shelf.

In the place on the settee where for so long had lain Mackie's book with its disturbing dust-cover, I now heaped all the books dealing with Henry VIII. Henry was to me now just a character in history. Naturally, I would have preferred to be commissioned to write my play about James Stewart, but if Henry Tudor could repair my fortunes as a playwright I was prepared to show him as much consideration as I had given to Mrs Gaskell. The mountain of James manuscript still lying on my table I filed by the simple process of dumping the whole lot upon the chair by the window. My head cleared remarkably when it had gone.

Research into Henry's affairs, character and mind gave me no trouble. Working in my usual way, I established dates and events, making a thorough study of the background of the divorce from Katherine and the marriage with Anne. Knowing so well the dynastic alliances of an earlier generation, I knew the causes of which I was now studying the effects. The remarkable thing was that I was able to put out of my head entirely the twenty-two-year-old Henry who had filled me with constant and terrible rage when I was writing of Flodden. Henry who had been James IV's brother-in-law and mortal enemy intruded nowhere in my picture of Henry as an older man. It was as though the two aspects existed upon separate planes. I remained without bias even when I found the older, developed character riddled with the vices already showing at eighteen – the moral cowardice, deceit and overweening vanity; he had worsened, not changed, but my duty as a playwright was to give him justice.

270

It was not difficult to feel a measure of warmth towards the writer of the engaging love-letters which exude a boyish happiness he himself can barely believe. It was impossible to describe his treatment of the unyielding Carthusians without red rage rising at the diabolical ingenuity of the tortures he devised – and probably witnessed, incognito, for amusement. Between the two extremes, Henry still came alive as a whole person. He came alive so clearly, so easily, that I could almost feel his presence in the room. (Why had this not happened in the case of James, a character so much more sympathetic?)

My work on the Henry manuscript was exacting, but it was a glorious sensation to find my way through history's pages merely as an observer – like a holiday in comparison with my recent experience with James. To have my working ability restored to full capacity filled me with gratitude.

While I could bend my mind to practical matters, I decided to rescue from the depository my bottle of brown ink. . . . I had just cleared the storage charges on my furniture, so I could go to the depository with a clear conscience. It moved me strangely to see my furniture shrouded beneath dust-sheets in a huge chamber as silent as a tomb. An elderly, gentle man moved the covers to find for me the drawer where I put the ink, still in its packaging, on that desperate day in 1961.

When I reached home I unwrapped the precious bottle. Flushing out of my pen the grey-black ink, I sluiced water through the ink sac many times before, ecstatically, I refilled my pen. When I wrote my name on a piece of paper it dried *brown*. . . . I felt as though another life had been restored to me.

I had worked well during October, but November saw the return of menstrual irregularity. There was no cause for it now that I could see, but it persisted, making my head invariably worse. To have a clear head at the end of November was vital, for Wendy had engaged me to speak at the St Andrew's dinner, as the second guest speaker after Professor Douglas Young. I went to ask my doctor for the hormonal pills I had used twice previously in emergencies. He prescribed them, but the problem was that they would not work in time to clear my head before the dinner. Remembering the effect they had had upon me on the earlier occasions, I decided not to take them until afterwards. My state of mental confusion when I went to that dinner is described in a letter written at the time: ' . . . it's like having every thought, word and action separated from me by a barrier, but all of it is inside my head so that I'm trying to reach me over the top of me – it's dreadful!'

There was no question of my cancelling the engagement. I was going to that dinner to speak as a playwright *for Scotland*. For Scotland I could get up from the dead, if I had to. That was the single thought dominating my mind as I dressed for the dinner in my black gown with the stark white stole across my throat.

Arriving early, I saw present two gentlemen, one of them Dr Stevenson. The other kissed my hand on introduction. This was something to which I had been accustomed since the age of fifteen, and to have my hand kissed was as natural to me as having it shaken. So I was exceedingly annoyed with myself on this particular occasion for – as I put it later – 'simpering like a *woman*!' In fact, the word simpering does not describe my behaviour, for all I did was smile charmingly – but the charm, I felt, was womanly, not regal. I worried about it for a long while afterwards.

I sat at the head table until my turn came, then I downed a glass of whisky, flung up a desperate prayer to St Andrew, and rose to my feet. To this day I cannot be sure what I said, but words poured from me: I pointed the comparison between my affluent life as a playwright in London, and my life these years later trying to write of universal man in Scotland. My speech ended with the vow never, no matter what the cost, to write of Scots life in terms pleasing to our English masters.

Amid thunderous applause, I leaned on the table, utterly exhausted. When Professor Young came to congratulate me, my question 'Was it really all right?' was a request for information. Later, when a woman came to ask me how I could speak with such fluency and eloquence entirely unaided by notes, I told her that I had spoken 'from a head which held no brain' and that her thanks for that speech should go to God, St Andrew and the man who invented *uisge beath*.

I still could not take the hormonal pills because on the day following the dinner I had another critical engagement – this time an interview, as a playwright, with a journalist. I quote again from my own letter: 'On the Sunday David Lilleker came to interview me. I warned him that I didn't know what I was saying, and explained bluntly why, but he said, "Just talk, and I'll sort it out." . . . Anyway, he's said he'll let me read his interview before he puts it into *The Edinburgh Weekly*.'

On Monday, 28 November, I took those pills I so much dreaded. My condition is described in the letter:

I said to my doctor today, the female one, 'If a horse felt the way I do, somebody would be merciful and shoot it.' She said, 'Yes, I know' – and meant it.

It has gone on for a fortnight this time. Or it will be a fortnight when I get the next three days over. And it's not as if there is anything I can do instead of Anne Bullen to use the time usefully, because I can't concentrate on manual tasks either. When I light the fire in the morning, I end up surrounded by a fence of buckets, shovels, fire-irons, fireguards, floor-cloths – every mortal thing in a great spread of litter I can't *bother* thinking how to sort away. So I leave them where they are, and go to make the bed – where I create the same sort of chaos in the bedroom. So I go back to the kitchen – which is a SHAMBLES – and add some more to that muddle, whilst I make a cup of coffee which I sit drinking among the fire-irons. Mercifully, I have no appetite, so I don't have to think about food.

At the end of which, it might be as well to mention to you that Anne Boleyn has at least got under way. I found a whole draft of dramatic assessments I'd made of characters, inter-relationships and known facts of character etc., plus some detective work to get at the truth of certain historical mysteries involved – all of which struck me as I read it as being so brilliantly INTELLIGENT, I couldn't believe that I had written it at all. Actually . . . I do remember writing it one Sunday night just after you'd commissioned me to do the job. It's all much too clever for me to understand in my present state, so I'll put it aside for later perusal. ALSO, though half-witted, I have made a start on the actual script – which exists as six foolscap pages. All in all, there is a very sharp brain, if I remember rightly, on the wrong side from me of this iron curtain my female hormones have erected across my brain.

During the course of writing this letter the mental blockage I describe began to clear away, which I mention on a later page:

Does it look to you whilst reading this letter as if a bit of my head has cleared? I felt it while on this page, as if concentration had got my internal steel curtain softening up in places so that I can feel the lumpy outline of intelligence on the other side of it – for all the world like pieces of sculpture shrouded in dust-sheets. Yes! even as I write, I can feel the use of *me* coming back to me – isn't that marvellous? There; you have been in on the birth of an historic occasion.

Then, with reference to physical health: 'Do you think I'll last? I sometimes wonder.'

Down the side of the letter I have written a vigorous marginal P.S. in my strong, brown, twentieth-century roundhand: 'My brain *has* come back to normal! So don't throw away this letter. It's one of the few graphic accounts of a female brain-cycle made during actual rotation that anyone has written, I should think. So as a male writer you might find it useful.'

The first pill had begun to take effect. The following day I took the second. Now came the darkening I knew to expect, when increasing depression was accompanied by a return of the mental obstruction so intense that it felt like a solid object in my head. It was now Tuesday 29 November, and I had to get through three more days of this. Also, I was expecting David Stevenson to lunch, his first visit, and in my present condition how to cook a meal for a guest, I had no idea. Then a wayward inspiration seized me, to put on my black tights and tunic so that I could clean the house. Then I made the discovery that the apparel gave me not only ease of movement, but a distinct lightening of the tension in my head. I wished I could have continued wearing them when my guest arrived so that I could converse more easily, but he was a slightly formal person and I did not know him very well, so, regretfully, I changed into a suit just before his arrival. When he came we talked of national matters, he proposing that I join the party, a suggestion I could not, as yet, accept. I lent him a copy of the new play *Message to Mittelplatz* which, I said, was my own way of fighting Scotland's battles. We arranged a second luncheon appointment for the following week when he would return the script. When he had gone, I changed back into the tunic and tights in order to wash the dishes.

Wearing the tights and tunic, which certainly helped me, I managed to battle through the next two days until my menstrual period began on the Thursday night. With tears of relief, I felt my mental blockage clear entirely, and set to work that night upon the script of *Anne Bullen*. I worked brilliantly all through the next day, and the next, which was Saturday. That evening I was to go to the usual party, for which I wore a dress. I felt deliciously light and feminine when I set out: by the time I returned the femininity had turned to raw hysteria. The backlash from the hormonal pills had arrived.

I knew the condition, for I had experienced it twice before after using those particular pills, but this time I was quite unable to deal with it. When I left the friends who had driven me home I was talking with savage despondency about my 'wasted life', though still in the strain of ironic humour which invited others to share my laughter at my own expense. One of them, more perceptive than I realised, asked, 'Will you be all right?' and I assured him that I would, refusing the offer of company. I closed the door, and then collapsed on the settee in paroxysms of weeping.

Common sense and experience knew what was the matter, but neither functions very well when the system is flooded with too many female hormones, be they naturally present or synthetically introduced. My animus which preserved the balance had been swamped. All I could think of was my lost female potential. Husband, home, children, I had thrown them all away. What use to me, I asked myself, was the *femme fatale* image which *I* never took seriously – or, if I did, contrived to stop its impact before it hurt anyone or damaged my usefulness to Scotland. The entity which put Scotland first was not on duty that evening; all that remained was a wretched, wailing female, aged thirty-seven, and sodden with self-pity.

Yet it was something more than the pills, as I knew; I had been watching my death-throes as Ada F. Kay for a long while. All the difference now was that I had been injected with extra femininity at a time when I knew already that it had no future. I went to the cupboard where I kept a quantity of salts of sorrel left from bleaching lace, the only means of self-slaughter that I had in the house. I mixed the crystals in water. Knowing them to be almost insoluble, I swirled them round with a spoon and drank down the mixture with the crystals in a state of suspension; I reflected wrily that I had remembered one useful term from my school chemistry lessons.

When I had swallowed the stuff, my wits returned. My reaction was an angry, 'That was a damn stupid thing to do!'

Well, it was done now, and I knew that potassium quadroxide, like cyanide, changes the chemical structure of the blood. There is no antidote. I went to my bed for an hour or two, then rose early to go out for my Sunday newspaper. In the shop I desperately wanted to tell the friendly newsagent's wife what I had done, but it seemed unreasonable to worry her with the situation on a Sunday morning when she was so busy. Returning home, I thought of calling a friend of mine, a doctor, who lived round the corner, but I knew she would be busy with her children. I truly was frightened for a short while, then I pulled myself together, adopting a completely realistic attitude: it was a predicament into which I had plunged myself, and there was no way out of it.

By this time I had begun to feel peculiar and very drowsy. I lay down on the settee and smoked a cigarette. I was now in a state of calm, prepared to die neatly. When I became uncertain in my hand movements I extinguished the cigarette. I wanted no holes burnt in the carpet, no fires to disturb my neighbours' Sabbath calm. I slid into oblivion.

From a very great distance an alarum disturbed my peace. It sounded like bells, but they were not the bells of heaven. Then gradually I acquired the feeling that the bell was from 'the other side' – and it was metallic. It was someone trying to reach me. Gradually it penetrated my great distance as *a telephone bell*. I came back to life quite suddenly and tumbled from the settee to the telephone on the sideboard. It was my mother asking, 'Ada, *are you all right?*' She had sensed something wrong with me, and the telephone had been ringing for a long time. I assured her that I was perfectly all right; I had just been asleep for a while. It was no use worrying her with the truth.

When our conversation ended I lay down again automatically to continue dying. Gradually, it dawned on me that the process had apparently stopped. Exasperated, I rose from the settee to make myself a cup of tea while I waited to see what would happen. I saw the ridiculous aspect of my situation, and even laughed at it while I drank my tea. But the presence of oxalic acid in the system is a 'pending' matter.

I rationalised the position. Having emerged from the coma or whatever it was, and finding myself alive, I should do something useful. However brief my time, I could do some work in it. I went to my typewriter and resumed my labour on the Anne Bullen script. It was then 7 p.m.

I worked until nine, and then the pain started in my kidneys. I gripped my chair, and worked on till midnight. The pain was terrible. I took extra sleeping-pills to dope myself till morning. By this time I was sure I would live, but to live with damaged kidneys would be no joke. This thought decided me to visit my doctor. The pain was so bad that I could barely sit in the bus for the journey across town.

Feeling an absolute fool, I told him I had taken potassium quadroxide. He laughed and said, 'I don't know that there is a quadroxide of potassium, is there? I'll look it up.' He did so, and his face changed. He assured me that by this time I had obviously survived it, and the pain in my kidneys was attributable to the waste matter clearing away; but he felt that the people at the poisons treatment centre ought to see me.

Within minutes I was on the bus, clutching a letter for the hospital, and feeling more of a fool by the minute. At the Royal Infirmary I found the appropriate department and handed over the letter. Then I sat in a corridor, wondering how soon I could go home. The hospital, I then discovered, had no intention of letting me go home. I was still protesting that I had a script to finish when I was being put to bed.

Wearing a hospital gown, I sat up in bed facing a group of doctors and nurses clustered round my bedside. I asked how soon I could go home. One of them spoke, 'You cannot go home today. You have a very dangerous substance inside you.' And, looking at their faces, I thought I detected an unspoken 'and what to do about it, we don't know. . . .'

I did not have my sleeping-pills. Nor my earplugs. I heard every happening through the long night in that ward, by its nature one where dramatic human happenings are prevalent. Every hour or so one of the nurses slipped into the side-ward where I lay, to find me awake. They let me smoke for lack of another occupation. In the end, they brought me a cup of tea whenever there was a brew-up. We became friendly during the course of that long night.

In the morning I was informed that I would have to appear before a medical board which would decide whether or not to discharge me. I had been through that before – in Edinburgh, in 1947. I knew what to expect. In my anxiety I made a slip; it just so happened that I had once met the head psychiatrist at a party, and when his name was mentioned I seized on it gratefully: 'Oh, thank God, he'll let me out!' I could have bitten out my tongue when I had said it; however, professional ethics saved the day, for the message was relayed and a stranger was substituted.

I wore no grand clothes to help me this time. I had no make-up on my face. I was alone, in a hospital night-gown and a hospital candlewick wrap, and a pair of hospital mules that slopped off at the heel; but as I put my hand on the boardroom door to open it, I had one powerful advantage — I knew the enemy. He was the man who had sent my body down to England, and his name was The Psychiatrist. He would never get me again.

I opened the door to find the walls lined with people, seated. At the far end was the presiding psychiatrist, who rose as I entered. He gave me his superior's apology for absence and asked me to sit down. He wanted me to tell him 'all about' it. I heard an ice-cold voice, my own, reply, 'I am not going to speak to you before all these people. I don't know them.' Instantly, they rose and he presented to me each in turn by name.

I had then no objection to sitting down to tell him as little as possible, as politely as I could. I explained about the hormonal pills. Asked did I have depressions, I replied that I had yet to meet a human being who did not have depressions. When he asked did I want psychiatric help, I replied, 'No thank you,' adding, 'I prefer to deal with my own problems.'

At the end of the short interview the company rose when I did, and I bowed my head formally to the assembly as I quitted the room in my draggled hospital regalia. Some minutes later I learned in the ward that I had been discharged. It had been a near escape. A kind, wee nurse helped me to dress, and insisted that I made up my eyes 'the way they looked when you came in'. I had no wish to waste time making up my face before I left, but I put on my eye-shadow to please her.

Then I went home to read the splendid article about me which David Lilleker had written in *The Edinburgh Weekly*. It had been rather a full week since that Sunday interview.

I wrote afterwards to the Infirmary a note of thanks for the care they took of persons who wasted their time on accidents which could have been avoided. My head was now clear and working in a rather formal, stately fashion.

On my next visit to the surgery I said to my doctor, 'While I'm well, I'll try to tell you precisely how I feel on the days when I cannot explain what is wrong with me. I feel like a pair of Siamese twins, when one twin is dead and the other has to go round trailing the dead body with

277

him.' I spoke light-heartedly, though choosing my words carefully, and my doctor, smiling, replied, 'You have given what sounds like a perfect description of schizophrenia!' We both laughed.

The day following my release from the poisons treatment centre was that on which David Stevenson was to return the script of *Mittelplatz* and take luncheon. I had donned my tunic and tights when I rose in the morning, and this time I was totally unable to make the change into a dress or suit. I can remember thinking, 'To hell with convention! If he does not know me as I am, that's just too bad.'

In the form of a wry joke against myself, I told him of my adventure with the salts of sorrel, for I was curious to know why it had not killed me. I began by asking whether as a doctor he met any cases of oxalic acid poisoning, to which he replied, 'Only on a mortuary slab.' The only explanation he could offer to account for my being the exception to the rule was the possibility that the form in which I had taken the poison was too insoluble to be properly absorbed into my system, and thus failed to enter my bloodstream in sufficient quantity to be effective. He then told me that during the First World War there had been several deaths resulting from the use of boiled rhubarb leaves as a substitute for cabbage. I thanked him for the tip. Next time, I said, I would just boil rhubarb leaves and drink the fluid.

He had appeared unsurprised by my slightly outré attire, and I took this as indication that I could now wear it on most occasions without causing too many raised eyebrows. My reservation had been due entirely to a natural self-consciousness about the display of a spectacular length of leg. I had never worn trousers, except for a few occasions on night call when I was an Army medical orderly, for trousers, I had felt, were a garment never upon my wavelength: tights were entirely different.

When James, my script-editor, came up to Edinburgh later in the week, he found a lithe, black-clad figure bursting with high spirits whom I introduced as 'the new me'. (I had now replaced the gold belt with one of plain brown leather.) He said, 'Marvellous! You look like a cadet from an élite cavalry school.' Laughing, I told him that had been exactly my own thought when I saw myself in the mirror. I added, 'One day I shall even get that horse!' We discussed for a moment the difficulties of keeping a horse in Morningside, but when I said, 'You wait. You'll see me yet, dressed like this, riding up Morningside Road!' I spoke with absolute conviction.

James was pleased to see me looking so well; even more pleased by the progress of the Anne Bullen script. I was at the same time revising *Message to Mittelplatz*, so my working capacity was tremendous. I told him that my tights and tunic were responsible: thus clad I felt businesslike and competent in a way which I had never felt before, even

278

during my B.B.C. days. It was as though a light inside me which had previously been used with a dimmer had now been switched to full voltage.

During December and January I worked with a terrible vigour upon Anne Bullen. My specialised knowledge of Europe's dynastic history gave me the edge over any playwright seeking Henry and Anne merely in terms of a love story. Love played its part, as did the need for a male heir; but the real reason why Anne married her Henry, after eight years' scheming, was that Katherine of Aragon was the aunt of Charles V, the most powerful man in Europe (despite his adenoids) and Charles V happened to sack Rome and capture the Pope just at the moment when Pope Clement VII was about to grant Henry Tudor his divorce from Katherine. It is doubtful whether Henry's passion for Anne would have lasted out those eight years had not the challenge to his ego worked like an aphrodisiac.

I laughed when I read those letters of Ferdinand of Aragon, now bereft of his Isabella. I knew the style of Ferdinand's letters as though I had myself received them. (I *had* received them.) Each letter was in a bundle containing at least four covering letters explaining to everyone to whom they were directed what to include and what to omit from any discourse. I could feel that bundle of letters in my hand and remember my own bewilderment as I read the several versions of fact which must be withheld from me . . . (Accidentally, the Spanish ambassadors' mail had arrived before the ambassadors!) This flash of memory inspired a device I used in the play, employing the hands of the palace archivists and the frame of pigeon-holes to link the events of Europe in an ironic pictorial commentary.

Seen against this background, the meteoric rise and fall of Anne and the destruction of others' lives in the process gave the theme the stature of classical tragedy. One could not like Anne, but I felt compassion for the asthmatic girl with the cloven finger who was either pregnant or recovering from childbirth at every moment when she most needed to have her wits about her. Hysterical, grown careless through acquisition of power, she had lost both her political and feminine cunning when both were required to keep Henry.

The subsidiary characters were no less real: George Bullen, Tom Wyatt – even Henry Percy, whom history barely mentions – all slipped out of their niches in time to tell me all about it. It was the way that characters aways came alive when I was writing of them: all, that is, except *James Stewart*. I knew them as a playwright.

My awareness of King Ferdinand of Aragon was upon a different plane entirely; even at the time I noticed the disparity.

Initially, I had some difficulty in locating the visual background for the characters I now knew so well. Hampton Court I had never visited – indeed, I had avoided it; I found myself unable to imagine Tudor palace interiors, which was curious in view of my formal education in Tudor architecture. From the point of view of the script this did not really matter, because it was the designer's job, not mine – and, as a playwright who had started young, I knew that one square of stone wall, with or without tapestry, could serve a multitude of scenes: but when writing I liked to see where my characters were standing.

Finally, I focused on two locations which were so clear in my mind that I knew they had existed. One was a gallery overlooking a green quadrangle; the other was more interesting, a small room which I described as 'Henry's study' although my head seemed to hold another, older name for it. Every detail of that room I could see clearly; a small chamber filled with maps and sea-charts, and careful drawings of ships. On the work-benches lining the walls was a litter of papers, carved wooden ship models, and in the place of prominence a small, locked, wooden cabinet which I knew contained dental pliers, a pestle and mortar, drugs in jars, and crude surgical instruments. The room held so many books of reference that at one time I had been obliged to find another home for them, and gave them to a monastery. Every newest invention of the Renaissance was packed into that room for royal consideration, together with a few uncompleted inventions belonging to its owner, on which he was still working. It was the room of a man passionately interested in everything. I knew that room so well that I used it for the scenes where I showed Henry plotting and planning with his close advisers.

I had made just one mistake, however. The room I visualised so clearly had never belonged to Henry Tudor. Oh no; it was the room where *I* had worked, the private turret chamber with the door which gave access to the roof-walk, my favourite thinking place. It was where I had gone to ponder those tortuous letters from King Ferdinand and Queen Isabella.

6

IN MID-JANUARY JAMES IV EDGED HIS WAY FURTHER INTO THE foreground. An old friend of mine, home on a visit from the United States, wanted me to meet her in London. When I told her, on the phone, that I could not afford the air fare, she asked, 'What's wrong with the train?' This flung me into a dilemma, how to explain my aversion to the land-route via Berwick and Newcastle. Then I was struck by a happy inspiration: if I made the real object of my visit *a search for King James's bones*, I could face the journey.

I travelled comfortably down to King's Cross, my pretext keeping me happy and excited all the way. In London I made sure that everyone knew the supposed purpose of my visit, though I took no steps to pursue the quest in any practical fashion. When asked on what evidence I based my theory that the Scots king's body was in the south of England, I was obliged to confess that my single textual reference came from Agnes Mure Mackenzie's *The Kingdom of Scotland*, namely, that James's body had been borne down to Henry, who had failed to give it burial.

I had made no effort whatever to extend my knowledge and had left Scotland without attempting to uncover any clues which might be there. On reaching London I became evasive if anyone tried to offer me practical suggestions about museum archives and libraries. In one who delighted in research, my lack of scientific method was remarkable. Those attempting to correct it met a stream of bland excuses why I could not pursue the matter. Had anyone pierced my armour of enthusiasm to discover how totally unreal was my intention of searching for King James's body, I would have been even more surprised than they.

My illusory quest gave me – in addition to a peaceful journey via Berwick and Newcastle – an excellent opportunity to propound my views upon the importance of Scotland as a sovereign nation in the light of its usefulness to Europe in the first decade of the sixteenth century. By linking my own visit to London with the presence of James's dead body, I came through as a living force into the twentieth century. My longest lecture on the subject was delivered straight out of the year 1513 in Diana's living-room in Leicester Square (where I had lived when newly married) to an audience of her visitors, comprising members of the Royal Ballet. They seemed interested (I hope they were!) and I made sure that by the end they knew precisely what that war with England was all about which had cost us so dear on 9 September 1513. At the end, one of the guests thanked me for a fascinating discourse and departed with the patently sincere wish, 'And I do hope you find your bones.' Half of me was embarrassed – they were not *my* bones, but I was grateful for his use of that possessive pronoun. Below this level, some deeper consciousness hugged the phrase 'your bones' – hugged it as a miser might his cache of gold. I had known them as my bones all the way down from Edinburgh in the train, but I would never myself have voiced ownership.

It was from Diana's flat that I made a telephone call to an old friend whom I had not seen for four years – John, who had been the best man at my ill-starred wedding. In consequence, I was invited out to Blackheath where he now lived, and we spent two days discussing the progress of our respective lives since our last meeting. We had both

281

much to say, and Scottish history was banished from my mind for forty-eight hours. On the Sunday we visited his parents for luncheon, for they had not seen me since 1960, and our talk was all of family matters. To their eyes I had not changed, for I was wearing formal clothes during my stay in London and had left the tunic and tights in Edinburgh.

On Sunday afternoon John suggested a walk over the heath to Greenwich Observatory; I had been delighted to learn that I was actually staying, as it were, on Henry Tudor's doorstep, for this brought me closer to the characters in the play. Crossing the heath we discussed the English Reformation, and the appalling way in which it had been handled; writing an unbiased play did not preclude my saying, 'The Church of England was founded so that Henry Tudor could marry his whore and legitimate his bastard, and then it has the impudence to excommunicate me because *I* am divorced!' My bitterness about my excommunication had deepened considerably during the time I had been writing about Henry.

We came to the edge of the heath beside the Observatory and I looked down upon the site once occupied by Henry's Palace of Placentia. A terrible depression came upon me, and I started shivering with *damp*, as though the unshed grave-tears had this time run into my bones causing mildew, and I said in a flat voice, almost casual, 'James the Fourth lies somewhere over there,' pointing my finger in the direction of the seamen's hospital building. Then I cried, 'Please, can we go now?' and started back, almost running in my anxiety to get away from the place.

Back in the security of the drawing-room, with tea and crumpets, my profound depression left me. When asked, academically, my reason for voicing the opinion that King James's bones were, or had been, at Greenwich, I replied by giving my own story of my terror of 'a chalk-soil grave in Kent' and the sensation, now familiar, of 'grave-damp in the bones of my soul'. John pointed out that Greenwich was not in Kent. This did not seem to matter to me. (In fact, we were subsequently to discover, Greenwich *was* in Kent – in the sixteenth century.) At no time during the discussion did I question why *my* extraordinary sense of being a dead body was related to *King James*.

The next day was John's birthday, so we made a small occasion of it. We agreed that I would come down to stay with him again in the March to celebrate my birthday, and during my visit he would take me to Hever Castle. My play about Anne Bullen would by that time be finished, but I was interested in seeing Hever where so much of the action took place.

I departed home to Scotland feeling happier in my relationship with Kent. In earlier days John and his father, Kentish men, had taken Peter and myself for an evening tour of the Kentish countryside in an effort to persuade me that it was not such a bad county as I maintained. I had been touched by their effort, but my inexplicable aversion to Kent stayed undiminished. What had now so suddenly changed my attitude was the dawning realisation that it was King James's bones I saw buried there, not Ada Stewart's.

On 3 March I flew down to London, my brain once more in the grip of its chronic obscurity. *Ann Bullen* was, I knew, the finest piece of dramatic writing I had ever yet achieved, but God alone knew how I had managed to accomplish it. My brain now felt as if it had split down the middle, like a cleft tree, with one side living and one dead. The only thing holding the two parts together was my dress of black tights and tunic, which I had worn through the writing of *Ann Bullen*, and that I was obliged to leave behind in order to go down to Kent in my role of the woman who had existed prior to June 1966.

I arrived at Blackheath with what I now termed invariably 'the steel shutter' wedged firmly across my brain. It was worse than I had ever known. I arrived on the Friday evening, having assured John that all the catering for our guests could be dealt with on the Saturday morning and afternoon. He knew he could rely on me because he remembered me as a capable hostess in former days. What I had not made allowance for was the terrible deterioration of my faculties. On the Saturday morning, I can remember going with him to Nicolson's in Bromley to buy food. To him I seemed perfectly all right, and he left me to do the ordering. Actually, my head was a total blank except for the conviction that I was provisioning an army. When we reached home I looked at the mountain of exotic foodstuffs piled on the kitchen table and burst into tears. I cried, 'But what can we give them to *eat*?' John stood back, dismayed: he had thought I had a menu in my head.

To this day it is recalled by those who were present as 'that glorious party'. What I remember is the horror of a kitchen filled with provisions that nobody would ever eat. The sight affected me with a profound melancholy, disturbing me to ghost-tears. Socially I was adequate, circulating graciously, talking eloquently – I even managed to give studied, sensible advice to two guests determined to pour out their psychological problems: what to do with that food totally defeated me. I was told repeatedly simply to forget it, but I was still trying to fill pastry-cases with cucumber and caviare when the earliest-departing guests came to say good night. Then I sat down amidst the heaps of provisions and began to cry, the great, baying grief now overlaid with notes of hysteria.

As it happened, we did have a psychiatrist in the house. Nick invaded the kitchen with two glasses in his hand, mine and his own, closing the door behind him. None of the guests had seen the state I was in when lying low in the kitchen, but the professional in Nick had doubtless spotted behind the façade of the smiling hostess a very sick person. He began gently, then turned on me the Freudian analyst's treatment. Reduced to hysterics, I can remember screaming, 'No, you're wrong!' And I knew he was wrong: half mad I might be, but there stood apart from my weeping self a strong, cogitant man in black hosen and doublet who sufficiently controlled the brain of the demented lady to enable her to tell Nick that my state of mind had nothing to do with my relationship with my father. Nick and I were on some kind of collision course, though I did not feel the impact until the word 'father' gave me a picture, fleetingly, of *another* father in a memory which fitted nowhere the period 1929–67.

On that visit to Blackheath I was forced to face the fact I would not recognise in Edinburgh, that I was very ill indeed. I said, cautiously, that I trusted Nick despite his Freudian approaches – which is to say a very great deal – and asked John to take me to him as a patient.

When he had heard the practical details of my bitter struggle to maintain my foothold in Scotland, Nick asked me why did I persist in trying to live there? The fact that I had no real home, no security, no money, were all problems created by my refusal to return to London. He pointed out that none of these difficulties had existed when I lived and worked in the south of England. What was there in Scotland which justified my act of professional suicide?

Stubbornly I said, 'I shall not leave Scotland.'

He made another suggestion. As a *temporary* measure would I not go down to London, earn enough money to restore my fortunes, and then return to Scotland? It was not, he pointed out, as though London was a foreign place to me; all my professional connections were there, and I had many friends in the south. Could I not for a limited period return?

He had touched my buried nerve. I shouted, 'Look, I have spent my whole life fighting to get back to Scotland. Nothing will make me leave now – *nothing.*'

He asked what good was I to Scotland in my present condition, half-fed and worried nearly out of my mind by financial problems.

I tried, inadequately, to explain the numerous unpaid good causes to which my life in Scotland was devoted. I told him of the host of people who found their way to my door in Steel's Place, to be encouraged by my own downright refusal to quit the scene of Scotland's battle for survival. Here I had great difficulty in maintaining my calm when telling this man in Kent what life was like for Scots after centuries of misrule from Westminster. Scotland's maladministration had to be experienced to be understood.

He asked why, in that case, was I bent on living there?

I cried, 'Because I have to!'

'Why?'

'*I have to!*'

'You don't have to. You're not a Scot—'

'*I am!*'

'You're not. You were born in Lancashire.'

There was a significant pause. Then he quietly resumed, 'You have nothing to gain by living there, have you?'

I was silent. Gain was something of which I never thought in relation to Scotland.

'You have no house in which to keep your furniture. You cannot sell your work up there. All you have is worry—'

'*I will not leave Scotland!*'

'No matter what it costs you?'

'No matter what it costs me.'

There was a pause, then he said mildly, 'Then there's not much I can do to help you, is there?'

'No.'

Again there was a pause. Then the Freudian analyst found his own explanation for the passion that was killing me: 'Obviously, you must have some man up there—'

I shouted at him, 'No! There's not a man. You have it all wrong. Don't you see? I have to live in Scotland *because Scotland does not exist unless I live there.*'

He had probed to find the truth and he had got it. Whether the statement surprised him as much as it surprised me I did not know, for it was the first time I had ever voiced it. It was an extraordinary reply, but it was the true one. All my days I had loved a nation more than I could love any living human person. The fact had never seemed strange to me, nor did it now in the consulting-room when I thought about it. I picked up my handbag, John helped me into my coat, and we departed.

I fled Kent directly afterwards, and psychiatry, my wiser instinct knowing that my best chance of survival lay in escaping across the Border as quickly as possible.

Immediately on arrival back in Steel's Place I donned the black tights and tunic. When I unpacked the suitcase I hung away the dress I had worn for the party, knowing I had no more use for it. The turquoise jewel I had so much wanted, knowing it had to go with me down to England for that party, I cast into my jewel-box never to be worn again. That was the moment when I knowingly cast off the identity of the modern lady: henceforward her clothes would be a disguise I wore when occasion required it. Such times were to become, in fact, increasingly rare.

285

I sent off to London for more pairs of black tights so that I did not require to wash my clothing every night. My drying-rack now became festooned constantly with black tights, sometimes as many as six pairs at a time. I had ceased entirely to wear the cuirass-styled foundation garment, neither my body nor my spirit having any further use for it. I began referring to my all-black costume as my 'battle-dress', for this was what it had become.

There was now a new person working at my typewriter whose ghost-hands no longer required the subterfuge of scribbling cryptic messages disguised as verse: there was no nocturnal poetry written during this period. He works overtly now, channelling our life's single passion into letters and play-scripts. I still watched my hands with curiosity, but their antiquity worried me no more. As long as they flew across the keys to convey our meaning, I did not care whose hands they were – and had been.

On 3 April I made my decision to join the Scottish National Party. I wrote to tell David Stevenson, with whom I had discussed the matter many times. I declared myself free of political ambition, but willing to address envelopes, help organise jumble sales and make cups of tea. I wanted to work at ground level with the rest of Scotland's people who felt as I did. I still saw my two roles separately, and my work as a national playwright remained for me the aspect of greater importance, but that did not preclude my being a Nationalist as well.

Just for the moment it seemed as though Scottish television drama had a future, for the three-year English occupation of the B.B.C.'s Glasgow studios had ended. One of the plays under consideration by The Television Drama Department was *The Year of Mrs Hannibal*. I took hope for this play which championed the indigenous culture when, on 31 March, I watched a twenty-minute experimental play in Gaelic – and I wrote on 5 April, 'Now that we have had a play in Gaelic about two halves of a split mind getting matey over a cup of cocoa, could we push the matter of a play written in Gaelic *and* English?'

All that *Mrs Hannibal* needed, I knew, was cutting, but the three-year delay had been too long for me. I was now more positively identified with Scotland's struggle for independence, and *Message to Mittelplatz* was my theme of 1967. This was to my mind essentially a stage play, not because it was unsuitable for television adaptation, but because I wanted it to reach live theatre audiences. That there was an audience for it I was certain, but how to push it past the barrier of English theatre directors and English-oriented managements was the problem.

Knowing that I was pushing my luck by submitting a play with a strongly nationalist theme, I was anxious to know in advance whether

286

it was likely to be faulted on artistic grounds. As I said at the time, 'If *Hamlet* had been written during a war with Denmark, you can rely on it that it would have been rejected on "artistic grounds"!' To get an unbiased opinion from someone who was not being asked to produce it, I sent it off to Ronald Mavor, Director of the Scottish Arts Council. It was desperately important to me to have the existence of this play somewhere recorded, in case it should vanish into oblivion: it was my voice of the twentieth century I was now trying to make heard, before it was too late.

The scripts of *Mittelplatz* had been despatched to three theatres, of which as yet only one had acknowledged its arrival. The slow, cumbrous machinery of the theatre was something which I was conditioned to accept, but in the case of this particular play I was filled with feverish impatience, increased since my return from England. It was this which decided me to send it to the B.B.C.: that play had to reach an audience, and I was fighting against time.

There came an immediate enthusiastic response. I knew better than to pin my hopes to anything in my profession, but this was one occasion when I had to break the rule. Only *Mittelplatz* stood between me and the James play which by this time I was hoping I might never need to write.

Since the September of 1966 the pages of the James play had lain on the chair in the window, gathering dust and the yellow patina of nicotine. The chair was wedged between my table and the window, difficult of access, and this inaccessibility had been a help to me while I was engaged on *Mittelplatz* and *Ann Bullen*. Now that both were finished, I viewed the heap of unsorted, spoiled manuscript with trepidation and a sense of guilt. While I awaited further news from the B.B.C. about *Mittelplatz* this was, ideally, the time to return to work on the James play, but my fear of it lingered. My head had worked well during *Ann Bullen* despite its severe afflictions, and the thought of what another session upon the James play might do to it filled me with apprehension.

I rationalised my fears. Would I, in fact, encounter the same difficulties? Was it possible that I had been unfair to James? After my exhaustive research for *Ann Bullen* I was shamed by the little scholarship I had shown in regard to James Stewart. I had not even bothered to read his letters, – though Wendy Wood had mentioned a volume containing them, a consideration owing to him no less than to Mrs Gaskell and Henry Tudor.

The more I thought of it, the more apparent it became that it had been a grave omission not to read the letters.

As though in answer to my thoughts there came a telephone call from Leslie, now working in Grant's manuscript department, to say that he had obtained the copy of Thomas Wyatt's collected poems for which I had asked. He then mentioned that there had come into the shop a copy of *The Letters of James IV*, published by the Scottish Historical Society, and would I like to have it? In fact, I could hardly refuse: if the letters were bent on reaching me, there was no way I could now avoid them.

We had not met for some while, so I invited Leslie to dinner on Tuesday, 11 April, when he would bring the books with him. All that day I was curiously excited, for by the evening I would have James's thoughts not merely in my head but in my hands to hold. When Leslie came I put the books unopened on the sideboard whilst I served dinner and we caught up on the lost conversation of more than a year. When he was leaving I asked what I owed him for the two books. He told me the price of the Wyatt poems; then he picked up the heavy volume published by the Scottish Historical Society and laid it in my hands. 'The *Letters*,' he said, 'belong to you. I want you to let me make you a present of them.' I protested, 'Leslie – no!' But he repeated, '*Please*.' I bowed my head and with silent nod accepted them.

When he was gone I hugged the volume in my arms, shaken by ghost-tears. I left the book unopened while I prepared myself for bed, wanting to delay the moment of reunion with those letters. Finally, I took the book to the settee where I sat and opened it. My immediate shock of disappointment baffled me. For an agonising moment I wondered what was wrong, and then realised that the letters *had been translated into English*.

Where had the life gone from them, the strong, dour tongue that I remembered? Edited, numbered, set neatly on a printed page, these were not my letters, though I did see one which even in translation carried the unmistakable stamp of my rhetorical style just as it occurs in my formal correspondence of the present day.

I sat for a while turning the book's pages, saddened by their *foreignness*. Then I came suddenly to wonder why the letters looked so different from what I had expected. What had I expected? Henry Tudor's letters had been presented in a similar fashion, and it had not occurred to me to wonder why *they* were not in manuscript. Why should I expect to see James IV's letters just as Paniter had taken them down, *with the ink still wet*?

Then strange things started happening in my head. The voice inside me read the words as plain 'auld Scots', so that I became confused and half-blinded by the printed characters, as though I had the beginnings of migraine. Hurriedly I put away the book, took my sleeping-pills and went to bed. The next day when I awakened the 'steel shutter' was lodged across my brain. I did not attempt to read the *Letters* again. Nor did I resume work on the James play. After a while the blockage in my head cleared a little.

Then my creative talent bloomed suddenly in a new and totally unexpected form: I, who throughout a lifetime had been renowned in my family as its one member totally devoid of musical talent, began to *compose songs*!

There was no question of unconscious plagiarism because no tune stays long enough in my head to make an impression there. The talent came out clear, strong, and totally original. I awoke, made my breakfast and washed dishes to the accompaniment of a rousing marching song. I hurriedly summoned a musical friend of mine, and together we composed a second and a third verse· then she took it away to her music teacher to be arranged. Its first public performance was in Haddington, where it met with success. (I was subsequently to hear it sung at an S.N.P. ceilidh in the theatre on Church Hill where tapping feet picked up the rhythm.)

My second song was composed single-handed. This too was a mustering song, but in it was a strongly *maternal* Scotland calling home her children to fight for their heritage. The tune had a Gaelic ring, very ancient, but none of my friends had heard it before.

Whence came my extraordinary new talent I had not the faintest idea, but I was extremely glad to have it: anything I could use in Scotland's cause was welcome. I asked David Stevenson if anyone in Scotland published rebel songs.

7

THIS VIGOROUS, ARTICULATE FIGURE AT WORK DURING APRIL and May is accompanied by its ghost, the two linked together by a pair of hands which can type nationalist letters but no longer sew buttons, and the black uniform I called my battledress. The periods when my head blotted out were lengthening, '. . . the tensions which used to last two or three days, now last for fifteen out of twenty-five. . . .' At no time was I ever unaware of what I was doing. When my head was at its worst I sat or lay on the settee, chain-smoking, totally conscious of my discomfort and my inability to perform the smallest task. When my head cleared I rushed immediately to my typewriter with a fervent, 'Thank God!'

My friends visited me a great deal, finding me as eloquent as ever (I did not let them find me when I was not!) but I felt myself now to be cut off, as though the barrier inside my head had somehow imposed itself between me and other people. My sense of isolation had become almost unendurable, when, during the second week of April, there came into my dark world a new companion – an infant mouse, who moved in to share the flat with me via a crevice in the plumbing. For several months my personal correspondence carried reports of this vital relationship without which I do not think I could have survived with sane mind my wellnigh intolerable predicament.

It is hard to say when the idea first consciously entered my mind that the discrepancy between my twin selves might have a rational explanation. I date it back to the evening when I crossed the hall to the bathroom and saw, as I had seen many times before, my figure reflected in the wardrobe mirror. Until that time I had always identified the tights and tunic I now wore as modern female dress, and it had never occurred to me to think of them as *doublet and hosen*. I had been arrested by the sight of my silhouette against the light from the living-room, and what flashed into my head was a portrait of a man in black medieval costume.

The thought must have alarmed me, for later, when I came from the bath naked into the living-room, I made a drawing of the upper part of my female torso which I saw reflected in the mirror above the fireplace. Head, shoulders and breasts, the likeness is a good one. It is styled 'Self-portrait' and dated meticulously 23 April 1967. My urgency shows in the drawing, the dashing pencil strokes, as though I recognised the need to record quickly the identity of Ada F. Kay, playwright, before she slipped away to join the shades.

The next day, 24 April, found me at work on '*Message to Mittelplatz*', re-writing, partly to renew my link with the play on which so much depended, and partly because I had a premonition that I should soon be hearing from the B.B.C. about it. Sure enough, word reached me on 26 April which indicated a warm and active response in more than one quarter. The main business of the letter was technical, concerning timing. Play spaces at that time were 30, 50, or 75 minutes and during the following year the stress would be upon the 50 minute slot to give outlet to the greatest number of writers. I was asked if '*Mittelplatz*' would work at that length, or at 75 minutes.

So far as I was concerned, '*Mittelplatz*' *had* to work at seventy-five minutes (or even fifty) – and, in fact, it could work easily at seventy-five, if efficiently adapted. I wrote back at once with the assurance that I could cut it to seventy-five minutes, and outlined the style of presentation I would use. My mind writing that letter was as clear and competent as it had ever been, which makes the more significant the alarming change which occurred the following day.

The cause of this sudden deterioration was a letter which I received from one of the theatres to which I had sent a script of '*Mittelplatz*' and I quote it because it is the style even more than the content which so profoundly affected me:

Dear Miss Kay,

Like yourself I am deeply exasperated by my failure to reply to your letters and to give you an answer about your play *Message to Mittelplatz*. Unlike you, I have cause to be deeply ashamed of this tardiness. I have read the play and it has been read by others and we all appreciate its worth while feeling ultimately that it would not fit in with our scheme of things. To elaborate would be offensive and presumptuous, but working as we do at very high pressure we feel it necessary that one of us should feel some kind of stirring of excitement at the prospect of everything we include in our programme; in this particular case a dismayed appreciation of its undoubted qualities.

I understand how offensive this letter must be to you and I am truly sorry to have been so long writing it. My only justification is that having read a play and keeping it in the office its reverberations occasionally reach out to one, but, alas, this has not happened in this case.

My immediate reaction was to rush to my typewriter to reply: 'Far from being offended by your letter, I was enchanted with it. Tell me, do you ever write for *Punch*?'

My hilarity was short-lived. As I stared at the letter it began to confuse me in much the same way as did textual reference to James, but for a different reason. My deepest problem of this time related to words, and the writer of this letter had used too many of them. At first I had seen the verbosity; later I began to wonder whether it was real, or existed merely in my own mind. The extraordinary and damaging effect is recorded in a letter subsequently sent to a friend: '. . . I must confess, when I read ——'s letter, it decided me to go inside: if I met people who used words the way he does, at least I'd know they were in there getting *cured*.'

What is madness has never been defined; approximations exist, as in the word 'normal', but normality at best is relative. When one has reached the stage of thinking that the rest of the world might be mad, it is usually wise to check upon one's own sanity. I telephoned to John in Kent, and Nick the psychiatrist, and the outcome of the conversations at that point was the suggestion that I should go to Blackheath to be treated by Nick. I set off to discuss this project with my doctor, but had a great deal of difficulty explaining the situation. He reminded me that on a previous occasion I had demanded psychiatric assistance and within twenty-four hours gone plunging back to the surgery, with a clear head, to reject it. However, my doctor told me, the decision was up to me; his own attitude was non-committal.

By 29 April my condition had so far deteriorated that I was asking

291

John and Nick in Kent to arrange for me hospital accommodation. Again I consulted my own doctor, and for the first time he did not advise against my going into hospital. When pressed with the question, 'What *would* you advise?' he answered, 'I think I would recommend it.' He had never said that before. Immediately I was on the telephone to Kent, where plans were now being made to have me admitted to Bexley Hospital as an emergency case.

Crazed though I might be, a part of my head still forming its own rational conclusions saw my predicament as being one brought upon me by circumstance as much as by my disorder within. A letter from Ronald Mavor at the Arts Council summed up the situation:

> I have just finished reading *Message to Mittelplatz*. It is full of ingenious and witty notions and has certainly enough droll incidents to keep any audience happy; I wish I could feel more optimistic about it.
>
> I must confess that I do not see where there exists an audience for this play. Your remarkable blend of Gothic farce and political satire might certainly come off in the right place and at the right time but I do not see the time or place for them just now. . . .

No play has an audience until a theatre puts it on, that is the crux of a playwright's dilemma. And *Mittelplatz* was *my last hope*.

Physically, I knew that I could not last out much longer. Underfed, overworked, my body no longer had the stamina to sustain the dynamic force working through it. In addition, 'the sheer nagging misery of living hand to mouth was more than my female hormones were prepared to stand on top of the strain of being subordinated to a male intellect.'

Everything now depended on the television production of *Message to Mittelplatz*. On 3 May there came an encouraging response to my suggestion that I could reduce the play to seventy-five minutes. Then came the rub: I would not get paid on a commissioning basis for the editing until after I had proved that the adaptation would work. Furthermore, the producer who liked the play was going away on holiday and our plan to discuss the style of adaptation would have to wait until he came back.

I shouted my despair: what on earth was I to live on while adapting *Mittelplatz*? Far worse was the news that I could not start work on it until June. A whole month lay ahead of me, idle except for. . . . My eyes travelled to the heaps of manuscript on the chair by the window. I think I had always known that it would come back to this, that circumstance would force me upon the course which I had hoped so desperately to avoid, back to Flodden. With time on my hands and no other ideas, I would have to try once more to write my play about James Stewart. Nobody could query my right to be nationalist when speaking out of the sixteenth century.

Resigned, I pulled the heap of manuscript from the chair, dusted it, and sat down to read. To my absolute horror I discovered that I could no longer read what I myself had written about King James. I can remember going round the house, touching objects for reassurance that I was still there. I shouted aloud, 'Why can't I do it?' 'Why can't I write this play?' Then I said, 'It's as difficult as trying to write a play about *myself*.' Then came to me a new and terrifying thought: *was that possibly what I was doing*?

Panic-stricken, I telephoned John, begging him to come for me at once. I was so frightened I was almost gibbering. He said he would telephone Nick immediately to arrange my admission to Bexley Hospital, and he himself would drive up to Edinburgh overnight on the fourth if I could just hold on for another thirty-six hours.

When I left the phone I steered myself through my nightly routine, concentrating carefully upon each task in an effort to calm myself. Gradually panic subsided. When I went to take my bath I sank into the water, relaxing my limbs and thinking that I need worry no more, for rescue was on its way. . . . And then the sight of my naked body lying in the old, long, metal bath-tub from which I had scoured the enamel suddenly electrified me with the memory of *something* – followed instantly by the realisation that Bexley was in *Kent*. I shouted, '*My grave in Kentish chalk soil!*' And I hurled myself from the bath so quickly that I was not even dry when I scrambled into my doublet and tights. I ran to my typewriter, and drafted a straight, coherent letter to the Scottish Arts Council demanding to know why, if a play were entertaining, it was not performed? For whom were we writing? I asked. So far as I understood my job, and William Shakespeare had understood it, we were writing to amuse an *audience*, not a handful of theatre directors engaged in entertaining themselves.

The next morning the Earl of Balfour walked into my gun-sights, through a letter in the correspondence column of *The Scotsman* from which I quote the paragraph which most incensed me:

I wonder how many of those who somewhat light-heartedly think it would be 'nice' to have 'some form of home rule' and 'some form of Scottish Parliament' realise that if their wishes were fulfilled then it would be virtually certain that never again would a Scottish M.P. sitting for a Scottish constituency hold the office of British Prime Minister, British Foreign Secretary or British Chancellor of the Exchequer.

293

I pushed aside my morning coffee and drew the typewriter towards me:

Sir,

In Lord Balfour's list of top jobs available to Scots as British citizens, he could have mentioned that several Scotsmen in their time have occupied the Throne – but the fact still remains that even our kings went south to get promotion.

May I respectfully suggest that what is wrong with the United Kingdom is not the mixed strain of nationalities but, basically, the imbalance of population; and the cure for this would seem to lie in the natural redistribution of U.K. citizens, which can come about only when Scotland, England and Wales have separate and equal focal points of administration?

Then, while it would be true that no Scot could, theoretically, become Prime Minister of England, there would be nothing to disqualify him from holding the highest post available in any federal parliament which the three units of territory agree to share between them. He would even, thereby, become the first truly 'British' Prime Minister.

I signed, sealed and stamped the letter and ran out to post it before making a replacement for that cold cup of coffee. Then I phoned several of my friends to discover that not in me alone was battle fervour kindled. His lordship looked like having a heavy bag of mail to answer in the correspondence columns.

Thereafter I spent a useful, busy day at the typewriter. I have no record of the total number of letters I wrote, but I remember that I had to go to the post office for extra supplies of postage stamps and that I put into the pillar box two separate piles of envelopes – all containing articulate, reasoned letters upon many subjects, variants on a single, unifying theme: independence. I had prepared a meal, but I was still busy at the typewriter when my rescuer arrived at 8 a.m. the next morning, exhausted after his marathon drive from Kent.

Of the demented lady he had come to save there was no trace; in her place there was a vigorous, defiant, black-clad warrior, flourishing a newspaper containing the Earl of Balfour's letter and roaring, '*This* is why I have to stay to fight!'

During the next twenty-four hours John heard a great deal about the maladministration of Scotland: but I said never a word about the extraordinary thought which had entered my mind about the possible link between James, King of Scots, and myself.

I did my best to make amends for his fruitless journey by giving him the best hospitality I could afford, and I was deeply penitent for

294

putting him to so much inconvenience. But when I had given him a parting hug of gratitude, my voice pealed triumphantly down the common stair, 'I don't go down to England this time, living or dead!'

For two days the correspondence columns of *The Scotsman* were filled with nationalists' replies to the Earl of Balfour – mine among them. It was the first overtly political letter which I had contributed. For me there was no looking back: I had broken my avowed rule, as a playwright, never to show my own colours. What most cheered me was the sight of so many people rallying to the cause of Scotland's independence; not since 1513 had I seen a mustering like it.

Of my private battle I said nothing, apart from a single, cryptic sentence appearing at the end of a letter to James Brabazon, which is the first and, so far as I know, the only reference made in writing to the suspicion now forming in my mind that James Stewart and I were indivisible. I had described, with much compassion for the traveller, John's heroic sortie to rescue me. Explaining my sudden change of mind caused by the thought of 'my grave in Kentish chalk soil', which had been my fear-cause for leaving London in 1960, I said, in brackets: '(I am beginning to have two minds about the cause of this phenomenon, and one of them takes me into gey deep waters)'.

My reluctance to venture into the 'gey deep waters' caused me to devote myself during the next few days to my battle for recognition as Ada F. Kay, playwright. The idea that I could actually be another person from a previous century was unthinkable. To squash the notion, I determined to make another assault on the James play, still hoping that I could somewhere isolate that elusive gentleman in a form – third person singular; gender, male; condition, dead – which I could recognise as a character in a *play*.

Determined to be ruthless with the fellow (and with my head) I went to the library to regain possession of R. L. Mackie's book, reasoning that an *un*sympathetic biographer would be more likely to create for me a character visibly separate from myself. After my previous experience, I knew the risk I was taking, but *anything* was preferable to entertaining the ghastly suspicion now forming in my mind.

I was still not prepared for the shock awaiting me. On attempting to read the text I discovered that English had become a foreign tongue: where there appeared quotations from contemporary records, in Middle Scots, those I could read with no difficulty. In the end, desperate to hear a voice in 'mine ain Scotis tongue' I turned to the chapter containing copious quotations from the poetry of Henryson and Dunbar. Here, for a while, I was relaxed and happy; ignoring the interpolations in modern English gibberish, my tongue rolled blissfully round the familiar lines by Henryson:

. . . Ane lytill Mous come till ane Rever syde;
Scho micht not waid, hir schankis were sa schort,
Scho culd not swim, scho had na hors to ryde:
Of verray force behovit hir to byde.
And to and ffra besyde that Rever deip
Scho ran, cryand with mony pietuous peip.

I hoped my friend the mouse behind the skirting-boards was listening, as I read aloud the splendid lines with a fluency that no modern English tongue could contrive, a fluency made the more remarkable by my increasing difficulty in rendering modern Scots. Then, for Mouse's benefit, I launched into another poem by Henryson:

. . . The uther Mous, that in the burgh can byde,
Was gild brother and made ane fre burges;
Tol fre als, but customemair or less,
And fredome had to ga quhairever scho list,
Amang the cheis in ark, and meill in kist . . .

And so on. This feat, I discover now, was even more astonishing in view of the fact that my only acquaintance with Henryson was through Mackie's book, and Mackie's book *does not contain the tale of the 'burges mous' from which I had been quoting.*

My head was terribly disturbed during the next few days, curtailing my activities in most directions. I made no further attempt to read Mackie's book, though I left it lying on the settee where I could take it up to look at the portraits. One day when I looked for the nth time at le Boucq's drawing on the cover in the hope of finding King James, I was horrified to see only a head-shaped blank upon the paper.

When Lawrence came that evening I picked up the book and, slamming my hand across the portrait, I roared, 'I'm beginning to wonder, did this bloody man *ever exist at all*?'

'Oh, he existed,' said Lawrence. 'Very much so.

When my visitor had departed I took up the book again and began to pluck at it, making small whimpering noises. It was, I felt, too much. I had worries enough without having to batter my tormented head against the problem of James Stewart's identity. Yet could I now ignore it? Was it possible that the key to my own now critical condition lay somewhere within the James-cypher?

My fear of remaining with my head blocked like this for ever was greater now even than my fear of venturing into the 'gey deep waters'. Carefully, I assembled the facts, beginning with my astonishing reply to Nick, over which I had pondered many times: 'Scotland does not exist unless I live there.' From my birth two motivating forces had shaped my every crucial action: duty towards Scotland and my terror

296

of being buried in the south of England. Neither made any sense whatever in terms of heredity, environment or my known personal experience. Could there be some other factor – call it *un*known personal experience – which had shaped my attitudes before my present life took hold of me?

Calmly now I pondered these questions, relating them to the other problematic identity, the character of James Stewart. Even to attempt to delve into this critical area produced tension in my head but I had to resolve the mystery at no matter what cost. I poured myself a measure of whisky to ease the pain in my head and put Mackie's book away from me upon the far chair, where it became just a book, an object.

Why did I have so much inside information about James apparently unknown to historians? (I was not and never had been mediumistic, so that possibility did not enter my head.) Why was he the only historical personage I had encountered in my whole writing life who never came alive for me as *himself*? Yet I could think his thoughts upon my typewriter, breaking my lifelong rule never to presume to know what dead men thought; what they had spoken one was permitted to guess, but the mind behind the words was a sealed repository. (For this reason I neither wrote, nor liked, historical novels.) Why should James be the sole exception? And why was it impossible to see James through others' writing? – a phenomenon I would expect to apply only to *oneself*.

These and many other questions came under scrutiny as I sat there thinking. What I could not face was the answer. I would have to take someone into my confidence, for I dare not be alone when I posed the final question. I waited until Lawrence visited me a week later, when I asked timidly, 'Can I talk to you?' Then I listed all the questions posed as above. At the end, I steeled myself to put the final question, feeling that it was a blasphemy to claim another human being's life and identity. Very diffidently, having difficulty with the words, I said, 'I have been thinking. . . .I know it sounds crazy, but . . .could James the Fourth be me?'

After a pause, Lawrence replied, 'Well, stranger things have happened.'

It was easier now I had said it; no sixteenth-century Scots soldier king, outraged by my presumption, came storming into my mind – as I would have expected had I been wrong. Nobody came in answer to my challenge, but a warmth stole through me as though I had opened a casement to admit the sun. In the long silence I said, 'If there is an answer to my question, there's only one place I shall find it. At Flodden.'

Lawrence said he would drive me there whenever I wished.

My head was a great deal easier after that conversation, and renewed vitality sent me charging away upon my twentieth-century warpath: Ronald Mavor's letter of 16 May was sympathetic, acknowledging the force of my argument, but it took the plight of Scottish playwrights not one step closer to solution. I viewed the Scottish Arts Council with some affection; over the years I had watched it try to do its best for drama in Scotland, but everywhere, it seemed to me, its intentions took a turn in the wrong direction. There was always a gap between real need and real assistance. I decided to go forth in person to tackle it in its stronghold in Rothesay Terrace.

The name Rothesay charged my batteries with supplementary energy as I strode in my black battledress through the May sunshine – I stood at least ten feet tall, and my presence surrounded me like crystalline armour. I came to be charming but utterly implacable: I had come this day to fight not for myself but for all of Scotland's playwrights, using my own experience to illustrate my argument.

Whether it was coincidence, or whether my words had taken effect, I cannot say, but later that week I saw announced in *The Scotsman* a new Scottish Arts Council scheme to aid theatres presenting new plays by Scottish authors. I voiced my appreciation to the Scottish Arts Council, but, at the risk of interfering in their affairs, I said I thought there remained a danger that somewhere along the line theatre directors who, with their eyes on a London West End production, would still give preference to plays by Scottish authors which dealt with human life as it was lived everywhere *but* in modern Scotland. Also, inevitably, there would be those Scots playwrights who would hasten to write plays pleasing to their English masters. I was to be proved right later when items in the press showed precisely the trend I had feared. For the first time I was bitter: I had fought until my bones were showing, but basically nothing changed. We were left, as before, with *Craig Compound* and hoots-i'-the-heather to represent a nation whose worn granite face remained suffering and unidentified.

Then I remembered that it was precisely a year since Grampian Television had invited me to re-submit *The Common Stair*, so I raked it out of the cupboard and sent it off to them.

Economic hardship beset me on every side. Unable to pay my furniture storage bill, I faced the risk of having my possessions sold to defray expenses. The threat to the Amboyna table sent me half out of my mind with worry. I promised payment in August, knowing that by that time I would have the adaptation of *Mittelplatz* completed. On 17 June the Inland Revenue, by Recorded Delivery, threatened to take me to court unless I paid immediately the outstanding sum of £22 7s. My face hardened as I read that one, and I shouted aloud, '*Let them*! And I will say in court what is the plight of a living dramatist in Scotland!'

Since my talk with Lawrence my head had been so clear and

competent that I had given no more thought to the vexed question of James Stewart's identity. When Lawrence mentioned, casually, that my visit to Flodden could be accommodated in his programme before his summer holiday, I said that it could wait until his return. The whole problem I had now packed away neatly into a far recess of my mind, meaning never to disturb it again if it could be avoided. My ruse was unsuccessful. On 23 June 1967 – the scribble is meticulously dated – the phantom poet of nocturnal working hours reappears on the scene after many months' absence. His style, however, has now changed. Imagery has vanished, and he makes plain the substance of his diatribe. The theme of the opening verse is James's struggle to maintain the balance of power in Christendom essential to its peace; then it switches suddenly to a scream of guilt from myself for the loss of a nation on the battlefield. Then, underneath the date, almost like a signature, I have written:

Where have I seen this God-sunk-type-nit before?
　　　　　　　unknown quantity before'?
Where have I seen this destiny before?

It is the first time the nocturnal versifier has written of James and the link is unambiguous. But it is the scrawled question at the end, ranging from the contemptuous to the sublime, which is the most revealing. The slangy, ironic epithet 'God-sunk-type-nit' belongs to the vocabulary of abusive encouragement I apply only to myself and *no one else*. My right to use it is something I guard jealously. I could not have used it in reference to James unless I was absolutely certain in my unconscious mind that I was writing of *myself*.

The next day I cheerfully slid the paper containing the verses into the correspondence midden, thinking no more about it as I reached for the script of *Mittelplatz*. I was not concerned now with King James. *The Common Stair* (I hoped) and *Mittelplatz* were my future. I had been working on the television adaptation for some days, intending to surprise my well-disposed producer with it when he returned from holiday. It had not been easy; my head had been confused while working upon the theme of a mock-king turning back into a real one, but I persevered. The script was shaping well, and the big cuts I had to make were proving as effective as I had hoped in my initial estimate. I was eager to show them in Glasgow, for they made my point that a shortened television version was feasible. I knew that all my worries would be over when *Mittelplatz* reached the screen.

Then, on 1 July came the thunderbolt: without waiting to see my adaptation, the B.B.C. had decided against presenting *Mittelplatz* – the reason given being that the play was too long to condense into the fifty-minute slot available.

I sat staring at the letter incredulously. Shock numbed even the pain in my head. No *Mittelplatz*. What now would become of me?

There was an attempt to soften the blow, the suggestion I should go through to Glasgow the following week to discuss any other ideas I might have. Truly, I had none. However, I would go if only as a courtesy.

On 3 July Grampian returned my serial synopsis for *The Common Stair*. James Buchan still thought it would make an excellent series, but felt that the project required the resources available to a big company. His letter ended 'Have you tried out the idea on Francis Essex of STV? If he could find the writers, I am sure he would be interested.'

Had the letter arrived upon any other morning, I might have heeded it. As it was, the postal delivery coincided with my hurried preparations to go to Glasgow, and I separated the letter – which I cast on to the midden – from the synopsis, which I put into my shoulder-bag. All I had to show as new work was a not very stimulating small satire called *The Happy Marriage* so I took *The Common Stair* to offer to the B.B.C. in Glasgow.

Like a ghost, all fight knocked out of me, I went to Glasgow. Gaunt-faced, wearing my now habitual black costume, my personality retracted utterly, *I failed to be seen* by my expectant host in the B.B.C. canteen where we were to meet for luncheon. We had not met since he produced my play *Hills Beyond the Smoke* in 1961, and it had not occurred to me that I had changed beyond recognition. He, too, had changed, and I was so ill that I failed to identify him. (We had actually sat waiting at different tables, we discovered afterwards.) When finally we ran each other to earth in his office, he was by this time due to attend a meeting; so, to spare me a wasted journey, he introduced me to Stewart Conn, the radio producer. I had not thought of writing for radio for a long time, but during the course of conversation I chanced to mention that I was working upon a play about James IV. Stewart told me that, if I could have it written in time, there was the St Andrew's Day slot waiting to be filled at the end of November.

The St Andrew's Day slot and the James play seemed to go together. But could I write it? What would happen if I did? I travelled home torn between hope and terror. I still had the synopsis, prepared the previous year, so I dusted it – literally – and posted it to Stewart Conn with a letter which put *me* back into the picture as a playwright writing about a character in history: whatever I privately suspected, there was no need to tell the B.B.C. about it.

Stewart wrote back in friendly fashion on 12 July:

I'd find it difficult to push through a commissioning without being able to give at least a suggestion of the play itself and the style of writing used.

In other words, how far are you prepared to go towards a radio script? Or a draft of one? I assure you of my own support – but I do need something firmer to go on.

So did I. After my recent experience with *Mittelplatz* my faith in the Corporation's ability to realise its members' good intentions had dwindled. (Just how badly the B.B.C. could behave when it was really trying I was to learn two years later when, at the last moment, my much-lauded *Ann Bullen* script was scrapped from the series because it was not sufficiently cosy.)

Stewart Conn's request was reasonable, but to be treated like a new, unproven writer went down badly with the author of *Red Rose for Ransom* and *The Man from Thermopylae*. My prickly pride I could swallow; my real worry was the dread I had of facing James Stewart yet again as a character in history. I meant to get out of writing that Flodden play if something on a modern theme found favour. Then, on 20 July, back came *The Common Stair*. The potential of the idea had been recognised but its presentation was beyond the scope of B.B.C. Scotland's budget. The series I had dubbed *Craig Compound* had, of course, been financed and approved by London, and my original ploy to by-pass Glasgow had been the right one even though it had not succeeded.

This was the time when I should have remembered James Buchan's advice about sending *The Common Stair* to STV but the letter was lost beneath the litter of James manuscript, still spread upon my table. My head was clouding too badly to make a search for it. And 22 July brought another rain of blows, this time from Pitlochry: with a constructive and kindly letter, came the return of *The Year of Mrs Hannibal* and the synopsis of the Flodden play. Kenneth Ireland thought the latter would make a good film if I 'collaborated with an experienced scenario writer'. I began to wonder if Ada F. Kay, experienced television writer had ever existed, or was she just a figment of James IV's imagination? When I roared, 'God help me!' I did not intend it as a prayer, but it was taken that way. Out of the blue, I received a phone call from Sunny, the soldier I had known on earlier battlefields, wanting my advice as a playwright.

Once I would have shied from this man who remembered me from a previous existence, but he was now the person I most wanted to see. Lawrence was due to go away on holiday on 30 July, for three weeks, and the prospect of having nobody with whom to discuss my dilemma terrified me. I had done nothing to further the project of going to Flodden but as long as I could continue saying, 'I must go soon,' I was moderately comforted. I had never once used the word 'reincarnation' in reference to my predicament; it was a word that made me think of Babylonian queens masquerading as garage attendants (or vice versa), whereas my own feeling was of *being* James. In a curious way, the previous incarnation for me was Ada F. Kay.

Although we had met but twice previously, the face of the man at my door was that of one of the oldest friends I had. I saw it clearly now beneath the steel 'bunnet' I had remembered across the centuries – it might have been yesterday. This time he saw me wearing my black battledress, and as I advanced to shake his hand I felt my lengthened stride to be distinctly mannish; talking to him, it amused me to see the familiar James Stewart mannerisms identify themselves. All trace had gone of the lady on stiletto heels whom he had first encountered.

I found it more difficult than I had expected to tell my tale to Sunny. It was easy enough to say that I had been a soldier, but I hated having to tell him *which* soldier. (I had groaned so often in the past, 'Why do they all claim to have been kings and queens?')

Sunny, as it turned out, was far more interested in me as a playwright. In a way I was glad: to talk about television technique was a safe, earthing subject. I had not really wanted to discuss reincarnation – still for me an uncomfortable word; simply, I was glad to know someone else who had far memories. My worst distress was that I had no contact with anyone who could say, 'Don't let it worry you. I can remember being hanged at Tyburn.'

Sunny departed with a load of play-scripts I lent him, and his letter received on 24 July cheered me greatly, paying just tribute to my skill as a dramatist which everyone else appeared to have forgotten. Also, he enclosed, 'a quid to buy some cigarettes but be sure to spare some of it to get yourself a bit of steak and a couple of eggs for a decent meal. You are far too pale. You've got to have shoulders to bear the harness for the battles that lie ahead.'

The promise of more battles reduced me nearly to tears, but I was moved by the generosity of my old comrade-in-arms, and obediently bought the steak and eggs. Seeing myself in the mirror, I reflected that Sunny was right. My face was chalk-white, thin and angular as never before, the bone structure showing clearly where the once-feminine curves of jaw and cheek had gone. It was like seeing through my living face a skull. The physical body was merging into its background like a rubbed pastel drawing.

These days I felt like a ghost when the sun mercilessly picked out my black-clad figure amongst the people in the street wearing summer dresses. In winter my outfit had been striking, much admired, but now it attracted unwelcome attention. I had been laughed at in the bus by a pack of uniformed schoolgirls. I was imprisoned in the black clothes, the sole garment which held my head together.

By the last week of July my allies – and my opponents – were all away on holiday; I was alone, ill and wretched. Then a telephone call from 'my Craigmillar folk' reminded me of a promise to visit them in the summer when they would take me to see 'their' castle. Not for the world would I have hurt them by saying that the last thing I wanted to do was visit Craigmillar Castle. I had no work on hand to justify excusing myself on the grounds that I was too busy.

In the warm sunshine, Elizabeth, her young Jimmy and I walked up the hill to the castle, through fields that were the last remnant of rural Craigmillar. For a moment I was happy, feeling the sun on my head, grateful that I was no longer obliged to wear *a cap*. Otherwise, my head was terrible, almost blotted out entirely. Then suddenly, as we reached the entrance gate, my whole manner changed. I went striding purposefully ahead to exchange words of greeting with the Ministry of Works custodian, then I was off across the greensward towards the main gate, Elizabeth and Jimmy at my heels almost forgotten.

There was now a tree growing in the inner court, but the tower standing before me was still recognisable. It did not seem to me a ruin as I rushed inside, certain of my welcome. Up the stair to the banqueting hall I led the way, and as we emerged at the top of the stair I was momentarily dazzled by the flickering, vivid, smoky yellow light cast by the roaring fire in the great fireplace. Then it was gone. I stood shocked, staring at the cold walls of a *ruin*. They were all gone, those people who had rushed to set meat and wine before me. I stood, unbearably desolate.

Elizabeth, coming up behind me, asked was I all right, but I did not answer. I stood gazing into the black shell of the main tower, with the floor of the banqueting hall now but a gaping hole down to what had been the kitchens. What had become of the smoky yellow light that I had seen so clearly when I entered?

I would until the very end fight to reject the evidence of my inward eyes. There *had to be* some other explanation for my 'optical illusions'. But even as I looked at the Ministry of Works' electric light-bulbs set high in the walls at strategic points, I knew that they could never have produced that unmistakable yellow, smoky glare of rush-lights and the reddish cast of flame shooting upward from a log-fire.

There was one other room, a bed-chamber, which I glimpsed momentarily looking as it did in days when I myself had used it. But when my friends came to stand beside me, there was just an empty room, of bare stone and thick with dust. Dumb and uninterested, I walked with Elizabeth and Jimmy round the rest of the castle, which held for me no reality. I was confused by walls which had not existed when I knew the place.

For me the saddest absence was when I emerged from the main gate, expecting to see my great black stallion, in scarlet and gold harness, held ready for me by his groom. He was the horse I could still remember at the age of seven, when I played my game of 'King's business' between the humps of marram grass. My love for that horse had been so great that I found it hard to believe that Craigmillar Castle did not have him somewhere waiting for me.

Horse, attendants, messengers from the Newhaven shipyard, all were gone. My castle was a ruin, and empty save for Elizabeth, Jimmy and the castle keeper. It had all been a very long time ago, and I felt as old and lonely as the years which had trickled away to dust since that banqueting fire had last been lighted.

Walking back for tea, a couple of teenage girls squawked with laughter at my black costume. Elizabeth was furious. She said, 'They dinnae ken who ye are!' Nor did she, I reflected bitterly; nor did anyone. Mine was the loneliness of a man who has outlived his generation – in my case, many generations. Elizabeth went on about 'folk who let down Craigmillar' but I said wearily, 'It doesn't matter. I'm used to it.' But the laughter had in fact hurt: accustomed as I was to the blight of my eternal battledress, I wanted those girls to know that I did not dress this way for fun, but because *I had to*. The garb was symptomatic of the disease.

After the visit to Craigmillar I felt I had so little left to lose that I might as well try my hand, yet again, upon the Flodden play I was supposed to be writing for the B.B.C. I was working this time, of course, entirely in sound, and there was no barrier between myself and the stair-women. I began their opening dialogue . . . and then there came pouring into my head a torrent of Scots so anciently audible that I found my typewriter lacked the keys to spell it. It showed the play would work, but it terrified the life out of me.

On 8 August I rose from my bed in a dreamlike state to face a day which held no future. I had gone to bed the night before knowing that I had but one more day to live.

In the forenoon there was a peal of the doorbell. When I went to answer it, I saw before me a small, hirsute man who introduced himself as the nationalist whom a mutual friend had sent to see me. I offered him lunch, the tin of Norwegian herring I had been too dispirited to eat for my meal the previous evening. Watching him eat, I thought how ironic it was that someone else should enjoy my own last dinner. My sense of death lay over every thought that came to me. When he had eaten, he told me that he was going to visit several people of our own political persuasion in the Borders and he thought I should go with him. I did not feel much like meeting more new people, but as it was a day when I had nothing left to do in all the world, I decided I might as well go down to the Borders. I took no coat; wearing just my battledress, I picked up my shoulder bag and gloves and went downstairs with him to the car.

The car was a curious, small, triangular vehicle, and, I soon realised, I was in the hands of a hair-raising driver. When the heat from the engine penetrated the thick, black nylon covering my calves, I asked how soon would we go up in flames? I was told the engine did 'warm up a little' but it was nothing to worry about. I sat tight, counting my last moments at frequent intervals: I am not a driver, but I can tell when death keeps missing me by inches. Fatalistically, I wondered if this journey had been the cause of my 'end of life' feeling when I retired the previous night.

At some point on the road which left Craigmillar Castle away to our left, he asked me suddenly, 'Have you been to Flodden?'

I caught my breath, then answered carefully, 'No.'

He said, 'Neither have I. I think we should go there.'

Icy perspiration broke out on the palms of my hands. I saw myself in a trap. How could I explain to this man whom I barely knew my single, very good reason for not wanting to go to Flodden? I had not realised until this moment that I had never meant to go to Flodden; I was much too terrified of the place. I shut my eyes and inwardly prayed he would forget to mention it again. However, he did mention it, much later, when we were crossing the Teviot. Cautiously I replied that Flodden was 'not one of my favourite places'.

To this he replied, 'It's not a favourite place of any Scot, but I feel it's a duty to see the battlefield at some time in one's life.'

Damn him. By including the word 'duty' he had presented the suggestion in the one form which made it impossible for me to refuse. I reflected with an inward, unpleasantly hollow laugh that I might have known that fate would find some way to get me to Flodden.

We visited various people and it was late when we arrived in Jedburgh, where he had his house. He had suggested I should stay there overnight so we could visit more people in the morning, then go on to Flodden. I had discovered by this time that the house contained no hostess – he was divorced – but with tomorrow's battlefield on my mind minor details like the propriety of sheltering beneath a stranger's roof unchaperoned seemed remarkably trivial. He prepared a meal of soup with raw onion in it, which was very palatable, and then we sat talking about Scotland.

I was desperate to be alone – my head had clouded so badly I had the greatest difficulty in conversing; the steel shutter was pressing forward so hard that I felt sure it must soon burst through the front of my face. At the same time I was terrified of solitude and the prospect of being awake until dawn with my own thoughts, so we went on talking.

305

Finally, I had to tell him that I wished to retire, for my head was agony with meaningless sentences circling inside it. He presented me with a pile of fresh sheets and showed me to a bedroom where he helped me to make up the bed. Then he retired, wishing me a good night.

When I had prepared myself for bed, I put my cigarettes and the ashtray within reach. Physically, I was glad to lie down, but my mind was filled with horror at the thought of the sleepless hours ahead of me. Expecting to be home at nightfall, I had, of course, not brought my sleeping-pills. I could do nothing other than smoke endless cigarettes as I lay beneath a pall of dread. . . . 'The battlefield tomorrow. . . .'

What would happen there? Would I truly discover the lost key to my identity? And if so, how? Or would my brain explode into sheer, stark madness? Worst of all, what if nothing whatever happened, and I had to spend the rest of my life framed in a doorway, one foot on the threshold of the twentieth century, the other caught by the heel in a world now dead to everyone but myself?

What happened in my head was so sudden that I almost heard the click as my vision switched. Ahead of me was a cluster of horsemen, amongst them the English standard-bearer on a white battle-charger. Then, as I lowered my head, I saw the mud-stained, creamy feather of its great feet, interrupted now by the intrusion of bodies before my eyes, and the movement of my own head as I lunged and parried. Up went my head as I heaved back my sword double-handed to slash at the staves of brown-bills – and framed in the angle between my forearms I saw for a second the standard-bearer's body on the horse directly ahead of me; the space cannot have been more than five yards. There was something else I saw behind the standard, a tub-like vehicle partially enclosed – but I meant to have that standard. There was a sudden, astonishing explosion in my face, like a bursting star, but the star had a shape, a winged shape, plummeting down. A *falcon*.

I was back in the room in Jedburgh, saying to myself, 'A falcon!' The battle symbol. How useful to have as a device and name for a resistance movement if such were ever required. Full of this idea I reached for another cigarette. I had lighted it, and saw it in my fingers burning like a red point in the dark, just as the next instalment overtook me. I was lying on my back, staring up at what seemed like a tunnel of staves and blades, and beyond them were hands and merciless faces of men intent on killing me. My left arm I raised to cover my head, to ward off the blows. All the hate of the world was concentrated on me in that moment, and *nobody was stopping it*. I howled, a howl of pure animal terror, as the blades thrust down upon me.

Then I found myself alone in a strange bedroom, with my screams fading on the air. A few minutes later my host came rushing into the room to discover, as he said, 'who was murdering you'.

I had no choice but to tell him what had happened. He went away to make some coffee. When he came back we talked upon the subject for a while, then he said in a matter-of-fact tone, 'So you are James IV?'

I said, 'Yes.' And now it came clear, and I was no longer frightened of it.

My new friend observed, 'You should have told me before. I wouldn't have known what you were talking about at one time, but a few years ago I had a similar experience in Greece' – and he went on to describe a clear memory similar to those which I had been having all my life. We had been talking for well over an hour before I noticed an extraordinary new phenomenon: the steel shutter within my head had gone. There was no longer a blockage in my brain: my head was clear from front to back.

We talked until it was daylight over Jedburgh, then he went to prepare breakfast before we set out upon our journey. I had no fear of the battlefield now. I had been through it already. I wanted to see the place quickly, to get it over. As we set off in the wee car it was raining. The windscreen wiper did not work. When my driver said, 'Can you see – is that a pedestrian ahead? I broke my glasses yesterday,' I took over as look-out. I reflected that, having survived the billhooks of the night before, albeit posthumously, there was no need to worry about trifles like broken glasses and non-functioning windscreen wipers.

I had one eerie moment as we passed a field of black-faced sheep, a flock of about four score. Unlike cows, sheep are incurious beasts, but these behaved as no other sheep I have ever seen. Eighty black faces turned to watch the road as we passed, and continued watching long after the little car had passed from their line of vision. It struck my mind to wonder if what they saw was not just myself but the passing of *the whole Scots army.*

Later I solved one of the puzzles from far back in my childhood. I saw 'the square hill where we camped' which had set my father searching through all his photographs. I said, 'That's Flodden Edge, isn't it?' It was.

As we neared our destination, my guide said, 'This I think is where they sited the artillery.' But I was not interested just then in what he said, for my eyes were upon a hill-slope away to my left. My companion told me to 'look out for a memorial', and I replied flatly, 'It's over there. On the left,' for I had just seen it upon the hill-slope which I had already recognised as the field where I fought.

We found our way past a small church to a wicket-gate at the side of the road. He stopped the car and stayed with it whilst I got out alone. I opened the gate and began to walk up the hill through the long grass. Some distance from the gate I was hit by an intense, this-is-me sensation, so strong that it made me gasp. I looked down at the ground

307

for a moment. My blood was soaked into that place. The soil and my feet knew each other. Then I plodded on, up to the tall. stone column bearing the inscription 'To the Brave of Both Nations'. Remembering the billhooks of the night before, I thought rather tiredly, 'Well, I had my share of it.' Unlike any other battlefield, it left me strangely unmoved; I knew it too well. Then, glancing away to my left, I sensed my comrades lying there beneath the earth – dear God, how many? All those who had helped me to make a nation. For a moment I was sad with envy, wishing that my lost bones shared their communal burial ground.

I turned and began my slow walk down the hill. It was quiet now, grassed over, so different from the scene that had lived so long in my head. A small, light rain fell upon my thin covering of nylon tunic. I felt wonderously light-hearted and my step quickened as I came striding down the hill. Now I would return to the contemporary world, and with my clear, new head I would work to rebuild my Scotland. I was not pleased to see two figures enter the wicket-gate. Just then I wished to encounter no one. Two elderly ladies started up the path towards me. At any other time, in any other place, I would have stepped into the long wet grass to give them right of way: but not here on this day. I stayed to the path allowing them to step aside for me. I bade them 'Good morning' and they stood, heads bent slightly, as they responded.

Then I opened the wicket-gate and stepped through into the twentieth century.

HAD I KNOWN AS I CAME DOWN THAT HILL WHAT AWAITED ME ON MY return I might not – so absurdly like my own soldier-hero of Thermopylae! – have been so confident of my welcome back into the living century. Of four letters lying behind the door, three were rejections of every modern story-line I had submitted. The full significance of this was lost on me just then, for, elated by the sudden acquisition of my new, clear head, I lost no time in writing to tell my parents and a few close friends how I had come by it.

It was during the writing of those letters that I became aware of small discrepancies between features of the battle-scene and my own, now conscious, effort to describe it. What were those vertical lines constantly before my eyes each way I turned my head, so natural to me at the time as James Stewart, now so foreign to my experience as Ada Kay? Were they pike staves? Streaks of rain? Neither, I realised, could have presented such uniform formation. Nor could I account for the presence on the English side of a contraption which I could now liken only to an Orkney armchair. I was to spend four whole days wrestling with the problem before the sight of a can-opener lying on the kitchen table, reminding me of those bill-hooks, suddenly fused together both parts of the memory: I had been fighting *inside armour*. Those vertical steel lines before my eyes were the slats of my visor-grille. (Had my term 'a steel shutter' been a coded clue, I wonder?) That accounted also for the curiously masked vision which I had tried to describe as 'seeing out of a tunnel'. (I never resolved the problem of the 'Orkney armchair' and omitted it from my memoirs: it was finally identified for me after publication of *Falcon* by a critic who observed that James Stewart would surely have known that the Earl of Surrey fought in a *battle chariot*.)

Now the human mind is capable of many marvels, but I doubt whether it has yet succeeded in inventing consciously for itself a problem which it is incapable of resolving. On grounds of logic I yielded up my last faint hope that the death recall might have been some kind of waking dream and that I could even yet escape the consequences of having been James Stewart.

There was no escape, as time was swiftly to prove when, following the rejection of all my modern synopses, there came a letter from Stewart Conn telling me to go ahead with the Flodden play. Unable to tell the B.B.C. of my predicament, desperate for work, I took up the script where I had left it. King James came alive in his first spoken sentence: now it was the turn of the other historical characters to become cardboard silhouettes. I had to abandon the radio play – but now everyone wanted James, and the next offer came from Perth Rep., through the Scottish Arts Council, commissioning a new play about James IV. I could not refuse again for the same reasons. Again the same thing happened. James came alive at once, but only James. Now my store of twentieth-century-learned history was lost to me behind a wall of time five centuries thick, and in my efforts to complete my task I took up again the books I had hoped to put aside. One thing there had changed. I knew now to look for *me* inside the pages – and there I was, my vices and virtues all recorded, each stressed according to the bias of the historian but all of them combining to present a clear picture of my own personality today as it was when other men knew it as James Stewart. All other historical presences, dates, facts now vanished behind unreadable text.

I was still battling to complete the play when I went down to London to discuss this present book with a publisher. Peter Davis liked the idea but showed more keen interest in the James memoirs. . . .

Since the publication of *Falcon, The Autobiography of His Grace James the 4 King of Scots* (in 1970) it has taken me seven years to fight my way out of that black battledress and the mud of Flodden. These years may be the subject of one more book, after which – I hope – I shall have finished.

Meanwhile, I leave my reader with a quotation which he may find, as I did, illuminating. I discovered it for the first time by chance when I was trying to remember which of the three gates of Stirling Castle (two constructed later by myself) had been the original main gate through which I had ridden out, as a boy clad in scarlet, with the rebels. For the purpose of the manuscript it did not matter in the least, but I was anxious to satisfy my own curiosity. (I had not visited Stirling Castle or any of the other palaces, nor was I to do so until after I had described them from memory.) It was late at night, libraries were closed, and I knew that no book of mine held a picture of Stirling Castle great gate. Then I remembered one book which I had never opened – H. V. Morton's *In Search of Scotland*. I went to get it. It fell open at a page where the author quotes from Stow's *Survey of London*. In the passage, Stow describes what was done to James's body after death, and my shocked, immediate thought was of *my tree drawings*.

I shall give the quotation not as it appears in H. V. Morton's book, but as I found it years later, in a small volume by G. Gregory Smith, *The Days of James IV*, where it is appended as a footnote which my reader, like myself, may find helpful – or disturbing.

'Then was the body disembowelled, embalmed and cered, and

secretly amongst other stuff conveyed to Newcastle. . . .' 'Then it was carried to London, to the monastery of the Carthusian monks at Bethlehem.' Polyd. Verg., xxvii., p. 642. Leo X in a letter to Henry VIII, 29 Nov. 1513 (Cotton. Vitell. B. 2, 54), gave permission for the interment in holy ground at St Paul's Cathedral; but nothing seems to have been done. Stow in his *Survey of London*, p. 539, says that since the dissolution of the house of Shene in the reign of Edward VI the body lay 'lapped in lead' in a waste room amongst old timber and rubble. 'Since the which time, workmen there, for their foolish pleasure, hewed off his head; and Lancelot Young, master glazier to Queen Elizabeth, feeling a sweet savour to come from thence, and seeing this same dried from all moisture, and yet the form remaining, with the hair of the head and beard red, brought it to London, to his house in Wood Street, where for a time he kept it for its sweetness, but in the end caused the sexton of that church (St Michael's) to bury it amongst other bones taken out of their charnel.'

Author's footnote: Since writing this book I have discovered that the church of St Michael, off Cheapside, was destroyed during the Great Fire of 1666.